HB
41
CUH
1985

D1645450

(*continued on back*)

INSTITUTE OF ECONOMICS
WITHDRAWN
OXFORD

Structural Sensitivity
in Econometric Models

WITHDRAWN

Structural Sensitivity in Econometric Models

EDWIN KUH

JOHN W. NEESE

PETER HOLLINGER

Massachusetts Institute of Technology
Center for Computational Research in Economics and
Management Science

ECONOMICS
LIBRARY
14 OCT 1985
WITHDRAWN
AND STATISTICS

JOHN WILEY & SONS

New York · Chichester · Brisbane · Toronto · Singapore

Copyright © 1985 by John Wiley & Sons, Inc.

All rights reserved. Published simultaneously in Canada.

Reproduction or translation of any part of this work
beyond that permitted by Section 107 or 108 of the
1976 United States Copyright Act without the permission
of the copyright owner is unlawful. Requests for
permission or further information should be addressed to
the Permissions Department, John Wiley & Sons, Inc.

Library of Congress Cataloging in Publication Data:

Kuh, Edwin.
    Structural sensitivity in econometric models.

    (Wiley series in probability and mathematical
statistics, ISSN 0271-6356. Applied probability
and statistics)
    Bibliography: p.
    Includes index.
    1. Econometrics.   2. Macroeconomics—Mathematical
models.   3. Inflation (Finance)—Mathematical models.
4. United States—Economic conditions—1945–   —Mathematical models.   I. Neese, John W., 1952–
II. Hollinger, Peter, 1952–   III. Title.
IV. Series.

HF141.K79 1984   330′.028   84-23431
ISBN 0-471-81930-1

Printed in the United States of America

10 9 8 7 6 5 4 3 2 1

Preface

This book assesses the worth of linear dynamic systems methods for probing the behavior of complex macroeconomic models. While our main purpose is methodological, we fully illustrate our approach in the context of one good medium-size econometric model, the Michigan Quarterly Econometric Model of the United States. We are better able to understand inflation by unraveling its crucial behavioral determinants from the welter of equations that typify such models. In the end, of course, the value of these techniques must be judged by how well they work, and we believe that they clearly show great promise. Among the suggested analytical procedures, the systematic study of parameter sensitivity has previously been neglected. It has proven to be a powerful device for ascertaining the essentials of model behavior, more so than customarily employed multipliers.

We began five years ago with the nonlinear parameter-perturbation analysis published in Kuh and Neese (1982). This book proceeds one further logical step to appraise the merits of linear systems analysis in the same context. This approach provides the added insights obtainable from the properties of characteristic roots and vectors. While the main mathematical theorems have existed for some years, using them to extract information about simultaneous-equation model structure is a nontrivial endeavor.

A high-quality FORTRAN code to compute characteristic roots and vectors, called EISPACK (1976), already existed when this research began, but this code needed to be augmented in several respects. Peter Hollinger wrote a model linearization code, and John Neese embedded EISPACK in a broader algorithmic framework that made EISPACK much more effective for sizable econometric models. Neese is also mainly responsible for writing the interface between the algorithmic code and the TROLL interactive modeling system. Both aspects were arduous, but the outcome, a TROLL task called LIMO (*li*near *mo*del analysis), makes an unusually wide range of linear system methods accessible to economists, operations researchers, engineers, and physical scientists, who rely on these analytical devices. While seldom applied to econometric models, linear analysis has been used in engineering and the physical sciences for some years.

Valuable suggestions were made about how to structure the LIMO program by the numerical analysts David Gay and Gene Golub, at Bell Laboratories and Stanford University, respectively. The suggestions of David Gay and Virginia Klema, MIT, greatly improved the content of Appendix 5A. Stephen O'Connell and Sean Doyle, MIT students, provided yeoman service as research assistants and critics of rough drafts. Much hard slogging was needed, and they contributed that willingly as well as their own ideas about what should be done. Sean Doyle deserves special thanks, since he bore the brunt of the work and is mainly responsible for writing Appendix 5A.

This book records many details. To overload a metaphor, you can't comprehend a forest unless you look closely at the trees. We have tried to look at both. Robert Eberlein, who wrote a Ph.D. thesis using a related approach, reviewed most of the manuscript. David Belsley, of Boston College, and Michael McCarthy, of the University of Pennsylvania, commented in detail on Chapter 2. Karen Martel typed the manuscript in her impeccable style with the patience of a saint; we are deeply appreciative. Micky DuPree meticulously proofread a complex and, at times, mysterious manuscript.

Research support from the Department of Energy's Energy Information Agency, under contract DE-AC02-76ER03069, provided welcome support for the development of LIMO, and we are grateful to the IBM Corporation for its part in the support of this research. Douglas Hale, who is the Director of EIA-QUAD, also gave us helpful criticism of LIMO documentation.

EDWIN KUH
JOHN W. NEESE
PETER HOLLINGER

Cambridge, Massachusetts
January 1985

Contents

Structural Sensitivity
in Econometric Models

CHAPTER 1

Essentials of
Model Structure

This introductory chapter sets the stage for a methodological study that we hope will deepen our understanding of econometric model structures. To serve these analytical purposes, the Michigan Quarterly Econometric Model of the U.S. price-war inflationary processes offers a convenient subject for study. The MQEM has been carefully designed and reflects much of what is good in current macroeconomic models. The surge in postwar model building has yielded many insights into economic structure and made forecasting a more systematic process. At the same time, some early aspirations held out for econometrics have been disappointed, especially the goal of providing deeper insights into economic structure. Modelers and model users alike often find it difficult to be confident about which equations or sectors are the strategic sources of model behavior, a disquieting state of affairs rendered all the harder by the large size of most current models.

1.1 THE GOAL OF MODEL UNDERSTANDING

Macroeconomics, like beauty, is in the eye of the beholder. From the outset, the subject is inherently controversial by virtue of the subjective/distributional aspects of policies that are its central concern. Choosing the "right" point on a Phillips curve—if the curve exists at all—requires, for example, a welfare judgment about the unemployed labor force versus retired individuals on fixed money incomes. Such controversies are compounded by profound disagreements about economic theory and behavior. Thus the possibly nonexistent Phillips curve is indicative of one such unresolved

1

theoretical–factual issue. The theory–behavior fissure has widened the area for polemics in academic and public discourse. Among well-known, important reasons for controversy, one of great concern is about "rules of evidence" or "empirical rules of the game." A consensus on that issue is absent. In this book we hope to show that there are sensible ways to increase agreement about some rules of evidence. These can help to promote clearer empirical confrontations of alternative theories. The objective component of social sciences is admittedly circumscribed by its subject matter, but in this book we present some ideas that should broaden that scope.

Computational power has expanded during the past 30 years, offering opportunities to enlarge the scale and complexity of econometric models. These benefits are associated with adverse side effects, however. The consequences of these new tools, for good and ill, will be weighed in the remainder of this chapter.

Macromodels have grown from small-scale academic exercises (expanded IS–LM curves, so to speak) to detailed models with 1000 or more equations. Model size increased initially in recognition of the violence done to perceived reality by excessive aggregation: investment, for example, is not a homogeneous blob, but a composite of plant, equipment, residential structures and inventories, each with its own buyers, sellers, financial markets, and dynamics. The first wave of model expansion occurred during the fifties and sixties. Stone and Croft's Cambridge growth model (1959) is a dynamic interindustry model designed to study alternative growth policies. Soon thereafter, the Brookings–SSRC project (Duesenberry et al., 1965) added industry detail to macroeconomic models. Behavior equations for numerous financial instruments designated by origin and ownership (e.g., corporate bonds held by households) have been estimated with Federal Reserve flow-of-funds data and are now important components of some macromodels. Since "the" energy crisis arrived, supply-side economics and its attendant production–price embodiment spawned further sectoral detail with more complex theoretical and empirical representations. The resurgence of balance-of-payments problems has had similar effects.

As members of a policy-oriented social science, economists respond swiftly to issues of the day. When a new, exciting, relevant problem appears, it soon surfaces in another set of equations. Since computing costs have long since ceased to be a serious barrier, movement has generally been in one direction: bigger. This disciplinary impetus has been reinforced by the growing commercialization of models, which are now big business.[†] Since

---

[†] In remarks given at a session on "Macroeconomic Models and Policy," (Econometric Society Third World Congress, Toronto, 1975), Tobin (1977, p. 760) makes a number of trenchant observations, some of which are echoed here. "In the meanwhile, the reputation of economics depends to a frightening degree on a handful of economists who are in the midst of current macroeconomic turmoil-forecasting, commenting, making policy, criticizing policy."

commercial model clientele have many diverse interests, it is sensible to accommodate their detailed needs, even when doing so adds little to basic knowledge about economic behavior or forecast accuracy. An equation added to a model for whatever reason can degrade model performance when it is improperly specified. Thus proliferation of this sort is at best innocuous for improved understanding of the central elements of macroeconomics.

These particular academic and commercial motives for expanded models can have merit: more thorough studying of newly perceived problems or catering to client needs should not be criticized, except possibly for encouraging sloppiness by spreading resources too thinly. There are, however, some serious adverse side effects of proliferation.

The first is that model management has become expensive, calling for resources well beyond the means of most universities to support on their own. In this regard economics stands in interesting contrast to some sciences, of which physics is a prime example. High-energy physics research requires extremely costly equipment. Since no conventional market exists for physics research, most experimental apparatus is owned by the government and its use shared among universities and government laboratories. Choices are wider in economics, and in the United States this fact has led to commercial dominance of macro modeling activities. Except for a few universities which sponsor their own model, students and faculty are unable to replicate, test, study, and learn about large-model behavior. Sometimes, indeed, large models are published, but passive examination is no substitute for "hands-on" access.

Moreover, most large models are heavily directed toward forecasting, since that is what most commercial clients want, rather than toward objective study of the economy. While commercial modelers are usually serious about the importance of theory and will incorporate new advances whenever possible, the paramount objective of forecasting is to squeeze down error variability. That objective is often (though not always) attained at the expense of structural validity, since high correlations with bizarre economic implications can take precedence over sounder economic interpretations accompanied by larger error variances.[†] This tradeoff is not always present and would be absent in an ideal world.

Another consequence of the preponderance of commercial modeling stems more narrowly from the proprietary nature of models. While cost considerations alone often suffice to preclude hands-on model operation, full access is often impossible in order to protect "business secrets." While commercial models are sometimes published, in the normal course of events

---

[†] The practice of using "add factors" (sometimes unjustifiably defended on the grounds that as prior information, they are a valid Bayesian concept) may help forecasts but to the detriment of structural understanding.

they are frequently modified, so that models have become obsolete by the time they appear in print. Also, publications seldom include data or precise definitions, so that replication is not possible anyway. Software inadequacy is another impediment to transferring or replicating large models, a problem that would be less formidable if the models were less gargantuan.

The worst drawback of equation proliferation is our inability to understand what the models are really about. For all practical purposes, even if we are fortunate enough to have hands-on access to an adequately documented model, we are limited to treating models like "black boxes." That is, one can observe the response of model outputs (endogenous variables) to model inputs (exogenous variables), usually via simulation, but one cannot observe the interactions among the model's equations that make it different from the sum of its individual parts (equations). Thus at one extreme we can study each equation and its statistical properties, while at the other only complete model behavior responses are available. The intervening crucial pieces of knowledge about the structural elements of the model, including simultaneity and the sources of model dynamics, cannot be studied in this way.

A related difficulty is that large models are a barrier to intuition. Initially we learn or teach macroeconomics by studying four admittedly oversimplified relations: the investment and consumption functions and the demand and supply functions for money. These have been boiled down to intersecting curves in income–interest-rate space that first appeared in Hicks' (1937) famous IS–LM exegesis of Keynes' *General Theory* (1936), or Modigliani's (1944) equally seminal treatment. Some recent business-cycle theory originated with the Hansen–Samuelson (Samuelson, 1939) multiplier–accelerator model that comprises a consumption function, an investment function, and an income identity. In the first two models cited, different qualitative comparative-equilibrium responses of income to monetary or fiscal policy could be calculated from different assumptions about the curvature of the underlying structural relations. From the third model, the boundary of dynamic stability could be trivially established for various parameter combinations. These remarks are not motivated by nostalgia for the 1930s or 1940s, but illustrate what is lost when we are restricted to black-box analysis. In more familiar terms, black-box analysis is equivalent to using a model's local reduced form to calculate multipliers, that is, it is equivalent to studying model behavior through simulation.[†]

[†]Exact reduced-form coefficients, of course, do not exist for nonlinear models, and the overwhelming majority of models in current use are nonlinear. Valid local approximations for "small enough" changes in exogenous variables can be computed, however, for linearized models.

This brings us full circle to remarks in the introductory paragraphs about the need for better rules of evidence. Theoretical controversies often involve small segments of a given large model. It is therefore not possible, by black-box analysis, to untangle an isolated change in specification from the large number of potential model interactions. It thus becomes impossible to devise a quantitative resolution of the controversy.

While we have seen that difficulties have arisen from the expansion of model size and complexity, that result is far from being the exclusive consequence of modelers' preferences. Macroeconomic theory and macro-models are closely intertwined, often unproductively however. Much macro theory is posed at a level of abstraction that prevents its application in an empirical setting. Some macro theory does not yield testable propositions, or involves intrinsically subjective elements of behavior with no direct observable counterpart: expectations are a prime example. Theory also is understandably vague about lag structure. Macro theory too tends to be either silent or contrived about institutions (e.g., wage-setting processes), so that the modelers are left to fend for themselves.

The main purpose of this study is to arrive at methods that will help us to understand better what really matters in a model—which equations and/or coefficients and/or exogenous variables most importantly influence endoge-nous variables of interest.[†] Chapter 2 spells out the framework to accom-plish this, provided econometric models are not excessively complex (though large) and the coefficients are sufficiently few, that is, the coefficient matrices are sparse. Since these conditions often prevail, we anticipate that relevant results will emerge.

We can, if we choose, proceed to a second objective of extracting a designated subset of interesting endogenous variables, together with the most important coefficients and exogenous variables, from the full model. This reduced-order, or compressed, model will contain relevant and accu-rate model information, especially if the full model decomposes approxi-mately into block-diagonal form. Ando, Fisher, and Simon (1963) have shown that it is practical to study block-structure dynamics separately in the short and intermediate term if the off-diagonal elements of the endogenous-variable matrix (assuming linearity) are sufficiently small. Fisher (1963) (reprinted in Ando et al., 1963) has extended these results to block-triangular form. It is sometimes possible, as we shall attempt to show, to arrive at compressed models sufficiently small to allow intuitive under-standing by the general research community. We shall explore some impli-cations of decomposability more thoroughly in Chapter 4.

[†] Deleau and Malgrange (1976) describe some related methods with similar purposes in mind.

A complementary approach that merges with the compressed-model perspective is to build small, strongly theory-based macromodels or "maquettes" (see Deleau et al., 1984). This contrasts with our objective of sifting out the essential elements of an existing large model.

While there are numerous reasons why small models are attractive, the most important one from our perspective was mentioned at the outset: to arrive at more widely acceptable rules of evidence in econometric modeling. If analytical methods of the sort we are going to propose are credible, in the sense that we can demonstrate convincingly that our approach successfully isolates the strategic elements of the original model, it should be possible either to arrive at a small, acceptable representation of the original, large model (or perhaps only important segments of it), or at least to describe the several aspects of a larger system that dominate its behavior. The former is possible when the model is decomposable, and the latter should be possible even when it is not. The small model will be more open to intuition and study by standard mathematical procedures for both structural- and reduced-form representations. Then discussion and controversy can, as they should, concentrate on the core model functions. These can be studied uncluttered by dozens of minor coefficients and relationships. Even if the final result remains a large model (though presumably smaller than the original), its strategic components will have been identified and can focus intuitive understanding.

1.2 MACROECONOMIC ISSUES

The purpose of this volume is twofold. First, as sketched out above, we want to devise more effective ways of understanding model structure. Second, we want to learn more about the inflationary process, and how fiscal and monetary policy instruments and exogenous prices affect prices, wages, and productivity. These are matters of paramount substantive interest in their own right. Moreover, the effectiveness of the model analysis procedures that we propose is most readily demonstrated by showing their relevance to a specific issue.

The major macroeconomic policy issue of the seventies is best summarized by the single word, stagflation—slow growth or recession, accompanied by high rates of inflation. While the mid eighties are less inflationary, that issue is one that will continue to haunt our perceptions and policies. We shall study inflationary processes using the Michigan Quarterly Econometric Model (MQEM) of the United States. The 1982 version we have used has 117 equations, divided about equally between behavioral equations and identities. It serves our methodological purposes well in that it is representative of the better medium-sized, well-known models.[†]

Since stagflation is an issue in its own right, we wish to learn more about it. How are wages, prices, and productivity related? How are wages and prices linked to production (real output, real GNP) and the monetary sector? How tight are these linkages? Can we decompose inflationary responses into raw-material price impacts and their further propagation through the wage and price setting mechanism embodied in the MQEM? Exogenous energy and food price increases have been named as major villains in the inflation saga. Earlier optimism that exogenous price shocks would quickly work their way through the system has dimmed. Today it is more common to believe that inflationary biases have been built into the system, so that exogenous shocks, via inflationary expectations coupled with cost-of-living escalator clauses, have long-lasting effects.[‡]

Another topic, of earlier vintage, concerns the potency, stabilization properties, and economic consequences of monetary and fiscal policy. We have a recent version of the MQEM which includes an augmented monetary sector. It contains equations relating the federal budget identity to debt, money creation, and interest rates. Several monetary–fiscal questions immediately come to mind. What are the relative strengths and timing of monetary and fiscal policy on output, prices, and interest rates?

Whatever we look at may be sensitive to nonlinearities. Price–wage behavior could depend, via a Phillips-curve mechanism, on how close the economy is to full employment. Thus, while we shall lean heavily on linear analysis, we are obligated to establish circumstances when the benefits of assuming linearity are nullified by strategic nonlinearities that were perceived by the modelers.

Some contemporary econometric and macroeconomic issues are beyond our reach. Rational-expectation models, which postdate the original structuring of the MQEM, are attempts to shore up the microeconomic foundations of macroeconomics. Lucas (1976) has argued that models like the MQEM that are not based on rational-expectation postulates cannot be used for policy analysis, or for that matter, viewed as a sensible representation of the economy. However, this position has in turn been questioned

---

[†] The proprietors of the MQEM, Professors Saul Hymans and Philip Howrey, participated with us in an interuniversity project on Model Reliability, for which their model often served as a focus. Their assistance in various forms is greatly appreciated.
[‡] The relative price stability in 1984 (5 years after the second OPEC crude-oil price escalation and the ensuing major demand-induced depression during the early 1980s), largely orchestrated by monetary policy, does not conflict with this statement.

with respect to its foundations and realism. Shiller (1978) and Gordon (1981) argue that the extreme equilibrium assumptions of this critique weaken its persuasiveness. Tobin (1983, p. 33) further points out that in order to generate fluctuations for these equilibrium business-cycle models, "... they have cyclical consequences only with the help of further arbitrary assumptions. Whether these are more or less objectionable, more or less 'ad hoc,' than the much-criticized Keynesian assumptions of wage and price inertia seems a question more of taste than principle." Still, the more explicit treatment of micro and macro linkages, especially expectations, remains high on the research agenda. Progress in rational-expectation model building, using examples comparable in scale to the highly aggregated Cowles Commission initial simultaneous-equation models of the early 1950s, have started to appear (Sims, 1980; Sargent, 1976, 1979), and soon we may hope to see better-articulated versions.[†][‡] The analytical methods of this study can be put to use in understanding the systematic structure of rational-expectation models as they are used here with more traditional, current-vintage macromodels such as the MQEM. For instance, if coefficients are endogenized to respond to policy actions, they become a special sort of endogenous variable that can be studied according to methods proposed in Chapter 2.

Another issue at the forefront of modeling is the treatment of disequilibrium. Fair and Jaffee (1972), Laffont and Monfort (1979), and Quandt (1982) have constructed models that allow for various types of disequilibrium, in contrast with some versions of rational expectations that (doubtfully, in the opinion of many, including ourselves) assume continuous equilibrium. Model behavior might then be discontinuous at the point where excess demand gives way to excess supply. The fixed-price models of Malinvaud (1977) and Benassy (1977) systematically relate macromodel disequilibrium foundations to short-run price inflexibility. Estimation issues

---

[†]Sims (1982, p. 334) while covering a number of methodological issues of model building, asserts: "However my view is that the rational expectations critique of econometric policy evaluation has sent the profession down a false trail. ... But the positive program of rational expectation econometrics, to estimate identified, structural models to be used in predicting the effects of change in policy rules while taking account of induced changes in expectational mechanisms, reproduces the main faults of standard econometric policy evaluation in exaggerated form." (Copyright © 1982 by D. Reidel Publishing Company, Dordrecht, Holland.) While Sims provides a rationale for vector autoregressions as his preferred alternative (not ours), these remarks of his, added to many others, should help to counteract a fairly widespread impression that rational-expectation perspectives are intellectually dominant.

[‡]A systematic review of this approach applied to the econometrics of macromodels appears in the lucidly written volume by Frederic Miskin (1983).

are difficult too, depending on how switching regression regimes are treated.[†] These more complex, realistic, and difficult disequilibria do not appear in the MQEM. In common with nearly all other macromodels, the only recognized disequilibrium in the MQEM happens through dynamic behavior reflected in the lag structure when the economy is not in a steady-state equilibrium.

The remaining chapters of the book proceed as follows. Chapter 2 is an overview of various methods we propose to pursue the objectives described above. Chapter 3 describes the Michigan Quarterly Econometric Model and the issues involved in its linearization, and offers some initial thoughts about its inflationary properties via simulation. The MQEM's linear homogeneous dynamics are described in Chapter 4. Chapter 5 uses linear systems analytic methods of Chapter 2 for linear-multiplier and parameter-perturbation analysis, and characteristic-root properties, to interpret the price–wage–productivity properties of the MQEM. Chapter 6 deals with reduced models, both to complete the research process outlined in Chapter 2 and as a matter of independent interest.

REFERENCES

Ando, Albert, Franklin M. Fisher, and Herbert A. Simon (1963). *Essays on the Structure of Social Science Models*, MIT Press, Cambridge, MA.

Benassy, Jean Pascal (1977). On Quality Signals and the Foundations of Effective Demand Theory, *Scandanavian Journal of Economics*, Vol. 79, pp. 147–168.

Deleau, Michel and Pierre Malgrange (1978). *L'Analyse Des Modèles Macro Economiques Quantitatifs*, Economica, Paris.

Deleau, Michel and Pierre Malgrange (1976). Analysis of Macroeconometric Dynamic Models, *Colloques Internationaux du CNRS*, No. 259.

Deleau, Michel, Pierre Malgrange, and Pierre Alain Muet (1982). A Study of Short Run and Long Run Properties of Macroeconomic Dynamic Models by Means of an Aggregative Core Model. In *Conference Proceedings of International Seminar on Recent Developments in Macroeconomic Modeling*, Pierre Malgrange and Pierre Alain Muet (Eds.), Blackwell, Oxford, 1984.

Duesenberry, J., G. Fromm, L. Klein, and E. Kuh (Eds.) (1965). *The Brookings Quarterly Econometric Model of the United States*, Rand McNally, Chicago, and North Holland, Amsterdam.

Fair, Ray and Dwight Jaffee (1972). Methods of Estimation for Markets in Disequilibrium, *Econometrica*, Vol. 40, pp. 497–514.

Gordon, Robert J. (1981). Output Fluctuations and Gradual Price Adjustment, *Journal of Economic Literature*, Vol. XIX, pp. 493–530 (June).

[†]An elegant review of the econometric theory and a number of practical issues of estimation appear in Quandt (1982).

Hazelwinkel, M. and A. H. G. Rinnoy Kan (Eds.) (1983). *Current Developments in the Interface*: *Economics, Econometrics, Mathematics*, Reidel, Dordrecht.

Keynes, John M. (1936). *The General Theory of Employment, Interest and Money*, MacMillan, New York.

Laffont, Jean-Jacques and A. Monfort (1979). Disequilibrium Econometrics in Dynamic Models, *Journal of Econometrics*, Vol. 11, pp. 353–363.

Lucas, Robert E. (1976). Econometric Policy Evaluation: A Critique. In *The Phillips Curve and Labor Markets*, K. Bruner and A. H. Meltzer (Eds.), pp. 19–46, Vol. 1 of a Supplementary Series to the *Journal of Monetary Economics*.

Lucas, Robert E. (1981). Tobin and Monetarism, *Journal of Economic Literature*, Vol. XIX, pp. 558–567 (June).

Malinvaud, Edmond (1977). *The Theory of Unemployment Reconsidered*, Blackwell, Oxford.

Miskin, Frederic S. (1983). *A Rational Expectations Approach to Macroeconometrics*: *Testing Policy Ineffectiveness and Efficient-Market Models*, Univ. of Chicago Press, Chicago.

Quandt, Richard E. (1982). Econometric Disequilibrium Models, *Communications in Statistics*: *Econometric Reviews*, Vol. 1, No. 1, pp. 1–63 (with discussions by D. F. Hendry, A. Monfort, and J.-F. Richard and reply by Quandt), Dekker, New York.

Samuelson, Paul A. (1939). Interactions Between the Multiplier Analysis and the Principle of Acceleration, *The Review of Economics and Statistics*, pp. 75–78 (May).

Sargent, Thomas J. (1979). *Macroeconomic Theory*, Academic, New York.

Sargent, Thomas J. (1976). A Classical Macroeconomic Model for the United States, *Journal of Political Economy*, Vol. 84, No. 2, pp. 207–237.

Shiller, Robert J. (1978). Rational Expectations and the Dynamic Structure of Macroeconomic Models, A Critical Review, *Journal of Money and Credit*, Vol. 4, pp. 1–44.

Sims, Christopher (1982). Scientific Standards in Econometric Modeling, in *Current Developments in the Interface*: *Economics, Econometrics, Mathematics*, M. Hazewinkel and A. H. G. Rinnoy Kan (Eds.), pp. 317–340, Reidel, Dordrecht.

Stone, Richard and Murray Croft (1959). *Social Accounting and Economic Models*, Bowes & Bowes, London.

Tobin, James (1977). Macroeconomic Models and Policy, in *Frontiers of Quantitative Economics*, M. D. Intrilligator (Ed.), Vol. IIIb, Contributions to Economic Analysis, Vol. 106, pp. 560–573.

Tobin, James (1983). Macroeconomics under Debate, Cowles Foundation Discussion Paper No. 669, Yale Univ.

Tobin, James (1980). *Asset Accumulation and Economic Activity*: *Reflections on Contemporary Economic Theory*, Yrao Johansson Lectures, Blackwell, Oxford.

CHAPTER 2

Procedures for Model Understanding

2.1 INTRODUCTION

Exhibit 2.1 serves as a frame of reference for subsequent model analysis and with it we can readily describe the distinction between a standard multiplier analysis and parameter-perturbation analysis. Given the initial conditions $\{E(\varepsilon_t) = 0, \ y_{t-i}\}$ together with values for x_t and x_{t-i} over the simulation period and known parameters β, we can generate deterministic simulation solutions period by period for the endogenous variables y_t, which are often designated as the "base case." In the usual multiplier calculations the β and endogenous-variable initial conditions are held constant while a new set of x_t, x_{t-i} are selected for a new simulation. The change (new minus base) in y is then compared with the change in x. In parameter perturbations, the x_t, x_{t-i} together with endogenous variable initial conditions remain at their base-case values while the chosen β are changed for each new simulation. The changes in y are now compared with the change in β.

We shortly make use of both approaches for understanding specific aspects of a given model. In the remainder of this section we briefly preview some of the principal concerns in understanding econometric models. Section 2.2 is about the potential advantages of linear system analysis; Section 2.3 describes linear dynamic models expressed in terms of their characteristic roots. It also derives measures of characteristic-root sensitivity to model coefficients. Section 2.4 merges the individual technical procedures that were discussed in Sections 2.2–2.3 into a coherent approach for analyzing model structure. We note that by comparing conclusions drawn from linear analysis with those from nonlinear simulations we can highlight distortions that might have arisen as a consequence of linearization. Section

<u>Notation</u>

$F(y_t, y_{t-i}, x_t, x_{t-i}; \beta) = 0$ Deterministic system of equations to be solved for y_t

                    y = endogenous variable vector
                    x = exogenous variable vector
                    β = parameter vector

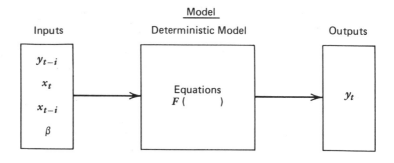

Analytical Approaches

Multiplier: Endogenous variable changes in response to
exogenous variable changes (black box)

Parameter perturbation: Endogenous variable changes in response
to parameter changes (structural)

Exhibit 2.1   Some elementary model concepts.

2.5 takes up the interpretation of first-order parameter sensitivity and its well-known and more widely applied counterpart, multiplier analysis. Appendix 2A goes beyond the single-equation illustrations of Section 2.5 to describe related analysis for systems of equations. Appendix 2B presents the basic algorithms for computing quantities needed by the linear analysis methods used in this study.

Choosing Strategic Elements in a Model

Experience with medium- and large-scale econometric models suggests that such models contain many elements (equations, variables) that have little effect on the model's more important endogenous variables, but whose sheer number overwhelms intuition. In this context, intuition about a model and identification of its strategic elements are closely related in practice. Our strategy for isolating strategic elements depends essentially on a systematic combination of multipliers, parameter perturbations, and linear systems analysis. We can identify what "really counts" by sorting all of the model's coefficients and exogenous variables into two categories: those with negligible influence, and those with large influence on all interesting endogenous variables. If the negligible coefficients and unimportant exogenous variables are a sizable fraction of the model's elements, the remaining elements, provided they are intellectually coherent, will allow more scope for intuition.

It should be possible, then, to condense large models into their essential elements, facilitating better and more basic understanding. Other approaches to reduce the impenetrability of most current macromodels are also being actively pursued. One such perspective is the core-model concept. Michel Deleau, Pierre Malgrange, and Pierre-Alain Muet (1982) have created a theory-based 26-equation model with numerical coefficients that explicitly incorporates steady-state constraints and detailed neoclassical constant-returns-to-scale production theory as part of an otherwise traditional macromodel. Rex Bergstrom and Clifford Wymer (1976) and Giancarlo Gandolfo (1981) have built theory-based core macromodels. They further hypothesize continuous time behavior, which has strong implications for estimation and interpretation of dynamics. Patrick Artus, Guy Laroque, and Gilles Michel (1984) have built a switching-regime core macromodel of the French economy that is predicated on fundamentally different disequilibrium behavior from lags that traditionally reflect disequilibrium. We construe our approach to be one of several (which also include rational expectations) that share one common tenet: a profound uneasiness with the foundations of current macromodels, and the need to probe or to rethink their structure.

With rare exceptions, closed-form analysis is only possible for models whose equations are strictly linear in variables and coefficients. In practice, however, models are seldom totally devoid of reciprocals, ratios, products, logarithms, or exponentials. Thus there are two possible (nonexclusive) approaches: simulation of the nonlinear model, and analysis of its linearized counterpart.

The most important concerns of a model ordinarily depend on what is at stake. Fifteen years ago, for example, price–wage behavior was of less interest than real output and employment. The response of real final demand to fiscal and monetary instruments was thought to matter most. Today, one might wish to concentrate on inflation. If it is true, as some economists believe, that for the short and intermediate run (say for 10 quarters) the real economy is weakly linked to price–wage rates of change, then it is practical to study the latter in isolation. What matters in such circumstances is whatever governs price–wage behavior. In either case (just the real sector, or just a price–wage sector) the end result is a compressed, partial model that can be most readily studied and understood in isolation. When it is practical to pare away sectors of lesser concern, particular sectors can be more easily understood.

2.2 LINEAR THEORY AND NONLINEAR MODELS

Linear analysis has two major advantages. One is that it enables the calculation of characteristic roots and vectors, which provide interesting information on which we will elaborate further. The second is cost: for a nontrivial but modest expenditure an entire model's parameter and exogenous-variable influence can be canvassed. While any single simulation of a medium-size model costs only a few dollars, a comprehensive evaluation requires perturbations for at least one parameter per equation and for each exogenous variable (to compute multipliers). Complete analysis thus quickly inflates simulation costs to high levels.

Linearization, though, puts potential limits on the scope of analytical conclusions.[†] As is well known, the behavior of a weakly nonlinear model with continuous low-order derivatives can be accurately mimicked by its linearized counterpart in the neighborhood of the solution or simulation path. Linear approximations for a highly nonlinear model will only hold for extremely small deviations from the simulation path, which correspondingly limits the range of validity of linear analysis. Few econometric models have severe nonlinearities; nevertheless, all are somewhat nonlinear, and the acceptable range of input variations in a given modeling situation is a practical judgment, though one susceptible to testing. Relevant insights about nonlinear models can often be extracted from linear approximations, even when the original model cannot be tracked precisely. Later we shall describe means to validate inferences based on linearization through comparisons with the nonlinear model. These comparisons should minimize fallacious conclusions drawn from the linearized version. Frequent relinearization is another way to guard against false inferences.

Most of the subsequent discussion will be about the deterministic equation systems. This limitation may appear unduly restrictive, especially after the seminal contributions of Frisch (1933) and Slutzky (1937). They showed that when nonoscillatory, damped linear deterministic dynamic systems are subjected to independently distributed random shocks, model outputs then resemble many economic time series that have irregular, persistent cycles, contrary to the behavior of their "unshocked" counterparts. These ideas were further supported by Adelman and Adelman (1959), who found that the early Klein–Goldberger model's simulation behavior resembled economic time series (with appropriate 7–10 year cycles) only when indepen-

---

[†]The limitations of nonlinear simulation methods should not be forgotten either. The main limitation is that simulation results can be extremely sensitive to exogenous-variable time paths. Furthermore, it is possible for nonlinear simulations to have no homogeneous solution, but only particular solutions.

dent random shocks were added. Howrey (1972) shows how cyclical behavior for a combined deterministic and stochastic process can be portrayed using spectral analysis (see also Wolters, 1980). Thus there are strong reasons why random shocks should not be neglected. Nevertheless, there remains the pressing need to attain a deeper understanding of the systematic parts of models. Since the stochastic responses of endogenous variables are channeled through a system's deterministic homogeneous dynamics, understanding such behavior is a primary concern of stochastic analysis as well.

Linearization

The following notation will be used to describe a nonlinear state-variable dynamic model:[†]

$$f_1(y_{1t}, \ldots, y_{Gt}; y_{1,t-1}, \ldots, y_{G,t-1}; x_{1t}, \ldots, x_{Kt}; \beta_1, \ldots, \beta_J) = \varepsilon_{1t},$$

$$\vdots$$

$$f_g(y_{1t}, \ldots, y_{Gt}; y_{1,t-1}, \ldots, y_{G,t-1}; x_{1t}, \ldots, x_{Kt}; \beta_1, \ldots, \beta_J) = \varepsilon_{gt},$$

$$\vdots$$

$$f_G(y_{1t}, \ldots, y_{Gt}; y_{1,t-1}, \ldots, y_{G,t-1}; x_{1t}, \ldots, x_{Kt}; \beta_1, \ldots, \beta_J) = \varepsilon_{Gt},$$

$$(2.2.1)$$

where f_g = one of G functional relationships each of which may be nonlinear.

y_{gt} = one of G current endogenous variables.

$y_{g,t-1}$ = one of the G endogenous variables lagged one period, (note that endogenous variables appear lagged at most once, since higher-order lags have been eliminated by introducing additional endogenous-variable definitions included in the G equations described above).

x_{kt} = one of K current exogenous variables (note that any lagged exogenous variables have been eliminated by introducing additional endogenous-variable definitions included in the G equations described above, *or* they have been disguised by redefining their time subscripts).

[†] For a helpful introduction to the concepts involved in this formulation, refer to Chapters 1–4 of Liu and Liu (1975). Also see Gelb (1974). The nonlinear state-variable model comes directly through redefinition of variables from a nonlinear structural-form model. The transformation to state-space form is treated more fully in Appendix 2B.

β_j = one of the J constant coefficients which appear in *any* of the G equations.

ε_{gt} = one of G additive error terms.

It is convenient to further compress the notation into vector form:

$$f(y_t, y_{t-1}, x_t, \beta) = \varepsilon_t, \tag{2.2.2}$$

where

$$f = \begin{pmatrix} f_1 \\ \vdots \\ f_g \\ \vdots \\ f_G \end{pmatrix}, \quad y_t = \begin{pmatrix} y_{1t} \\ \vdots \\ y_{gt} \\ \vdots \\ y_{Gt} \end{pmatrix}, \quad y_{t-1} = \begin{pmatrix} y_{1,t-1} \\ \vdots \\ y_{g,t-1} \\ \vdots \\ y_{G,t-1} \end{pmatrix}, \quad x_t = \begin{pmatrix} x_{1t} \\ \vdots \\ x_{kt} \\ \vdots \\ x_{Kt} \end{pmatrix}$$

$$\beta = \begin{pmatrix} \beta_1 \\ \vdots \\ \beta_j \\ \vdots \\ \beta_J \end{pmatrix}, \quad \varepsilon_t = \begin{pmatrix} \varepsilon_{1t} \\ \vdots \\ \varepsilon_{gt} \\ \vdots \\ \varepsilon_{Gt} \end{pmatrix} \tag{2.2.3}$$

Deterministic simulation is the period-by-period solutions of this equation system with $\varepsilon_t \equiv 0$. Simulation thus consists of solving a set of (usually nonlinear) simultaneous equations for the current values of the endogenous variables, conditional on the model's coefficients, exogenous variables, and initial conditions or prior-period solutions for lagged endogenous variables.

A linearization of this equation system around the simulation path creates the basis for linear analysis that yields quantitative insights akin to those obtained from simulation, plus others as well. A clear exposition about linearizing econometric models appears in Klein and Goldberger (1955).[†] The familiar first-order Taylor-series approximation to the model's nonlinear structural form around the baseline simulation is

$$D_t \Delta y_t = E_t \Delta y_{t-1} + F_t \Delta x_t + G_t \Delta \beta, \tag{2.2.4}$$

where $\Delta y_t, \Delta y_{t-1}, \Delta x_t, \Delta \beta$ are deviations around the baseline simulation,

[†] More detailed aspects of implementation are presented in the appendices to this chapter.

and

$$D_t(y_t, y_{t-1}, x_t, \beta) \equiv \left(\frac{\partial f}{\partial y_t}\right), \tag{2.2.5}$$

$$E_t(y_t, y_{t-1}, x_t, \beta) \equiv -\left(\frac{\partial f}{\partial y_{t-1}}\right), \tag{2.2.6}$$

$$F_t(y_t, y_{t-1}, x_t, \beta) \equiv -\left(\frac{\partial f}{\partial x_t}\right), \tag{2.2.7}$$

$$G_t(y_t, y_{t-1}, x_t, \beta) \equiv -\left(\frac{\partial f}{\partial \beta}\right). \tag{2.2.8}$$

Though the D, E, F, and G matrices are generally time-varying as noted, we shall drop the time subscript for now, commenting later on this time dependence.

Assuming that D is invertible, which is usually true for econometric models, we may obtain the reduced-form deviation model:

$$\Delta y_t = D^{-1}E\Delta y_{t-1} + D^{-1}F\Delta x_t + D^{-1}G\Delta\beta, \tag{2.2.9}$$

$$\Delta y_t = A\Delta y_{t-1} \quad + B\Delta x_t \quad + C\Delta\beta, \tag{2.2.10}$$

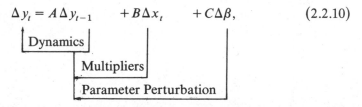

Regular multiplier analysis (in which $\Delta\beta = 0$) traces out the effects on model outputs Δy_t induced by changes in model inputs, Δx_t. These are transmitted through the reduced-form dynamics coefficients A and reduced-form exogenous-variable coefficients B. Parameter-perturbation analysis at this level of generality resembles multiplier analysis: coefficient changes operate through reduced-form coefficients C and dynamics coefficients A on endogenous model outputs, for $\Delta x = 0$.

It is easy to understand why multiplier analysis has for so long been the dominant mode of analysis, to the comparative neglect of parameter perturbation: this reliance has its origins in the methods ordinarily used in creating such models.[†] As a matter of course, most econometricians con-

---

[†] The authors at various times have engaged in this task. It is hard work, and the following comments should not be construed as belittling such enterprises.

struct a model one equation at a time, working to arrive at results in accord with economic theory and which also possess desirable statistical properties. Then individual equations are combined into a complete model, which is provisionally approved when complete model simulations display acceptable behavior. Arriving at a model in this manner does not provide assurances that the model has sensible steady-state properties, and the information it gives about model dynamics is often restrictive.[†] Since standard simulations are equivalent to multiplier analysis, in effect multipliers are employed as diagnostic devices to examine full model behavior. Finally, the accepted model is ready for its intended use: forecasts and/or policy analysis. Once again, these are scenarios generated by simulation of the complete nonlinear model, using alternative sets of exogenous variables and/or policy parameters.

Understanding the relations between economic theory and behavior through a model is yet another objective. Where this is the main purpose, parameter perturbations should be given especially serious consideration. Since economic intuition and comprehension are most closely linked to structural equations and not the reduced form, parameter perturbations of structural coefficients ought to receive more attention. Multipliers in a linear model (or simulation analogues of a linearized model) are made up of scrambled structural coefficients (e.g., the elements of $D^{-1}E = A$ and $D^{-1}F = B$) and ordinarily lack intuitive content relevant to interpretation of model structure.[‡]

2.3   LINEAR MODELS REEXPRESSED USING CHARACTERISTIC ROOTS

A linearized model's time response is conveniently expressed in terms of its reduced form [equation (2.1.10)]. Given initial conditions Δy_{t_0}, and time paths for exogenous variable and coefficient perturbations $\Delta x_s, \Delta \beta_s$ for $t_0 < s \leq t_0 + n$ $(n \geq 1)$, the endogenous-variable response $\Delta y_{t_0 + n}$ at $t_0 + n$

[†] More technically, only particular solutions are usually presented and homogeneous dynamics are usually neglected.

[‡] If a particular model has low parameter sensitivity for endogenous variables of interest, then the Lucas critique (1976)—that parameters change in response to the stochastic behavior of variables of concern to individual agents—will have less potential practical importance. Conversely, if significant policy parameters induce large responses, the potential importance of Lucas's observations will be all the greater. Even more to the point, parameters thought to be endogenous should be treated that way from the outset.

is given by the familiar convolution formula:

$$\Delta y_{t_0+n} = A^n \Delta y_{t_0} + \sum_{s=0}^{n-1} A^s \{ B\Delta x_{t_0+n-s} + C\Delta\beta_{t_0+n-s} \}. \quad (2.3.1)$$

This formula is frequently used with $\Delta y_{t_0} = 0$ and $\Delta\beta_s = 0$ ($s = t_0, \ldots, t_0 + n$) is conventional reduced-form multiplier analysis. We shall discuss some of its other uses later in this chapter.

A more illuminating way to understand the linearized model's dynamic behavior is obtained by reexpressing equation (2.3.1) using the characteristic roots and vectors of the dynamics matrix A. These are defined by the following formulas:[†]

$$Ar_g = r_g\lambda_g \quad (g = 1,\ldots,G), \quad (2.3.2)$$

$$l'_g A = \lambda_g l'_g \quad (g = 1,\ldots,G), \quad (2.3.3)$$

where λ_g = is characteristic root of A (a complex-valued scalar).
r_g = the right characteristic vector associated with λ_g.
l_g = the left characteristic vector associated with λ_g.

Equations (2.3.2) and (2.3.3) are equivalent to

$$AR = R\Lambda, \quad (2.3.4)$$

$$L'A = \Lambda L', \quad (2.3.5)$$

where $\Lambda = G \times G$ diagonal matrix with the characteristic roots on its diagonal.
R = the $G \times G$ matrix of right characteristic vectors.
L = the $G \times G$ matrix of left characteristic vectors.

We are free to normalize the characteristic vectors so that

$$L'R = RL' = I, \quad (2.3.6)$$

where I = the $G \times G$ identity matrix.

From equations (2.3.4), (2.3.5), and (2.3.6) we can express A in terms of its

[†]We assume in this section that A possesses a full set of G roots and vectors, as the exposition would be unfruitfully complicated by considering the defective case.

characteristic roots and vectors:

$$A = R\Lambda L'$$

$$= \sum_{g=1}^{G} r_g \lambda_g l'_g. \tag{2.3.7}$$

A corresponding expression for powers of the matrix A relates the characteristic roots and vectors to the dynamic behavior of the linearized model:[†]

$$A^s = R\Lambda^s L'$$

$$= \sum_{g=1}^{G} r_g \lambda_g^s l'_g. \tag{2.3.8}$$

Substituting equation (2.3.8) into the convolution formula in equation (2.3.1) yields

$$\Delta y_{t_0+n} = \sum_{g=1}^{G} r_g \left\{ \lambda_g^n l'_g \Delta y_{t_0} + \sum_{s=0}^{n-1} \lambda_g^s l'_g \left(B\Delta x_{t_0+n-s} + C\Delta \beta_{t_0+n-s} \right) \right\}. \tag{2.3.9}$$

Thus, for any single root λ_g, the portion of endogenous-variable response associated with λ_g is

$$\left(\Delta y_{t_0+n} | \lambda_g \right) = r_g \left\{ \lambda_g^n l'_g \Delta y_{t_0} + \sum_{s=0}^{n-1} \lambda_g^s l'_g \left(B\Delta x_{t_0+n-s} + C\Delta \beta_{t_0+n-s} \right) \right\}. \tag{2.3.10}$$

When the responses of a particular endogenous variable associated with a given characteristic root are large, we have isolated a variable–root association that warrants further scrutiny by methods described in the next section.

Characteristic-Root Sensitivity

When a particular characteristic root holds our interest, we may want to know where it originates in the model structure. We must start by determining which modeling decisions are mostly prominently associated with this root in the linearized model. This information, along with the additional

---

[†]A valuable text by William Baumol (1979) provides background on how characteristic roots help describe dynamic behavior.

knowledge about where elements of the linearized model come from in the original model, provides the answer we seek.[†]

Let the total differential of λ_g with respect to the a_{ij}'s be given by

$$\Delta\lambda_g \cong \sum_{i=1}^{G} \sum_{j=1}^{G} \frac{\partial\lambda_g}{\partial a_{ij}} \Delta a_{ij}, \qquad (2.3.11)$$

where $\Delta\lambda_g, \Delta a_{ij}$ = changes in λ_g and a_{ij}.

A scaling issue arises in interpreting equation (2.3.11). We are looking for those Δa_{ij} which produce the largest contributions to $\Delta\lambda_g$; these a_{ij} are the imputed sources of λ_g. To interpret the contributions, the Δa_{ij} must be comparable. If we measure relative contributions by $\partial\lambda_g/\partial a_{ij}$, we implicitly scale the Δa_{ij} so that they have the same absolute magnitude. However, a more reasonable scaling might be identical relative magnitudes. In this case the relative contributions are $(\partial\lambda_g/\partial a_{ij})a_{ij}$.[‡] Appendix 2B, Section 2B.7 demonstrates that $\lambda_g = \sum_{i=1}^{G}\sum_{j=1}^{G}(\partial\lambda_g/\partial a_{ij})a_{ij}$ exactly, so that one can interpret each relative contribution defined below (2.3.11) as a share of that particular root contributed by a_{ij}. If the partial-derivative notation of (2.3.11) is replaced by Δ purely for didactic purpose, we see that each individual relative contribution can be thought of as $\Delta\lambda_g/(\Delta a_{ij} \div a_{ij})$, that is, the change in λ_g per unit small relative change in the coefficient a_{ij}. It follows immediately that elasticities $(\partial\lambda_g/\partial_{ij})a_{ij}/\lambda_g$ sum to unity, which offers another potentially interesting normalization.

In any case $\partial\lambda_g/\partial a_{ij}$ is an essential ingredient. A formula for this partial derivative can be obtained from equations (2.3.2) and (2.3.3). First differentiate equation (2.3.2) with respect to a_{ij}:

$$\frac{\partial A}{\partial a_{ij}} r_g + A \frac{\partial r_g}{\partial a_{ij}} = \frac{\partial r_g}{\partial a_{ij}} \lambda_g + r_g \frac{\partial\lambda_g}{\partial a_{ij}}. \qquad (2.3.12)$$

Then premultiply both sides of this expression by l'_g:

$$l'_g \frac{\partial A}{\partial a_{ij}} r_g + l'_g A \frac{\partial r_g}{\partial a_{ij}} = l'_g \frac{\partial r_g}{\partial a_{ij}} \lambda_g + l'_g r_g \frac{\partial\lambda_g}{\partial a_{ij}}. \qquad (2.3.13)$$

[†]Chapters 4 and 5 study the MQEM in depth from these several perspectives on model structure.

[‡]If a_{ij} equals zero, this and similar normalizations (e.g., elasticities) fail. We then must get whatever information we can from the derivative itself. This becomes a practical issue whenever we wish to evaluate the influence of a coefficient a_{ij} that previously had been set to zero, by making it nonzero.

Note from (2.3.6) that $l'_g r_g = 1$, which simplifies the last term above. This property will be used in subsequent expressions. Using equation (2.3.3), this equation reduces to

$$l'_g \frac{\partial A}{\partial a_{ij}} r_g = \frac{\partial \lambda_g}{\partial a_{ij}}, \tag{2.3.14}$$

from which it follows, given the form of $\partial A / \partial a_{ij}$, that

$$\frac{\partial \lambda_g}{\partial a_{ij}} = l'_{ig} r_{jg}, \tag{2.3.15}$$

where l_{ig} = the ith element of l_g.

        r_{jg} = the jth element of r_g.

It is often preferable to consider perturbations in D and E matrix entries from the linearized structural form, since these entries are most easily related to elements of the original structural model. For these perturbations, the relevant linear approximations are the following:

$$\Delta \lambda_g \cong \sum_{i=1}^{G} \sum_{j=1}^{G} \frac{\partial \lambda_g}{\partial d_{ij}} \Delta d_{ij}, \tag{2.3.16}$$

$$\Delta \lambda_g \cong \sum_{i=1}^{G} \sum_{j=1}^{G} \frac{\partial \lambda_g}{\partial e_{ij}} \Delta e_{ij}. \tag{2.3.17}$$

Formulas for $\partial \lambda_g / \partial d_{ij}$ and $\partial \lambda_g / \partial e_{ij}$ are presented in Appendix 2B. The same interpretation in terms of relative contributions summing to λ_g and elasticities summing to unity also holds for D- and E-matrix root sensitivities.

2.4 SORTING-OUT PROCEDURES

We now provide an overview of how we shall use linear analysis, which will often be complemented by nonlinear analysis. The latter is often critical for large exogenous-variable changes or large parameter perturbations, in order to understand model nonlinearities or to test implications of linear analysis. The reader is referred to Exhibit 2.2 for the diagrammatic counterpart to this discussion. Starting with the original nonlinear structural model, the first step is linearization. Second, the linearized structural model is put into

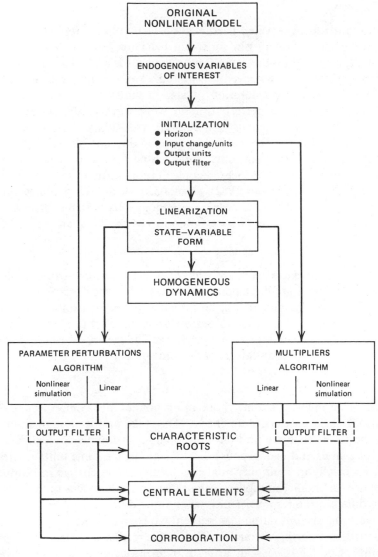

Exhibit 2.2 Sorting-out options.

state-space deviation form. Third, this set of equations is converted to its reduced form, discussed above as equation (2.2.10). Fourth, the matrix A in this equation is modified according to the characteristic-root, characteristic-vector decomposition of equations (2.3.7)–(2.3.10). While obviously none of these transformations is relevant for simulation of the nonlinear model, those described next are essential for both approaches.

Time Horizon

The time horizon over which perturbation results are computed is clearly problem-dependent. Interest in short-run behavior—at least four quarters, at most eight quarters—dictates a lower bound for a possible horizon; the long-run horizon is less convention-bound. Another major consideration must be the strength and duration of lags in the system, which determine how long it takes for a perturbation to work through the system. More experimentation and experience is required with this process to arrive at useful rules of thumb. The next chapter contains one such effort. If the model has roots greater than unity, longer time periods may be needed to observe when explosive influences become dominant. In an earlier version of the MQEM (Kuh and Neese, 1982), simulations of the full nonlinear model stabilized—in the sense that nearly all endogenous variables had smooth time paths when model inputs were smooth—by twelve quarters.

Deterministic or Random Changes

Even though most coefficients are statistical estimates, one can still choose to treat parameters as "best point estimates" that most accurately reflect theory, prior beliefs, and so on, and then proceed to explore the model response sensitivity to small perturbations in them. That is what we shall do subsequently. Associated large changes in the endogenous variables indicate which coefficients are the strategic ones in the models.[†]

Scaling

Another issue involves scaling. Four main possibilities come to mind. The first is to look at unscaled differences. These take on meaning in situations where the input changes have an unambiguous economic context. Second, when exogenous and endogenous variables are in the same units it is often useful, especially in multiplier analysis, to divide the change in output by the change in input (multipliers calculated for incommensurate units are usually difficult to interpret). Third, when units differ, it is often convenient to measure inputs and outputs as percentage changes and then to compute arc elasticities. Fourth, one might wish to scale response according to typical variability. Similar issues can arise in regression analysis, where "beta" coefficients are computed to remove both scale and units. Beta scaling and related issues are discussed further in Section 2.5.

[†] In an earlier paper Kuh and Neese (1982) looked at what happens to model output sensitivity when one parameter in an equation changes and the rest in that equation are optimally readjusted (in the sense of minimum-variance constrained least squares) according to the estimated coefficient covariances. Pagan and Shannon (1983) present several interesting and original measures of stochastic sensitivity. Fair (1980) uses stochastic simulation to assess model specification. In short, these aspects of sensitivity are also now becoming available.

Size and Type of Change

The size and type of change (impulse or step input) raise further issues. Small changes, provided that they are large enough to exceed the limits of machine precision, ought to be given serious consideration. Large changes will become entangled with model nonlinearities, so that obtaining an understanding of first-order effects—that are also highly probable—sometimes motivates a resort to small changes when studying nonlinear models (the issue is irrelevant for linear systems of equations). Then, large changes should be studied to learn about the importance of nonlinearities.[†] Elsewhere (Kuh and Neese, 1982), we studied parameter perturbations ranging from 0.001 to 10%. We found that 0.1 or 1% perturbations worked well, in the sense that these parameter changes met our basic small-change criterion: yielding elasticities outside of machine noise that were minimally affected by nonlinearities.

It is thought desirable sometimes to make statistically based parameter changes—for example, by considering the covariance matrix of estimated parameters to be multivariate normal and then randomly extracting new coefficients from this joint distribution. This distinctly different approach has merit for some purposes related to our own. Such a procedure, however, would often lead to large changes outside the bounds of linearity (which is not necessarily incorrect). It therefore conflicts with or complements what we are after—effective ways to determine linear components of behavior and then investigate whether or not inferences about model structure based on linear analysis are valid in nonlinear circumstances. Thus, while we are not opposed to this approach, we have set it aside as not germane to our perspective.

In addition, one will often want to combine coefficient changes. In a distributed-lag relation for instance, all lags in combination could have a strong effect, even when individual coefficients do not. Particularly, since we use filtering (see below), it is important not to bias reported results against model structures where such combinations arise naturally.

Both economic and technical considerations influence the choice between an impulse and a step response. From an economic perspective, an impulse input can be thought of as a one-time stochastic shock (either to parameters or to exogenous inputs), whose effects are then traced through the system over time. Furthermore, when coefficients of the matrix A are varied, an impulse change alters the dynamics for just one period, whereas a step input causes a permanent change in a dynamics coefficient. Again, from an economic point of view, a step input change can be thought of as the

---

[†] In the next chapter, some measures proposed by Zellner and Peck (1973) to gauge the extent of nonlinearity and symmetry are computed for the MQEM.

introduction of a new mode of behavior and its ramified effects on the economy through the model's dynamics.

The main technical aspects are these: Dynamics are easier to visualize for impulse responses, and level magnitudes are most easily perceived with step inputs. Since, even for stable responses, level magnitudes (even normalized ones) can be vastly different, there are practical technical grounds for relying most often on impulse inputs, since the resultant outputs are less inclined to "run off the graph" for stable systems with slow dynamics (e.g., a first-order lag of 0.99 has a profound long-run effect on levels).

Filter Choice

Filtering is intended to reduce the largely superfluous information from a given computer run. Computer output is voluminous even for medium-size models, so that condensation helps both computer storage and visual scanning when extraneous or small entries are eliminated. Thus, while not mandatory, filtering is extremely valuable for understanding and interpretation. Furthermore, the filter cutoffs should be small, carefully chosen values so as to reduce the risk of overlooking some response of substance.

To illustrate how we shall proceed in practice, let us suppose that for parameter perturbations each coefficient change is 1% and outputs are measured in percent, so that their ratio is an arc elasticity. In our experience many elasticities will be zero, while many others will be of order of magnitude 10^{-4} or less. Since economic data are seldom accurate to more than four significant digits, elasticities less than 10^{-4} can reasonably be treated as zero.[†] About half the results fall into these two extreme categories, but what of the remainder? Broadly speaking, only a small proportion of the remainder are likely to count. Sometimes isolating influential from less influential parameters enables the modeler to concentrate his resources most effectively on the ones that matter, leaving the rest of the model unchanged.[‡] More quantitative comments can be made that are based on previous experience with an earlier, slightly different version of the MQEM. The proportion of elasticities in excess of 1 was about 6% at impact, and the proportion above 5 was about 1%. As longer-run (potentially explosive) dynamics become more important, the share of large elasticities increased: generally speaking, even after 24 quarters only 16% of the recorded A matrix entries for elasticities exceeded 5.

[†] Wilkinson (1965) has shown that perturbations in data are related to the relative change in coefficients in an estimation context. Thus very small elasticities from a numerical point of view can be treated as zero.

[‡] If *a priori* beliefs are contradicted by the perturbation outcomes—a coefficient expected to be highly influential turns out not to be, or *vice versa*—then this approach to model structure analysis is especially appealing.

Thus our experience uniformly indicates that even in circumstances where large responses are most probable, at least half the elasticities are 10^{-4} or less, and furthermore, that the remainder are heavily skewed—a handful of really sizable elasticities and a modest fraction of medium-size ones. We therefore will mainly use filters of either 0.05 or 0.10, with slight need to worry about overlooking strategic magnitudes. We can test the reasonableness of these cutoffs by setting below-cutoff values to zero in the original nonlinear model and comparing the resulting simulation with endogenous-model responses for the full, uncensored model. We call this comparison *corroboration*. If the endogenous variable time paths are close, the filtering process can be judged to have been effective. Since some nonlinearities can behave very differently from their linearized counterparts, the basic approach we have adopted can fail; hence the need for corroboration in the sense used here. The final box in Exhibit 2.2 represents this step. The comparison is made in order to validate our research strategy for a given model, not the model itself.

Multiplier analysis involves the same considerations for horizon, impulse response, step response, and filter size. As with parameter combinations, there are often combinations of exogenous-variable changes that make more sense than one-at-a-time changes. While it is possible to combine results from several individual perturbations after the fact, it is often more reasonable to look at fiscal–monetary policy combinations than at the individual variations in particular policy instruments.

Homogeneous Dynamics

Multiplier analysis and parameter perturbations respectively indicate how exogenous-variable and parameter changes affect current endogenous variables. As illustrated in equation (2.3.10), these effects always operate through the model's dynamics. Dynamic structure is worthy of separate investigation for three reasons. First, dynamic responses in isolation provide informative background that illuminates multiplier and parameter perturbation analysis. Second, the dynamics show which sectors are earliest in the causal structure and how dynamic coupling changes through time. Third, stochastic responses are dominated by the homogeneous dynamics.

Characteristic-Root Decomposition

According to (2.3.10), endogenous responses are associated with individual characteristic roots, either in the context of multipliers or parameter perturbations. For multipliers, the links involve sums of characteristic-root powers, left characteristic vectors, and reduced-form coefficients, that is, the elements of B in (2.3.10). For parameter perturbations we need the coefficients from C plus the other elements mentioned.

These linkages enable us to pinpoint where specific dynamics interact with exogenous variables in multiplier analysis. Alternatively, we can locate which characteristic roots are associated with parameter perturbations that appear most critical to interesting endogenous variable responses.

Characteristic-Root Sensitivities

Characteristic-root sensitivity analysis has two aims. The first is to know how the equation structure generates particular roots. Even with low filtering levels, the sensitivities are often few in number. In these instances it is straightforward to locate the coefficients which contribute most to a particular root and examine their related equations. Equations are seldom tightly coupled dynamically, so that a given root is often about the same as the first-order or Koyck lag in a specific equation; when tight coupling does occur, this simple association breaks down. Also, roots with imaginary parts often have many large sensitivities. This observation appears to be systematically related to the previously mentioned condition.

Second, information about root sensitivities can be usefully combined with linear-multiplier or parameter-perturbation analysis. Often a given endogenous variable is driven by a few exogenous variables operating through a few important characteristic roots. One can thus spin an interpretive yarn beginning with the exogenous-variable, characteristic-root associations, and then examine the structure of those roots. The same approach can be applied to parameter perturbations.

Corroboration

In this monograph we are exploring fresh ways to understand econometric models, including linear system analysis. These have been sketched qualitatively above. While we believe that nonlinearities will seldom lead to false inferences from linearized models, this possibility should not be ruled out. Corroboration here means that comparisons of the behavior predicted by the linearized version hold up in practice for the nonlinear model. For instance, linear analysis could indicate that a subset of coefficients and/or exogenous variables are inconsequential. We can then set these to zero in the nonlinear model and observe if the resulting simulation path changes little: if so, the information from the linear model was not misleading. Or, linear analysis might indicate that a subset of variables is weakly coupled to the rest of the model. We can then compare simulations from the isolated nonlinear subset of equations with simulations of the complete nonlinear model. When the two solutions are close, inferences drawn from the linearized system have conveyed appropriate information. If the linear methods we use consistently provide correct insights, this sort of corroboration will become less important than it is currently in the early stages of our experimentation.

2.5 FIRST-ORDER SENSITIVITY ANALYSIS FOR A SINGLE EXPLICIT EQUATION

In this section we work through a simple example to give a preview of multiplier and parameter-sensitivity concepts and a closer look at elasticity and beta scaling.[†] Equations of different functional forms have different dynamic properties, and some (such as first differenced equations) may require different scalings to make interpretation easier. For simplicity, we begin by considering the single, reduced-form equation

$$y_t = \beta_0 + \beta_1 y_{t-1} + \beta_2 x_t, \tag{2.5.1}$$

where y_t and y_{t-1} are current and one-period lagged values of an endogenous variable, x_t is exogenous, and $\beta_0, \beta_1, \beta_2$ are constant coefficients. It is assumed that an initial condition y_{t_0}, a time path for x_t (x_s, $t_0 \leq s \leq t_0 + N$, for integer N), and coefficient values are given so that a solution or simulation time path for y_t is defined (y_s, $t_0 \leq s \leq t_0 + N$).

We begin with a first-order Taylor series expansion of equation (2.5.1) in the vicinity of the simulation time path:

$$dy = \frac{\partial f}{\partial \beta_0} d\beta_0 + \frac{\partial f}{\partial \beta_1} d\beta_1 + \frac{\partial f}{\partial y_{t-1}} dy_{t-1} + \frac{\partial f}{\partial \beta_2} d\beta_2 + \frac{\partial f}{\partial X_t} dX.$$

$$\tag{2.5.2}$$

In the case of the linear equation (2.5.1) this becomes

$$\Delta y_t = \Delta \beta_0 + \Delta \beta_1 y_{t-1} + \beta_1 \Delta y_{t-1} + \Delta \beta_2 x_t + \beta_2 \Delta x_t. \tag{2.5.3}$$

Note that in this case the series expansion directly leads to a reduced-form deviation model [see equation (2.2.10)].

Scaling

To aid interpretation, the variates in equation (2.5.3) (the deviations) are then scaled, according to our criterion of "interesting" variation, by rewrit-

[†]Appendix 2A treats perturbation analysis of systems of equations that are both time varying and time invariant.

ing it as

$$\frac{\Delta y_t}{\text{scale}(\Delta y_t)} = \left[\frac{\text{scale}(\Delta \beta_0) \cdot 1}{\text{scale}(\Delta y_t)} \right] \frac{\Delta \beta_0}{\text{scale}(\Delta \beta_0)}$$

$$+ \left[\frac{\text{scale}(\Delta \beta_1) \cdot y_{t-1}}{\text{scale}(\Delta y_t)} \right] \frac{\Delta \beta_1}{\text{scale}(\Delta \beta_1)}$$

$$+ \left[\frac{\beta_1 \text{scale}(\Delta y_{t-1})}{\text{scale}(\Delta y_t)} \right] \frac{\Delta y_{t-1}}{\text{scale}(\Delta y_{t-1})}$$

$$+ \left[\frac{\text{scale}(\Delta \beta_2) \cdot x_t}{\text{scale}(\Delta y_t)} \right] \frac{\Delta \beta_2}{\text{scale}(\Delta \beta_2)}$$

$$+ \left[\frac{\beta_2 \text{scale}(\Delta x_t)}{\text{scale}(\Delta y_t)} \right] \frac{\Delta x_t}{\text{scale}(\Delta x_t)}. \qquad (2.5.4)$$

Each right-hand-side term is the product of a variable's or parameter's scaled deviation (outside brackets) and its scaled deviation proportion (inside brackets). "Scaled-deviation proportion" means the number of units of "interesting" variation in the l.h.s. variable caused by a unit "interesting" variation in the associated r.h.s. variable. These proportions are evaluated along the original model simulation time paths and are therefore time-varying in general.

Interesting variations reflected in a scale measure take several forms. Elasticities are widely used, and these are just the scaled changes divided by the levels. Another scaled measure would be the ratio of a change to the variable's standard deviation. While we are attracted to a particular variant of standard deviation scaling called "beta scaling," there is no unique best scale: the investigator must choose a scale most relevant for his immediate purposes.

Adopting the shorthand

$$\text{prop}(\Delta \beta_0, \Delta y_t) \quad \text{for} \quad \frac{\text{scale}(\Delta \beta_0) \cdot 1}{\text{scale}(\Delta y_t)}$$

and similarly for other terms, and rearranging, equation (2.5.4) can be written in the format of equation (2.2.11):

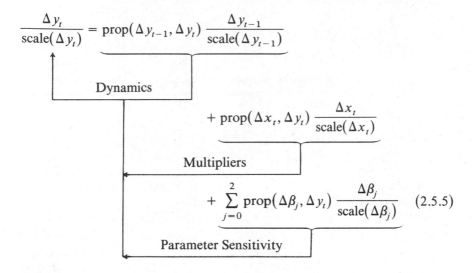

$$\frac{\Delta y_t}{\text{scale}(\Delta y_t)} = \underbrace{\text{prop}(\Delta y_{t-1}, \Delta y_t) \frac{\Delta y_{t-1}}{\text{scale}(\Delta y_{t-1})}}_{\text{Dynamics}}$$

$$\underbrace{+ \text{prop}(\Delta x_t, \Delta y_t) \frac{\Delta x_t}{\text{scale}(\Delta x_t)}}_{\text{Multipliers}}$$

$$\underbrace{+ \sum_{j=0}^{2} \text{prop}(\Delta \beta_j, \Delta y_t) \frac{\Delta \beta_j}{\text{scale}(\Delta \beta_j)}}_{\text{Parameter Sensitivity}} \quad (2.5.5)$$

Homogeneous dynamics are governed by $\text{prop}(\Delta y_{t-1}, \Delta y_t) = \beta_1 \text{scale}(\Delta y_{t-1})/\text{scale}(\Delta y_t)$. If we choose $\text{scale}(\Delta y_{t-1}) \cong \text{scale}(\Delta y_t)$, this proportion is close to β_1, the dynamics coefficient in the model equation (2.5.1). The two nonhomogeneous parts of the expression, the multiplier and parameter-sensitivity forcing functions, are governed by the exogenous-variable deviation proportion and the parameter deviation proportions, respectively.

When we employ elasticity scaling [i.e., $\text{scale}(\Delta y_t) = y_t$], the scaled deviation proportions have a "level share" interpretation. Equation (2.5.5) becomes (writing out the proportions)

$$\%\Delta y_t = \frac{\beta_1 y_{t-1}}{y_t} \%\Delta y_{t-1} + \frac{\beta_2 x_t}{y_t} \%\Delta x_t + \frac{\beta_0}{y_t} \%\Delta \beta_0$$

$$+ \frac{\beta_1 y_{t-1}}{y_t} \%\Delta \beta_1 + \frac{\beta_2 x_t}{y_t} \%\Delta \beta_2. \quad (2.5.6)$$

The proportions are now r.h.s.-variable shares in the original model equation (2.5.1). They are "level shares," that is, the proportions of the level y_t that are set by y_{t-1}, x_t, β_0, β_1, and β_2. We note that β_2's level share is identical to x_t's level share; the same relation holds for β_1 and y_{t-1}. The dynamics are governed by y_{t-1}'s level share, which is close to β_1 only when y_t has a smooth time path.

Beta scaling requires a qualitatively different interpretation. In this case equation (2.5.5) becomes

$$\frac{\Delta y_t}{S(\Delta y_t)} = \frac{\beta_1 S(\Delta y_{t-1})}{S(\Delta y_t)} \cdot \frac{\Delta y_{t-1}}{S(\Delta y_{t-1})}$$

$$+ \frac{\beta_2 S(\Delta x_t)}{S(\Delta y_t)} \cdot \frac{\Delta x_t}{S(\Delta x_t)} + \frac{S(\Delta \beta_0)}{S(\Delta y_t)} \cdot \frac{\Delta \beta_0}{S(\Delta \beta_0)}$$

$$+ \frac{S(\Delta \beta_1) y_{t-1}}{S(\Delta y_t)} \cdot \frac{\Delta \beta_1}{S(\Delta \beta_1)} + \frac{S(\Delta \beta_2) x_t}{S(\Delta y_t)} \cdot \frac{\Delta \beta_2}{S(\Delta \beta_2)} \qquad (2.5.7)$$

where $S(\Delta y_t)$ is the standard deviation of Δy_t. These proportions are closely related to beta coefficients in regression analysis.

Beta coefficients (not to be confused with the symbol β used to designate population parameters or coefficients in other contexts) are least-squares estimates based on data vectors transformed to have zero mean and unit standard deviation: $\tilde{y}_t = (y_t - \bar{y})/S_y$ and $\tilde{x}_{jt} = (x_{jt} - \bar{x}_j)/S_{x_j}$—that is, $\hat{\tilde{y}} = \tilde{x}\beta$ in conventional matrix notation. Beta coefficients remove scale from measured responses in regression for reasons similar to those cited above, so that we have borrowed this term for our purposes. In least-squares matrix notation, where $\hat{y} = x\hat{b}$ for unscaled data, we have for an individual beta coefficient $\hat{\beta}_j = \hat{b}_j S_{x_j}/S_y$. Then if a large $\hat{b}_j$ originated as an arithmetic consequence of small x_j variability relative to y variability, this effect on $\hat{b}_j$ is suitably compensated by using $\hat{\beta}_j$ instead.

Multipliers in Elasticity Form

We illustrate some multiplier concepts in the context of an impulse response with elasticity scaling. Referring to equation (2.5.6), this response is defined to be the time path followed by $\%\Delta y_t$ in response to a one-period perturbation of x_t, say at time t_1, with unchanged coefficients. Defining $\eta(y_t, x_{t_1}) \equiv \%\Delta y_t/\%\Delta x_{t_1}$, we have

$$\eta(y_t, x_{t_1}) = \frac{\beta_1 y_{t-1}}{y_t}\eta(y_{t-1}, x_{t_1}), \qquad t > t_1,$$

$$\eta(y_{t_1}, x_{t_1}) = \frac{\beta_2 x_{t_1}}{y_{t_1}}, \qquad t = t_1. \qquad (2.5.8)$$

Equation (2.5.8) shows that the impact elasticity $\eta(y_{t_1}, x_{t_1})$ is identical to x_t's impact exogenous-variable share $\beta_2 x_{t_1}/y_{t_1}$.

Beyond impact the previous-period endogenous variable shares clearly play a part. Taking the n-period interim elasticity $\eta(y_{t_1+n}, x_{t_1})$ as an example:

$$\eta(y_{t_1+n}, x_{t_1}) = \frac{\beta_1 y_{t_1+n-1}}{y_{t_1+n}} \cdot \frac{\beta_1 y_{t_1+n-2}}{y_{t_1+n-1}} \cdot \ldots \cdot \frac{\beta_1 y_{t_1}}{y_{t_1+1}} \left(\frac{\beta_2 x_{t_1}}{y_{t_1}} \right)$$

$$= \frac{\beta_1^n y_{t_1}}{y_{t_1+n}} \left(\frac{\beta_2 x_{t_1}}{y_{t_1}} \right). \tag{2.5.9}$$

Here $\beta_1^n y_{t_1}/y_{t_1+n}$ is the share of the lagged endogenous variable n periods back in determining y_{t_1+n}. This share multiplies $\beta_2 x_{t_1}/y_{t_1}$, which is the exogenous-variable share on impact. Thus the interim impulse elasticity is a scaling of the impact exogenous-variable share. We see that for a given equation, impact shares contain a lot of information about relative importance.

The dynamics parameter β_1 is of primary importance in determining interim elasticity scaling, although the reference time path for y_t normally modifies β_1's effect. The sole exception is when y_t remains at a constant level. Then equation (2.5.9) becomes

$$\eta(y_{t_1+n}, x_{t_1}) = \beta_1^n \left(\frac{\beta_2 x_{t_1}}{y_{t_1}} \right). \tag{2.5.10}$$

From (2.5.10) it is clear that for sluggish dynamics (i.e., β_1 positive and close to 1, which is a common occurrence) interim impulse elasticities remain close to their impact values; for swift dynamics (i.e., β_1 close to 0) the impact elasticity soon decays.

On the other hand, y_t's reference time path can have a marked effect when y_t is growing, as is more often the case. If we assume constant growth for simplicity [i.e., that $y_{t_1+n} = y_{t_1}(1 + r)^n$], we have

$$\eta(y_{t_1+n}, x_{t_1}) = \left(\frac{\beta_1}{1 + r} \right)^n \frac{\beta_2 x_{t_1}}{y_{t_1}}. \tag{2.5.11}$$

Parameter Sensitivity in Elasticity Form

Elasticity responses to parameter perturbations provide useful information concerning model structure. So far this section has only dealt with equations in linear form [like (2.5.1)]. However, since different functional forms have distinctly different deterministic properties, we extend the analysis here. Starting with the total differential of equation (2.5.2), we eliminate the elements that are irrelevant for the response to an impulse perturbation at t_1 in the parameter β_2 of equation (2.5.1), and convert to elasticity form:

$$\eta(y_t, \beta_2) \equiv \frac{\beta_2}{y_t} \cdot \frac{dy_t}{d\beta_2} = \frac{\beta_2}{y_t}\left(\frac{\beta_1 dy_{t-1}}{d\beta_2} + x_t\right) \tag{2.5.12}$$

$$= \beta_1\left(\frac{\beta_2}{y_t}\frac{dy_{t-1}}{d\beta_2}\right) + \frac{\beta_2 x_t}{y_t}. \tag{2.5.13}$$

The transformation in (2.5.14) below enables (2.5.13) to be rewritten in the straightforward way it appears in (2.5.15):

$$\frac{\beta_2}{y_t} \cdot \frac{dy_{t-1}}{d\beta_2} \equiv \left(\frac{dy_{t-1}}{d\beta_2} \cdot \frac{\beta_2}{y_{t-1}}\right)\left(\frac{y_{t-1}}{y_t}\right) \equiv \eta(y_{t-1}, \beta_2)\left(\frac{y_{t-1}}{y_t}\right) \tag{2.5.14}$$

$$\eta(y_{t_1}, \beta_2) = \frac{\beta_2 x_{t_1}}{y_{t_1}}, \qquad t = 1,$$

$$\eta(y_t, \beta_2) = \frac{\beta_1 y_{t-1}}{y_t}\eta(y_{t-1}, \beta_2), \qquad t > 1. \tag{2.5.15}$$

The other elasticities can be written equivalently as

$$\eta(y_{t_1}, \beta_0) = \frac{\beta_0}{y_t}, \qquad t = 1,$$

$$\eta(y_t, \beta_0) = \frac{\beta_1 y_{t-1}}{y_t}\eta(y_{t-1}, \beta_0), \qquad t > 1;$$

$$\eta(y_{t_1}, \beta_1) = \frac{\beta_1 y_{t_0}}{y_t}, \qquad t = 1, \tag{2.5.16}$$

$$\eta(y_t, \beta_1) = \frac{\beta_1 y_{t-1}}{y_t}\eta(y_{t-1}, \beta_1), \qquad t > 1. \tag{2.5.17}$$

Note that on impact these elasticity parameter responses have the following useful property:

$$\eta(y_{t_1}, \beta_0) + \eta(y_{t_1}, \beta_1) + \eta(y_{t_1}, \beta_2) = \frac{\beta_0 + \beta_1 y_{t_0} + \beta_2 x_{t_1}}{y_{t_1}} = 1. \tag{2.5.18}$$

In the linear case, an impact parameter elasticity can be interpreted as the "relative share" which contributes to the solution of the l.h.s. endogenous variable. Suppose instead that the original equation is in log-level form:

$$\ln y_t = \beta_0 + \beta_1 \ln y_{t-1} + \beta_2 \ln x_t. \qquad (2.5.19)$$

We then apply the total differential of equation (2.5.2), and again transform to elasticity form:

$$\eta(y_t, \beta_2) \equiv \frac{\beta_2}{y_t} \cdot \frac{dy_t}{d\beta_2} = \left(\frac{\beta_2}{y_t}\right)\left((\ln x_t)y_t + \beta_1 \frac{y_t}{y_{t-1}} \cdot \frac{dy_{t-1}}{d\beta_2}\right),$$

$$\eta(y_{t_1}, \beta_2) = \beta_2 \ln x_{t_1}, \qquad\qquad t = 1,$$
$$\eta(y_t, \beta_2) = \beta_1 \eta(y_{t-1}, \beta_2), \qquad t > 1. \qquad (2.5.20)$$

Similarly, the other elasticity responses to impulse perturbations in the coefficients at t are

$$\eta(y_{t_1}, \beta_0) = \beta_0, \qquad\qquad\qquad t = 1,$$
$$\eta(y_t, \beta_0) = \beta_1 \eta(y_{t-1}, \beta_0), \qquad t > 1; \qquad (2.5.21)$$
$$\eta(y_{t_1}, \beta_1) = \beta_1 \ln y_{t_0}, \qquad\qquad t = 1,$$
$$\eta(y_t, \beta_1) = \beta_1 \eta(y_{t-1}, \beta_1), \qquad t > 1. \qquad (2.5.22)$$

There is an important difference between the linear and log-level elasticities at impact. The log-level analogue of equation (2.5.18) sums to

$$\eta(y_{t_1}, \beta_0) + \eta(y_{t_1}, \beta_1) + \eta(y_{t_1}, \beta_2) = \beta_0 + \beta_1 \ln y_{t_0} + \beta_2 \ln y_{t_1}$$

$$= \ln y_{t_1}. \qquad (2.5.23)$$

Thus the elasticity responses to perturbations in the parameters of equation (2.5.19) can be made arbitrarily large (and thus more influential in a model simulation) by simply rescaling the variables. While such rescalings are innocuous for the purpose of estimation (only the constant term changes), the magnitudes of variables in nonlinear equations can and do have a large influence on a model's deterministic behavior. This issue of scaling does not arise with linear equations, since the impact sum of parameter perturbations is always unity.

A closely related issue arises in the MQEM, where the modelers often resort to first-differenced logarithmic equations. While one could write the impact elasticity as equation (2.5.23), it is customary instead to renormalize:

$$\Delta \ln y_t = \beta_0 + \beta_1 \ln x_t. \tag{2.5.24}$$

The sum of impact parameter elasticities is then $\Delta \ln y_t$. Elasticities based on this normalization lack a useful economic interpretation. If y_t of equation (2.5.24) is a price level, then $\eta(y_t, \beta_1)$ measures the percentage change of the *level* y_t in response to a percent change in β_1. A more useful normalization in this and related contexts is to measure the percentage change in the inflation *rate* in response to a perturbation. This is easily done by defining a new rate-of-change variable z_t:

$$z_t = \ln y_t - \ln y_{t-1}. \tag{2.5.25}$$

Equation (2.5.24) then becomes

$$z_t = \beta_0 + \beta_1 \ln X_t, \tag{2.5.26}$$

and the parameter elasticities [$\eta(z_{t_1}, \beta_0)$ and $\eta(z_{t_1}, \beta_1)$] sum to unity. This transformation is also useful for the interpretation of multipliers.

Homogeneous Dynamics in Elasticity Form

Single-equation homogeneous dynamics have been used earlier to derive parameter and multiplier sensitivities. Here, for simplicity, we consider equations with only one lagged r.h.s. dependent variable. Taking first the linear equation (2.5.1), we see that the elasticity response to perturbations in y_{t_0} is

$$\eta(y_{t_1}, y_{t_0}) = \frac{\beta_1 y_{t_0}}{y_{t_1}}, \qquad t = t_1,$$

$$\eta(y_t, y_{t-1}) = \left(\frac{\beta_1 y_{t-1}}{y} \right) \eta(y_{t-1}, y_{t-2}), \qquad t > t_1. \tag{2.5.27}$$

Similarly, for the log-level equation (2.5.19) the response reduces to

$$\eta(y_{t_1}, y_{t_0}) = \beta_1, \qquad t = t_1,$$

$$\eta(y_t, y_{t-1}) = \beta_1 \eta(y_{t-1}, y_{t-2}), \qquad t > t_1. \tag{2.5.28}$$

An interesting general relationship immediately follows: for any functional form, an impulse perturbation of ψ (where ψ can be a lagged endogenous variable, exogenous variable, or parameter) has an elasticity response defined as

$$\eta(y_{t_1}, \psi) = \frac{dy_{t_1}}{d\psi} \cdot \frac{\psi}{y_{t_1}}, \qquad\qquad t = 1,$$

$$\eta(y_t, \psi) = \eta(y_t, y_{t-1})\eta(y_{t-1}, \psi), \qquad t > 1. \qquad (2.5.29)$$

So, while impact elasticities (the forcing function) differ according to the source of the perturbation and the functional form of the equation, the general form for all elasticity impulse responses in later periods reduces to the product of the previous period's elasticity and the current period's elasticity share of the lagged dependent variable. This observation is implicit in equation (2.5.5).

Parameter Sensitivities in Beta Scaled Form

To illustrate beta scaling we turn to the response to a step parameter perturbation for the linear equation (2.5.1). This is often appropriate for multipliers, just as elasticity scaling is in parameter-perturbation calculations. Referring to equation (2.5.7), this response is defined to be the time path followed by $\Delta y_t / S(\Delta y_t)$ in reaction to a once-and-for-all perturbation, beginning at time t_1, of a single coefficient while all other coefficients and the exogenous variable are unaltered. Defining

$$\text{beta}(y_t, \beta_j) = \frac{\Delta y_t}{S(\Delta y_t)} \div \frac{\Delta \beta_j}{S(\Delta \beta_j)}, \qquad (2.5.30a)$$

we have for β_0

$$\text{beta}(y_t, \beta_0) = \frac{\beta_1 \cdot S(\Delta y_{t-1})}{S(\Delta y_t)} \cdot \text{beta}(y_{t-1}, \beta_0) + \frac{S(\Delta \beta_0)}{S(\Delta y_t)}, \qquad t > t_1,$$

$$\text{beta}(y_{t_1}, \beta_0) = \frac{S(\Delta \beta_0)}{S(\Delta y_{t_1})}, \qquad\qquad t = t_1.$$

$$(2.5.30b)$$

Since $S(\Delta y_{t-1}) \cong S(\Delta y_t)$ most of the time, this expression simplifies for $t > t_1$ to

$$\text{beta}(y_t, \beta_0) \cong \beta_1 \text{beta}(y_{t-1}, \beta_0) + \frac{S(\Delta \beta_0)}{S(\Delta y_t)}. \qquad (2.5.31)$$

Similarly, for the other two coefficients, β_1 and β_2, we have for $t > t_1$

$$\text{beta}(y_t, \beta_1) \cong \beta_1 \text{beta}(y_{t-1}, \beta_1) + \frac{S(\Delta\beta_1)y_{t-1}}{S(\Delta y_t)}, \qquad (2.5.32)$$

$$\text{beta}(y_t, \beta_2) \cong \beta_1 \text{beta}(y_{t-1}, \beta_2) + \frac{S(\Delta\beta_2)x_t}{S(\Delta y_t)}. \qquad (2.5.33)$$

For each coefficient step perturbation, the impact beta is equal to the coefficient's impact share of the parameter standard deviation.

Beyond impact, the step-response interim beta is illustrated for β_0:

$$\text{beta}(y_{t_1+n}, \beta_0) = \left[\frac{\beta_1^n S(\Delta y_{t_1})}{S(\Delta y_{t_1+n})} \right] \frac{S(\Delta\beta_0)}{S(\Delta y_{t_1})}$$

$$+ \left[\frac{\beta_1^{n-1} S(\Delta y_{t_1+1})}{S(\Delta y_{t_1+n})} \right] \frac{S(\Delta\beta_0)}{S(\Delta y_{t_1+1})} + \cdots + \frac{S(\Delta\beta_0)}{S(\Delta y_{t_1+n})}.$$

$$(2.5.34)$$

There are $n + 1$ products of lagged-endogenous-variable standard-deviation shares with lagged-parameter standard-deviation shares, of which the first is identical to the impulse response. We notice that the step response is the sum of $n + 1$ consecutive impulse responses, the first occurring at time t_1, and the last at time $t_1 + n$.[†]

As with elasticity scaling, the dynamics parameter β_1 is the primary determinant of interim betas, while the time path for $S(\Delta y_t)$ may modify β_1's effect. This is seen by rewriting equation (2.5.34):

$$\text{beta}(y_{t_1+n}, \beta_0) = \left[\sum_{s=0}^{n} \beta_1^s \right] \frac{S(\Delta\beta_0)}{S(\Delta y_{t_1+n})}. \qquad (2.5.35)$$

Only when $S(\Delta y_{t_1})$ remains at a constant level is β_1 the sole contributing factor. Then equation (2.5.35) becomes

$$\text{beta}(y_{t_1+n}, \beta_0) = \left[\sum_{s=0}^{n} \beta_1^s \right] \frac{S(\Delta\beta_0)}{S(\Delta y_{t_1})}. \qquad (2.5.36)$$

[†] This is clearly an illustration of the well-known fact that superposition holds for linear systems.

However, if $S(\Delta y_t)$ grows at a constant rate, that is, $S(\Delta y_{t_1+n}) = (1 + r)^n S(\Delta y_{t_1})$, then we have

$$\text{beta}\left(y_{t_1+n}, \beta_0\right) = \frac{1}{(1 + r)^n} \left[\sum_{s=0}^{n} \beta_1^s\right] \frac{S(\Delta \beta_0)}{S(\Delta y_{t_1})}. \qquad (2.5.37)$$

Positive rates of growth diminish betas; negative rates increase them.

Conclusion

Traditional methods for analyzing econometric structures consist of simulations and inspection of multipliers and simulation errors. This chapter and its technical appendices propose a more comprehensive set of procedures. Given the methods themselves and the traditional sparsity of macroeconometric-model coefficient matrices, we believe that our scope of understanding can be greatly enhanced and that we and the reader will have learned much more about the essentials of model structure than before. Simulations and multipliers have a clear place in this process, but in a different frame of reference.

REFERENCES

Adelman, Irma and Frank L. Adelman (1959). The Dynamic Properties of the Klein–Goldberger Model, *Econometrica*, Vol. 27, pp. 596–625.

Artus, Patrick, Guy Laroque, and Gilles Michel (1984). Estimation of a Quarterly Macroeconomic Model with Quantity Rationing. In *Conference Proceedings of International Seminar on Recent Developments in Macroeconomic Modeling* (Paris), Pierre Malgrange and Pierre Alain Muet (Eds.), Blackwell, Oxford.

Baumol, William (1979). *Economic Dynamics: An Introduction*, 3rd edition, Macmillan, New York.

Bergstrom, Rex and Clifford Wymer (1976). A Model of Disequilibrium Neoclassical Growth and Its Application to the United Kingdom, in *Statistical Inference in Continuous Time Economic Models*, A. R. Bergstrom (Ed.), North-Holland, Amsterdam, pp. 267–327.

Fair, Ray C. (1980). Estimating the Predictive Accuracy of Econometric Models, *International Economic Review*, Vol. 21, pp. 355–378, (June).

Frisch, Ragner (1933). Propagation Problems and Impulse Problems in Dynamic Economics. In *Economic Essays in Honor of Gustav Cassel*, Allen and Unwin, London.

Gandolfo, Giancarlo (1981). *Qualitative Analysis and Econometric Estimation of Continuous Time Dynamic Models*, North-Holland, Amsterdam.

Gelb, Arthur (Ed.) (1974). *Applied Optimal Estimation*, MIT Press, Cambridge, MA.

Howrey, Philip (1972). Dynamic Properties of a Condensed Version of the Wharton Model. In *Econometric Models of Cyclical Behavior*, Vol. 2, B. G. Hickman (Ed.), National Bureau of Economic Research, New York, pp. 601–671.

Klein, L. R. and Arthur S. Goldberger (1955). *An Econometric Model of the United States, 1929–1952*, North-Holland, Amsterdam.

Kuh, Edwin and John Neese (1982). Parameter Sensitivity, Dynamic Behavior and Model Reliability: An Initial Exploration with the MQEM Monetary Sector. In *Proceedings of the Econometric Society European Meeting 1979, Selected Econometric Papers—in Memory of Stefan Valavanis*, E. G. Charatsis (Ed.), The Athens School of Economics and Business Science, Athens.

Pagan, A. R. and J. H. Shannon (1983). Sensitivity Analysis for Linearized Computable General Equilibrium Models, mimeo, Australian National University.

Sims, Christopher (1980). Macroeconomics and Reality, *Econometrica* Vol. 48, pp. 1–48, (January).

Slutzky, Eugen (1937). The Summation of Random Causes as the Source of Cyclic Processes, *Econometrica*, Vol. 5, p. 105.

Wolters, Jurgen (1980). Business Cycle Stabilization Policies in a Small Econometric Model of the FRG, *European Economic Review*, Vol. 14, pp. 9–43.

Zellner, Arnold and Stephen C. Peck (1973). Simulation and Experiments with a Quarterly Macroeconomic Model of the U.S. Economy. In *Econometric Studies of Macro and Monetary Relations*, A. A. Powell and R. A. Williams (Eds.), North-Holland, pp. 149–168.

APPENDIX 2A.   LINEAR TIME-INVARIANT SYSTEMS OF EQUATIONS

In this chapter we have considered some implications of the time-invariant equation-system properties of linearized models and have gone into further interpretive depth with a single linear time-invariant reduced-form equation. This appendix augments aspects of Chapter 2 in the following ways. First, we consider the general time-varying first-order approximation to the properties of a nonlinear system of equations. We emphasize the share interpretation that initially arose in the single-equation elasticity case. Second, we enlarge on the time-invariant properties of linearized systems.

2A.1   FIRST-ORDER PERTURBATION DYNAMICS

As in the single-equation case illustrated in Section 2.5, we shall restrict ourselves to "small" parameter perturbations and appeal to first-order analysis.[†] A first-order approximation to the model's nonlinear dynamics (in the vicinity of the baseline simulation) is found by evaluating the total

---

[†] With only minor changes, this appendix corresponds to Kuh and Neese (1982, pp. 128–133). The emphasis is on elasticities here. Other scaling would not affect the general qualitative conclusions about matrix properties of perturbation analysis for linear time-invariant systems.

differential of (2.2.2) (with $\varepsilon_t = 0$) along the baseline path:

$$dy_t = A_t(y_t, y_{t-1}, x_t, \beta)\, dy_{t-1}$$
$$+ B_t(y_t, y_{t-1}, x_t, \beta)\, dx_t$$
$$+ C_t(y_t, y_{t-1}, x_t, \beta)\, d\beta, \qquad (2A.1)$$

where it has been assumed as before that the $G \times G$ matrix $(\partial f/\partial y_t)$ is invertible for all t of interest:

$$A_t(y_t, y_{t-1}, x_t, \beta) \equiv -\left(\frac{\partial f}{\partial y_t}\right)^{-1}\left(\frac{\partial f}{\partial y_{t-1}}\right), \qquad (2A.2)$$

$$B_t(y_t, y_{t-1}, x_t, \beta) \equiv -\left(\frac{\partial f}{\partial y_t}\right)^{-1}\left(\frac{\partial f}{\partial x_t}\right), \qquad (2A.3)$$

$$C_t(y_t, y_{t-1}, x_t, \beta) \equiv -\left(\frac{\partial f}{\partial y_t}\right)^{-1}\left(\frac{\partial f}{\partial \beta}\right). \qquad (2A.4)$$

Given an infinitesimal perturbation in a single parameter β_j at time $t_0 + 1$, equation (2A.1) indicates that

$$\frac{dy_t}{d\beta_j} = \begin{cases} 0 & \text{for } t = t_0, \\ A_t \dfrac{dy_{t-1}}{d\beta_j} + (C_t)_{\cdot j} & \text{for } t \geq t_0 + 1, \end{cases} \qquad (2A.5)$$

where $(C_t)_{\cdot j}$ denotes the jth column of C_t and where it is assumed that the initial condition y_{t_0} and the exogenous-variable time paths x_t are independent of the parameters.

2A.2   ELASTICITIES AND "SHARES" INTERPRETATION

The elasticity of y_g with respect to β_j is derived from equation (2A.5) as

$$\eta(y_g, \beta_j)_t \equiv \frac{dy_{gt}}{d\beta_j}\frac{\beta_j}{y_{gt}} =$$

$$\begin{cases} 0 & \text{for } t = t_0, \qquad (2A.6a) \\ (A_t)_{g\cdot}\dfrac{dy_{t-1}}{d\beta_j}\left(\dfrac{\beta_j}{y_{gt}}\right) + c_{gj,t}\left(\dfrac{\beta_j}{y_{gt}}\right) & \text{for } t \geq t_0 + 1, \qquad (2A.6b) \end{cases}$$

where $(A_t)_g$. denotes the gth row of A_t and where $c_{gj,t}$ denotes the (g, j)th entry of C_t. Moreover, since

$$\frac{dy_{i,t-1}}{d\beta_j}\left(\frac{\beta_j}{y_{gt}}\right) \equiv \frac{y_{i,t-1}}{y_{gt}}\eta\left(y_i, \beta_j\right)_{t-1}, \tag{2A.7}$$

the first term on the right-hand side of equation (2A.6b) can be expressed in terms of previous-period elasticities. Consequently, equation (2A.6) can be rewritten as

$$\eta\left(y_g, \beta_j\right)_t = \begin{cases} 0 & \text{for} \quad t = t_0, \quad (2A.8a) \\[2ex] \sum_{i=1}^{G}\left(\frac{a_{gi,t}y_{i,t-1}}{y_{gt}}\right)\eta\left(y_i, \beta_j\right)_{t-1} \\[1ex] \quad + \dfrac{c_{gj,t}\beta_j}{y_{gt}} & \text{for} \quad t \geq t_0 + 1, \quad (2A.8b) \end{cases}$$

where $a_{gi,t}$ is the (g, i)th entry of A_t.

At this point we observe that in the general case the parameter-perturbation elasticity has a "shares" interpretation which is analogous to that discussed above in the simple, single-equation case. The general $\eta(y_g, \beta_j)$'s homogeneous dynamics depend on the previous-period elasticity of each endogenous variable in a proportion which is a *first-order approximation* to that variable's share in determining y_{gt}, that is, $a_{gi,t}y_{i,t-1}/y_{gt}$. Likewise, its forcing function is a first-order approximation to β_j's share in determining y_{gt}, that is, $c_{gj,t}\beta_j/y_{gt}$.

This basic "shares" analogy carries one most of the way from understanding the small-perturbation parameter sensitivity of the single-equation, explicit, linear time-invariant system discussed in Section 2.5 of Chapter 2 to understanding that of a multiequation, implicit, nonlinear time-varying system. Partly to demonstrate this proposition, and partly to point out aspects of the general problem which require further consideration, we now focus on one specialization of the multiequation, linear, explicit, time-invariant system for the general problem.

2A.3   DETAILS FOR AN EXPLICIT, TIME-INVARIANT MULTIEQUATION SYSTEM

The system is written

$$f = y_t - Ay_{t-1} - Bx_t = 0. \tag{2A.9}$$

As in the single-equation case, linearity in the parameters ensures that the first-order approximate shares are exact. We first consider y_g's elasticity with respect to representative exogenous and endogenous variable coefficients appearing in the y_g-equation. For b_{gk}, the (g, k)th entry of B, we have

$$
\eta(y_g, b_{gk})_t = \begin{cases} 0 & \text{for} \quad t = t_0, \quad (2A.10a) \\[2em] \displaystyle\sum_{i=1}^{G}\left(\frac{a_{gi}y_{i,t-1}}{y_{gt}}\right)\eta(y_i, b_{gk})_{t-1} \\[1em] \quad + \dfrac{b_{gk}x_{kt}}{y_{gt}} & \text{for} \quad t \geq t_0 + 1, \quad (2A.10b) \end{cases}
$$

and for a_{gn}, the (g, n)th entry of A,

$$
\eta(y_g, a_{gn})_t = \begin{cases} 0 & \text{for} \quad t = t_0, \quad (2A.11a) \\[2em] \displaystyle\sum_{i=1}^{G}\left(\frac{a_{gi}y_{i,t-1}}{y_{gt}}\right)\eta(y_i, a_{gn})_{t-1} \\[1em] \quad + \dfrac{a_{gn}y_{n,t-1}}{y_{gt}} & \text{for} \quad t \geq t_0 + 1. \quad (2A.11b) \end{cases}
$$

Equations (2A.10) and (2A.11) show that the dynamics term of the first-order difference equation for the elasticity in the vector case is analogous to that in the scalar case. The current-period elasticity of y_g again depends on its own previous-period elasticity in a proportion equaling its previous-period endogenous-variable share. The difference is that it also depends on all the other endogenous variables' previous-period elasticities according to their respective previous-period shares in determining y_g. The forcing-function or parameter-share terms are identical to those in the simple case of Section 2.5; consequently, the impact elasticities are also identical.

However, if we instead consider y_g's elasticity with respect to parameters which do not appear in the y_g-equation, then the forcing-function terms drop out, since the parameter shares in y_g are nil:

$$
\eta\left(y_g, b_{mk}\right)_t = \begin{cases} 0 & \text{for } t = t_0, & (2A.12a) \\[2ex] \displaystyle\sum_{i=1}^{G}\left(\frac{a_{gi}y_{i,t-1}}{y_{gt}}\right)\eta\left(y_i, b_{mk}\right)_{t-1} & \text{for } t \geq t_0 + 1, \quad m \neq g, \\ & (2A.12b) \end{cases}
$$

and

$$
\eta\left(y_g, a_{mn}\right)_t = \begin{cases} 0 & \text{for } t = t_0, & (2A.13a) \\[2ex] \displaystyle\sum_{i=1}^{G}\left(\frac{a_{gi}y_{i,t-1}}{y_{gt}}\right)\eta\left(y_i, a_{mn}\right)_{t-1} & \text{for } t \geq t_0 + 1, \quad m \neq g. \\ & (2A.13b) \end{cases}
$$

Hence, the impact elasticities are zero.

Interim-elasticity expressions analogous to those in equation (2.5.8) are easily derived for this vector case [see equations (2A.10b) and (2A.12b) respectively], showing that the n-period interim elasticities are once again the sum of n products of lagged-endogenous-variable shares with lagged-parameter shares [see (2.5.9) for the single-equation analogue]:

$$
\eta\left(y_g, b_{gk}\right)_{t_0+n} = \left[\left[A^{n-1}\right]_{gg}\frac{y_{g,t_0+1}}{y_{g,t_0+n}}\right]\frac{b_{gk}x_{k,t_0+1}}{y_{g,t_0+1}}
$$
$$
+ \left[\left[A^{n-2}\right]_{gg}\frac{y_{g,t_0+2}}{y_{g,t_0+n}}\right]\frac{b_{gk}x_{k,t_0+2}}{y_{g,t_0+2}} + \cdots + \frac{b_{gk}x_{k,t_0+n}}{y_{g,t_0+n}},
$$

$$(2A.14)$$

$$
\eta\left(y_g, b_{mk}\right)_{t_0+n} = \left[\left[A^{n-1}\right]_{gm}\frac{y_{m,t_0+1}}{y_{g,t_0+n}}\right]\frac{b_{mk}x_{k,t_0+1}}{y_{m,t_0+1}}
$$
$$
+ \left[\left[A^{n-2}\right]_{gm}\frac{y_{m,t_0+2}}{y_{g,t_0+n}}\right]\frac{b_{mk}x_{k,t_0+2}}{y_{m,t_0+2}} + \cdots
$$
$$
+ \left[\left[A\right]_{gm}\frac{y_{m,t_0+n-1}}{y_{g,t_0+n}}\right]\frac{b_{mk}x_{k,t_0+n-1}}{y_{m,t_0+n-1}}. \qquad (2A.15)
$$

(Since b_{mk} does not appear in the y_g-equation, its current-period parameter share is zero.)

As before, we rewrite equations (2A.14) and (2A.15) to better illuminate the importance of the dynamics parameters (elements of A) in determining interim-elasticity magnitudes:

$$\eta(y_g, b_{gk})_{t_0+n} = \left[[A^{n-1}]_{gg} x_{k,t_0+1} + [A^{n-2}]_{gg} x_{k,t_0+2} + \cdots + x_{k,t_0+n} \right]$$

$$\times \frac{b_{gk}}{y_{g,t_0+n}}, \qquad (2A.16)$$

$$\eta(y_g, b_{mk})_{t_0+n} = \left[[A^{n-1}]_{gm} x_{k,t_0+1} + [A^{n-2}]_{gm} x_{k,t_0+2} + \cdots \right.$$

$$\left. + [A]_{gm} x_{k,t_0+n-1} \right] \frac{b_{mk}}{y_{g,t_0+n}}. \qquad (2A.17)$$

For x_{kt} roughly constant over $t_0 + 1 \le t \le t_0 + n$ we have

$$\eta(y_g, b_{bk})_{t_0+n} \cong \left[\sum_{i=0}^{n-1} [A^i]_{gg} \right] \frac{b_{gk} x_{k,t_0+n}}{y_{g,t_0+n}}, \qquad (2A.18)$$

$$\eta(y_g, b_{mk})_{t_0+n} \cong \left\{ \left[\sum_{i=0}^{n-1} [A^i]_{gm} \right] - 1 \right\} \frac{b_{mk} x_{k,t_0+n}}{y_{g,t_0+n}}. \qquad (2A.19)$$

For x_{kt} growing at a roughly constant rate r,

$$\eta(y_g, b_{bk})_{t_0+n} \cong \left[\sum_{i=0}^{n-1} \left[\frac{A^i}{(1+r)^i} \right] \right]_{gg} \frac{b_{gk} x_{k,t_0+n}}{y_{g,t_0+n}}, \qquad (2A.20)$$

$$\eta(y_g, b_{mk})_{t_0+n} \cong \left\{ \left[\sum_{i=0}^{n-1} \left[\frac{A^i}{(1+r)^i} \right] \right]_{gm} - 1 \right\} \frac{b_{mk} x_{k,t_0+n}}{y_{g,t_0+n}}. \qquad (2A.21)$$

Hence, in the constant-level steady state,

$$\bar{\eta}(y_g, b_{bk}) = \left[[I - A]^{-1} \right]_{gg} \frac{b_{gk} x_t}{\bar{y}_t}, \qquad (2A.22)$$

$$\bar{\eta}(y_g, b_{mk}) = \left\{ \left[[I - A]^{-1} \right]_{gm} - 1 \right\} \frac{b_{mk} \bar{x}_k}{\bar{y}_g}, \qquad (2A.23)$$

and in the constant-growth steady state,

$$\tilde{\eta}(y_g, b_{bk}) = \left[\left[I - \frac{A}{1+r}\right]^{-1}\right]_{gg} \frac{b_{gk}\tilde{x}_{ks}}{\tilde{y}_{gs}}, \tag{2A.24}$$

$$\tilde{\eta}(y_g, b_{mk}) = \left\{\left[\left[I - \frac{A}{1+r}\right]^{-1}\right]_{gm} - 1\right\} \frac{b_{gm}\tilde{x}_{ks}}{y_{gs}}, \tag{2A.25}$$

where, as before, the overbars denote constant-level steady-state values, the tildes denote constant-growth steady-state values, and $\tilde{x}_{ks}$, $\tilde{y}_{gs}$ are evaluated at an arbitrary time $s \gg t_0$.

APPENDIX 2B. SENSITIVITY ANALYSIS OF EQUATION SYSTEMS AND RELATED COMPUTATIONAL ISSUES

This appendix fills in some mathematical details omitted from Chapter 2 and describes aspects of the computational algorithms we have used.[†] It is divided into three main parts:

Notation. This section describes model notation and the translation to state-space form.

Basic Building Blocks. In these sections, elementary linear algebra is used to derive the basic matrices on which the sensitivity analysis is built. The matrices of linearized coefficients in their structural form, their transformation to reduced form, and the partial root decomposition of the dynamics matrix are covered here. An important issue is the choice of root cutoff.

Model Diagnostic Tools. These are the results of sensitivity analysis. The time responses of the model and techniques for isolating the origin of dynamic behavior that is of interest are derived here.

[†] This appendix has been copied, with only minor changes, from the Research Background of the TROLL LIMO manual, Center for Computational Research in Economics and Management Science, MIT Technical Report No. 34.

Notation

2B.1 NOTATION FOR STRUCTURAL-FORM MODEL

The following notation will be used to describe a *deterministic structural-form model*:

$$f\left(\{y_{g,t}, \ldots, y_{g,t-M_g}\}, \{x_{k,t}, \ldots, x_{k,t-N_k}\}, \{\beta_j\}\right) = 0,$$

$$g = 1, \ldots, G, \quad k = 1, \ldots, K, \text{ and } j = 1, \ldots, J,$$

$$(2B.1.1)$$

where f = a vector of G functional relations.

$y_{g,t}$ = one of G endogenous variables.

$x_{k,t}$ = one of K exogenous variables.

β_j = one of J constant coefficients.[†]

M_g = the maximum lag in y_g appearing in any of the G functional relations.

N_k = the maximum lag in x_k appearing in any of the G functional relations.

Finally, $\{z_h\}$ $(h = 1, \ldots, H)$ is short for $z_1, z_2, \ldots, z_h$.

2B.2 STATE-SPACE REPRESENTATION OF A STRUCTURAL-FORM MODEL

A great deal of analysis is available to study state-space system of equations, that is, those in which endogenous variables appear lagged at most once and exogenous variables only appear unlagged. Happily, any structural-form model in the form of equation (2B.1.1) can be reexpressed in the state-space form. The state-space representation is not unique; we present our particular choice, one whose use is widespread.

The transformation of the structural-form model to its state-space representation involves defining additional endogenous variables and associated equations.[‡] As mentioned above, endogenous variables can have lags no

---

[†] Time-varying coefficients may be treated as exogenous variables.
[‡] Liu and Liu (1975), Aoki (1976), Chow (1975).

greater than one in the state-space representation. We define *endogenous-variable constructs* to reexpress higher-order lags as first-order lags in constructed variables. This is best illustrated by an example. Suppose we have an equation that contains an endogenous variable lagged twice:

$$\ln y_t = \beta_1 \ln y_{t-2}. \tag{2B.2.1}$$

Then define the new endogenous variable yc, where

$$yc_t = y_{t-1}, \tag{2B.2.2}$$

so that the original equation can be rewritten as a system of two equations containing only first-order lags:

$$\ln y_t = \beta_1 \ln yc_{t-1},$$

$$yc_t = y_{t-1}. \tag{2E.2.3}$$

Still other endogenous variables are defined to ensure that exogenous variables have no lags at all in the state-space representation. Thus, exogenous-variable constructs are defined to reexpress exogenous-variable lags as first-order lags in constructed endogenous variables. Suppose we have an equation that contains an exogenous variable lagged twice:

$$\ln y_t = \beta_1 \ln x_{t-2}. \tag{2B.2.4}$$

Then we define two new endogenous variables xc1 and xc2, where

$$xc1_t = x_t,$$

$$xc2_t = xc1_{t-1},$$

so that the original equation can be rewritten as a system of three equations containing no lagged exogenous variables:

$$\ln y_t = \beta_1 \ln xc_{t-1}^2,$$

$$xc1_t = x_t,$$

$$xc2_t = xc1_{t-1}. \tag{2B.2.5}$$

From the two examples we infer that $M_g - 1$ endogenous-variable constructs (equations) must be defined to express, in the state-space form,

Exhibit 2B.1   Key to notation.[a]

D	Total derivative
P	Partial derivative
Y	Endogenous variables
X	Exogenous variables
BETA	Parameters
C	Construct variables
L	Lagged variables

Examples

$$\text{DYDYL}_t = \frac{dy_t}{dy_{t-1}},$$

$$\text{PFPBETA}_t = \frac{\partial f}{\partial \beta_t}$$

$$\text{DYCDYCL}_t = \frac{d\, yc_t}{d\, yc_{t-1}}$$

[a] These notation rules are used in the remainder of this appendix.

an endogenous variable that appears with maximum lag M_g in the structural-form model. Similarly, N_k exogenous-variable constructs are needed for an exogenous variable with maximum lag N_k. Moreover, the additional equations required to define the endogenous and exogenous variable constructs are simple linear relations.

Thus we can express the original model as three systems of equations which together constitute the *state-space representation of the structural-form model*. The first system reexpresses the original equation (2B.1.1):

$$f(y_t;\; y_{t-1}, yc_{t-1}, xc_{t-1};\; x_t;\; \beta) = 0; \tag{2B.2.6}$$

a second defines the endogenous variable constructs:[†]

$$yc_t = \text{DYCDYL} \cdot y_{t-1} + \text{DYCDYCL} \cdot yc_{t-1};$$

and a third defines the exogenous variable constructs:

$$xc_t = \text{DXCDXCL} \cdot xc_{t-1} + \text{DXCDX} \cdot x_t,$$

[†] The conversion of the TROLL model to space-state form requires some additional notation. See Exhibit 2B.1.

where f = a vector of G functional relations.

y_t = a vector of G endogenous variables.

yc_t = a vector of $G_{yc} = \sum_{g=1}^{G}(M_g - 1)$ endogenous-variable constructs.

xc_t = a vector of $G_{xc} = \sum_{k=1}^{K} N_k$ exogenous-variable constructs.

x_t = a vector of K exogenous variables.

β = a vector of J constant coefficients.

DYCDYL = a $G_{yc} \times G$ matrix.

DYCDYCL = a $G_{yc} \times G_{yc}$ matrix.

DXCDXCL = a $G_{xc} \times G_{xc}$ matrix.

DXCDX = a $G_{xc} \times K$ matrix.

Note that f, M_g, and N_k are identical to the entities defined in equation (2B.1.1), and

$$
y_t = \begin{pmatrix} y_{1t} \\ \vdots \\ y_{gt} \\ \vdots \\ y_{Gt} \end{pmatrix}, \quad
x_t = \begin{pmatrix} x_{1t} \\ \vdots \\ x_{kt} \\ \vdots \\ x_{Kt} \end{pmatrix}, \quad
\beta = \begin{pmatrix} \beta_1 \\ \vdots \\ \beta_j \\ \vdots \\ \beta_J \end{pmatrix}.
$$

The matrices DYCDYL, DYCDYCL, DXCDXCL, DXCDX have mostly zero entries, with a few scattered ones.

Basic Building Blocks

2B.3   LINEARIZED STATE-SPACE REPRESENTATION OF STRUCTURAL-FORM MODEL

Linearization of the state-space model around a simulation path provides the basis for our linear analysis. A simulation path, of course, is found by solving the (generally nonlinear) set of equations (2B.1.1) or (2B.2.6) for the current values of the endogenous variables, conditional on the model's coefficients, exogenous variables, and/or initial conditions or prior-period solutions for lagged endogenous variables. We wish to emphasize that one's choice for simulation path in linearization is important, since the linearized model will be strictly accurate only for small deviations of endogenous variables, exogenous variables, and coefficients from their values in the simulation. Hence, simulation defines a reference or baseline time path to which linearized-model behavior is linked. The intimacy of that link, that is, the size of the deviations for which the behavior of the linearized model accurately mimics that of the original model, depends on the original model's degree of nonlinearity.

From a mathematical point of view, there is no rigorous basis for inferences about the global dynamic character of a nonlinear model from its linearized counterpart. The information content will however be greatest when a system is relinearized at each point in time. This can be prohibitively expensive, but periodic relinearization, together with corroboration tests that are developed in Chapter 6, provides safeguards against potentially misleading information due to nonlinearities. Since in most econometric models nonlinearities are weak, in practice the time-varying linearized-model coefficients do not change much from period to period. Thus valid and valuable information can be extracted from the linearized versions of nonlinear models.

A clear exposition about linearization of econometric models can be found in Klein and Goldberger (1955). We depart from conventional practice by considering coefficient changes in addition to endogenous- and exogenous-variable changes. The familiar first-order Taylor series approximation to the model's (nonlinear) state-space form [equation (2B.2.6)] about the baseline simulation is

$$\text{PFPY}_t \cdot \Delta y_t = \text{PFPYL}_t \cdot \Delta y_{t-1} + \text{PFPYCL}_t \cdot \Delta yc_{t-1}$$

$$+ \text{PFPXCL}_t \cdot \Delta xc_{t-1} + \text{PFPX}_t \cdot \Delta x_t$$

$$+ \text{PFPBETA}_t \cdot \Delta \beta,$$

$$\Delta yc_t = \text{DYCDYL} \cdot \Delta y_{t-1} + \text{DYCDYCL} \cdot \Delta yc_{t-1},$$

$$\Delta xc_t = \text{DXCDXCL} \cdot \Delta xc_{t-1} + \text{DXCDX} \cdot \Delta x_t, \qquad (2B.3.1)$$

where Δy_t, Δyc_t, Δxc_t, Δx_t, and $\Delta \beta$ are deviations around the baseline simulation, and where

$$\text{PFPY}_t \equiv \left(\frac{\partial f}{\partial y_t} \right), \qquad \text{a } G \times G \text{ matrix,}$$

$$\text{PFPYL}_t \equiv -\left(\frac{\partial f}{\partial y_{t-1}} \right), \qquad \text{a } G \times G \text{ matrix,}$$

$$\text{PFPYCL}_t \equiv -\left(\frac{\partial f}{\partial yc_{t-1}} \right), \qquad \text{a } G \times G_{yc} \text{ matrix,}$$

$$\text{PFPXCL}_t \equiv -\left(\frac{\partial f}{\partial xc_{t-1}} \right), \qquad \text{a } G \times G_{xc} \text{ matrix,}$$

$$\text{PFPX}_t \equiv -\left(\frac{\partial f}{\partial x_t} \right), \qquad \text{a } G \times K \text{ matrix,}$$

$$\text{PFPBETA}_t \equiv -\left(\frac{\partial f}{\partial \beta} \right), \qquad \text{a } G \times J \text{ matrix.}$$

We can rewrite equation (2B.3.1) in a more concise form by combining Δy_t, Δyc_t, and Δxc_t into a single vector Δz_t. This form we call the *linearized state-space representation of the structural model*:

$$D_t \cdot \Delta z_t = E_t \cdot \Delta z_{t-1} + F_t \cdot \Delta x_t + G_t \cdot \Delta \beta, \qquad (2B.3.2)$$

where

$$\Delta z_t = \left(\begin{array}{c} \Delta y_t \\ \hline \Delta yc_t \\ \hline \Delta xc_t \end{array} \right),$$

a vector of $G + G_{yc} + G_{xc}$ endogenous-variable deviations;

$$D_t = \left[\begin{array}{c|c|c} \text{PFPY} & 0 & 0 \\ \hline 0 & \text{IYC} & 0 \\ \hline 0 & 0 & \text{IXC} \end{array} \right],$$

a square matrix of order $G + G_{yc} + G_{xc}$ (IYC and IXC are identity matrices of orders G_{yc} and G_{xc}, respectively);

$$
E_t = \begin{bmatrix}
\text{PFPYL}_t & \text{PFPYCL}_t & \text{PFPXCL}_t \\
\hline
\text{DYCDYL} & \text{DYCDYCL} & 0 \\
\hline
0 & 0 & \text{DXCDXCL}
\end{bmatrix},
$$

a square matrix of order $G + G_{yc} + G_{xc}$;

$$
F_t = \begin{bmatrix}
\text{PFPX}_t \\
\hline
0 \\
\hline
\text{DXCDX}
\end{bmatrix},
$$

a $(G + G_{yc} + G_{xc}) \times K$ matrix; and

$$
G_t = \begin{bmatrix}
\text{PFPBETA}_t \\
\hline
0 \\
\hline
0
\end{bmatrix},
$$

a $(G + G_{yc} + G_{xc}) \times J$ matrix.

2B.4   LINEARIZED STATE-SPACE REPRESENTATION OF REDUCED-FORM MODEL

An explicit equation for the current endogenous variables can be found by solving the first system of equations in (2B.3.1) for Δy_t:

$$
\Delta y_t = \text{DYDYL}_t \cdot \Delta y_{t-1} + \text{DYDYCL}_t \cdot \Delta y c_{t-1}
$$

$$
+ \text{DYDXCL}_t \cdot \Delta x c_{t-1} + \text{DYDX}_t \cdot \Delta x_t
$$

$$
+ \text{DYDBETA}_t \cdot \Delta \beta, \tag{2B.4.1}
$$

where

$$
\text{PFPY}_t^{-1} \cdot \text{PFPYL}_t \equiv \text{DYDYL}_t
$$

defines DYDYL_t, a $G \times G$ matrix,

$$
\text{PFPY}_t^{-1} \cdot \text{PFPYCL}_t \equiv \text{DYDYCL}_t
$$

defines DYDYCL_t, a $G \times G_{yc}$ matrix,

$$
\text{PFPY}_t^{-1} \cdot \text{PFPXCL}_t \equiv \text{DYDXCL}_t
$$

defines DYDXCL$_t$, a $G \times G_{xc}$ matrix,

$$\text{PFPY}_t^{-1} \cdot \text{PFPX}_t \equiv \text{DYDX}_t$$

defines DYDX$_t$, a $G \times K$ matrix, and

$$\text{PFPY}_t^{-1} \cdot \text{PFPBETA}_t \equiv \text{DYDBETA}_t$$

defines DYDBETA$_t$, a $G \times J$ matrix. When PFPY$_t$ is of full rank (as is generally the case with properly specified econometric models), this equation is uniquely determined. Failure of this rank condition violates assumptions of this algorithm.

Joining equation (2B.4.1) with the last two parts of equation (2B.3.1), we form the *linearized state-space representation of the reduced-form model*:

$$\Delta z_t = A_t \Delta z_{t-1} + B_t \Delta x_t + C_t \Delta \beta, \qquad (2B.4.2)$$

where

$$
A_t = \left[
\begin{array}{c|c|c}
\text{DYDYL}_t & \text{DYDYCL}_t & \text{DYDXCL}_t \\
\hline
\text{DYCDYL}_t & \text{DYCDYCL}_t & 0 \\
\hline
0 & 0 & \text{DXCDXCL}_t
\end{array}
\right],
$$

a square matrix of order $G + G_{yc} + G_{xc}$;

$$
B_t = \left[
\begin{array}{c}
\text{DYDX}_t \\
\hline
0 \\
\hline
\text{DXCDX}
\end{array}
\right],
$$

a $(G + G_{yc} + G_{xc}) \times K$ matrix; and

$$
C_t = \left[
\begin{array}{c}
\text{DYDBETA}_t \\
\hline
0 \\
\hline
0
\end{array}
\right],
$$

a $(G + G_{yc} + G_{xc}) \times J$ matrix.

If there is a perturbation to the system represented by (2B.4.2) at time t, so that $\Delta z_t \neq 0$ (it does not matter if the perturbation comes from $A_t \Delta z_{t-1}$, $B \Delta x_t$, or $C_t \Delta \beta$), and there are no further perturbations to the system, then

$$\Delta z_{t+1} = A_t \Delta z_t,$$

$$\Delta z_{t+2} = A_t \Delta z_{t+1} = A_t \cdot [A_t \Delta z_t] = A_t^2 \Delta z_t,$$

which leads to

$$\Delta z_{t+n} = A_t^n \Delta z_t. \qquad (2B.4.3)$$

The matrix A is called the *dynamics matrix*, and is the only link between the past behavior of the model and its state in the current period.

2B.5   PARTIAL CHARACTERISTIC-ROOT DECOMPOSITION OF THE DYNAMICS MATRIX A

The calculation of the matrix A_t^n by direct multiplication can be costly and introduce unacceptable numerical inaccuracies. An alternative method of calculating A_t^n is to decompose the matrix A_t into its characteristic roots and vectors, which have the following well-known property:

$$A_t^n = R_t \Lambda_t^n L_t^T, \qquad (2B.5.1)$$

where R_t = the matrix of right characteristic vectors.

$\quad L_t$ = the matrix of left characteristic vectors.

$\quad \Lambda_t$ = a diagonal matrix with the characteristic roots on the diagonal.

The direct calculation of Λ_t to the power n is much more accurate and inexpensive than raising the original matrix A_t to that power. The matrix Λ_t contains other useful information: the roots inform one of the stability or instability of the model, and the techniques of Sections 2B.7 and 2B.8 make it possible to associate the dynamic behavior of A_t with elements of the original model. A problem that makes both the computations and the presentation more complicated is that many numerical problems are encountered calculating the *full* decomposition shown in equation (2B.5.1). Thus equation (2B.5.1) is *not* computed. Instead, a *partial* decomposition is computed that has much more stable numerical properties. This procedure is described in a general way in this section and is covered in detail in Section 2B.10 and in the references cited at the end of this Appendix.

We begin by making our definitions more complete. For any square $N \times N$ matrix (such as A_t), a right characteristic vector r is defined to be a vector of length N satisfying the equation

$$A_t r = r\lambda \qquad (2B.5.2)$$

with λ a scalar. λ is called the characteristic root associated with r.

In general, for real matrices, the characteristic vectors and roots may be complex numbers. However, since complex characteristic roots will only occur in conjugate pairs, it is possible to represent complex vectors and roots with real numbers. To do this, note that the complex column vector r may be expressed as a combination of two column vectors:

$$r = r_1 + ir_2 \qquad (2B.5.3)$$

with r_1 and r_2 real and i representing the square root of minus one. Similarly, the characteristic root of r is

$$\lambda = \rho \pm i\mu \qquad (2B.5.4)$$

with ρ and μ real. The characteristic equation (2B.5.2) then becomes

$$A_t(r_1 + ir_2) = (r_1 + ir_2)(\rho + \mu i). \qquad (2B.5.5)$$

So, equating real and imaginary parts, we have

$$A_t r_1 = \rho r_1 - \mu r_2$$

and

$$A_t r_2 = \rho r_2 + \mu r_1$$

respectively. In matrix notation this becomes

$$A_t[r_1 \;\vdots\; r_2] = [r_1 \;\vdots\; r_2]\begin{bmatrix} \rho & \mu \\ -\mu & \rho \end{bmatrix} \qquad (2B.5.6)$$

with r_1 and r_2 combined into a $N \times 2$ matrix, and the root for this characteristic vector is a 2×2 block with the real part of the root on the main diagonal and the complex part off the diagonal. A real root (one with a zero complex component) is treated as a special case of the complex. Since the complex part of the root is zero, only a one-column right characteristic vector is needed, and the block describing the root is a 1×1 block that contains the root itself. So the real-root equivalent of (2B.5.6) is

$$A_t[r] = [r] \cdot \lambda. \qquad (2B.5.7)$$

The algorithm keeps track of which roots (and therefore which columns) are complex, so that the correct operations are made.

If we have a full set of distinct characteristic vectors for the matrix A_t, we can write

$$A_t R_t = R_t \Lambda_t, \qquad (2B.5.8)$$

where R_t is a real square $N \times N$ matrix whose columns are the right characteristic vectors of A (a single column for a real root, twin columns for a complex one); Λ_t is a real square $N \times N$ block-diagonal matrix containing all the characteristic roots on the diagonal, with a single 1×1 block for real roots and a 2×2 block containing the complex conjugate pair for complex roots [the 2×2 block of equation (2B.5.6)]. All entries in the matrices in (2B.5.8) are real; complex numbers are known by their location. This, of course, saves a substantial amount of storage space.

Two problems can arise in the characteristic-vector–root decomposition of a square nonsymmetric matrix such as the dynamics matrix A_t shown in equation (2B.5.8). One problem is that repeated roots that lack the same number of characteristic vectors can occur as a consequence of model structure. In our experience this does not happen frequently in real-world econometric models. Should this situation arise, special solution procedures, not implemented here, are needed.

A related problem arises from numerical considerations: when two or more characteristic roots have magnitudes much smaller than the largest roots in the system, it is often difficult or impossible for any finite-precision algorithm to distinguish the neighboring vectors. This problem arises in medium- and large-size econometric models.

To overcome this problem, we have constructed a *partial* characteristic-root–vector decomposition which only calculates vectors for the roots whose magnitudes exceed a prespecified cutoff level. Problems arising from structural multiple-root degeneracies described in the previous paragraph will also be avoided when the multiplicities arise for roots whose magnitudes fall below the cutoff level.

The partial decomposition involves many transformations that will be dealt with only generally here. Section 2B.10 and its references should be consulted for more detail by the adventurous reader.

The matrix A_t is transformed into the Schur form matrix S:

$$A_t \tilde{R}_t = \tilde{R}_t S_t, \tag{2B.5.9}$$

where S_t is a real square $N \times N$ upper-block-triangular Schur matrix (not diagonal) containing the characteristic roots on the diagonal [1×1 blocks containing the root for real roots, 2×2 blocks containing the conjugate pair in a block as in equation (2B.5.6)] with zeros below the diagonal. $\tilde{R}_t$ is an orthonormal real square $N \times N$ matrix. (So $\tilde{R}_t^T = \tilde{R}^{-1}$.) The columns of $\tilde{R}$ are *not* the right characteristic vectors of A_t.

The order of characteristic vectors is arbitrary, so the algorithm orders the roots along the diagonal by modulus from largest to smallest,[†] while the

---

[†] The modulus of a real characteristic root is given by the absolute value of the root. The modulus of a complex root $\lambda = \rho \pm \mu i$ is given by $\sqrt{\rho^2 + \mu^2}$. It is easy to see that the real case is a special case of the complex with $\mu = 0$, so that the modulus for the real root is $\sqrt{\lambda^2} = |\lambda|$.

matrix S_t is being created. For a useful introduction to Schur matrices, see Bellman (1970, p. 202).

Many econometric models have zero and near-zero roots. Because this will introduce numerical defectiveness in the calculation of characteristic vectors, a small positive root cutoff is chosen interactively by the user which will partition the matrix S_t into above-cutoff and below-cutoff parts. This is simply done because the roots are in the descending order along the diagonal:

$$A_t \cdot [\tilde{R}_{1,t} \mathbin{\vdots} \tilde{R}_{2,t}] = [\tilde{R}_{1,t} \mathbin{\vdots} \tilde{R}_{2,t}] \begin{bmatrix} S_{1,t} & \vdots & S_{12,t} \\ \hline 0 & \vdots & S_{2,t} \end{bmatrix} \qquad (2\text{B}.5.10)$$

[which is identical to equation (2B.5.9) except that it is partitioned],

where $S_{1,t}$ = a real $H_{AC} \times H_{AC}$ upper-triangular Schur matrix (H_{AC} is the dimension representing above-cutoff roots) containing the above-cutoff roots on the diagonal, with 1×1 blocks for real roots and 2×2 blocks for complex roots.

$S_{2,t}$ = a real $H_{BC} \times H_{BC}$ upper-triangular Schur matrix (H_{BC} is the dimension representing below-cutoff roots) containing the below-cutoff roots on the diagonal, with 1×1 blocks for real roots and 2×2 blocks for complex roots. (Note: $H_{AC} + H_{BC} = N$, the dimension of A_t.)

$S_{12,t}$ = a real $H_{AC} \times H_{BC}$ matrix associated with nondynamic coupling in the matrix A_t.

$\tilde{R}_{1,t}$ = a real matrix associated with the above-cutoff roots, whose columns are *not* the right characteristic vectors of A_t.

$\tilde{R}_{2,t}$ = a real matrix associated with the below-cutoff roots, whose columns are *not* the right characteristic vectors of A_t.

The partition $S_{12,t}$ is zeroed out by the transformation T_4 described in Section 2B.10. The right characteristic vectors are then calculated for the above-cutoff roots represented by the matrix $S_{1,t}$. This results in

$$A_t \cdot [R_{1,t} \mathbin{\vdots} \tilde{R}_{2,t}] = [R_{1,t} \mathbin{\vdots} \tilde{R}_{2,t}] \begin{bmatrix} \Lambda_{1,t} & \vdots & 0 \\ \hline 0 & \vdots & S_{2,t} \end{bmatrix}, \qquad (2\text{B}.5.11)$$

where $R_{1,t}$ = a real matrix whose H_{AC} columns are right characteristic vectors of A_t associated with the above-cutoff roots.

$\tilde{R}_{2,t}$ = a real matrix associated with the below-cutoff roots whose H_{BC} columns are *not* characteristic vectors of A_t.

$\Lambda_{1,t}$ = a real square $H_{AC} \times H_{AC}$ block-diagonal matrix containing the above-cutoff roots with 1×1 blocks containing real characteristic roots and 2×2 blocks defining complex conjugate root pairs (the blocks are ordered by modulus).

$S_{2,t}$ = a real square $H_{BC} \times H_{BC}$ upper block-triangular matrix (not diagonal) containing the below-cutoff roots with 1×1 blocks on the diagonal for the real roots and 2×2 blocks for the complex conjugate root pairs (the blocks are ordered by modulus).

We note in passing that the larger roots are "more interesting" than the smaller roots in the sense that "most of A_t^n," especially as n increases, is contributed by the larger roots.[†] For a successful decomposition $[R_{1,t} \vdots \tilde{R}_{2,t}]$ is invertible; we denote the transpose of its inverse by $[(R^{1,t})^T \vdots (\tilde{R}^{2,t})^T]$. Then (2B.5.5) is the equation for A_t, yielding

$$A_t = [R_{1,t} \vdots \tilde{R}_{2,t}] \begin{bmatrix} \Lambda_{1,t} & \vdots & 0 \\ \cdots & + & \cdots \\ 0 & \vdots & S_{2,t} \end{bmatrix} \begin{bmatrix} R^{1,t} \\ \tilde{R}^{2,t} \end{bmatrix},$$

$$= R_{1,t}\Lambda_{1,t}R^{1,t} + \tilde{R}_{2,t}S_{2,t}\tilde{R}^{2,t}. \tag{2B.5.12}$$

Since the roots in $S_{2,t}$ are smaller than those in $\Lambda_{1,t}$, the first term in equation (2B.5.12) will normally contribute more than the second.

Finally, we define (and the algorithm computes) an analogous left-hand decomposition:

$$\begin{bmatrix} L_{1,t}^T \\ \tilde{L}_{2,t}^T \end{bmatrix} \cdot A_t = \begin{bmatrix} \Lambda_{1,t} & \vdots & 0 \\ \cdots & + & \cdots \\ 0 & \vdots & S_{2,t} \end{bmatrix} \begin{bmatrix} L_{1,t}^T \\ \tilde{L}_{2,t}^T \end{bmatrix}, \tag{2B.5.13}$$

where $L_{1,t}^T = R^{1,t}$, and its rows define left characteristic vectors.
$\tilde{L}_{2,t}^T = \tilde{R}^{2,t}$ and its rows do not define left characteristic vectors.

The matrix $L_{1,t}^T$ is computed by inverting $R_{1,t}$. If the matrix $R_{1,t}$ is ill conditioned,[‡] this may introduce inaccuracies into the system. The condition number of $R_{1,t}$ is calculated so that the user can determine if the conditioning is acceptable. See the discussion in Appendix 5A for more information about the MQEM and sources of ill-conditioning within it.

[†] Furthermore, the algorithm has been extended to prevent large contributions from the characteristic vectors associated with small roots from degrading computational accuracy—see the discussion following equation (2B.10.4).
[‡] It is important to note that $R_{1,t}$ will not be an orthogonal matrix unless A_t is symmetric. This is rarely the case with econometric models.

Model Diagnostic Tools

2B.6 TIME RESPONSE OF A REDUCED-FORM MODEL: INITIAL CONDITION, IMPULSE OR STEP MULTIPLIER, OR PARAMETER-PERTURBATION RESPONSE

We begin with the linearized state-space reduced-form model whose coefficients have been evaluated for a particular time period:

$$\Delta z_t = A\,\Delta z_{t-1} + B\Delta x_t + C\Delta\beta. \qquad (2B.6.1)$$

Then, given an initial condition (at time t_0) for the endogenous-variable deviations (Δz_{t_0}), time paths for the exogenous-variable deviations (Δx_s, $t_0 < s$), and values for parameter deviations ($\Delta\beta$), a time response for the endogenous-variable deviations is defined:

$$\Delta z_{t_0+n} = A^n \Delta z_{t_0} + \sum_{s=0}^{n-1} A^s \cdot \left\{ B\Delta x_{t_0+n-s} + C\Delta\beta \right\}, \qquad (2B.6.2)$$

where $t_0 + n$ = the current time period.

s = the running time index for the perturbed values of Δx between $t_0 + 1$ and $t_0 + n$.

Since variables have different units and variabilities, we need to consider scaling inputs and outputs in ways that make interpretation easier. Suppose we scale the variables in equation (2B.6.2) such that input and output deviations are comparable for some particular purpose:

$$\Delta\tilde{z}_{t_0+n} = A^n \Delta\tilde{z}_{t_0} + \sum_{s=0}^{n-1} A^s \cdot \left\{ B\Delta\tilde{x}_{t_0+n-s} + C\Delta\tilde{\beta} \right\}, \qquad (2B.6.3)$$

where $\Delta\tilde{z}_{g,t} \equiv \Delta z_{g,t}/\text{scale}(\Delta z_{g,t})$ for $g = 1, \ldots, G + G_{yc} + G_{xc}$,

$\Delta\tilde{x}_{k,t} \equiv \Delta x_{k,t}/\text{scale}(\Delta x_{k,t})$ for $k = 1, \ldots, K$,

$\Delta\tilde{\beta}_j \equiv \Delta\beta_j/\text{scale}(\Delta\beta_j)$ for $j = 1, \ldots, J$.

Equation (2B.6.3) can be specialized to the *homogeneous response*, in which $\Delta\tilde{x}_s = 0$ ($t_0 < s$) and $\Delta\tilde{\beta} = 0$:

$$\Delta\tilde{z}_{t_0+n} = A^n \Delta\tilde{z}_{t_0}; \qquad (2B.6.4)$$

the *multiplier response*, in which $\Delta \tilde{z}_{t_0} = 0$ and $\Delta \tilde{\beta} = 0$:

$$\Delta \tilde{z}_{t_0+n} = \sum_{s=0}^{n-1} A^s B \Delta \tilde{x}_{t_0+n-s}; \qquad (2B.6.5)$$

and the *parameter perturbation response*, in which $\Delta \tilde{z}_{t_0} = 0$ and $\Delta \tilde{x}_s = 0$ ($t_0 < s$):

$$\Delta \tilde{z}_{t_0+n} = \sum_{s=0}^{n-1} A^s C \Delta \tilde{\beta}. \qquad (2B.6.6)$$

Responses for arbitrary perturbations are not computed. Rather, only responses to the initial-condition perturbations (homogeneous response), and to impulse or step perturbations of exogenous variables (multipliers), or parameters (parameter sensitivity) can be calculated. This is not restrictive for a linear time-invariant reduced-form model, because superposition arguments ensure that the response to an arbitrary perturbation can be constructed from that to an impulse or a step perturbation. Consequently, the impulse or step responses contain all the information of any other responses.

The algorithm provides three scaling options: elasticity, beta, and user-constructed. The first two types of scaling will often be appropriate and are available as options; the third gives the user flexibility to specify "arbitrary" scaling vectors. In elasticity scaling each variable's deviation is divided by its level: for example, $\Delta \tilde{z}_{g,t} \equiv \Delta z_{g,t} / z_{g,t}$. Beta scaling divides each delta by a measure of the associated variable's standard deviation: for example, $\Delta \tilde{x}_{k,t} \equiv \Delta x_{k,t} / s.d.(\Delta x_{k,t})$. Scaling methods are discussed further in Section 2.5. The subsequent illustrations use elasticities.

The homogeneous or initial-condition perturbation response has already been presented in equation (2B.6.4). For the homogeneous response, we choose an endogenous variable to view at $t_0 + n$, (say z_{g,t_c+n}) and an endogenous variable to perturb at time t_0 (say z_{i,t_0}). The elasticity η is

$$\eta(z_{g,t_0+n}, z_{i,t_0}) \equiv \lim_{\Delta z_{i,t_0} \to 0} \left\{ \frac{\Delta z_{g,t_0+n}}{\Delta z_{i,t_0}} \cdot \frac{z_{i,t_0}}{z_{g,t_0+n}} \right\}$$

$$= [A^n]_{gi} \frac{z_{i,t_0}}{z_{g;t_0+n}}, \qquad (2B.6.7)$$

where $[A^n]_{gi} =$ the row-g, column-i entry of A^n.

The multiplier generated by an *impulse* (i.e., one-period perturbation) *in the exogenous variables* at time $t_0 + 1$ is

$$\Delta \tilde{z}_{t_0+n} = A^{n-1} B \Delta \tilde{x}_{t_0+1}. \qquad (2B.6.8)$$

From equation (2B.6.8) we can derive the elasticity of z_g at time $t_0 + n$ with respect to an impulse perturbation in x_k at $t_0 + 1$:

$$
\eta\left(z_{g,t_0+n}, x_{k,t_0+1}\right) \equiv \lim_{\Delta x_{k,t_0+1} \to 0} \left\{ \frac{\Delta z_{g,t_0+n}}{\Delta x_{k,t_0+1}} \cdot \frac{x_{k,t_0+1}}{z_{g,t_0+n}} \right\}
$$

$$
= [A^{n-1}]_{g.} \cdot [B]_{.k} \frac{x_{k,t_0+1}}{z_{g,t_0+n}}, \qquad (2B.6.9)
$$

where $[A^{n-1}]_{g.}$ = row g of A^{n-1}.

$[B]_{.k}$ = column k of B.

The multiplier generated by a *step perturbation in the exogenous variables* at time $t_0 + 1$ (a once-and-for-all change of magnitude $\Delta \tilde{x}$) is

$$\Delta \tilde{z}_{t_0+n} = \sum_{s=0}^{n-1} A^s B \Delta \tilde{x}. \qquad (2B.6.10)$$

An elasticity expression is not well defined in this case, since a constant exogenous-variable perturbation generally corresponds to a time-varying percentage change in exogenous variables.

However, we can derive an elasticity expression for a constant-percentage perturbation in the exogenous variables. Then the multiplier becomes

$$\Delta \tilde{z}_{t_0+n} = \sum_{s=0}^{n-1} A^s B \cdot \omega x_{t_0+n-s}, \qquad (2B.6.11)$$

where ω is the constant fraction by which x is perturbed. Hence, the elasticity of z_{g,t_0+n} with respect to a constant-percentage perturbation in x_k (beginning at $t_0 + 1$) is

$$
\eta\left(z_{g,t_0+n}, x_k\right) \equiv \lim_{\omega \to 0} \left\{ \frac{\Delta z_{g,t_0+n}}{z_{g,t_0+n}} \div \omega \right\}
$$

$$
= \sum_{s=0}^{n-1} [A^s]_{g.} \cdot [B]_{.k} \frac{x_{k,t_0+n-s}}{z_{g,t_0+n}}. \qquad (2B.6.12)
$$

A reasonable approximation to (2B.6.12) is computed, which factors out the final term from the summation operator, thereby greatly simplifying computation. This approximation is

$$\eta\left(z_{g,t_0+n}, x_k\right) \cong \sum_{s=0}^{n-1} [A^s]_g \cdot [B]_{\cdot k} \frac{\bar{x}_k}{z_{g,t_0+n}}, \qquad (2B.6.13)$$

where $\bar{x}_k$ is the mean of x over user-specified bounds.

The parameter sensitivity responses are analogous to the multiplier results. The response to an *impulse parameter perturbation* at time $t_0 + 1$ is

$$\Delta \tilde{z}_{t_0+n} = A^{n-1} C \Delta \tilde{\beta}. \qquad (2B.6.14)$$

Hence, the elasticity of z_{g,t_0+n} with respect to an impulse in β_j is

$$\eta\left(z_{g,t_0+n}, \beta_j\right) = [A^n]_g \cdot [C]_{\cdot j} \frac{\beta_j}{z_{g,t_0+n}}. \qquad (2B.6.15)$$

The parameter sensitivity response to a *step parameter perturbation* of magnitude $\Delta \tilde{\beta}$ beginning at time $t_0 + 1$ is

$$\Delta \tilde{z}_{t_0+n} = \sum_{s=0}^{n-1} A^s C \Delta \tilde{\beta}. \qquad (2B.6.16)$$

Unlike the multiplier case, an elasticity expression for the step parameter perturbation is well defined, since the coefficients are constant through time. Thus the elasticity of z_{g,t_0+n} with respect to a step perturbation in β_j is

$$\eta\left(z_{g,t_0+n}, \beta_j\right) = \sum_{s=0}^{n-1} [A^s]_g \cdot [C]_{\cdot j} \frac{\beta_j}{z_{g,t_0+n}}. \qquad (2B.6.17)$$

2B.7   PARTIAL CHARACTERISTIC-ROOT DECOMPOSITION OF TIME RESPONSES OF A LINEARIZED REDUCED-FORM MODEL

Time responses of the linearized reduced-form model can be decomposed into responses associated with individual characteristic roots. Such decompositions provide useful diagnostic information for the study of model structure.

Decompositions of all the time responses presented in Section 2B.6—that is, responses to initial-condition perturbations and to impulse or step perturbations of exogenous variables or parameters—are all calculated for a time-invariant version of the linearized reduced-form model. All of these decompositions can be found by substituting an expression for powers of the decomposed dynamics matrix A into the response equations from Section 2B.6. We begin deriving this expression from a time-invariant version of equation (2B.5.12) (and renumber the equation for convenience):

$$A = R_1 \Lambda_1 R^1 + \tilde{R}_2 S_2 \tilde{R}^2. \tag{2B.7.1}$$

[Recall that $R^1 = (R^{-1})^T = L^T$.] Powers of A are simply related to powers of Λ_1 and S_2:

$$A^n = R_1 \Lambda_1^n R^1 + \tilde{R}_2 S_2^n \tilde{R}^2. \tag{2B.7.2}$$

The part of equation (2B.7.2) involving Λ_1^n can be broken down further as a consequence of the block diagonality of Λ_1. If we (loosely) denote the 1×1 and 2×2 blocks by λ_h, where there are H such blocks whose orders sum to H_{AC}, we have

$$R_1 \Lambda_1^n R^1 \equiv \sum_{h=1}^{H} [R_1]_{\cdot h} \cdot \lambda_h^n \cdot [R^1]_{h \cdot}, \tag{2B.7.3}$$

where

$[R_1]_{\cdot h}$ is one column if λ_h is 1×1, and two columns if λ_h is 2×2.
$[R^1]_{h \cdot}$ is similarly one row if λ_h is 1×1, and two rows if λ_h is 2×2.

Hence, we write A^n as

$$A^n = \sum_{h=1}^{H} [R_1]_{\cdot h} \cdot \lambda_n^n \cdot [R^1]_{h \cdot} + \tilde{R}_2 S_2^n \tilde{R}^2. \tag{2B.7.4}$$

Time-response decompositions are derived by substituting equation (2B.7.4) into the response equations from Section 2B.6. Rather than present an exhaustive list of decompositions, we shall concentrate on the initial-condition-perturbation response decomposition.

First we derive the decomposed response. Substituting equation (2B.7.4) into equation (2B.6.4), we have

$$\Delta \tilde{z}_{t_0 + n} = \left\{ \sum_{h=1}^{H} [R_1]_{\cdot h} \cdot \lambda_h^n \cdot [R^1]_{h \cdot} + \dot{\tilde{R}}_2 S_2^n \tilde{R}^2 \right\} \Delta \tilde{z}_{t_0}. \tag{2B.7.5}$$

From this expression we identify the part of the response that is associated with a given above-cutoff root λ_n:

$$\left(\Delta \tilde{z}_{t_0+n} | \lambda_h\right) = [R_1]_{\cdot h} \cdot \lambda_h^n \cdot [R^1]_{h\cdot} \cdot \Delta \tilde{z}_{t_0}, \qquad (2B.7.6)$$

and the part associated with the below-cutoff roots:

$$\left(\tilde{z}_{t_0+n} | S_2\right) = \tilde{R}_2 S_2^n \tilde{R}^2 \Delta \tilde{z}_{t_0}. \qquad (2B.7.7)$$

Second we derive the decomposed response in elasticity form. Substituting equation (2B.7.4) into the elasticity expression (2B.6.7), we identify the portion of the elasticity that comes from λ_h:

$$\eta\left(z_{g,t_0+n}, z_{i,t_0} | \lambda_h\right) = [R_1]_{gh} \cdot \lambda_h^n \cdot [R^1]_{hi} \cdot \frac{z_{i,t_0}}{z_{g,t_0+n}}, \qquad (2B.7.8)$$

and the part that comes from S_2:

$$\eta\left(z_{g,t_0+n}, z_{i,t_0} | S_2\right) = [\tilde{R}_2]_g \cdot S_2^n [\tilde{R}^2]_{\cdot i} \frac{z_{i,t_0}}{z_{g,t_0+n}}. \qquad (2B.7.9)$$

2B.8 CHARACTERISTIC-ROOT SENSITIVITY TO LINEARIZED-MODEL COEFFICIENTS

The derivatives of a characteristic root with respect to elements of the linearized model's coefficient matrices can be used to pinpoint the elements of model structure which determine behavior associated with the root.

Since the root sensitivity of a complex root would be a complex number, and this would make interpretation of the results difficult, LIMO instead calculates either the sensitivity of the modulus of the root *or* the sensitivity of the period of the root with respect to the linearized coefficients. The first part of this section deals with the modulus sensitivities.

Equation (2B.5.12) defines LIMO's partial characteristic-root decomposition of A_t. As a first step, extract the portion relevant to λ_h (one of the above-cutoff roots) from a time-invariant version of equation (2B.5.12):

$$A \cdot [R_1]_{\cdot h} = [R_1]_{\cdot h} \cdot \lambda_h. \qquad (2B.8.1)$$

For convenience, we represent the column vector $[R_1]_{\cdot h}$ by the simpler symbol r_h:

$$A r_h = r_h \lambda_h \qquad (2B.8.2)$$

Taking the derivative of equation (2B.8.2) with respect to an arbitrary scalar γ, we have

$$\frac{\partial A}{\partial \gamma} \cdot r_h + A \cdot \frac{\partial r_h}{\partial \gamma} = \frac{\partial r_h}{\partial \gamma} \cdot \lambda_h + r_h \cdot \frac{\partial \lambda_h}{\partial \gamma}. \qquad (2B.8.3)$$

Equation (2B.8.3) can be simplified by premultiplying both of its sides by l'_h, where l_h is defined to be the left characteristic vector associated with λ_h:

$$l'_h A = \lambda_h l'_h. \qquad (2B.8.4)$$

(Here, l_h is the column $[L_1]_{.h}$ in the usual notation and l'_h is the transpose of l_h.) Performing the premultiplication, we find

$$l'_h \cdot \frac{\partial A}{\partial \gamma} \cdot r_h + l'_h \cdot A \cdot \frac{\partial r_h}{\partial \gamma} = l'_h \cdot \frac{\partial r_h}{\partial \gamma} \cdot \lambda_h + l'_h \cdot r_h \cdot \frac{\partial \lambda_h}{\partial \gamma}. \qquad (2B.8.5)$$

We know by postmultiplying both sides of equation (2B.8.4) by $\partial r_h / \partial \gamma$ that

$$l'_h \cdot A \cdot \frac{\partial r_h}{\partial \gamma} = l'_h \cdot \frac{\partial r}{\partial \gamma} \cdot \lambda_h. \qquad (2B.8.6)$$

Hence, equation (2B.8.5) simplifies to

$$l'_h \cdot \frac{\partial A}{\partial \gamma} \cdot r_h = l'_h \cdot r_h \cdot \frac{\partial \lambda_h}{\partial \gamma}. \qquad (2B.8.7)$$

Finally, solving for $\partial \lambda_h / \partial \gamma$, we have the characteristic-root sensitivity equation:

$$\frac{\partial \lambda_h}{\partial \gamma} = \frac{l'_h \cdot \dfrac{\partial A}{\partial \gamma} \cdot r_h}{l'_h \cdot r_h}. \qquad (2B.8.8)$$

We can specialize equation (2B.8.8) for γ equal to the i, jth element of the matrix A:

$$\frac{\partial \lambda_h}{\partial a_{ij}} = \frac{l'_h \cdot \dfrac{\partial A}{\partial a_{ij}} \cdot r_h}{l'_h \cdot r_h} = \frac{(l_h)_i \cdot (r_h)_j}{l'_h \cdot r_h}, \qquad (2B.8.9)$$

where $(l_h)_i$ is the ith element of l_h, and $(r_h)_j$ is similarly the jth element of r_h. LIMO computes left and right characteristic vectors normalized so that

$L^T R = 1$, whence $l'_h r_h = 1$. This further simplifies (2B.8.9) to

$$\frac{\partial \lambda_h}{\partial a_{ij}} = (l_h)_i (r_h)_j. \tag{2B.8.10}$$

Root sensitivities for real roots can also be given a geometric interpretation. We can put equation (2B.8.10) into matrix form:

$$P_h = \frac{\partial \lambda_h}{\partial A} = r_h l'_h. \tag{2B.8.11}$$

The spectral projection P_h is simply the outer product of the right and left characteristic vectors for λ_h. P_h is a nonsymmetric projection matrix into the space of r_h. This interpretation of root sensitivities becomes useful in isolating sources of ill-conditioning in the solution of characteristic roots.

Root sensitivity to the linearized structural form D and E matrix entries additionally develops out of the definition of A:

$$DA = E. \tag{2B.8.12}$$

From equation (2B.8.11),

$$\frac{\partial D}{\partial \gamma} \cdot A + D \cdot \frac{\partial A}{\partial \gamma} = \frac{\partial E}{\partial \gamma}. \tag{2B.8.13}$$

For γ equal to the i, jth entry of D, equation (2B.8.12) shows that[†]

$$\frac{\partial A}{\partial d_{ij}} = -D^{-1} \cdot \frac{\partial D}{\partial d_{ij}} \cdot A. \tag{2B.8.14}$$

For γ equal to the i, jth entry of E,

$$\frac{\partial A}{\partial e_{ij}} = D^{-1} \cdot \frac{\partial E}{\partial e_{ij}}. \tag{2B.8.15}$$

Root sensitivity to D matrix entries is found by substituting equation (2B.8.14) into the sensitivity equation (2B.8.8) for $\gamma = d_{ij}$:

$$\frac{\partial \lambda_h}{\partial d_{ij}} = \frac{-l'_h D^{-1} \cdot \dfrac{\partial D}{\partial d_{ij}} \cdot A r_h}{l'_h r_h}$$

$$= -\lambda_h \cdot (l'_h D^{-1})_i (r_h)_j. \tag{2B.8.16}$$

[†] Note in what follows that $\partial D/\partial e_{ij} = \partial E/\partial d_{ij} = 0$.

Similarly for root sensitivity to E matrix entries:

$$\frac{\partial \lambda_h}{\partial e_{ij}} = \frac{l_h' D^{-1} \cdot \dfrac{\partial E}{\partial e_{ij}} \cdot r_h}{l_h' r_h}$$

$$= \left(l_h' D^{-1} \right)_i (r_h)_j. \qquad (2B.8.17)$$

These modulus root sensitivities have two useful scaling representations: elasticity and relative. The familiar elasticity scaling can be interpreted as the percentage change of the root in response to a percent change in the i, jth entry of the matrix A, D, or E (depending on which is being examined). In elasticity form, these root sensitivities are

$$\eta(\lambda_h, a_{ij}) \equiv \frac{\partial |\lambda_h|}{\partial a_{ij}} \cdot \frac{a_{ij}}{|\lambda_h|} \qquad \text{for } A, \qquad (2B.8.18)$$

$$\eta(\lambda_h, d_{ij}) \equiv \frac{\partial |\lambda_h|}{\partial d_{ij}} \cdot \frac{d_{ij}}{|\lambda_h|} \qquad \text{for } D, \qquad (2B.8.19)$$

$$\eta(\lambda_h, e_{ij}) \equiv \frac{\partial |\lambda_h|}{\partial e_{ij}} \cdot \frac{e_{ij}}{|\lambda_h|} \qquad \text{for } E, \qquad (2B.8.20)$$

where the root magnitudes are real. For the matrix A the relative scaling is the response (change) in λ_h to a relative change in a_{ij}:

$$\omega(\lambda_n, a_{ij}) = \frac{\partial \lambda_h}{\partial a_{ij}} \cdot a_{ij}, \qquad (2B.8.21)$$

and the D and E scalings are computed similarly. Note that the real root sensitivities in elasticity form have attractive additive properties across elements of A, D, or E. Noting that $l_h' A r_h = \Sigma_i \Sigma_j (l_h)_i a_{ij} (r_h)_j$, we have [substituting (2B.8.9) into (2B.8.18) and summing]

$$\sum_{i,j} \eta(\lambda_h, a_{ij}) = \frac{l_h' A r_h}{l_h' r_h \lambda_h}, \qquad (2B.8.22)$$

from which it follows, since r_h is a right characteristic vector of A associated with λ_h, that $A r_h = \lambda_h r_h$ and

$$\sum_{i,j} \eta(\lambda_h, a_{ij}) = 1. \qquad (2B.8.23)$$

Similarly, $\Sigma_{i,j}\eta(\lambda_h, d_{ij}) = -1$ and $\Sigma_{i,j}\eta(\lambda_h, e_{ij}) = 1$. These properties make the interpretation of root sensitivities straightforward.

The period sensitivities are somewhat more complicated. The periodicity τ_h of λ_h is defined to be

$$\tau_h = \frac{2\pi}{\arctan(\mu_h/\rho_h)}, \tag{2B.8.24}$$

where ρ_h is the real part of the root λ_h, and μ_h is its imaginary component. Taking the derivative of τ_h with respect to an arbitrary scalar γ, we have

$$\frac{\partial \tau_h}{\partial \gamma} = \frac{-2\pi}{[\arctan(\mu_h/\rho_h)]^2} \cdot \frac{1}{1 + (\mu_n/\rho_n)^2} \times \frac{1}{\rho_h^2}\left(\rho_h \frac{\partial \mu_h}{\partial \gamma} - \mu_h \frac{\partial \rho_h}{\partial \gamma}\right).$$

$$\tag{2B.8.25}$$

After some tedious algebra, this simplifies to

$$\frac{\partial \tau_h}{\partial \gamma} = \frac{(\tau_h)^2}{2\pi|\lambda_h|^2}\left(-\rho_h \frac{\partial \mu_h}{\partial \gamma} + \mu_h \frac{\partial \rho_h}{\partial \gamma}\right). \tag{2B.8.26}$$

As with the modulus sensitivities, we can specialize the scalar to the i, jth element of A, D, or E. Here we focus on A:

$$\frac{\partial \tau_h}{\partial a_{ij}} = \frac{(\tau_h)^2}{2\pi|\lambda_h|^2}\left\{-\rho_h\left[(l_{1h})_i(r_{2h})_j + (l_{2h})_i(r_{1h})_j\right]\right.$$

$$\left. + \mu_h\left[(l_{1h})_i(r_{1h})_j + (l_{2h})_i(r_{2h})_j\right]\right\}, \tag{2B.8.27}$$

where the right and left characteristic vectors are each a combination of two vectors as described in the discussion after equation (2B.5.3), with the first part associated with the real portion of the characteristic root and the second with the complex portion. The distinction between real and complex portions of the characteristic vectors was omitted for clarity in the modulus case.

Again, parallel to the structure of the modulus sensitivities, the period sensitivities can be scaled as elasticities or by relative scaling. Illustrating this with the elasticity sensitivity with respect to the matrix A, we have

$$\eta(\tau_h, a_{ij}) = \frac{\partial \tau_h}{\partial a_{ij}} \cdot \frac{a_{ij}}{\tau_h}. \tag{2B.8.28}$$

An interesting relationship is that the elasticity sensitivities are directly proportional to the period of the root. Similarly, the period root sensitivities (the root sensitivities with respect to the imaginary component) sum to zero in the elasticity form of A. This is an intuitive result as a percent change in every element of A is the same as multiplying A by a constant, which does not change the periodicity of any of the roots.

2B.9 WILKINSON CONDITION NUMBERS

Wilkinson condition numbers (the reciprocal of Wilkinson's s-numbers) are a measure of the rate of change of each characteristic root with respect to perturbations in the matrix A. These condition numbers provide an index of the numerical decomposability of that root from the rest of the system and an upper bound on the magnitude of the root sensitivities of Section 2B.8; they are also an interesting diagnostic for the decomposed time responses of Section 2B.7. See Chan, Feldman, and Parlett (1977) and Wilkinson (1965) in the references at the end of this appendix. A caveat on their usage is at the end of this section. The use of Wilkinson condition numbers in perturbation analysis of Λ is dealt with in Appendix 5A.

LIMO computes the Wilkinson condition numbers in the following manner:

$$\text{COND}(\lambda_h) = \frac{\|l_h\| \|r_h\|}{l_h' r_h} = \frac{1}{\cos \theta_h}, \tag{2B.9.1}$$

λ_h = the hth characteristic root.

l_h = the left characteristic vector associated with λ_h.

r_h = the right characteristic vector associated with λ_h.

θ_h = the angle between the pair of left and right characteristic vectors (in the plane formed by the vectors) associated with λ_h.

Hence $\text{COND}(\lambda_h)$ has a minimum of 1 when $\theta_h = 0$, and increases as θ_h increases to 90°. The angle θ_h has the following interpretation: If $\theta_h = 0$ for a pair of characteristic vectors associated with a root λ_h, the right characteristic vector r_h is perpendicular to all other characteristic vectors in the matrix A. This is easily shown by recalling that $RL^T = I$, which means that $l_h \perp r_j$ for all $h \neq j$. It then immediately follows that if $\text{COND}(\lambda_h) = 1$, then l_h is parallel to r_h. Thus r_h is perpendicular to all r_j for $j \neq h$. As $\text{COND}(\lambda_h)$ (and thus θ_h) increases, r_h is no longer orthogonal to the other right characteristic vectors.

What this means in the context of LIMO is that if $\theta_h = 0$, then the behavior associated with this root is completely numerically independent (completely decomposable) from the rest of the system. As θ_h increases [and as COND(λ_h) increases], the calculation of characteristic vectors for that root becomes more ill conditioned. Wilkinson condition numbers serve the useful function of isolating the roots of A that are numerically independent of the rest of the system.

Wilkinson condition numbers also have an intimate relationship with the root sensitivities of Section 2B.8. The unscaled root-sensitivity matrix can be interpreted as a projection matrix into the space of r_h:

$$P_h = \frac{\partial \lambda_h}{\partial A} = r_h l_h'. \qquad (2B.9.2)$$

Using the fact that P_h is of rank one, it can be shown that the Frobenius norm of P_h is the Wilkinson condition number:

$$\|P_h\|_F = \sqrt{\sum_i \sum_j \left(P_{h_{ij}} \right)^2} = \text{COND}(\lambda_h). \qquad (2B.9.3)$$

Since the individual elements of P_h are the root sensitivities $\partial \lambda_h / \partial a_{ij}$ defined in equation (2B.8.10), the Wilkinson condition numbers are simply

$$\text{COND}(\lambda_h) = \sqrt{\sum_i \sum_j \left(\frac{\partial \lambda_h}{\partial a_{ij}} \right)^2}. \qquad (2B.9.4)$$

This is an intuitive result since COND(λ_h) is an upper bound on the rate of change of λ_h to perturbations in A and $\partial \lambda_h / \partial a_{ij}$ is a measure of the sensitivity of λ_h to perturbations in individual elements of A.

Often COND(λ_h) will be large (above 10^3) when there are near-multiple roots (i.e., two or more roots that are nearly numerically indistinguishable).

A particular reason that Wilkinson condition numbers are of interest is that they provide a valuable aid to interpreting the decomposed time responses of Section 2B.7. Rewriting equation (2B.7.5), we have

$$\left(\Delta \tilde{z}_{t_0+n} | \lambda_h \right) = [R_1]_{\cdot h} \cdot \lambda_h^n \cdot [L_1]_h^T \Delta \tilde{z}_{t_0}. \qquad (2B.9.5)$$

Since ill-conditioning occurs with the interactions of two or more roots, two roots that have high Wilkinson condition numbers also may have projection matrices that project into nearly parallel spaces but in opposite directions. The decomposed responses of a variable to a perturbation for two such roots could be large, and close to being equal and opposite in sign.

2B.10   COMPUTATIONAL ASPECTS

Characteristic-Root–Vector Decompositions and Defective Matrices

If a matrix does not have as many linearly independent characteristic vectors as it has characteristic roots, it is called "defective" in numerical-analysis literature (Golub and Wilkinson, 1976). A symmetric matrix cannot be defective. However, a nonsymmetric matrix (such as the dynamics matrix A) *can* be defective when it has repeated roots. Repeated roots are a necessary *but not sufficient* condition for a nonsymmetric matrix to be defective.

A defective dynamics matrix can arise in two ways in LIMO. The first is *structural*: the original nonlinear model may have been specified in a way that dictates repeated roots lacking the same number of linearly independent characteristic vectors. The second is numerical: when two or more characteristic roots have magnitudes much smaller than the largest roots in the system, it is often difficult or impossible for any finite-precision algorithm to distinguish the neighboring vectors.

We believe that unavoidable structurally defective dynamics matrices are unusual for linearized real-world econometric models, apart from those associated with multiple zero roots. As a first example of an avoidable defective condition, sometimes the MQEM contains equations of the form $\Delta z_{1t} = \alpha + \beta \Delta z_{2t}$ which arise in first-differenced equations for estimation purposes. This automatically creates a unit root, even when the original level version of such an equation is static.

Two other examples follow:

1. Model:

$$\mathrm{RS}_t = \alpha\,\mathrm{RS}_{t-1},$$

$$\mathrm{INV}_t = \beta\,\mathrm{INV}_{t-1} + \delta\,\mathrm{RS}_{t-3}.$$

Reduced form:

$$\begin{pmatrix} \mathrm{RS}_t \\ \mathrm{INV}_t \\ \mathrm{RS}_{t-1} \\ \mathrm{RS}_{t-2} \end{pmatrix} = \begin{bmatrix} \alpha & 0 & 0 & 0 \\ 0 & \beta & 0 & \delta \\ 1 & 0 & 0 & 0 \\ 0 & 0 & 1 & 0 \end{bmatrix} \begin{pmatrix} \mathrm{RS}_{t-1} \\ \mathrm{INV}_{t-1} \\ \mathrm{RS}_{t-2} \\ \mathrm{RS}_{t-3} \end{pmatrix}.$$

Roots:

$$\{\alpha, \quad \beta, \quad 0, \quad 0\}.$$

The reader can verify that there is only one independent characteristic vector associated with the two zero roots: $(0, 1, 0, -\beta/\delta)^T$. This case is similar to one that we have come across. The essence of the structural "defect" is that two extra lags in RS are carried along purely to determine INV—which, in turn, never affects RS.

2. Model:

$$C_t = \alpha Y_{t-1},$$

$$I_t = \gamma(Y_{t-1} - Y_{t-2}),$$

$$Y_t = C_t + I_t.$$

Reduced form:

$$\begin{pmatrix} C_t \\ I_t \\ Y_t \\ Y_{t-1} \end{pmatrix} = \begin{bmatrix} 0 & 0 & \alpha & 0 \\ 0 & 0 & \gamma & -\gamma \\ 0 & 0 & \alpha + \gamma & -\gamma \\ 0 & 0 & 1 & 0 \end{bmatrix} \begin{pmatrix} C_{t-1} \\ I_{t-1} \\ Y_{t-1} \\ Y_{t-2} \end{pmatrix}.$$

Roots:

$$\{0, \quad 0, \quad \lambda_3, \quad \lambda_4\},$$

where

$$\lambda_3, \lambda_4 = \frac{(\alpha + \gamma) \pm \sqrt{(\alpha + \gamma)^2 - 4\gamma}}{2}.$$

For $\alpha = 0.75$ and $\gamma = 0.25$, we have $\lambda_3 = \lambda_4 = 0.5$, and these multiple roots possess only one characteristic vector: $(3, -1, 2, 4)^T$. The structural defect is highly coincidental, as it depends entirely on a fortuitous choice for α and γ. In analyzing half a dozen empirical econometric models, apart from first-differenced equations, we have never encountered structural defects associated with nonzero roots.

While structurally defective dynamics matrices are rare, numerically defective matrices are the rule rather than the exception. One way of assessing whether a matrix is numerically defective is to solve for its roots and vectors. If the root–vector decomposition can be performed, then calculate the condition number of the matrix of characteristic vectors (i.e., the ratio of the largest to the smallest singular value; see Belsley, Kuh, and Welsch, 1980, Appendix 2B, for an expository discussion). The best condition number is one, and the worst condition number is infinity. The best is achieved for linearly independent characteristic vectors; the worst is approached when any two vectors approach linear dependence. For computations with 16-digit accuracy, a condition number greater than 10^8 is cause for concern. Our experience is that condition numbers greater than 10^8 are commonplace in moderate-size econometric models.[†]

LIMO's Partial Characteristic-Root–Vector Decomposition Algorithm

LIMO's partial characteristic-root–vector decomposition algorithm is designed to take advantage of three common features of linearized structural econometric models:

1. There are many nondynamic identities.
2. Interesting parts of the dynamics matrix are not structurally defective.
3. The dynamics matrix is numerically defective.

We know that for each nondynamic identity appearing in the model there will be one zero characteristic root in the dynamics matrix A. The algorithm deflates (removes) these known zero roots from A before finding the remaining, "unknown" roots. This reduces the order of the problem.

Because the dynamics matrix is so often numerically defective, we do not attempt to compute vectors for all roots. As discussed in Section 2B.10.1, numerical defects arise primarily out of the wide range of root magnitudes. We can therefore avoid the defects by choosing a modulus cutoff and not computing vectors for roots below it.

Since econometric-model dynamics matrices are not often structurally defective, numerical defects are unlikely to crop up in connection with sensibly selected cutoffs. Any structural defects in roots of modulus below the cutoff will not harm the partial decomposition.

The germ of the idea for this algorithm originates with Bavely and Stewart's BDIAG algorithm (1979). Our original intent was to use BDIAG itself; however, we found it to be considerably more expensive in our application than conventional decomposition algorithms. By taking advantage of special structure we have built a considerably more economical algorithm that retains most of the desirable numerical properties.

A sketch of the algorithm follows in the next subsection with references to state-of-the-art code used by LIMO. More details appear in the remainder of this section. Recognition of the three common attributes of econometric

[†] Moler and VanLoan (1978) discuss this method of assessing nearness to a defective matrix. They do so in connection with a study of how to compute the exponential of a matrix (see pp. 820, 821 of their study).

models described at the beginning of this subsection can sharply reduce the total amount of computation and increase the precision with which characteristic roots and vectors are computed.

Basic Outline of Partial Characteristic-Root–Vector Decomposition Algorithm[†]

1. Apply left similarity transformation to break the matrix A into two dynamically disjoint blocks:[‡]

    (i)   One containing known, zero roots (identities and exogenous variable constructs).

    (ii) The other containing unknown roots:

$$A \overset{T_1}{\to} \left[\begin{array}{c|c} \text{Unknown} & \text{Nondynamic} \\ \text{roots} & \text{coupling} \\ \hline & \text{Known} \\ 0 & \text{zero} \\ & \text{roots} \end{array}\right].$$

T_1 depends on the structure of the particular model.

2. Apply right orthogonal similarity transformation to put "unknown roots" submatrix into real upper block-triangular (Schur) form:

$$\left[\begin{array}{c|c} \text{Unknown} & \text{Nondynamic} \\ \text{roots} & \text{coupling} \\ \hline & \text{Known} \\ 0 & \text{zero} \\ & \text{roots} \end{array}\right] \overset{T_2}{\to} \left[\begin{array}{c|c} \text{Schur} & \text{Nondynamic} \\ \text{form} & \text{coupling} \\ \hline & \text{Known} \\ 0 & \text{zero} \\ & \text{roots} \end{array}\right].$$

T_2 is found by means of the EISPACK routines ORTHES and ORTRAN (Smith et al., 1976) and G. W. Stewart's HQR3 and EXCHNG codes (Stewart, 1976). This transformation also puts the diagonal blocks of the Schur form in order of descending modulus. Each block is associated with one real characteristic root or one complex conjugate pair of roots.

[†] In this subsection time subscripts have been omitted.
[‡] A *left similarity transformation* of $\tilde{A}$ to A is $L^T A L^{-T} = \tilde{A}$, and a *right similarity transformation* is $R^{-1} A R = \hat{A}$.

3. Choose a characteristic-root magnitude cutoff and partition accordingly:

$$
\begin{bmatrix}
\text{Schur form} & \text{Nondynamic coupling} \\
0 & \begin{array}{c}\text{Known}\\\text{zero}\\\text{roots}\end{array}
\end{bmatrix}
$$

$$
\xrightarrow{T_3}
\begin{bmatrix}
\begin{array}{c}\text{Schur form,}\\\text{above-cut-}\\\text{off roots}\end{array} & \text{Nondynamic coupling} & \text{Nondynamic coupling} \\
0 & \begin{array}{c}\text{Schur form,}\\\text{below-cut-}\\\text{off roots}\end{array} & \text{Nondynamic coupling} \\
0 & 0 & \begin{array}{c}\text{Known}\\\text{zero}\\\text{roots}\end{array}
\end{bmatrix} \cdot
$$

This partitioning is expressed as a right similarity transformation T_3 for convenience. In matrix form, T_3 is merely an appropriately partitioned identity matrix.

4. Apply right similarity transformation to zero out "nondynamic coupling" submatrices associated with above-cutoff roots.

$$
\begin{bmatrix}
\begin{array}{c}\text{Schur form,}\\\text{above-cut-}\\\text{off roots}\end{array} & \text{Nondynamic coupling} & \text{Nondynamic coupling} \\
0 & \begin{array}{c}\text{Schur form,}\\\text{below-cut-}\\\text{off roots}\end{array} & \text{Nondynamic coupling} \\
0 & 0 & \begin{array}{c}\text{Known}\\\text{zero}\\\text{roots}\end{array}
\end{bmatrix}
$$

$$
\xrightarrow{T_4}
\begin{bmatrix}
\begin{array}{c}\text{Schur form,}\\\text{above-cut-}\\\text{off roots}\end{array} & 0 & 0 \\
0 & \begin{array}{c}\text{Schur form,}\\\text{below-cut-}\\\text{off roots}\end{array} & \text{Nondynamic coupling} \\
0 & 0 & \begin{array}{c}\text{Known}\\\text{zero}\\\text{roots}\end{array}
\end{bmatrix} \cdot
$$

T_4 is found by means of Bartels and Stewart's (1972) code SHRSLV and SYSSLV. Their code has been modified to take account of special structure and sparsity.

5. Find left (LVEC) and right (RVEC) similarity transformations of "Schur form, above-cutoff roots" submatrix to real block-diagonal form:

$$
\begin{bmatrix} \text{Schur form,} \\ \text{above-cut-} \\ \text{off roots} \end{bmatrix} \begin{array}{c} \text{RVEC} \\ \rightarrow \\ \text{LVEC} \end{array} \begin{bmatrix} \text{Real block-} \\ \text{diagonal,} \\ \text{above-cut-} \\ \text{off roots} \end{bmatrix}
$$

These transformations are found using a version of Chan, Feldman, and Parlett's (1977) code CONDIT, modified to save the transformation matrices.

6. From T_1, T_2, T_3, T_4 and LVEC or RVEC assemble left (L) or right (R) overall similarity transformations for A:

$$
A \begin{array}{c} R \\ \rightarrow \\ L \end{array}
\begin{bmatrix}
\begin{array}{c}\text{Real block-}\\\text{diagonal,}\\\text{above-cut-}\\\text{off roots}\end{array} & 0 & 0 \\
\hline
0 & \begin{array}{c}\text{Schur form,}\\\text{below-cut-}\\\text{off roots}\end{array} & \begin{array}{c}\text{Nondynamic}\\\text{coupling}\end{array} \\
\hline
0 & 0 & \begin{array}{c}\text{Known}\\\text{zero}\\\text{roots}\end{array}
\end{bmatrix}
$$

$$
= \begin{bmatrix}
\Lambda_1 & 0 & 0 \\
\hline
0 & S_{22} & S_{23} \\
\hline
0 & 0 & S_{33}
\end{bmatrix}.
$$

Note that

$$
R = T_1^{-T} T_2 T_3 T_4 \cdot
\begin{bmatrix}
\text{RVEC} & 0 & 0 \\
0 & I & 0 \\
0 & 0 & I
\end{bmatrix}
\equiv [R_1 \mid R_2 \mid R_3],
$$

$$
L = T_1 T_2 T_3 T_4^{-T} \cdot
\begin{bmatrix}
\text{LVEC} & 0 & 0 \\
0 & I & 0 \\
0 & 0 & I
\end{bmatrix}
\equiv [L_1 \mid L_2 \mid L_3].
$$

Point 6 indicates the nature of the overall similarity transformations, which have the following relation to the A-matrix equations (2B.5.10) and (2B.5.11) in Section 2B.5:

Section 2B.10		Sections 2B.1–2B.9
A	$\leftrightarrow$	A_t
Λ_1	$\leftrightarrow$	$\Lambda_{1,t}$
$\begin{bmatrix} S_{22} & \vdots & S_{23} \\ \text{---} & + & \text{---} \\ 0 & \vdots & S_{33} \end{bmatrix}$	$\leftrightarrow$	$S_{2,t}$
R_1	$\leftrightarrow$	$R_{1,t}$
$\begin{bmatrix} R_2 \vdots R_3 \end{bmatrix}$	$\leftrightarrow$	$R_{2,t}$
L_1	$\leftrightarrow$	$L_{1,t}$
$\begin{bmatrix} L_2 \vdots L_3 \end{bmatrix}$	$\leftrightarrow$	$L_{2,t}$

Powers and Sums of Powers of A_t

Computing powers (and sums of powers) of a square matrix X can lead to highly inaccurate results due to roundoff errors, and it can be expensive. Since LIMO's time responses (see Section 2B.6) are functions of powers and sums of powers of the dynamics matrix A for a fixed linearization evaluation date, these difficulties are important. Rounding errors *can be* (but are not necessarily) severe when the condition number of X is large (Moler and VanLoan, 1978, pp. 810, 811); since A almost always contains zero or near-zero characteristic roots, it can be expected to have a very large condition number. Computational cost grows as the cube of the order of X; A's order is often quite large (100–400) for medium-size econometric models. LIMO lessens the impact of these difficulties by:

1. Employing the partial characteristic-root–vector decomposition to reduce roundoff errors.
2. Using knowledge of the structure of the decomposition to reduce the effective order of matrix multiplications.
3. Not calculating further powers of the part of A associated with the below-cutoff roots when these powers cease making a significant contribution relative to that of powers of the above-cutoff-roots part.

A general motivation for using matrix decomposition techniques to compute matrix powers is presented in Moler and VanLoan (1978).[†] The form of LIMO's decomposition was presented in Section 2B.7 in connection

[†] See, in particular, methods 14, 15, and 18 in Section 6 of Moler and VanLoan's paper (1978).

with the partial characteristic-root decomposition of the linearized model's time response. Equation (2B.7.2) is reproduced here for convenience:

$$A^n = R_1 \Lambda_1^n R^1 + \tilde{R}_2 S_2^n \tilde{R}^2. \tag{2B.10.1}$$

Since the decomposition vectors are normalized so that $L_1^T = R_1^{-1}$ and $\tilde{L}_2^T = \tilde{R}_2^{-1}$, the equation (2B.10.1) can be rewritten

$$A^n = R_1 \Lambda_1^n L_1^T + \tilde{R}_2 S_2^n \tilde{L}_2^T. \tag{2B.10.2}$$

Using equation (2B.10.2) minimizes rounding errors when the decomposition of A is accurate because Λ_1 and S_2 have desirable structures. Since Λ_1 is block-diagonal, computing Λ_1^n merely involves raising 1×1 and 2×2 blocks to the power n; given that the diagonal blocks are associated with characteristic roots of modulus above a cutoff selected to restrict the range of roots in Λ_1, the accuracy of these powered blocks is easily maintained. S_2 has the form

$$S_2 = \begin{bmatrix} S_{22} & S_{23} & S_{24} \\ 0 & 0 & \text{PFPXCL2} \\ 0 & 0 & \text{DXCDXCL} \end{bmatrix}. \tag{2B.10.3}$$

Thus,

$$S_2^n = \begin{bmatrix} S_{22}^n & S_{22}^{n-1} & \Psi_n \\ 0 & 0 & \text{PFPXCL2} \cdot \text{DXCDXCL}^{n-1} \\ 0 & 0 & \text{DXCDXCL}^n \end{bmatrix}, \tag{2B.10.4}$$

where

$$\Psi_n \equiv \sum_{m=1}^{n} S_{22}^{n-m} S_{24} \cdot \text{DXCDXCL}^{m-1}$$

$$+ \sum_{m=2}^{n} S_{22}^{n-m} S_{23} \text{PFPXCL2} \cdot \text{DXCDXCL}^{m-2}.$$

Accurately computing the second- and third-row partitions of S_2^n is relatively easy because PFPXCL2 and DXCDXCL are very sparse matrices. The first-row partition is more troublesome; however, inaccuracies in S_{22}^n are often inconsequential, since the norm of S_{22} (and S_{22}^n) must be small relative to that of Λ_1 given that S_{22} contains only below-cutoff roots. To the extent that inaccuracies in S_{22}^n matter, we have the computational advantage that S_{22} (and S_{22}^n) is a Schur matrix; all computations with S_{22} are performed in double precision with extended-precision inner products.

Recognizing the structure of the partial root–vector decomposition enables savings in computational expense. In particular, code has been incorporated into LIMO that creates powers and sums of powers of the block diagonal matrix Λ_1. Multiplications involving sparse matrices PFPXCL2 and DXCDXCL are handled by sparse-matrix routines. The zeros in S_2^n [see equation (2B.10.4)] are explicitly recognized.

Considerable savings can result from calculating only those powers of S_2 that make significant contributions relative to the same powers of Λ_1. Referring to equation (2B.10.3), the submatrices S_{22}, S_{23}, and S_{24} are often large (order 50–200) for medium-size econometric models, and they are not sparse. The warning above (see the first paragraph of this section) about order-n^3 costs applies to computing powers of S_2. Since the norm of S_{22} is less than that of Λ_1 by our choice of root modulus cutoff, there is a power n such that the contribution of S_{22}^n to A^n will be far less than that of Λ_1^n. This concept is made precise in the context of computing a linearized model time response.

We begin with the scaled time response from equation (2B.6.3):

$$\Delta \tilde{z}_{t_0+n} = A^n \Delta \tilde{z}_{t_0} + \sum_{s=0}^{n-1} A^s \cdot \left\{ B \Delta \tilde{x}_{t_0+n-s} + C \Delta \tilde{\beta} \right\}. \quad (2B.10.5)$$

Substituting for A^n and A^s the expressions for their partial root–vector decompositions from equation (2B.10.2), we obtain

$$\Delta \tilde{z}_{t_0+n} = \left[R_1 \Lambda_1^n L_1^T + \tilde{R}_2 S_2^n \tilde{L}_2^T \right] \Delta \tilde{z}_{t_0}$$

$$+ \sum_{s=0}^{n-1} \left[R_1 \Lambda_1^s L_1^T + \tilde{R}_2 S_2^s \tilde{L}_2^T \right] \left\{ B \Delta x_{t_0+n-s} + C \Delta \beta \right\}. \quad (2B.10.6)$$

Taking infinity norms and rearranging terms yields an expression

$$\|\Delta \tilde{z}_{t_0+n}\| \le \|R_1\| \cdot \left[\|\Lambda_1^n\| \cdot \|L_1^T \Delta \tilde{z}_{t_0}\| \right.$$

$$+ \sum_{s=0}^{n-1} \|\Lambda_1^s\| \cdot \left\| L_1^T \cdot \left\{ B \Delta \tilde{x}_{t_0+n-s} + C \Delta \tilde{\beta} \right\} \right\| \bigg]$$

$$+ \|\tilde{R}_2\| \cdot \left[\|S_2^n\| \cdot \|\tilde{L}_2^T \Delta \tilde{z}_{t_0}\| \right.$$

$$+ \sum_{s=0}^{n-1} \|S_2^s\| \cdot \left\| \tilde{L}_2^T \cdot \left\{ B \Delta \tilde{x}_{t_0+n-s} + C \Delta \tilde{\beta} \right\} \right\| \bigg].$$

$$(2B.10.7)$$

To enable comparing relative contributions of Λ_1^s and S_2^n, we need to make some assumptions. Our choice of assumptions is:[†]

1. $10\|L_1^T \Delta \tilde{z}_{t_0}\| \geq \|\tilde{L}_2^T \Delta \tilde{z}_{t_0}\| \equiv b(z_{t_0})$.
2. $10\|L_1^T \cdot \{B\Delta\tilde{x}_{t_0+n-s} + C\Delta\tilde{\beta}\}\| \geq \|\tilde{L}_2^T \cdot \{B\Delta\tilde{x}_{t_0+n-s} + C\Delta\beta\}\| \equiv b(x_{t_0+n-s})$.
3. $b(x_{t_0+n-s})$ does not vary greatly with s.
4. $\|S_2^s\|$ is monotonically nonincreasing with s (i.e., S_2 has no roots with modulus exceeding 1).

The first two assumptions simplify equation (2B.10.7) to

$$
\|\Delta\tilde{z}_{t_0+n}\| \leq \|R_1\| \cdot \left[\|\Lambda_1^n\| \frac{b(z_{t_0})}{10} + \sum_{s=0}^{n-1} \|\Lambda_1^s\| \frac{b(x_{t_0+n-s})}{10} \right]
$$
$$
- \|\tilde{R}_2\| \cdot \left[\|S_2^n\| b(z_{t_0}) + \sum_{s=0}^{n-1} \|S_2^s\| b(x_{t_0+n-s}) \right].
$$

$$(2B.10.8)$$

Assumptions 3 and 4 imply that the absolute contribution of each term in $\sum_{s=0}^{n-1}\|S_2^s\|b(x_{t_0+n-s})$ mainly decreases with s. This makes the idea of dropping terms associated with larger s reasonable.

Making a term-by-term comparison of Λ_1^s and S_2^s contributions to $\|\Delta\tilde{z}_{t_0+n}\|$ in equation (2B.10.8), we have

$$
\rho_s \equiv \frac{\|\Delta\tilde{z}_{t_0+n}\| \text{ from } S_2^s}{\|\Delta\tilde{z}_{t_0+n}\| \text{ from } \Lambda_1^s} = 10 \times \frac{\|\tilde{R}_2\| \cdot \|S_2^s\|}{\|R_1\| \cdot \|\Lambda_1^s\|}. \qquad (2B.10.9)
$$

We choose to set the S_2^s contributions to zero for all s beyond that for which

$$
\rho_s < \text{tol}, \qquad (2B.10.10)
$$

where tol = a user-supplied tolerance.

Equations (2B.10.9) and (2B.10.10) amount to saying that S_2 is set to zero when

$$
\|S_2^s\| < \text{tol} \cdot \frac{\|R_1\| \cdot \|\Lambda_1^s\|}{10\|R_2\|}. \qquad (2B.10.11)
$$

[†] While arbitrary, these inequalities could be verified in a given problem.

Denoting the largest characteristic root of Λ_1 (or A) as λ_{max}, $\|\Lambda_1^s\|$ may be replaced by $|\lambda_{max}|^s$:

$$\|S_2^s\| < \text{tol} \cdot \frac{\|R_1\| \cdot |\lambda_{max}|^s}{10\|\tilde{R}_2\|}. \tag{2B.10.12}$$

In LIMO's RTPOWSUM command, the user is prompted for a value of tol which through equation (2B.10.12) determines when additional powers of S_2 can be set to zero (not computed). LIMO chooses a default value of 10^{-3} for tol; given the conservative nature of the bound in equation (2B.10.12), we are reasonably assured of three digits of accuracy in computing time responses.

REFERENCES

Bartels, R. H. and G. W. Stewart (1972). Algorithm 432, The Solution of the Matrix Equation $AX - SB = C$, *Communications of the Association for Computing Machinery*, Vol. 15, No. 9, pp. 820–826.

Bavely, Connice A. and G. W. Stewart (1979). An Algorithm for Computing Reducing Subspaces by Block Diagonalization, *SIAM Journal of Numerical Analysis*, Vol. 16, No. 2, pp. 359–367.

Belsley, David A., Edwin Kuh, and Roy E. Welsch (1980). *Regression Diagnostics: Identifying Influential Data and Sources of Collinearity*, Wiley, New York.

Chan, S. P., R. Feldman, and B. N. Parlett (1977). "Algorithm 517: A Program for Computing the Condition Numbers of Matrix Eigenvalues without Computing Eigenvectors [F2], *ACM Transactions on Mathematical Software*, Vol. 3, No. 2, pp. 186–203.

Cline, A. K., C. B. Moler, G. W. Stewart, and J. H. Wilkinson (1979). An Estimate for the Condition Number of a Matrix, *SIAM Journal of Numerical Analysis*, Vol. 16, No. 2, pp. 368–375.

Duff, I. S. (1981). Algorithms for Obtaining a Maximum Transversal, *ACM Transactions on Mathematical Software*, Vol. 7, No. 3, pp. 315–330.

Duff, I. S. and J. K. Reid (1978). An Implementation of Tarjan's Algorithm for Block Triangularization of a Matrix, *ACM Transactions on Mathematical Software*, Vol. 4, No. 2, pp. 137–147.

Golub, G. H. and J. H. Wilkinson (1976). Ill-Conditioned Eigensystems and the Computation of the Jordan Canonical Form, *SIAM Review*, Vol. 18, No. 4, pp. 578–619.

Flamm, David S. and Robert A. Walker (undated). Corrections to Algorithm 506: HQR3 ... ", mimeo.

Moler, C. and C. VanLoan (1978). Nineteen Dubious Ways to Compute the Exponential of a Matrix, *SIAM Review*, Vol. 20, No. 4, pp. 801–836.

Neese, John W., Peter Hollinger, and Edwin Kuh (1983). TROLL Program LIMO, (Linear Model Analysis), Technical Report # 34, Center for Computational Research in Economics and Management Science, Massachusetts Institute of Technology, Cambridge, Mass.

Smith, B. T., J. M. Boyle, J. H. Dongarra, B. S. Garbow, Y. Ikebe, V. C. Klema, and C. B. Moler (1976). *Matrix Eigensystem Routines*, EISPACK *Guide*, 2nd ed., Springer, New York.

Stewart, G. W. (1976). Algorithm 506 HQR3 and EXCHNG: Fortran Subroutines for Calculating and Ordering the Eigenvalues of a Real Upper Hessenberg Matrix [F2], *ACM Transactions on Mathematical Software*, Vol. 2, No. 3, pp. 275–280.

Tarjan, Robert (1972). Depth First Search and Linear Graph Algorithms, *SIAM Journal of Computing*, Vol. 1, pp. 146–160.

Wilkinson, J. H. (1965). *The Algebraic Eigenvalue Problem*, Oxford U. P., Oxford.

CHAPTER 3

Some Properties of the MQEM

The proprietors of the MQEM, Saul Hymans and Harold Shapiro, wrote a succinct overview of their model in the *International Economic Review* (1974). This article has recently been superseded by an article by Terrence Belton, Saul Hymans, and Carla Lown in a volume edited by Shapiro and Fulton (1985). We quote liberally from the early part of this article [referred to hereafter as BHL (1985)] and urge those interested in greater depth to read it in its entirety. More details about model characteristics will be presented in the context of particular analytical issues.

Section 3.1 is an overview of the model. Since price and wage dynamics are the principal concern, major price and wage relationships are discussed in most detail. Section 3.2 is about the initialization of linearization, and tests, including those developed by Arnold Zellner and Stephen Peck (1973), to characterize the model responses in terms of symmetry and nonlinearity. These tests are then applied to the MQEM. Section 3.3 is a preliminary view of cost-push inflation. Appendix 3A has tabulations comparing endogenous variables having raw-material cost-push effects with smoothed alternative paths, and Appendix 3B discusses price, wage, and productivity equations in more depth than the main body of the text.

We have deliberately omitted a literature review on wage, prices, and productivity, which is secondary to our principal purpose, the analysis of inflation behavior in a complete model context. This monograph is long enough as it is, and furthermore, the price–wage–productivity relations are in reasonably close accord with many of their counterparts elsewhere.

3.1 OVERVIEW OF THE MQEM

"MQEM is a medium-size nonlinear model designed primarily for short-term forecasting and policy analysis. There are 61 stochastic equations and 56 equations representing identities and constructions. The short-term nature of the model results from the basic structural characteristic that output is primarily expenditure-determined. The supply constraints in the model operate on productivity and prices, and through the effects of inflation, relative prices, the real money stock, and interest rates feed back on real expenditures. The model focuses on the determination of the principal variables in the National Income and Product Accounts, major monetary aggregates and interest rates, prices, and employment and productivity. The most important exogenous variables are nominal government expenditures (other than unemployment benefits and interest payments which are endogenous), exports and foreign prices, crude materials and agricultural prices, and the monetary base."[†] (BHL, 1985.)

Wages and Prices

"This group of 15 equations contains the two behavioral relationships which explain the basic wage rate and price level in the model, specifically, compensation per hour and the implicit output deflator, both for the private nonfarm sector. These two variables then serve as the principal variables in explaining the 12 implicit deflators which relate to various components of GNP as reflected in the National Income and Product Accounts.

"Compensation per Hour. The wage equation in the model, which explains the rate of change of money wage, is an expanded version of the Phillips–Lipsey mechanism. Wage changes respond to the employment of capital, both human and physical, through the inclusion of a weighted average of the employment rate (human capital) and capacity utilization (physical capital) with weights $\frac{2}{3}$ and $\frac{1}{3}$, respectively. Wage changes also respond to the recent (short-term) rate of price inflation in the consumption sector, a long-term inflation rate, and the change in the minimum wage rate. The elasticity of wage changes with respect to price changes is about 0.4 in the short run, and increases to about 0.85 in the long run.

"Output Deflator, Private Nonfarm GNP. The rate of inflation in the private nonfarm sector of the economy is determined primarily by the rate of increase of standard unit labor cost. The latter is measured by the rate of increase of hourly compensation (averaged over four quarters) less the trend rate of growth of productivity (which adjusts actual average productivity for short-term variations in GNP growth and capacity utilization). In addition, the rate of inflation depends on the level of capacity utilization and price 'shocks' deriving from the behavior of farm prices and crude materials prices, including oil."[†] (BHL, 1985.)

[†] From Howard T. Shapiro and George A. Fulton, (1985).

Exhibit 3.1 lists the model's current structure in outline form, classifying equations into six major groups. These provide some notion about aggregation levels and model structure. Exhibit 3.2 is a complete list of endogenous variables and their definitions. Behavioral equations are distinguished from definitional variables. We have added some logarithmic rate-of-change variables for wages, prices, and some other key variables to facilitate interpretation.

Exhibit 3.1   The MQEM: Main equation groups and principal endogenous variables.[a]

Block & Endogenous Variables	Units of Measurement	Contains Lagged Dependent Variable	Maximum Lag
A. Wages and Prices (Indexes)			
Compensation per hour	1977 = 100	Yes	3
Private nonfarm GNP deflator	1972 = 100	Yes	3
12 GNP component deflators	1972 = 100	8 of 12	6
B. Productivity and Employment			
Output per man-hour, private sector	1977 = 100	No	16
Employment rate, males 20 and over	percent	No	16
Aggregate unemployment rate	percent	No	1
C. Expenditures (Annual Rates)			
Consumption			
Auto Sales	10^6 units	Yes	4
Autos, new	10^9 1972 $	No	4
Autos, net used and parts	10^9 1972 $	Yes	16
Furniture and Household Equipment	10^9 1972 $	Yes	16
Other durables	10^9 1972 $	Yes	16
Nondurables	10^9 1972 $	Yes	16
Services	10^9 1972 $	No	16
Investment			
Business fixed structures	10^9 1972 $	Yes	5
Equipment			
Agriculture	10^9 1972 $	Yes	5
Production	10^9 1972 $	Yes	5

Exhibit 3.1 Continued.

Block & Endogenous Variables	Units of Measurement	Contains Lagged Dependent Variable	Maximum Lag
Other	10^9 1972 $	Yes	5
Residential construction	10^9 1972 $	Yes	5
Housing starts	10^3 units	Yes	3
Inventory	10^9 1972 $	Yes	16
Imports	10^9 1972 $	Yes	16
D. *Income Flows (Annual Rates)*			
Private Wages and Salaries	10^9 $	No	16
Profits	10^9 $	No	16
Dividends	10^9 $	Yes	16
Other labor income	10^9 $	Yes	16
Nonfarm proprietor income	10^9 $	No	16
Farm proprietor income	10^9 $	No	16
Govt. unemployment benefits	10^9 $	No	16
E. *Monetary Sector*			
M1BPLUS	10^9 $	Yes	2
M2BPLUS	10^9 $	Yes	16
90-day Treasury Bill rate	%/year	Yes	2
Budget identity	10^9 $	No	6
4 term structure equations	%/year	Yes	6
F. *Output Composition*			
Services component of Real GNP	10^9 1972 $	Yes	16
Manufacturing index of industrial production	1967 = 100	Yes	16
Index of available capacity in manufacturing	1967 = 100	Yes	2

[a]Source: BHL (1985).

Exhibit 3.2 Symbols and definitions of MQEM endogenous variables.[a]

MQEM[b] Equation No.	Symbol	Relation
A. Wages and Prices		
		Behavior Equations
A1	JCMH	Compensation per man-hour, business nonfarm sector, 1977 = 100

Exhibit 3.2 Continued

MQEM[b] Equation No.	Symbol	Relation
A4	PCDA	Deflator for consumption of autos and parts, 1972 = 100
A5	PCDFE	Deflator for consumption of furniture and household equipment, 1972 = 100
A3	PCDO	Deflator for consumption of other durables, 1972 = 100
A6	PCN	Deflator for nondurable consumption, 1972 = 100
A12	PCPI	Consumer Price Index (CPI), 1967 = 100
A7	PCS	Deflator for consumption of services, 1972 = 100
A11	PG	Deflator for total government purchases of goods and services, 1972 = 100
A9	PINC	Deflator for business fixed investment, nonresidential structures, 1972 = 100
A14	PIPDAG	Deflator for business fixed investment, producers' durables, agriculture, 1972 = 100
A15	PIPDO	Deflator for business fixed investment, producers' durables, other, 1972 = 100
A13	PIPDQ	Deflator for business fixed investment, producers' durables, production, 1972 = 100
A10	PIRC	Deflator for investment in residential construction, 1972 = 100
A2	PPNF	Deflator for business nonfarm GNP, 1972 = 100

Identities

	JCMHD	Index of real compensation per man-hour = $JCMH/(PC/100)$
	PC	Deflator for personal consumption, 1972 = 100
	PGNP	Implicit price deflator for GNP, 1972 = 100
	PIBF	Deflator for investment in nonresidential construction, 1972 = 100
	PIPD	Deflator for business fixed investment, producers' durables, 1972 = 100
	RPPERM	Permanent rate of inflation, eight period average, quarterly percent rate
	ULC77	Unit labor cost = $100 \times (JCMN/QMH77)$, 1977 = 100
	DLJCMH[c]	Logarithmic growth rate of JCMH
	DLJCMHD[c]	Logarithmic growth rate of JCMHD
	DLPC[c]	Logarithmic growth rate of PC
	DLPCDA[c]	Logarithmic growth rate of PCDA
	DLPCDFE[c]	Logarithmic growth rate of PCDFE
	DLPCDO[c]	Logarithmic growth rate of PCDO
	DLPCN[c]	Logarithmic growth rate of PCN
	DLPCPI[c]	Logarithmic growth rate of PCPI
	DLPCS[c]	Logarithmic growth rate of PCS
	DLPG[c]	Logarithmic growth rate of PG
	DLPGNP[c]	Logarithmic growth rate of PGNP
	DLPIBF[c]	Logarithmic growth rate of PIBF

Exhibit 3.2 Continued

MQEM[b]		
Equation No.	Symbol	Relation
	DLPINC[c]	Logarithmic growth rate of PINC
	DLPIPD[c]	Logarithmic growth rate of PIPD
	DLPIPDAG[c]	Logarithmic growth rate of PIPDAG
	DLPIPDO[c]	Logarithmic growth rate of PIPDO
	DLPIPDQ[c]	Logarithmic growth rate of PIPDQ
	DLPIRC[c]	Logarithmic growth rate of PIRC
	DLPPNF[c]	Logarithmic growth rate of PPNF
	DLULC77[c]	Logarithmic growth rate of ULC77

B. Productivity and Employment

Behavior Equations

B1	QMH77	Index of output per hour of all persons, used in YPWS and RUM equations, business nonfarm sector, 1977 = 100
B3	RUG	Global unemployment rate, percent
B2	RUM	Unemployment rate, males 20 and over, percent

Identities

	QHT1	Current productivity growth, used in JCMH equation quarterly rate
	QMHT	Trend growth rate of productivity, average of QHT1 over previous 8 quarters, annual rate (used in PPNF equation)
	REM	Employment rate, males 20 and over ≡ 100% − RUM
	DLQMH77[c]	Logarithmic growth rate of QMH77

C. Consumption and Investment

Behavior Equations

C1	AUTOS[d]	Units of new auto retail sales
C2	CDAN72[d]	Personal consumption expenditures on new autos, 1972 $
C3	CDAO72	Other auto consumption expenditures, 1972 $
C4	CDFE72	Consumption of furniture and household equipment, 1972 $
C5	CDO72	Consumption of other durables, 1972 $
C6	CN72	Consumption of nondurables, 1972 $
C7	CS72	Consumption of services, 1972 $
C7	HOUSES	Private housing starts, seasonally adjusted annual rates, thousands
C9	IBFNC72	Nonresidential investment, structures, 1972 $
C10	IINV72	Inventory investment, 1972 $
C15	IPDAG72	Real nonresidential investment, producers' durables, agriculture, 1972 $
C14	IPDO72	Real nonresidential investment producers' durables, other, 1972 $

89

Exhibit 3.2 Continued

MQEM[b] Equation No.	Symbol	Relation
C19	IPDQ72	Real nonresidential investment, producers' durables, production, 1972 $
C11	IRC72	Residential fixed investment, 1972 $
C13	M72	Imports, 1972 $
		Identities
	C	Personal consumption expenditures, current $
	C72	Personal consumption expenditures, 1972 $
	CDA72	Consumption of autos and parts, 1972 $, = CDAN72 + CDAO72
	FS	Final sales, current $
	FS72	Final sales, 1972 $
	FSMF72	Final sales of manufactured goods, 1972 $
	FSNMF72	Final sales of nonmanufactured goods, 1972 $
	GNP	Gross national product
	GNP72	Gross national product, 1972 $
	GNPERM72	Five-quarter moving weighted average of GNP72
	GNPAVEQ	Six-quarter moving average of GNP72
	IBF	Nonresidential fixed investment
	IBF72	Nonresidential fixed investment, 1972 $
	IBFNC	Nonresidential investment, structures
	IBFPD	Nonresidential investment, producers' durable equipment
	IBFPD72	Nonresidential investment, producers' durable equipment, 1972 $
	IINV	Inventory investment
	IRC	Residential fixed investment
	M	Imports
	Q	Present values of house payments, mortgage factor in IRC72 equation
	SINV72	Real business inventories = (4 × current stock)
	UCEAVEQ	Ratio of six-quarter moving average of UCKPDQ/JCMH
	UCKNC	User cost of capital, investment in nonresidential structures
	UCKPDQ	User cost of capital, producer durables, production

D. Income Flows[e]

		Behavior Equations
D16	GINTF	Net interest paid by government, federal
D12	TCF[d]	Corporate profits tax accruals, federal
D13	TCSL	Corporate profits tax accruals, state and local
D8	TIBF	Indirect business tax and nontax liability, federal
D9	TIBSL	Indirect business tax and nontax liability, state and local
D14	TPSL	Personal tax and nontax payment, state and local
D10	TSIF	Contributions for social insurance, federal

Exhibit 3.2 Continued

MQEM[b]

Equation No.	Symbol	Relation
D11	TSIP	Personal contributions for social insurance
D6	YCP + KCAC	Corporate profits with IVA and KCCA + KCAC
D4	YFP	Farm proprietors' income with inventory valuation and capital-consumption allowance adjustment
D3	YNFP	Nonfarm proprietors' income with inventory valuation and capital consumption allowance adjustment
D2	YOL	Other labor income
D7	YPDIV	Corporate dividend payments
D1	YPWS	Private wages and salaries
D5	YUNB	Government unemployment benefits paid

Identities

	GTRP	Government transfers (domestic)
	NIASF	Consolidated government surplus or deficit, federal
	NIASSL	Consolidated government surplus or deficit, state and local
	RHSAVE	Personal savings rate, percent
	STAT	Statistical discrepancy, national-income accounts
	TC	Corporate-profits tax accruals
	TIB	Indirect business tax and nontax liability
	TIP	Personal tax and nontax payments
	TSI	Total social-insurance contributions
	YCBT	Corporate profits before taxes
	YD	Disposable personal income
	YD72	Disposable personal income = $YD/(PC/100)$, 1972 \$
	YP	Personal income
	YPERM72	Permanent income, 1972 \$
	YT72	Transitory income, 1972 \$

E. Monetary Sector[f]

Behavior Equations

E3	FDCUR	Currency held by public plus unborrowed reserves
E6	GCBDD	Federal government deposits at nonfederal reserve banks
E9	GDEBTM	Market value of federal debt held by private investors
E5	GDEBTP	Gross public debt of U.S. Treasury held by private investors
E4	MRAM	Reserve-adjustment magnitude, applied to monetary base
E16	M1BPLUS	M1B plus savings accounts (measured as ratio of M2PLUS)
E1	M2PLUS	M2 plus short-term treasury securities (not held by money-market mutual funds)
E11	RAAA	Corporate AAA bond interest rate, long-term private sector rate
E15	RCD	90-day certificate of deposit rate, market yield

Exhibit 3.2 Continued

MQEM[b] Equation No.	Symbol	Relation
E12	RCP	4 to 6 month commercial paper rate (see RCPCD in identities below)
E10	RG5	5-year government bond rate
E2	RTB[d]	90-day treasury bill rate
		Identities
	DISC	Compound discount rate used in GDEBTM equation
	MULT	Multiplier of GINTF in GDEBTM equation
	RBASE	Growth rate of monetary base (annual rate)
	RCPCD	RCP from 1954 1 to 1962 4 and RCD from 1963 1 on
	RM2PLUS	Growth rate of M2PLUS $= 100 \times [\text{M2PLUS}/\text{M2PLUS}(-1)]^4 - 100$

F. Output Composition

		Behavior Equations
F3	JCAP	Index of available capacity in manufacturing
F2	JIPM	Federal Reserve index of industrial production in manufacturing, 1967 = 100
F1	SERVE72	Service component of GNP, 1972 $
		Identities
	JCU	Federal Reserve index of capacity utilization in manufacturing (1967 = 1.00) = JIPM/JCAP

[a] Symbols are listed alphabetically, so that MQEM equation numbers (column 1) are not in numerical order.

[b] Coefficient symbols within a given equation, which first appear in Chapter 5, follow the equation number, e.g., A1.1, A1.2, ... We have copied the exact designations of equation symbols as they appear in the MQEM version provided us. Incomplete numerical sequences arise, apart from inadvertent errors on our part, because some identities were given equation symbols but most were not. To minimize confusion, no identities have been given symbol designations; thus there are some gaps in equation numbers.

[c] These definitions were computed as $\Delta \log z_t = \ln z_t - \ln z_{t-1}$, where $\ln z_t - \ln z_{t-1} = \ln z_t(z_{t-1}) \cong (z_t - z_{t-1})/z_{t-1}$. Inclusion of these variables allows us to examine the model response in terms of growth rates of key endogenous variables.

[d] Autoregressive corrections have been explicitly incorporated.

[e] Unless otherwise noted, national-income-account flow variables are at annual rates, measured in billions (10^9) of current dollars, and seasonally adjusted.

[f] All interest rates are measured in percent per annum.

Source of Dynamics

The dynamic behavior of the MQEM stems from two sources: the specification of persistence effects and partial adjustment phenomena in individual equations, and how different equations are linked in the overall model. In Chapter 4 we examine the homogeneous dynamic structure of the complete model using the methods developed in Chapter 2. In this section we provide a brief discussion of the dynamic specification of individual equations and equation groups. For this purpose we shall decompose the model along the analytically convenient lines suggested in the BHL (1985) article. We thus consider in turn six main equation groups: wages and prices (14 stochastic equations and one identity), productivity and employment (3), expenditures (15), income flows (16), monetary sector (11), and output composition (3).

The wages-and-prices group, described above, derives much of its dynamic behavior from the presence of one-period-lagged dependent variables in eight of the twelve price-deflator equations. A pervasive wage–price interaction occurs through the appearance of the implicit output price deflator PPNF in most of the deflator equations, and indirectly through the presence of a lagged permanent inflation rate (an eight-period moving average of the consumer price inflation rate) in the compensation-per-man-hour equation, JCMH. The PPNF equation includes a lagged average unit-labor-cost variable.[†]

Important dynamic effects in the small productivity-and-employment group include the effect of capital accumulation on productivity (approximated by a six-period distributed lag on investment) and the effect of real GNP growth, lagged one and two periods, on the employment rate. Employment and productivity are linked directly through the appearance of productivity growth in the employment equation. Productivity affects prices through the unit-labor-cost variable in the PPNF equation.

Real expenditures for consumption, investment, and imports are derived from stock adjustment or distributed-lag relationships which lead naturally to the appearance of lagged dependent variables as explanatory variables. Important additional dynamics linking the real and monetary sectors of the model occur in the nonresidential-investment equations: the traditional monetary mechanism appears in the delayed (up to 10 quarters) effect of real interest rates on investment, and shorter-term credit-market conditions enter through short distributed lags on the interest differential between corporate bonds and 90-day certificates of deposit. Dynamic real-sector

---

[†]Appendix 3B contains all price, wage, and productivity equations including numerical coefficients and equation-specific variable definitions, with some further comments on equation structure.

influences on the components of aggregate demand include traditional acceleration terms (GNP growth) in some of the investment equations and permanent income terms (involving five-period moving averages of income flows) in some of the components of consumption.

The income-flows sector has the least articulated dynamic structure. "Accounted for in this block of the model are a variety of components of national and personal income, including private wages and salaries, corporate profits, proprietor incomes, and various tax flows."[†] (BHL, 1985). Personal disposable income, YP, is the key variable passed from this group to the rest of the model. YP enters the consumption equations in the expenditures group. In the income-flows group, YP is assembled straightforwardly from current values of economic activity variables and tax rates.

"Of primary importance in the MQEM monetary sector are a money supply equation and a set of money (or liquidity) demand equations which jointly determine the 90-day Treasury Bill rate. In addition, the sector includes a set of term structure equations and a government budget identity which links monetary and fiscal policy."[†] (BHL, 1985.) A key dynamic influence in the monetary sector stems from a partial adjustment mechanism in the overall liquidity demand equation (the demand for M2 plus short-term treasury securities) which introduces a lagged dependent variable. The demand for money (a modified version of MIB) as a fraction of total liquidity is then explained by the current Treasury Bill rate (RTB) and a two-quarter distributed lag on both RTB and the dependent variables. Short delays of monetary magnitudes and interest rates thus play an important role in determining the current interest rate, which then exerts an influence in the current and two subsequent periods on long-term interest rates in the term structure equations.

The final small block of three equations "explains sector outputs and output indexes used elsewhere in the model. These include the services component of GNP, the manufacturing index of industrial production and the index of available capacity in manufacturing."[†] (BHL, 1985.) Each of the equations in this block contains a lagged dependent variable. The index of capacity utilization that emerges from this block has an important influence on short-term dynamics in the productivity, compensation per hour, and output price-deflator equations.

Multipliers

Responses of the MQEM to fiscal and monetary stimuli are in Exhibits 3.3 and 3.4, respectively. Starting with an impact multiplier of 0.90 on real

[†] From Howard T. Shapiro and George A. Fulton, (1985).

GNP (first column of Exhibit 3.3) from a sustained increase in nondefense government purchases of $10 billion *current* dollars, the GNP multiplier reaches a peak of 1.44 in the fifth period. It then slowly tails off to 0.58 in period 40. Belton et al. attribute the declining multiplier to the price and interest rate increases induced by the fiscal stimulus (BHL, 1985.). Investment gets crowded out in the long pull, while consumption does not.

Exhibit 3.3 Fiscal policy multipliers from a permanent $10-billion increase in nondefense government purchases.[a]

Quarter	Deviations from Control Government Purchases ΔG72 $(10^9$ 1972 $)$	Deviations from Control Normalized by ΔGFO					
		GNP72	GNP	C72	IBF72	PGNP	RTB
1	11.68	0.90	0.89	.06	0	0	.004
2	11.47	1.19	1.18	.15	.06	0	.01
3	11.35	1.34	1.34	.23	.14	.00	.01
4	11.14	1.42	1.38	.27	.20	.001	.01
5	10.88	1.44	1.51	.30	.22	.004	.01
6	10.68	1.43	1.57	.34	.23	.01	.01
7	10.59	1.41	1.63	.36	.23	.02	.01
8	10.44	1.39	1.71	.38	.23	.03	.01
9	10.19	1.35	1.80	.40	.22	.04	.01
10	10.07	1.31	1.88	.42	.21	.05	.01
11	9.98	1.29	1.99	.44	.20	.06	.01
12	9.76	1.28	2.14	.47	.19	.08	.01
⋮	⋮	⋮	⋮	⋮	⋮	⋮	⋮
16	9.11	1.18	2.80	.53	.17	.14	.01
20	8.22	0.93	3.62	.53	.12	.24	.01
24	7.62	0.78	4.86	.59	.06	.35	.01
28	7.18	0.84	6.06	.68	.06	.42	.01
32	6.72	0.86	7.42	.79	.07	.50	.01
36	6.21	0.77	8.78	.87	.05	.59	.02
40	5.75	0.58	9.91	.87	.002	.69	.03

[a]Source: Belton et al. (1985).

Their monetary results are harder to evaluate (see Exhibit 3.4), since the responses are not normalized, although their "basic monetary" policy of increasing the monetary base 10% above its historical level leads to a much larger proportion of investment in the increment in GNP after 40 periods than the fiscal policy simulation. This result accords with many current beliefs and standard economic theory.

3.2 INITIALIZATION

Rationale

The selection of linearization procedures depends on the purposes served by the linearized model. Our primary aim is to establish which model elements are mostly responsible for the inflationary process, especially during the 1970's.

Since we want to see what happens when powerful transients impinge on "normal" economic behavior, we might try to generate steady-state growth

Exhibit 3.4   Effect of a permanent 10% increase in the monetary base.[a]

Quarter	Change in							
	MBASE	GNP72	GNP	C72	IBF72	M1BPLUS	PGNP	RTB
1	7.05	0	0	0	0	1.66	0	−.23
2	7.18	0.24	0.23	0.15	0	3.18	0	−.43
3	7.33	0.92	0.90	0.47	0.05	4.41	0	−.50
4	7.45	2.01	1.93	0.88	0.19	5.33	0	−.48
5	7.62	3.23	3.24	1.26	0.44	5.86	0.001	−.38
6	7.77	4.29	4.37	1.52	0.78	6.30	0.003	−.37
7	7.93	5.09	5.28	1.74	1.11	6.97	0.007	−.41
8	8.00	5.68	5.94	1.96	1.37	7.59	0.016	−.39
9	8.18	6.03	6.58	2.19	1.57	7.98	0.030	−.34
10	8.33	6.23	7.05	2.39	1.71	8.29	0.050	−.35
11	8.46	6.29	7.46	2.55	1.79	8.68	0.076	−.36
12	8.66	6.25	7.81	2.70	1.84	9.10	0.110	−.35
16	9.35	6.28	10.29	3.34	1.87	12.43	0.304	−.60
20	10.20	7.35	15.01	3.88	2.39	15.18	0.602	−.56
24	10.92	6.88	19.26	4.15	2.74	17.07	0.954	−.41
28	11.72	5.17	22.11	3.93	2.39	18.98	1.222	−.35
32	12.73	3.70	24.43	3.56	1.96	21.01	1.403	−.41
36	13.91	3.95	27.89	3.65	1.89	25.42	1.469	−.65
40	15.06	6.30	33.17	4.34	2.56	30.91	1.418	−.76

[a]Source: Belton et al. (1985).

behavior as the norm from which departures caused by economic shocks can most effectively be observed. In its strong form this means that all exogenous inputs should grow at the same geometric rate for a long enough time to eliminate most transient behavior, and that the model structure should exhibit constant returns to scale. Most empirical macromodels, including the MQEM, are not constrained to have constant returns to scale, which impedes the rigorous merger of growth models with macromodels.[†‡] Furthermore, growth rates among exogenous variables in the pre-oil-embargo period differ greatly. We have instead settled for less than the necessary conditions for neoclassical growth models by requiring "smooth, typical" growth of exogenous inputs. The anticipated smooth behavior of endogenous outputs thus becomes the basic criterion for behavior to be deemed suitable at the time of initialization. This approach preserves numerous aspects of historical behavior as well as the likelihood that many of the model's endogenous variable paths will closely resemble steady growth; therefore, actual historical transient behavior will not distort linearization and characteristic roots and vectors calculated from the linearized model.

Actual Process

The 96 exogenous variables include 56 "regular" variables and 40 dummy variables. As explained soon, these have been separated into three sorts of typical preinitialization behavior. Subjective judgments about initialization were reached by scanning time plots for each exogenous variable.

More concretely, our procedure will be to construct smooth exogenous variables for the preinitialization simulation period 1969 1 to 1973 2 that are based upon stylized, typical behavior of these variables over the period 1957 2 to the linearization data 1973 2. These in turn are expected to generate simulated exogenous variables that attain smooth growth paths by the linearization period, 1973 2. Since the longest lag (for one variable only) in the MQEM is 16 quarters, initial-condition effects should be small by 1973 2 and most endogenous variables should display smooth behavior or highly damped oscillations.[§]

Exogenous variables have been separated into categories as follows: Type 1 exogenous variable behavior is well represented by constant geometric

---

[†] The work of Deleau et al. (1984) mentioned in Chapter 2 is, however, a step in that direction.
[‡] Another approach to arrive at "standard behavior" is to linearize the model at a sequence of time periods and average the sequence of linearized coefficients. This has been proposed by B. Friedman (1975) and should also reduce undesirable effects of historical fluctuations in data on the calculated linearized coefficients. His approach is especially suitable for his research into optimal control of cyclical macromodels.
[§] This latter effect will be nullified if the model is dynamically unstable, or weakened if its homogeneous dynamics cause significant oscillations.

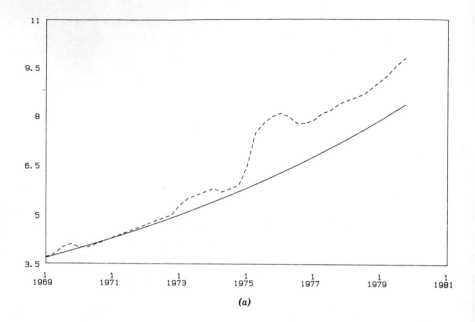

(a)

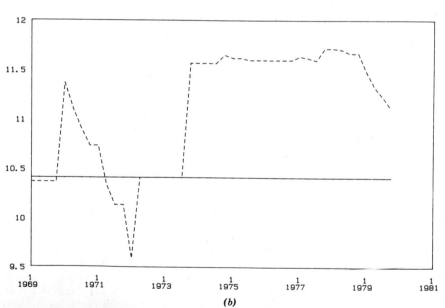

(b)

Exhibit 3.5 Examples of the three types of smoothed exogenous variable. Historical: dashed lines; smoothed: solid lines. (a) BTRP; (b) GOLD; (c) DASTRIKE.

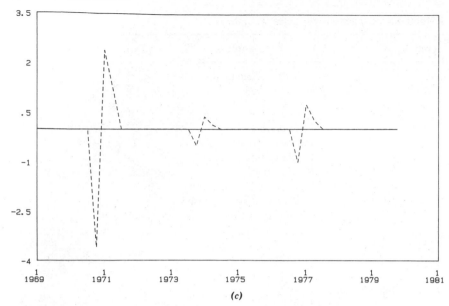

(c)

Exhibit 3.5 Historical: dashed lines; smoothed: solid lines. (a) BTRP; (b) GOLD; (c) DASTRIKE.

growth rate for the period 1957 2 to 1967 2 (the trend growth between two cyclical peaks). Type 2 exogenous variables had irregular behavior that could not be sensibly represented by simple geometric growth. To arrive at smooth behavior during the initialization period a constant typical level during the interval 1969 1 to 1973 2 was selected for this category. Type 3 exogenous variables were either dummy variables or acted very much like them, that is, they were constant most of the time, with only occasional departures. The predominant typical value during the interval 1969 1 to 1973 2 (usually zero) was chosen in these instances. Examples of each of the three types are graphically illustrated in Exhibit 3.5. Most variables were readily fitted into one category, and their nature is tabulated in Exhibit 3.6.

If smooth exogenous variables constructed in this way were close to their historical values in 1973 2, no further adjustments were made. If, however, their 1973 2 smooth values were far from their 1973 2 actual values, the smooth values were recalculated (e.g., new growth rates or different constant levels were chosen) so that they were close enough to satisfy us. With all exogenous variables thus calibrated, a full model simulation was made starting in 1969 1 with actual initial conditions for all lagged variables in that period plus smooth exogenous variables thereafter. The simulation spanned the period 1969 1 to 1973 2 for linearized purposes. The simulation output for 1973 2 was then used to evaluate the linearized coefficients.

Exhibit 3.6 Exogenous variables: Initialization.[a]

Symbol	Definition	Type	Initialization
	Part I. Regular Variables		
A. Monetary			
GOLD	Gold stock	2	CONST = 10.41
MBASE	Inclusive monetary base	1	$g = 1.00985$
RDIS	Discount rate, Federal Reserve Bank of N.Y.	2	CONST = 5.0
RRDEM	Reserve requirements on demand deposits, based on banks with deposits over $400 million	2	CONST = 17.5
SDR	Allowance for special drawing rights	2	CONST = 0.4
B. Government Outlays			
EGOV	Government employment	1	$g = 1.00648$
GAID	Grants-in-aid	1	$g = 1.035$
GDIVSL	Dividends received by government, state and local	2	CONST = 0.30
GFD	Government purchases: defense, federal	1	$g = 1.0085$
GFO	Government purchases: nondefense, federal	1	$g = 1.0256$
GINTSL	Net interest paid by government, state and local	1	$g = 1.04501$
GSL	Government purchases, state and local	1	$g = 1.0235$
GTRF	Government transfers to foreigners	1	$g = 1.006$
GTROF	Government transfers minus YUNB, federal	1	$g = 1.0275$
GTRSL	Government transfers, state and local	1	$g = 1.022$
GWALDF	Government wage accruals less disbursements, federal	3	CONST = 0
GWALDSL	Government wage accruals less disbursements, state and local	3	CONST = 0

Exhibit 3.6   Continued

Symbol	Definition	Type	Initialization
YGWS	Government wage and salary disbursements	1	$g = 1.02$
C. Taxes or Revenues			
SLCSF	Subsidies less current surplus of government enterprises, federal	1	$g = 1.0129$
SLCSSL	Subsidies less current surplus of government enterprises, state and local	1	$g = 1.01425$
TCFR	Statutory corporate tax rate, federal	2	CONST $= 0.48$
TCO	Treasury currency outstanding	1	$g = 1.0058$
TDEPRAG	Depreciation rate for tax purposes, agricultural equipment	2	CONST $= 0.36364$
TDEPRNC	Depreciation rate for tax purposes, nonresidential construction	2	CONST $= 0.066$
TDEPRO	Depreciation rate for tax purposes, other equipment	2	CONST $= 0.211$
TDEPRQ	Depreciation rate for tax purposes, production equipment	2	CONST $= 0.211$
TITCR	Investment tax credit	2	CONST $= 0.07$
TPNS	Dummy for nonwithheld surcharge	3	CONST $= 0$
TSIFR	Total Social Security tax rate	2	CONST $= 0.096$
TSISL	Total contributions for social insurance, state and local	1	$g = 1.02346$
WCEIL	Wage ceiling for Social Security tax rate	2	CONST $= 7.8$
D. Prices			
PAUTO	CPI for new autos, 1967 $= 100$	1	$g = 1.002$
PCRUDE	WPI for crude matls less raw food and feed stocks, 1967 $= 100$	2	CONST $= 100$

Exhibit 3.6   Continued

Symbol	Definition	Type	Initialization
PFP	Gross domestic farm-product deflator, 1972 = 100	1	$g = 1.00562$
PGAS	CPI for gasoline and motor oil, 1967 = 100	1	$g = 1.00285$
PIINV	Deflator for inventory investment, 1972 = 100	1	$g = 1.0031$
PM	Deflator for imports, 1072 = 100	1	$g = 1.0028$
PX	Deflator for exports, 1972 = 100	1	$g = 1.0035$
WUSMIN	U.S. minimum wage	1	$g = 1.0084$

E. Income and Income Adjustments, Transfers

Symbol	Definition	Type	Initialization
BTRP	Business transfer payments	1	$g = 1.01927$
HINT	Interest paid by consumers to business	1	$g = 1.02079$
HTRF	Personal transfers to foreigners	2	CONST = $1.0 billion
IVA	Corporate inventory valuation adjustment	2	CONST = 3.0
KCA	Capital consumption allowances and adjustments	1	$g = 1.01437$
KCAC	Corporate capital-consumption allowances with capital-consumption adjustment	1	$g = 1.0135$
KCCA	Corporate capital-consumption allowance	2	CONST = 0
NINT	Net interest	1	$g = 1.03332$
WALD	Wage accruals less disbursements	2	CONST = 0
YPINT	Personal interest income	1	$g = 1.02473$
YPRENT	Rental income of persons with capital-consumption adjustment	1	$g = 1.00786$

F. Other

Symbol	Definition	Type	Initialization
AUTOSIZE	Ratio of number of small-auto sales to total number of auto sales	2	CONST = 0.47
JGPM	Index of gallons per mile for new cars, 1965 = 100	2	CONST = 1.20

102

Exhibit 3.6 Continued

Symbol	Definition	Type	Initialization
JICS	Index of consumer sentiment, 1965 = 100	2	CONST = 90
X72	Exports, 1972 $	1	$g = 1.0095$
DATE	Quarterly calender date		LINEAR TREND
TIME	Time, = 1.0 in 1954 1, increasing by 1 per quarter		LINEAR TREND

Part II. Dummy Variables

Symbol	Definition	Type	Initialization
DAPACTM	Dummy for Canadian auto pact	2	CONST = 4.0
DASTRIKE	Dummy to reflect impact of auto strikes	3	CONST = 0
DAUTO	Dummy for AUTOS equation to reflect 1975 auto rebates and reaction to higher auto prices in 1974	3	CONST = 1.0
DEX65	Dummy for change in federal excise-tax law	2	CONST = 0
DFPR	Dummy for RUG equation to reflect shift in relation of RUM and RUG	2	CONST = 22.6
DFROFF	Dummy for removal of price control	3	CONST = 0
DFRZ1	Dummy for phase 1 of wage–price freeze	3	CONST = 0
DFRZ2	Dummy for phase 2 of wage–price freeze	3	CONST = 0
DFRZ3	Dummy for phase 3 of wage–price freeze	3	CONST = 0
DGPAY	Dummy for government pay raises	3	CONST = 0
DJGPM	Dummy for increased awareness of gasoline costs	2	CONST = 0
DM72DOCK	Dummy for impact of dock strikes on imports	3	CONST = 0
DM72SS	Dummy for impact of steel strikes on imports	3	CONST = 0
DPGAS	Dummy for PGAS series before it existed, in PCN equation	2	CONST = 0
DPROP13	Dummy in TIBSL equation for effect of Proposition 13	3	CONST = 0
DRAM	Dummy for the impact of change in structure of		

103

Exhibit 3.6 Continued

Symbol	Definition	Type	Initialization
	reserve requirements on reserve-adjustment magnitude (MRAM)	3	CONST = 0
DSEAS1	Seasonal dummy, = 1 in 1st quarter, −1 in 4th	3	CONST = 0
DSEAS2	Seasonal dummy, = 1 in 2nd quarter, −1 in 4th	3	CONST = 0
DSEAS3	Seasonal dummy, = 1 in 3rd quarter, −1 in 4th	3	CONST = 0
DSPRD	Dummy for RTB−RCP spread	3	CONST = 0
DTCF	Dummy for the effect of federal corporate-tax-law changes	3	CONST = 0
DTEX	Dummy for changes in excise taxes	3	CONST = 0
DTIB	Dummy for changes in indirect business taxes	3	CONST = 0
DTP	Dummy for personal-tax equation	3	CONST = 0
DTPR	Dummy for personal-tax rate	3	CONST = 0
DTSI	Dummy for revenue effect of a change in Social Security tax law	3	CONST = 0
DUBEXT	Dummy for the extension of unemployment benefits > 26 weeks	3	CONST = 0
DUM74	Dummy in IPDO72 equation	3	CONST = 0
DUM75	Dummy in GDEBTP equation	3	CONST = 0
DVNDOWN	Dummy for the impact of Vietnam War winddown on employment	2	CONST = 0
DVNUP	Dummy for the impact of Vietnam War windup on employment	2	CONST = 0
D5467	Dummy for change in trend of productivity	3	CONST = 0
D6873	Dummy for change in trend of growth of productivity	3	CONST = 1
D79	Dummy for change in trend of growth of productivity	3	CONST = 0
D5864	Dummy in JCAP equation	3	CONST = 0

Exhibit 3.6 Continued

Symbol	Definition	Type	Initialization
D66	Dummy in MIBPLUS equation	3	CONST = 1
D674	Dummy for state personal-income-tax law changes	3	CONST = 1
D7074	Dummy in JCAP equation	3	CONST = 1
D711	Dummy for state personal-income-tax law changes	3	CONST = 1
D763	Dummy in IRC72 equation	3	CONST = 0

[a]With rare exceptions, we have retained the categories and definitions that appear in BHL (1985).

Exhibits 3.7–3.11 show that most macroeconomic national account output series, together with wages and prices, had smooth paths and were close to their 1973 2 historical values, which is what we wanted to accomplish. In these exhibits an endogenous variable is generated in two ways: with smoothed input dynamics, and with its actual historical MQEM simulation values. Some (GNP72, C72, IBFPD72, IBFNC72) settle immediately into smooth

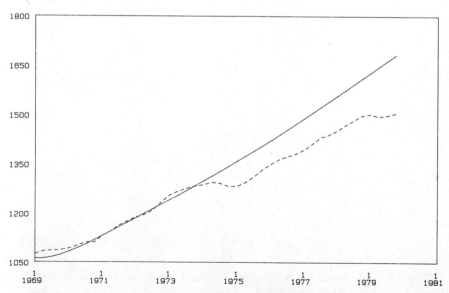

Exhibit 3.7 GNP72: Actual (dashed line) and generated by smooth inputs (solid line), 1969 1 to 1979 4.

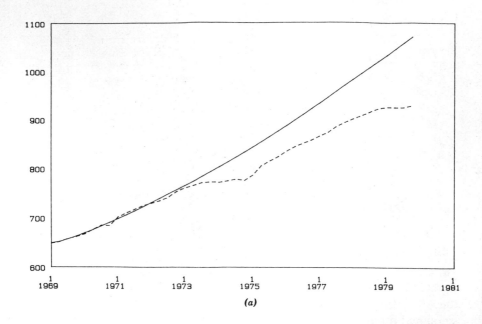

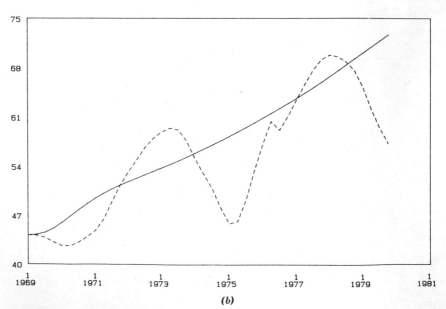

Exhibit 3.8 (*a*) C72 and (*b*) IRC72: Actual (dashed lines) and generated by smooth inputs (solid lines), 1969 1 to 1979 4.

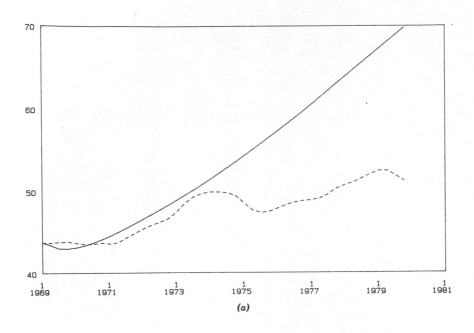

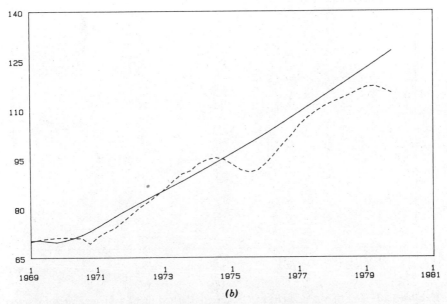

Exhibit 3.9 (*a*) IBFNC72 and (*b*) IBFPD72: Actual (dashed lines) and generated by smooth inputs (solid lines), 1969 1 to 1979 4.

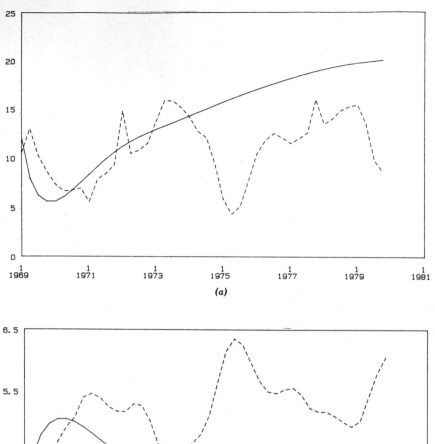

Exhibit 3.10 (*a*) IINV72 and (*b*) RUG: Actual (dashed lines) and generated by smooth inputs (solid lines), 1969 1 to 1979 4.

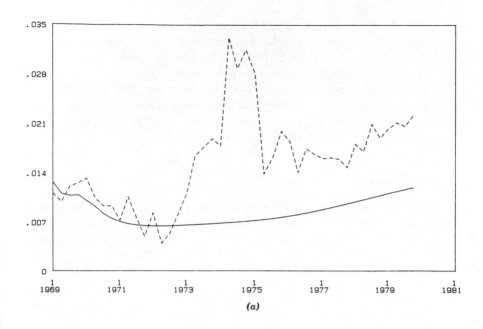

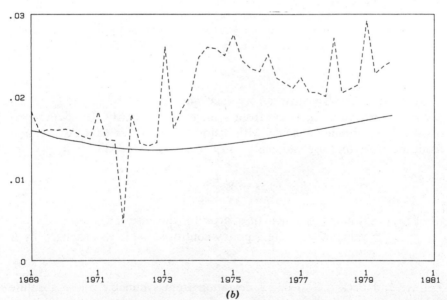

Exhibit 3.11 (*a*) $\Delta \ln$ PPNF and (*b*) $\Delta \ln$ JCMH: Actual (dashed lines) and generated by smooth inputs (solid lines), 1969 1 to 1979 4.

109

growth and stay that way, while others (IINV72, IRC72) have highly damped oscillations. In its smooth version, RUG approaches an asymptote far below its historical counterpart. In Exhibit 3.11, $\Delta \ln$ PPNF and $\Delta \ln$ JCMH have smooth, shallow U-shaped responses. These paths, further discussed below, satisfy our intent to obtain smooth outputs that are near 1973 2 output levels, but are not consistent with the attainment of steady-state behavior; the latter is not essential for our main purpose, which is to obtain sensible smooth behavior at the time the model is linearized.

Tests of Linearity and Symmetry

In an article describing techniques to exercise "a model strenuously in simulation experiments in order to discover possible model defects" (p. 167), Arnold Zellner and Stephen Peck (1973) devised measures of relative symmetry and linearity of models

to determine the extent to which induced changes in the model's endogenous variables are symmetric and/or linear. Symmetry is of interest for its own sake while a finding of linearity or near-linearity may be useful in efforts to simplify the model's structure. Also, since the effects of both relatively small and large changes are reported, we gain information on both the local and global properties of the model. We believe that it is very important to understand local and global properties of a model before it is used for serious policy analysis (Zellner and Peck, 1973, p. 152).

These measures calculate an average quantity of the extent to which perturbations cause departures from symmetry or linearity. The *base run* is obtained by running the model with historically observed data. A deviation from the base run for a variable y in quarter t is defined by

$$\delta y_{t,\Delta} = y_{t,\Delta} - y_{t,b}, \qquad (3.2.1)$$

where $y_{t,b}$ = value of y in the tth quarter for the base run.
$\quad\quad y_{t,\Delta}$ = value of y_t where a policy control variable was changed by Δ units.

Zellner and Peck then define a deviation from symmetry whose absolute value is

$$\gamma_t = |\delta y_{t,\Delta} + \delta y_{t,-\Delta}|. \qquad (3.2.2)$$

The mean absolute deviation from symmetry is then the arithmetic average of the γ_t's:

$$\bar{\gamma} = \frac{1}{T} \sum_{t=1}^{T} \gamma_t, \tag{3.2.3}$$

where T is the number of periods in the run. This measure of relative symmetry is scaled by absolute deviations from the base run. One element of this scale is

$$\phi_t = \frac{|\delta y_{t,\Delta}| + |\delta y_{t,-\Delta}|}{2}. \tag{3.2.4}$$

ϕ_t is then averaged to produce an overall scale measure called DIST:

$$DIST = \frac{1}{T} \sum_{t=1}^{T} \phi_t. \tag{3.2.5}$$

As the end result of their symmetry measure, they compute the relative measure of SYM:

$$SYM = \frac{\bar{\gamma}}{DIST}. \tag{3.2.6}$$

A value of SYM near zero indicates high symmetry in the response of the model to changes in the policy control variable, and a larger value indicates less symmetry.

The measure of linearity is defined similarly. Using the same definitions of deviations from the base run as in SYM [equation (3.2.1)], we get an absolute measure of linearity from the difference between scaled responses with different perturbations:

$$\eta_t = \delta y_{t,10\Delta} - 10\,\delta y_{t,\Delta}, \tag{3.2.7}$$

$$\bar{\eta} = \frac{1}{T} \sum_{t=1}^{T} |\eta_t|. \tag{3.2.8}$$

To illustrate the concept in equation (3.2.7), deviations are compared for perturbations that differ by a factor of 10, with the original deviation Δ multiplied by a factor of 10. Note that if the system were perfectly linear, $\eta_t = 0$ for all t.

To calculate a new relative measure of linearity, we first define a new DIST function:

$$\text{DIST}_l = \frac{1}{2} \sum_{t=1}^{T} \frac{|\delta y_{t,10\Delta}| + 10\delta y_{t,\Delta}|}{T}, \qquad (3.2.9)$$

which leads to the relative measure

$$\text{LIN} = \frac{\bar{\eta}}{\text{DIST}_l}. \qquad (3.2.10)$$

Again, if the response to the perturbations were perfectly linear, LIN = 0, since every element in DIST$_1$ will be zero.

In our tests of the MQEM the values of perturbations for SYM were $\pm .01$ and $\pm .10$, and for LIN were ± 10. These measures were calculated over 10- and 40-quarter intervals, and are compiled for variables of interest in Exhibit 3.12.

The response of the MQEM to perturbations in the exogenous policy variables MBASE (inclusive monetary base, billions of current dollars, season-

Exhibit 3.12 Zellner–Peck symmetry and linearity measures.[a]

					Step Perturbations of GFO					
		GNP72		PPNF		RAAA		RTB		RUG	
	Δ	10Q	40Q	10Q	40Q	10Q	40Q	10Q	40Q	10Q	40Q
SYM	$\pm.01$	.0053	.0138	.0506	.0598	.0112	.0192	.0137	.0281	.0271	.0596
	$\pm.10$	.0026	.0156	.0155	.0272	.0028	.0051	.0039	.0094	.0095	.0308
LIN	$+10$	.0037	.0221	.0239	.0165	.0050	.0067	.0075	.0220	.0174	.0497
	-10	.0025	.0067	.0132	.0161	.0044	.0123	.0054	.0134	.0114	.0277

					Step Perturbations of MBASE					
		GNP72		PPNF		RAAA		RTB		RUG	
	Δ	10Q	40Q	10Q	40Q	10Q	40Q	10Q	40Q	10Q	40Q
SYM	$\pm.01$	.0173	.0118	.1193	.0179	.0174	.0142	.0170	.0116	.0134	.0189
	$\pm.10$	.1729	.1410	.1761	.0662	.1749	.1329	.1730	.1187	.1851	.1663
LIN	$+10$	.0757	.0694	.1515	.0529	.0748	.0568	.0743	.0521	.0990	.0866
	-10	.0803	.0651	.1115	.0324	.0831	.0621	.0821	.0552	.0756	.0681

[a]LIN and SYM are defined in the text. 10Q and 40Q refer to periods (quarters) after original perturbation.

ally adjusted), and GFO (federal nondefense purchases of goods and services, billions of current dollars) was both highly symmetric and highly linear, in fact much more symmetric and linear than the responses of the Federal Reserve–MIT–Penn (FMP) model that was studied by Zellner and Peck.

The most nonlinear and nonsymmetric responses occur in the variable PPNF (private nonfarm implicit price deflator), although here also the comparable Zellner–Peck calculations indicated less linearity and symmetry for the FMP model than for the MQEM.

Parameter Sensitivity to Different Linearizations

In addition to the Zellner–Peck tests, we have also linearized the MQEM at three dates after 1973 2: 1975 2, 1977 2, and 1979 2. Several computations were made in parallel for each date. These include impact elasticities for the homogeneous responses that will be described in Chapter 4, and multiplier and parameter perturbations, which are the subject matter of Chapter 5. The outcome is in broad conformity with the Zellner–Peck tests, namely, that the MQEM does not appear to have strong nonlinearities.

The homogeneous responses at the three later dates were extremely similar. Exhibit 3.13 shows own-impact elasticity responses for several major variables. These reflect substantial stability for the various linearizations.

Impact-multiplier elasticities in Exhibit 3.14 for several endogenous responses to two exogenous variables, GFO (nonmilitary federal government expenditures) and MBASE (inclusive monetary base), also display compatibility at each of the four linearization dates.[†] Finally, in Exhibit 3.15, we note that impact-elasticity coefficient perturbations are most sensitive to alternative linearizations. Many coefficients are quite stable, while some are not.

Exhibit 3.13 Selected own-impact homogeneous elasticity responses at different linearization dates.

	1973 2	1975 2	1977 2	1979 2
JCMH	1.027	1.029	1.032	1.035
PPNF	1.013	1.015	1.018	1.023
QMH77	1.014	1.012	1.012	1.012
RAAA	0.911	0.911	0.912	0.913
RTB	0.746	0.747	0.747	0.747
RUG	0.469	0.468	0.471	0.477

[†]A noticeable response change among the various linearization dates is observed for productivity growth (DLQMH77) to the exogenous variable GFO.

Exhibit 3.14 Selected impact-multiplier elasticity responses at different linearization dates.

	GFO				MBASE				PFP			
	1973 2	1975 2	1977 2	1979 2	1973 2	1975 2	1977 2	1979 2	1973 2	1975 2	1977 2	1979 2
DLPPNF	0	0	0	0	0	0	0	0	0	0	0	0
DLJCMH	0	0	0	0	0	0	0	0	0	0	0	0
DLQMH77	2.83	2.64	2.38	1.90	0	0	0	0	−0.87	−0.88	−0.86	−0.76
GNP72	0.03	0.03	0.02	0.02	0	0	0	0	0	0	0	0
RTB	0.02	0.02	0.02	0.02	−0.94	−0.88	−0.83	−0.78	0	0	0	0
RUG	−0.18	−0.17	−0.16	−0.14	0	0	0	0	0.05	0.05	0.05	0.05

Exhibit 3.15 Elasticity responses to own-parameter perturbations at different linearization dates.

LHS	Coterm[a]	Coeff.	1973 2	1975 2	1977 2	1979 2
DLJCMH	Intercept	A1.0	.784	.732	.670	.610
	$(\ln PC(-1) - \ln PC(-3))$	A1.2	.194	.191	.198	.214
	Factor utilization rate	A1.3	-.241	-.173	-.118	—
	RPPERM	A1.6	.243	.226	.226	.241
DLPPNF	Intercept	A2.0	-.678	-.606	-.489	-.391
	JIPM/JCAP = weighted av.	A2.5	.823	.925	.962	.981
	Rate of change (JCMH − QMH77)	A2.6	.825	.642	.483	.374
DLQMH77	Intercept	B1.0	-14.588	-16.041	-17.044	-16.196
	Dummy	B1.2	0.997	1.096	1.165	1.107
	log JCU	B1.5	1.780	1.512	1.266	0.961
	$(\ln GNP72 - \ln GNP72(-1))$	B1.6	1.204	1.364	1.425	1.282
	Nonagri. investment: weighted average	B1.7	11.584	13.044	14.193	13.794

Exhibit 3.15 Continued.

LHS	Coterm[a]	Coeff.	1973 2	1975 2	1977 2	1979 2
RAAA	Intercept	E11.0	−.466	−.459	−.488	−.434
	RTB	E11.1	.202	.202	.202	.200
	RTB(−1)	E11.2	−.194	−.194	−.193	−.192
	PPNF/PPNF(−2)	E11.7	.489	.482	.472	.460
	RAAA(−1)	E11.8	.902	.901	.899	.898
RTB	Intercept	E2.0	−.848	−.847	−.845	−.844
	log RDIS	E2.4	1.648	1.645	1.642	1.639
	log RDIS(−1)	E2.5	−.914	−.912	−.910	−.909
	log MBASE	E2.6	−1.764	−1.792	−1.820	−1.849
	log M1BPLUS	E2.7	2.497	2.530	2.564	2.602
	log RTB(−1)	E2.8	.477	.481	.486	.492
RUG	Intercept	B3.0	—	.109	.124	.131
	Time	B3.1	.179	.229	.286	.327
	RUM	B3.3	.285	.236	.182	.147

[a]"Coterm" designates combinations of variables (e.g., a ratio) associated with a coefficient. The more straightforward word "variable" suffices when such combinations are absent.

None change sign, and all remain the same order of magnitude. Since our approach is to look at the broad picture and avoid fine distinctions (at best, models are coarse approximations to reality), we are inclined to believe that conclusions arrived at subsequently are not impaired by these observed consequences of nonlinearities. Where linearization made a difference, which was not often, it is noted in context later on.

3.3   PRICE SHOCKS: A PREVIEW OF INFLATION IN THE MQEM

As a prelude to an intensive investigation of the MQEM's inflationary implications, we next look at food- and petroleum-supply shock effects on the MQEM. To do this most cleanly, all exogenous variables were set at their smoothed values (constant, or geometric growth rates) beginning in 1969 1 and continuing until 1972 1. Thereafter, only the two critical exogenous price variables PFP (farm price index) and PCRUDE (price index of crude oil) are reset to their historical values, and the simulation resumes. Exhibit 3.16 shows the smoothed and historical series for $\Delta \ln$ PFP and $\Delta \ln$ PCRUDE.

Exhibits 3.17 through 3.22 summarize the response of the MQEM to our stylized shocks in the key prices PFP and PCRUDE.[†] Since the graphs contain a good deal of information, our written remarks will be brief.

As expected, the effects on inflation are strong. $\Delta \ln$ PPNF, the basic endogenous price's rate of change (Exhibit 3.17), reacts swiftly to the combined food–petroleum price accelerations early in the period: this inflation measure approximately doubles and does so immediately; then it returns to or falls below the smoothed-path inflation rate in 1975. The money-wage rate of change $\Delta \ln$ JCMH (Exhibit 3.18) initially follows a similar path, although with a delay, but then drops well below the smooth path in 1976 1 and remains there subsequently. The real wage falls (Exhibit 3.18) as prices respond more rapidly than wages for 2 years. Then the real-wage rate of change stabilizes around the smooth path until 1978, when it falls below it once more, since wage-rate increases did not keep up with the renewed inflation. Note that the smoothed real-wage rate of growth stabilizes at 0.7% per quarter or about 2.8% annually.

The explanation for this result, we believe, arises from definite interactions between price–wage behavior and the real sector as conditioned by the general stance of monetary policy. Exhibit 3.19 shows GNP72 and IINV72, while Exhibit 3.20 shows the unemployment rate (RUG) and capacity utili-

---

[†] Tabulated value for 53 endogenous variables, both price-shocked and smooth, appear in Appendix 3A of this chapter. The selected list covers all price and wage variables and a broadly representative list of other MQEM variables.

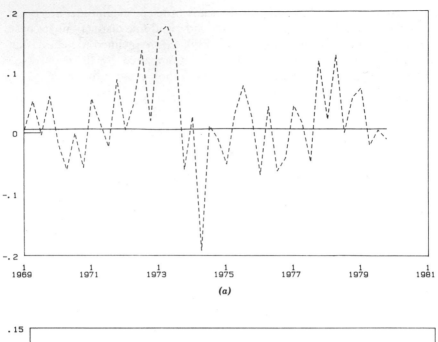

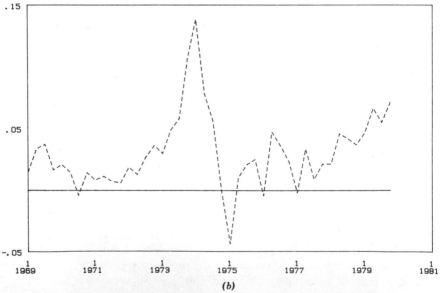

Exhibit 3.16 (*a*) Δ ln PFP and (*b*) Δ ln PCRUDE: Actual (dashed lines) and smooth values (solid lines), 1969 1 to 1979 4.

118

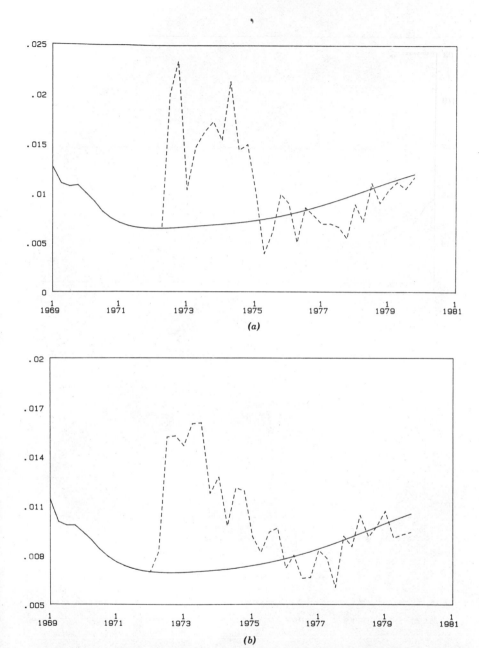

Exhibit 3.17 (*a*) Δ ln PPNF and (*b*) Δ ln PC: Price-shock (dashed lines) and smooth simulation responses (solid lines), 1969 1 to 1979 4.

119

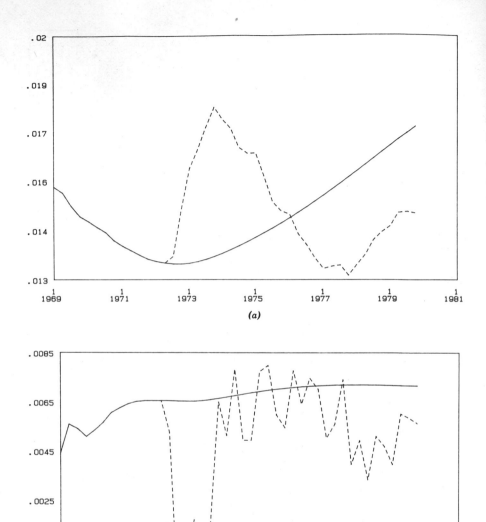

Exhibit 3.18 (*a*) Δ ln JCMH and (*b*) Δ ln JCMHD: Price-shock (dashed lines) and smooth simulation responses (solid lines), 1969 1 to 1979 4.

120

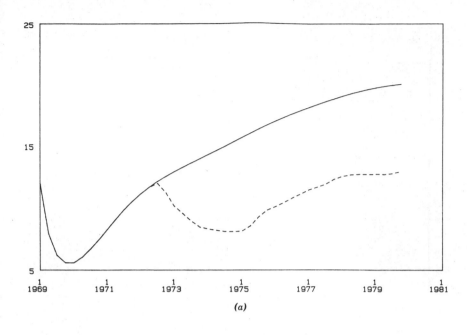

(a)

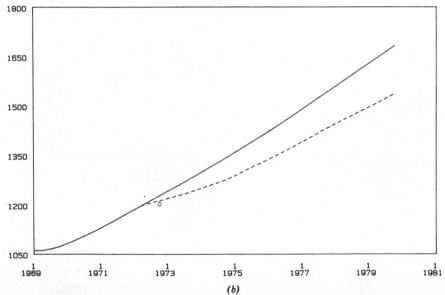

(b)

Exhibit 3.19 (a) IINV72 and (b) GNP72: Price-shock (dashed lines) and smooth (solid lines) simulation responses, 1969 1 to 1979 4.

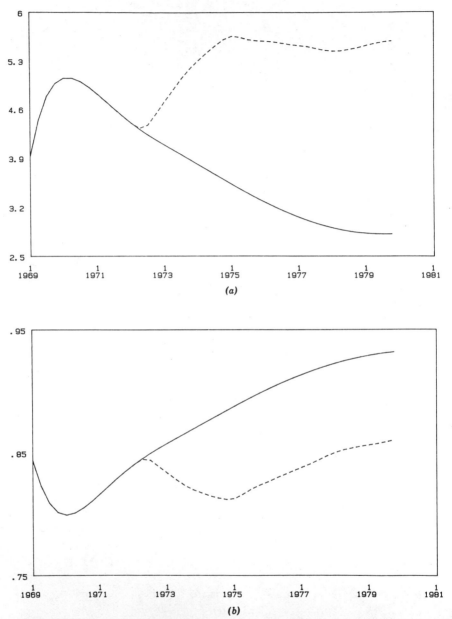

Exhibit 3.20 (*a*) RUG and (*b*) JCU: Price-shock (dashed lines) and smooth (solid lines) simulation responses, 1969 1 to 1979 4.

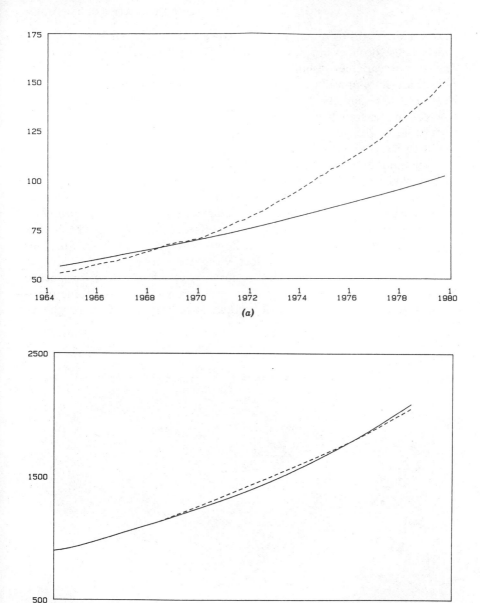

Exhibit 3.21 (*a*) GNP and (*b*) MBASE: Smoothed, with price-shocked (dashed lines) and historical magnitudes (solid lines).

123

zation (JCU). All these series tell a consistent story—that supply-price shocks cause declines in real output until the beginning of 1975, after which real output variables resume fairly stable growth, but at somewhat lower rates than those prevailing in the smooth simulations. Thus, unemployment rises until 1975 and stabilizes in the vicinity of $5\frac{1}{2}\%$ in the price-shock case, whereas in the smoothed simulations it falls continuously, approaching an asymptote of $2\frac{3}{4}\%$ at the end of the simulation period. Exhibit 3.21 shows the historical and smoothed path of the exogenous monetary base (MBASE) and the smooth and price-shocked paths of the nominal GNP. It appears that the stylized "nonaccommodating" monetary policy in our price-shocked simulation may have led to a cap on nominal-GNP growth, leading to severe output responses in the face of the price shocks. More expansionary monetary or fiscal policy would have offset these declines. Man-hour productivity, QMH77 in Exhibit 3.22, shows more productivity growth after 1974 with the price shock than it does without the price shock.

Because of lower output, Phillips-curve effects hold the price-shocked growth rate of compensation $\Delta \ln$ JCMH well below its smooth counterparts. In turn, upward pressures on final-product prices (PPNF, PC) from exogenous

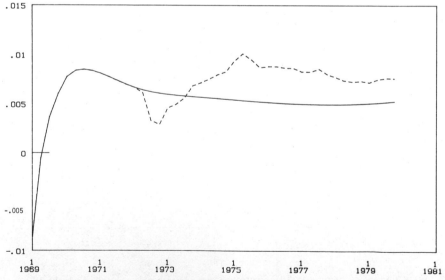

Exhibit 3.22 $\Delta \ln$ QMH77 price-shocked (dashed lines) and smooth simulations (solid lines).

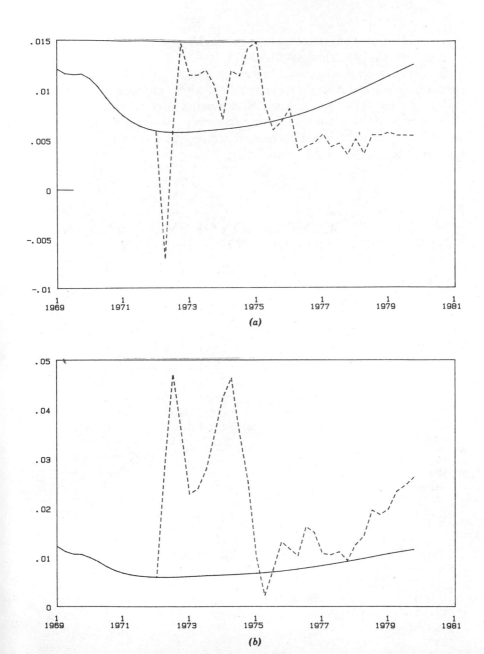

Exhibit 3.23 (*a*) Δ ln PIPD and (*b*) Δ ln PINC: Price-shock (dashed lines) and smooth (solid lines) simulation responses, 1969 1 to 1979 4.

price shocks are largely offset by lower wages, so that the shocked $\Delta \ln$ PPNF "tracks" the smooth $\Delta \ln$ PPNF after 1975.

Investment goods prices for $\Delta \ln$ PIPD (producers' durables) and $\Delta \ln$ PINC (structures) in Exhibit 3.23 both respond quickly to the supply-price shocks and then, after 1975–1976, follow different paths from each other and from their respective smoothed analogues. We simply wish to note the diversity among sectoral price indices, while recognizing that the initial responses resemble each other and $\Delta \ln$ PPNF.

APPENDIX 3A. COMPARISON OF SMOOTHED AND PRICE-SHOCKED SIMULATIONS, 1969–1979

List of endogenous variable symbols.

Exhibit 3A.1	Exhibit 3A.2	Exhibit 3A.3	Exhibit 3A.4
DLPPNF	DLPCDO	DLPIPD	IBF72
DLULC77	DLPCDA	DLPIPDQ	IBFPD72
DLJCMH	DLPCDFE	DLPIPDAG	IBFNC72
DLJCMHD	DLPCN	DLPIPDO	SINV72
DLPGNP	DLPCS	QMH77	IINV72
DLPCPI	DLPG	QMHT	IRC72
DLPC	DLPINC	QHT1	JCAP
DLPIRC	DLPIBF	RUG	JCU

Exhibit 3A.5	Exhibit 3A.6	Exhibit 3A.7
C72	M2PLUS	UCKNC
CDA72	M1BPLUS	UCKPDQ
CDO72	RTB	GNP
CDFE72	RCD	GNP72
CS72	RAAA	YPWS
CN72	NIASF	YCBT
YD72	NIASSL	
M72		

Exhibit 3A.1 Price rate-of-change variables: Comparison of smoothed and shocked simulations.

		DLPPNF		DLULC77		DLJCMH		DLJCMHD		DLPGNP		DLPCPI		DLPC		DLPIRC	
		Smth	Shck	Smth	Shck	Smth	Shck	Smth	Shck	Smth	Shck	Smth	Shck	Smth	Shck	Smth	Shck
1969	1	.0126	.0126	.0244	.0244	.0158	.0158	.0044	.0044	.0096	.0096	.0126	.0126	.0114	.0114	.0122	.0122
	2	.0111	.0111	.0161	.0161	.0156	.0156	.0056	.0056	.0104	.0104	.0117	.0117	.0100	.0100	.0097	.0097
	3	.0108	.0108	.0116	.0116	.0152	.0152	.0054	.0054	.0104	.0104	.0109	.0109	.0098	.0098	.0097	.0097
	4	.0109	.0109	.0089	.0089	.0149	.0149	.0051	.0051	.0105	.0105	.0106	.0106	.0098	.0098	.0097	.0097
1970	1	.0100	.0100	.0070	.0070	.0148	.0148	.0054	.0054	.0101	.0101	.0100	.0100	.0094	.0094	.0098	.0098
	2	.0092	.0092	.0062	.0062	.0146	.0146	.0057	.0057	.0096	.0096	.0094	.0094	.0089	.0089	.0098	.0098
	3	.0081	.0081	.0059	.0059	.0144	.0144	.0061	.0061	.0090	.0090	.0087	.0087	.0084	.0084	.0097	.0097
	4	.0075	.0075	.0058	.0058	.0142	.0142	.0063	.0063	.0085	.0085	.0082	.0082	.0079	.0079	.0095	.0095
1971	1	.0070	.0070	.0059	.0059	.0140	.0140	.0064	.0064	.0081	.0081	.0078	.0078	.0076	.0076	.0092	.0092
	2	.0067	.0067	.0061	.0061	.0139	.0139	.0065	.0065	.0078	.0078	.0076	.0076	.0074	.0074	.0089	.0089
	3	.0065	.0065	.0064	.0064	.0137	.0137	.0066	.0066	.0076	.0076	.0074	.0074	.0072	.0072	.0086	.0086
	4	.0064	.0064	.0066	.0066	.0136	.0136	.0066	.0066	.0075	.0075	.0073	.0073	.0071	.0071	.0084	.0084
1972	1	.0064	.0064	.0069	.0069	.0136	.0136	.0066	.0063	.0074	.0086	.0072	.0075	.0070	.0073	.0082	.0336
	2	.0064	.0183	.0071	.0093	.0135	.0136	.0065	.0013	.0074	.0142	.0072	.0132	.0070	.0122	.0081	.0095
	3	.0064	.0197	.0072	.0112	.0135	.0144	.0065	.0019	.0074	.0171	.0072	.0179	.0069	.0163	.0080	.0117
	4	.0065	.0118	.0074	.0109	.0135	.0160	.0065	.0044	.0074	.0125	.0072	.0125	.0069	.0116	.0080	.0148
1973	1	.0066	.0106	.0075	.0107	.0135	.0162	.0065	.0025	.0074	.0135	.0073	.0148	.0070	.0137	.0080	.0159
	2	.0066	.0149	.0077	.0111	.0135	.0165	.0066	.0007	.0075	.0159	.0073	.0171	.0070	.0158	.0080	.0187
	3	.0067	.0162	.0078	.0117	.0136	.0174	.0066	.0013	.0075	.0166	.0073	.0174	.0070	.0161	.0081	.0206
	4	.0067	.0170	.0080	.0114	.0137	.0181	.0066	.0064	.0076	.0145	.0074	.0125	.0071	.0117	.0082	.0271

Exhibit 3A.1 Continued.

		DLPPNF		DLULC77		DLJCMH		DLJCMHD		DLPGNP		DLPCPI		DLPC		DLPIRC	
		Smth	Shck	Smth	Shck	Smth	Shck	Smth	Shck	Smth	Shck	Smth	Shck	Smth	Shck	Smth	Shck
1974	1	.0068	.0149	.0081	.0107	.0138	.0178	.0067	.0052	.0076	.0149	.0074	.0135	.0071	.0126	.0084	.0309
	2	.0069	.0210	.0083	.0100	.0139	.0175	.0068	.0079	.0077	.0143	.0075	.0101	.0072	.0096	.0085	.0241
	3	.0070	.0141	.0085	.0090	.0140	.0169	.0068	.0049	.0077	.0140	.0075	.0128	.0072	.0119	.0087	.0212
	4	.0071	.0148	.0087	.0085	.0142	.0167	.0069	.0049	.0078	.0135	.0076	.0125	.0073	.0118	.0089	.0148
1975	1	.0072	.0100	.0089	.0073	.0143	.0166	.0069	.0076	.0079	.0101	.0077	.0094	.0074	.0090	.0091	.0101
	2	.0073	.0038	.0091	.0059	.0144	.0159	.0070	.0079	.0080	.0079	.0078	.0082	.0075	.0081	.0093	.0153
	3	.0075	.0059	.0093	.0058	.0146	.0153	.0070	.0059	.0082	.0091	.0079	.0096	.0076	.0093	.0095	.0151
	4	.0076	.0098	.0095	.0063	.0147	.0150	.0071	.0054	.0083	.0102	.0081	.0100	.0077	.0096	.0098	.0145
1976	1	.0078	.0088	.0097	.0061	.0149	.0149	.0071	.0078	.0084	.0084	.0082	.0074	.0078	.0071	.0100	.0107
	2	.0080	.0049	.0099	.0055	.0151	.0143	.0071	.0064	.0086	.0081	.0083	.0083	.0079	.0079	.0103	.0155
	3	.0083	.0085	.0102	.0054	.0152	.0140	.0071	.0075	.0088	.0080	.0085	.0068	.0081	.0066	.0105	.0135
	4	.0085	.0077	.0104	.0050	.0154	.0136	.0072	.0070	.0090	.0078	.0087	.0069	.0082	.0066	.0108	.0115
1977	1	.0087	.0068	.0106	.0050	.0156	.0133	.0072	.0050	.0092	.0084	.0089	.0087	.0084	.0083	.0111	.0082
	2	.0090	.0068	.0108	.0052	.0158	.0134	.0072	.0056	.0094	.0082	.0091	.0082	.0086	.0078	.0114	.0117
	3	.0093	.0065	.0110	.0049	.0159	.0134	.0072	.0074	.0096	.0070	.0093	.0062	.0087	.0060	.0117	.0091
	4	.0096	.0054	.0112	.0051	.0161	.0131	.0072	.0040	.0098	.0086	.0095	.0098	.0089	.0092	.0120	.0102
1978	1	.0098	.0088	.0114	.0058	.0163	.0135	.0072	.0049	.0100	.0091	.0097	.0091	.0091	.0085	.0123	.0101
	2	.0101	.0071	.0115	.0064	.0165	.0138	.0072	.0033	.0103	.0101	.0099	.0113	.0093	.0104	.0127	.0131
	3	.0104	.0110	.0117	.0070	.0167	.0142	.0072	.0051	.0105	.0103	.0101	.0098	.0095	.0091	.0130	.0132
	4	.0107	.0090	.0119	.0072	.0169	.0145	.0072	.0047	.0108	.0104	.0103	.0106	.0097	.0098	.0133	.0132
1979	1	.0110	.0103	.0120	.0075	.0171	.0147	.0072	.0040	.0110	.0113	.0106	.0116	.0099	.0107	.0137	.0146
	2	.0113	.0111	.0122	.0076	.0173	.0151	.0072	.0060	.0112	.0107	.0108	.0097	.0101	.0091	.0140	.0173
	3	.0116	.0104	.0123	.0075	.0175	.0151	.0072	.0058	.0115	.0107	.0110	.0099	.0103	.0093	.0143	.0165
	4	.0119	.0116	.0124	.0075	.0177	.0151	.0072	.0056	.0117	.0112	.0112	.0101	.0105	.0094	.0147	.0182

Exhibit 3A.2 Price rate-of-change variables: Comparison of smoothed and shocked simulations.

		DLPCDO		DLPCDA		DLPCDFE		DLPCN		DLPCS		DLPG		DLPINC		DLPIBF	
		Smth	Shck	Smth	Shck	Smth	Shck	Smth	Shck	Smth	Shck	Smth	Shck	Smth	Shck	Smth	Shck
1969	1	.0121	.0121	.0056	.0056	.0070	.0070	.0100	.0100	.0135	.0135	.0137	.0137	.0123	.0123	.0132	.0132
	2	.0100	.0100	.0053	.0053	.0067	.0067	.0088	.0088	.0129	.0129	.0125	.0125	.0112	.0112	.0118	.0118
	3	.0090	.0090	.0052	.0052	.0062	.0062	.0085	.0085	.0125	.0125	.0123	.0123	.0107	.0107	.0114	.0114
	4	.0086	.0086	.0052	.0052	.0060	.0060	.0085	.0085	.0124	.0124	.0124	.0124	.0107	.0107	.0112	.0112
1970	1	.0081	.0081	.0050	.0050	.0057	.0057	.0081	.0081	.0119	.0119	.0117	.0117	.0100	.0100	.0109	.0109
	2	.0076	.0076	.0048	.0048	.0051	.0051	.0076	.0076	.0113	.0113	.0111	.0111	.0092	.0092	.0101	.0101
	3	.0069	.0069	.0046	.0046	.0043	.0043	.0070	.0070	.0108	.0108	.0103	.0103	.0082	.0082	.0091	.0091
	4	.0064	.0064	.0044	.0044	.0036	.0036	.0066	.0066	.0103	.0103	.0097	.0097	.0074	.0074	.0083	.0083
1971	1	.0060	.0060	.0043	.0043	.0031	.0031	.0063	.0063	.0099	.0099	.0094	.0094	.0069	.0069	.0076	.0076
	2	.0057	.0057	.0042	.0042	.0027	.0027	.0061	.0061	.0096	.0096	.0092	.0092	.0065	.0065	.0071	.0071
	3	.0055	.0055	.0042	.0042	.0025	.0025	.0060	.0060	.0094	.0094	.0090	.0090	.0063	.0063	.0067	.0067
	4	.0054	.0054	.0042	.0042	.0023	.0023	.0059	.0059	.0092	.0092	.0090	.0090	.0061	.0061	.0064	.0064
1972	1	.0054	.0054	.0042	.0042	.0022	.0022	.0059	.0065	.0091	.0091	.0089	.0089	.0060	.0273	.0062	.0052
	2	.0053	.0098	.0042	.0069	.0022	.0068	.0059	.0143	.0090	.0120	.0089	.0181	.0060	.0432	.0060	.0192
	3	.0053	.0123	.0042	.0073	.0022	.0114	.0059	.0217	.0090	.0136	.0090	.0192	.0061	.0297	.0060	.0189
	4	.0054	.0104	.0042	.0054	.0023	.0099	.0059	.0120	.0089	.0124	.0090	.0131	.0061	.0221	.0060	.0151
1973	1	.0054	.0091	.0042	.0051	.0023	.0071	.0060	.0186	.0089	.0117	.0091	.0121	.0062	.0194	.0060	.0133
	2	.0054	.0101	.0042	.0061	.0024	.0077	.0060	.0225	.0089	.0127	.0091	.0154	.0062	.0231	.0061	.0152
	3	.0055	.0111	.0042	.0064	.0024	.0095	.0061	.0216	.0090	.0136	.0092	.0165	.0063	.0276	.0062	.0174
	4	.0055	.0118	.0043	.0066	.0025	.0105	.0061	.0096	.0090	.0145	.0092	.0171	.0064	.0346	.0062	.0190

Exhibit 3A.2 Continued.

		DLPCDO		DLPCDA		DLPCDFE		DLPCN		DLPCS		DLPG		DLPINC		DLPIBF	
		Smth	Shck	Smth	Shck	Smth	Shck	Smth	Shck	Smth	Shck	Smth	Shck	Smth	Shck	Smth	Shck
1974	1	.0056	.0114	.0043	.0061	.0025	.0102	.0061	.0119	.0091	.0145	.0093	.0155	.0064	.0420	.0063	.0195
	2	.0056	.0134	.0043	.0075	.0026	.0120	.0062	.0020	.0091	.0161	.0093	.0202	.0065	.0461	.0064	.0243
	3	.0057	.0118	.0043	.0060	.0026	.0112	.0062	.0093	.0092	.0152	.0094	.0149	.0066	.0346	.0065	.0198
	4	.0057	.0113	.0043	.0061	.0027	.0097	.0063	.0095	.0093	.0149	.0095	.0154	.0067	.0250	.0066	.0180
1975	1	.0058	.0093	.0044	.0050	.0028	.0076	.0063	.0048	.0094	.0135	.0096	.0117	.0068	.0100	.0067	.0127
	2	.0059	.0060	.0044	.0036	.0029	.0035	.0064	.0059	.0095	.0112	.0097	.0069	.0069	.0022	.0068	.0058
	3	.0060	.0054	.0044	.0041	.0030	.0017	.0065	.0100	.0096	.0106	.0098	.0086	.0071	.0074	.0070	.0062
	4	.0061	.0066	.0045	.0050	.0032	.0033	.0066	.0094	.0098	.0112	.0099	.0116	.0073	.0131	.0072	.0088
1976	1	.0062	.0068	.0045	.0047	.0033	.0042	.0067	.0031	.0099	.0112	.0101	.0108	.0074	.0116	.0074	.0092
	2	.0063	.0054	.0046	.0038	.0035	.0028	.0068	.0069	.0101	.0100	.0102	.0078	.0076	.0103	.0076	.0060
	3	.0064	.0061	.0046	.0047	.0036	.0028	.0069	.0029	.0102	.0103	.0104	.0106	.0079	.0162	.0079	.0085
	4	.0066	.0061	.0047	.0045	.0038	.0033	.0071	.0031	.0104	.0101	.0106	.0099	.0081	.0150	.0082	.0084
1977	1	.0067	.0058	.0047	.0043	.0040	.0030	.0072	.0080	.0106	.0097	.0108	.0093	.0084	.0107	.0085	.0073
	2	.0069	.0057	.0048	.0043	.0042	.0027	.0074	.0071	.0108	.0094	.0110	.0093	.0086	.0105	.0088	.0064
	3	.0071	.0055	.0048	.0042	.0045	.0025	.0075	.0029	.0110	.0092	.0112	.0091	.0089	.0111	.0091	.0069
	4	.0073	.0050	.0049	.0039	.0047	.0019	.0077	.0117	.0112	.0087	.0114	.0082	.0092	.0093	.0094	.0055
1978	1	.0075	.0061	.0050	.0047	.0049	.0028	.0079	.0090	.0114	.0094	.0116	.0109	.0095	.0126	.0098	.0077
	2	.0077	.0059	.0050	.0043	.0052	.0032	.0080	.0141	.0116	.0092	.0119	.0095	.0098	.0143	.0102	.0075
	3	.0079	.0073	.0051	.0052	.0054	.0044	.0082	.0091	.0119	.0101	.0121	.0125	.0101	.0196	.0105	.0106
	4	.0080	.0072	.0052	.0048	.0057	.0049	.0084	.0109	.0121	.0101	.0123	.0110	.0104	.0187	.0109	.0103
1979	1	.0082	.0076	.0052	.0051	.0059	.0050	.0085	.0127	.0123	.0105	.0126	.0120	.0107	.0198	.0113	.0110
	2	.0084	.0081	.0053	.0053	.0062	.0057	.0087	.0077	.0126	.0110	.0128	.0126	.0110	.0234	.0116	.0122
	3	.0086	.0080	.0054	.0051	.0064	.0058	.0089	.0080	.0128	.0111	.0130	.0121	.0113	.0246	.0120	.0127
	4	.0088	.0084	.0054	.0054	.0067	.0061	.0090	.0078	.0130	.0115	.0132	.0130	.0116	.0262	.0124	.0133

Exhibit 3A.3 Comparison of smoothed and shocked simulations.

		DLPIPD		DLPIPDQ		DLPIPDAG		DLPIPDO		QMH77		QMHT		QHT1		RUG	
		Smth	Shck	Smth	Shck	Smth	Shck	Smth	Shck	Smth	Shck	Smth	Shck	Smth	Shck	Smth	Shck
1969	1	.0121	.0121	.0129	.0129	.0147	.0147	.0109	.0109	86.3	86.3	.0152	.0152	.0041	.0041	3.93	3.93
	2	.0116	.0116	.0137	.0137	.0146	.0146	.0107	.0107	86.2	86.2	.0154	.0154	.0042	.0042	4.45	4.45
	3	.0116	.0116	.0140	.0140	.0144	.0144	.0104	.0104	86.5	86.5	.0155	.0155	.0044	.0044	4.79	4.79
	4	.0116	.0116	.0143	.0143	.0143	.0143	.0104	.0104	87.1	87.1	.0158	.0158	.0045	.0045	4.97	4.97
1970	1	.0112	.0112	.0141	.0141	.0137	.0137	.0098	.0098	87.7	87.7	.0161	.0161	.0046	.0046	5.05	5.05
	2	.0104	.0104	.0135	.0135	.0128	.0128	.0090	.0090	88.5	88.5	.0166	.0166	.0047	.0047	5.05	5.05
	3	.0093	.0093	.0125	.0125	.0115	.0115	.0080	.0080	89.2	89.2	.0170	.0170	.0047	.0047	5.00	5.00
	4	.0083	.0083	.0114	.0114	.0104	.0104	.0070	.0070	90.0	90.0	.0175	.0175	.0047	.0047	4.92	4.92
1971	1	.0075	.0075	.0104	.0104	.0095	.0095	.0063	.0063	90.7	90.7	.0179	.0179	.0048	.0048	4.82	4.82
	2	.0069	.0069	.0096	.0096	.0088	.0088	.0058	.0058	91.4	91.4	.0183	.0183	.0049	.0049	4.71	4.71
	3	.0065	.0065	.0089	.0089	.0083	.0083	.0054	.0054	92.1	92.1	.0187	.0187	.0051	.0051	4.60	4.60
	4	.0061	.0061	.0084	.0084	.0080	.0080	.0051	.0051	92.8	92.8	.0190	.0190	.0053	.0053	4.49	4.49
1972	1	.0059	.0063	.0080	.0033	.0078	.0078	.0050	.0110	93.4	93.4	.0194	.0194	.0056	.0056	4.40	4.40
	2	.0058	.0064	.0078	.0107	.0077	.0163	.0049	.0039	94.0	93.8	.0199	.0199	.0058	.0058	4.31	4.41
	3	.0058	.0131	.0076	.0163	.0077	.0217	.0049	.0111	94.6	94.1	.0205	.0205	.0060	.0060	4.23	4.53
	4	.0058	.0113	.0075	.0157	.0077	.0188	.0050	.0089	95.1	94.5	.0211	.0211	.0063	.0062	4.15	4.67
1973	1	.0058	.0099	.0075	.0147	.0078	.0164	.0050	.0074	95.7	95.1	.0219	.0219	.0065	.0065	4.08	4.78
	2	.0059	.0108	.0075	.0160	.0079	.0182	.0051	.0081	96.3	95.6	.0227	.0227	.0067	.0066	4.01	4.91
	3	.0060	.0117	.0076	.0174	.0080	.0202	.0052	.0088	96.8	96.1	.0236	.0236	.0069	.0068	3.94	5.06
	4	.0060	.0103	.0077	.0179	.0081	.0217	.0052	.0063	97.4	96.8	.0245	.0244	.0071	.0069	3.87	5.19

131

Exhibit 3A.3 Continued.

		DLPIPD		DLPIPDQ		DLPIPDAG		DLPIPDO		QMH77		QMHT		QHT1		RUG	
		Smth	Shck	Smth	Shck	Smth	Shck	Smth	Shck	Smth	Shck	Smth	Shck	Smth	Shck	Smth	Shck
1974	1	.0061	.0067	.0078	.0164	.0082	.0210	.0053	.0017	98.0	97.5	.0254	.0252	.0073	.0070	3.80	5.31
	2	.0062	.0117	.0079	.0199	.0083	.0251	.0054	.0073	98.5	98.2	.0263	.0259	.0075	.0071	3.73	5.43
	3	.0063	.0112	.0080	.0191	.0084	.0222	.0055	.0072	99.1	99.0	.0272	.0266	.0077	.0072	3.66	5.53
	4	.0064	.0141	.0081	.0199	.0085	.0212	.0056	.0113	99.6	99.8	.0280	.0272	.0080	.0073	3.59	5.62
1975	1	.0066	.0148	.0083	.0188	.0086	.0172	.0057	.0132	100.1	100.7	.0289	.0277	.0082	.0074	3.52	5.67
	2	.0067	.0084	.0084	.0136	.0088	.0107	.0059	.0065	100.7	101.8	.0297	.0282	.0084	.0075	3.45	5.66
	3	.0069	.0059	.0086	.0109	.0090	.0089	.0060	.0039	101.2	102.7	.0306	.0286	.0086	.0076	3.39	5.62
	4	.0071	.0067	.0089	.0111	.0092	.0107	.0062	.0049	101.7	103.6	.0314	.0290	.0088	.0077	3.32	5.61
1976	1	.0073	.0081	.0091	.0113	.0095	.0110	.0064	.0067	102.3	104.5	.0322	.0294	.0090	.0078	3.26	5.60
	2	.0076	.0038	.0094	.0083	.0098	.0083	.0067	.0016	102.8	105.5	.0331	.0298	.0092	.0079	3.20	5.58
	3	.0078	.0043	.0097	.0084	.0101	.0095	.0069	.0022	103.3	106.4	.0339	.0302	.0094	.0080	3.15	5.56
	4	.0081	.0046	.0101	.0082	.0104	.0095	.0072	.0028	103.8	107.3	.0348	.0306	.0097	.0082	3.10	5.53
1977	1	.0084	.0055	.0105	.0082	.0107	.0089	.0075	.0043	104.4	108.2	.0356	.0310	.0099	.0083	3.05	5.52
	2	.0088	.0042	.0109	.0074	.0111	.0086	.0078	.0026	104.9	109.1	.0365	.0315	.0101	.0084	3.01	5.50
	3	.0091	.0046	.0113	.0073	.0115	.0082	.0081	.0033	105.4	110.0	.0374	.0320	.0103	.0086	2.97	5.47
	4	.0095	.0035	.0117	.0063	.0119	.0072	.0084	.0020	105.9	110.9	.0382	.0324	.0105	.0087	2.93	5.45
1978	1	.0099	.0050	.0122	.0074	.0123	.0092	.0088	.0036	106.4	111.8	.0391	.0329	.0107	.0088	2.90	5.43
	2	.0103	.0036	.0127	.0068	.0127	.0089	.0091	.0016	107.0	112.6	.0399	.0335	.0109	.0090	2.88	5.44
	3	.0107	.0055	.0132	.0086	.0132	.0116	.0095	.0034	107.5	113.4	.0408	.0340	.0111	.0091	2.85	5.46
	4	.0111	.0055	.0137	.0088	.0136	.0115	.0098	.0033	108.1	114.2	.0416	.0345	.0114	.0093	2.84	5.48
1979	1	.0115	.0058	.0142	.0095	.0140	.0124	.0102	.0035	108.6	115.0	.0425	.0351	.0116	.0094	2.83	5.51
	2	.0119	.0055	.0147	.0100	.0145	.0135	.0105	.0027	109.2	115.9	.0433	.0356	.0118	.0096	2.82	5.54
	3	.0123	.0055	.0152	.0102	.0149	.0135	.0109	.0027	109.7	116.8	.0441	.0362	.0120	.0097	2.82	5.56
	4	.0127	.0054	.0157	.0107	.0153	.0144	.0112	.0023	110.3	117.7	.0450	.0368	.0122	.0099	2.82	5.57

Exhibit 3A.4 Comparison of smoothed and shocked simulations.

		IBF72		IBFPD72		IBFNC72		SINV72		IINV72		IRC72		JCAP		JCU	
		Smth	Shck	Smth	Shck	Smth	Shck	Smth	Shck	Smth	Shck	Smth	Shck	Smth	Shck	Smth	Shck
1969	1	114.0	114.0	70.2	70.2	43.8	43.8	988	988	11.95	11.95	44.20	44.20	126.1	126.1	.8434	.8434
	2	113.8	113.8	70.4	70.4	43.4	43.4	996	996	7.93	7.93	44.31	44.31	127.5	127.5	.8231	.8231
	3	113.0	113.0	70.0	70.0	43.0	43.0	1002	1002	6.19	6.19	44.61	44.61	128.8	128.8	.8092	.8092
	4	112.6	112.6	69.7	69.7	43.0	43.0	1008	1008	5.59	5.59	45.19	45.19	130.1	130.1	.8015	.8015
1970	1	113.3	113.3	70.2	70.2	43.1	43.1	1014	1014	5.59	5.59	46.00	46.00	131.3	131.3	.7994	.7994
	2	114.3	114.3	71.0	71.0	43.4	43.4	1020	1020	6.06	6.06	46.91	46.91	132.4	132.4	.8013	.8013
	3	115.6	115.6	71.9	71.9	43.7	43.7	1026	1026	6.73	6.73	47.83	47.83	133.6	133.6	.8055	.8055
	4	117.2	117.2	73.1	73.1	44.1	44.1	1034	1034	7.51	7.51	48.69	48.69	134.8	134.8	.8110	.8110
1971	1	119.0	119.0	74.5	74.5	44.5	44.5	1042	1042	8.32	8.32	49.48	49.48	136.0	136.0	.8172	.8172
	2	120.9	120.9	76.0	76.0	45.0	45.0	1051	1051	9.13	9.13	50.17	50.17	137.2	137.2	.8235	.8235
	3	122.9	122.9	77.5	77.5	45.5	45.5	1061	1061	9.89	9.89	50.78	50.78	138.5	138.5	.8296	.8296
	4	124.9	124.9	78.9	78.9	46.0	46.0	1072	1072	10.58	10.58	51.33	51.33	139.8	139.8	.8353	.8353
1972	1	126.9	126.9	80.3	80.3	46.6	46.6	1083	1083	11.18	11.18	51.83	51.79	141.1	141.1	.8406	.8404
	2	128.8	128.8	81.7	81.7	47.1	47.1	1095	1095	11.70	11.63	52.31	52.19	142.5	142.5	.8454	.8411
	3	130.7	130.3	83.0	82.8	47.7	47.5	1107	1106	12.16	11.21	52.77	52.61	143.9	143.9	.8498	.8374
	4	132.6	131.4	84.3	83.6	48.3	47.7	1119	1116	12.57	10.29	53.25	53.15	145.3	145.3	.8540	.8337
1973	1	134.5	132.2	85.6	84.3	48.9	47.9	1132	1126	12.95	9.90	53.73	53.87	146.8	146.6	.8579	.8307
	2	136.4	133.1	86.9	85.0	49.5	48.1	1146	1136	13.31	9.57	54.23	54.70	148.2	148.0	.8618	.8273
	3	138.3	134.0	88.2	85.8	50.1	48.2	1159	1145	13.66	9.10	54.74	55.53	149.7	149.3	.8656	.8236
	4	140.3	134.9	89.6	86.6	50.7	48.3	1173	1153	14.00	8.65	55.28	56.29	151.3	150.6	.8693	.8206
1974	1	142.4	135.8	91.0	87.4	51.4	48.4	1188	1162	14.34	8.47	55.83	56.96	152.8	151.9	.8730	.8180
	2	144.5	136.7	92.4	88.2	52.1	48.5	1202	1170	14.68	8.33	56.40	57.58	154.4	153.2	.8768	.8155
	3	146.6	137.6	93.8	89.1	52.8	48.5	1217	1178	15.03	8.22	56.99	58.17	156.0	154.5	.8805	.8137
	4	148.7	138.5	95.2	90.0	53.5	48.5	1233	1187	15.37	8.19	57.59	58.75	157.7	155.7	.8842	.8124

Exhibit 3A.4 Continued.

		IBF72		IBFPD72		IBFNC72		SINV72		IINV72		IRC72		JCAP		JCU	
		Smth	Shck	Smth	Shck	Smth	Shck	Smth	Shck	Smth	Shck	Smth	Shck	Smth	Shck	Smth	Shck
1975	1	150.9	139.3	96.7	90.8	54.2	48.5	1249	1195	15.72	8.20	58.20	59.32	159.3	157.0	.8879	.8131
	2	153.2	140.3	98.2	91.8	55.0	48.5	1265	1203	16.06	8.60	58.83	59.82	161.0	158.2	.8915	.8166
	3	155.5	141.6	99.7	93.0	55.7	48.6	1281	1213	16.39	9.32	59.47	60.17	162.8	159.4	.8950	.8207
	4	157.8	143.0	101.3	94.2	56.5	48.8	1298	1223	16.71	9.88	60.13	60.30	164.5	160.7	.8984	.8239
1976	1	160.1	144.3	102.8	95.3	57.3	49.0	1315	1233	17.03	10.16	60.80	60.26	166.3	161.9	.9017	.8269
	2	162.5	145.6	104.4	96.4	58.1	49.2	1332	1243	17.34	10.51	61.48	60.14	168.1	163.2	.9049	.8301
	3	164.9	146.9	106.0	97.4	58.9	49.5	1350	1254	17.63	10.89	62.18	60.00	170.0	164.4	.9079	.8331
	4	167.3	148.2	107.6	98.4	59.7	49.9	1368	1265	17.91	11.23	62.90	59.90	171.9	165.7	.9108	.8361
1977	1	169.7	149.6	109.3	99.4	60.5	50.2	1386	1277	18.18	11.57	63.63	59.87	173.8	167.0	.9135	.8389
	2	172.2	151.0	110.9	100.4	61.3	50.6	1404	1289	18.43	11.80	64.38	59.89	175.7	168.3	.9161	.8417
	3	174.7	152.5	112.6	101.5	62.1	51.0	1423	1301	18.67	12.05	65.14	59.97	177.7	169.7	.9185	.8450
	4	177.2	154.0	114.2	102.6	63.0	51.4	1442	1313	18.89	12.46	65.92	60.10	179.7	171.0	.9207	.8483
1978	1	179.7	155.7	115.9	103.9	63.8	51.8	1461	1326	19.10	12.70	66.72	60.26	181.8	172.4	.9227	.8511
	2	182.2	157.4	117.6	105.1	64.7	52.3	1480	1339	19.29	12.84	67.53	60.44	183.8	173.8	.9246	.8533
	3	184.8	159.0	119.3	106.3	65.5	52.7	1500	1352	19.46	12.88	68.35	60.65	185.9	175.2	.9263	.8548
	4	187.3	160.6	121.0	107.5	66.3	53.1	1519	1365	19.62	12.86	69.19	60.91	188.0	176.6	.9278	.8561
1979	1	189.9	162.1	122.7	108.6	67.2	53.5	1539	1377	19.76	12.88	70.04	61.24	190.2	178.0	.9291	.8571
	2	192.5	163.6	124.4	109.7	68.1	53.9	1559	1390	19.88	12.84	70.90	61.63	192.3	179.4	.9302	.8582
	3	195.0	165.1	126.1	110.8	68.9	54.3	1579	1403	19.98	12.92	71.77	62.06	194.5	180.9	.9312	.8596
	4	197.6	166.7	127.8	112.0	69.8	54.6	1599	1416	20.07	13.06	72.65	62.52	196.7	182.3	.9319	.8611

Exhibit 3A.5 Comparison of smoothed and shocked simulations.

		C72		CDA72		CDO72		CDFE72		CS72		CN72		YD72		M72	
		Smth	Shck	Smth	Shck	Smth	Shck	Smth	Shck	Smth	Shck	Smth	Shck	Smth	Shck	Smth	Shck
1969	1	649	649	41.76	41.76	13.93	13.93	35.43	35.43	283.7	283.7	274.3	274.3	710	710	62.3	62.3
	2	652	652	40.01	40.01	14.01	14.01	35.71	35.71	286.7	286.7	275.6	275.6	715	715	62.9	62.9
	3	657	657	40.3	40.3	14.12	14.12	36.04	36.04	289.8	289.8	277.0	277.0	720	720	63.4	63.4
	4	663	663	41.02	41.02	14.24	14.24	36.41	36.41	292.9	292.9	278.6	278.6	725	725	63.9	63.9
1970	1	670	670	41.91	41.91	14.38	14.38	36.84	36.84	296.1	296.1	280.3	280.3	732	732	64.5	64.5
	2	676	676	42.89	42.89	14.53	14.53	37.32	37.32	299.5	299.5	282.2	282.2	739	739	65.3	65.3
	3	684	684	43.86	43.86	14.7	14.7	37.87	37.87	302.9	302.9	284.3	284.3	746	746	66.2	66.2
	4	691	691	44.84	44.84	14.88	14.88	38.46	38.46	306.4	306.4	286.6	286.6	755	755	67.3	67.3
1971	1	699	699	45.79	45.79	15.08	15.08	39.09	39.09	310.0	310.0	289.1	289.1	763	763	68.5	68.5
	2	707	707	46.7	46.7	15.29	15.29	39.75	39.75	313.6	313.6	291.6	291.6	773	773	69.8	69.8
	3	715	715	47.57	47.57	15.51	15.51	40.44	40.44	317.4	317.4	294.3	294.3	782	782	71.1	71.1
	4	724	724	48.4	48.4	15.74	15.74	41.15	41.15	321.2	321.2	297.2	297.2	792	792	72.5	72.5
1972	1	732	732	49.19	49.19	15.97	15.97	41.87	41.86	325.0	325.0	300.1	299.9	802	802	74.0	73.9
	2	741	738	49.95	49.93	16.22	16.14	42.6	42.42	329.0	328.5	303.1	301.4	812	805	75.4	75.3
	3	750	743	50.7	50.18	16.47	16.32	43.34	42.9	332.9	331.9	306.1	301.9	823	808	76.9	76.4
	4	758	750	51.42	50.44	16.73	16.5	44.09	43.41	337.0	335.6	309.3	303.8	833	815	78.4	77.4
1973	1	768	755	52.15	50.87	16.99	16.74	44.85	43.93	341.1	339.1	312.5	304.6	844	821	79.9	78.3
	2	777	760	52.88	51.44	17.26	16.98	45.63	44.43	345.2	342.5	315.8	305.0	855	827	81.5	79.2
	3	786	765	53.62	51.89	17.54	17.21	46.41	44.93	349.4	345.9	319.1	305.5	866	832	83.0	80.0
	4	796	772	54.37	52.2	17.82	17.36	47.2	45.42	353.7	349.3	322.6	307.7	878	837	84.6	80.8
1974	1	805	778	55.14	52.36	18.11	17.52	48.01	45.9	358.0	352.8	326.1	309.4	890	841	86.2	81.6
	2	815	786	55.93	52.63	18.4	17.6	48.83	46.35	362.4	356.3	329.6	312.6	902	845	87.9	82.4
	3	825	792	56.74	52.75	18.7	17.73	49.67	46.81	366.9	360.0	333.3	314.7	914	850	89.6	83.2
	4	835	799	57.57	53.14	19.01	17.88	50.52	47.3	371.4	363.8	337.0	316.7	927	856	91.3	84.1

Exhibit 3A.5 Continued.

		C72		CDA72		CDO72		CDFE72		CS72		CN72		YD72		M72	
		Smth	Shck	Smth	Shck	Smth	Shck	Smth	Shck	Smth	Shck	Smth	Shck	Smth	Shck	Smth	Shck
1975	1	846	807	58.41	53.57	19.33	18.06	51.39	47.85	375.9	367.9	340.8	319.5	939	864	93.0	85.1
	2	856	815	59.28	54.14	19.65	18.3	52.26	48.5	380.6	372.1	344.7	322.3	952	874	94.8	86.3
	3	867	823	60.17	54.88	19.97	18.56	53.15	49.15	385.2	376.3	348.7	324.5	966	884	96.6	87.5
	4	878	831	61.07	55.5	20.3	18.8	54.06	49.79	390.0	380.5	352.7	326.8	979	892	98.5	88.9
1976	1	889	840	61.99	55.91	20.64	19.03	54.97	50.43	394.8	384.9	356.8	330.2	993	902	100.4	90.2
	2	900	849	62.92	56.34	20.98	19.29	55.9	51.08	399.7	389.3	360.9	333.0	1007	912	102.3	91.6
	3	912	858	63.87	56.92	21.33	19.52	56.83	51.72	404.6	393.8	365.2	336.5	1021	922	104.3	93.1
	4	923	868	64.83	57.44	21.68	19.76	57.78	52.35	409.6	398.4	369.5	340.0	1035	932	106.2	94.6
1977	1	935	877	65.81	57.96	22.04	20.02	58.73	52.97	414.7	403.0	373.8	342.8	1049	942	108.2	96.1
	2	947	886	66.8	58.46	22.4	20.28	59.69	53.58	419.8	407.7	378.2	345.8	1064	952	110.3	97.6
	3	959	896	67.81	58.99	22.77	20.55	60.66	54.23	425.0	412.6	382.7	349.6	1078	964	112.3	99.2
	4	971	904	68.82	59.57	23.14	20.85	61.64	54.85	430.2	417.3	387.2	351.9	1093	974	114.4	100.8
1978	1	983	914	69.85	60.14	23.51	21.13	62.61	55.46	435.5	422.1	391.7	354.8	1108	984	116.5	102.5
	2	996	922	70.88	60.63	23.88	21.43	63.6	56.05	440.9	426.8	396.3	356.9	1123	993	118.7	104.1
	3	1008	931	71.93	61.11	24.26	21.7	64.58	56.63	446.3	431.5	400.9	359.8	1138	1003	120.8	105.6
	4	1021	939	72.98	61.55	24.64	21.98	65.57	57.2	451.8	436.2	405.6	362.5	1153	1013	123.0	107.2
1979	1	1033	948	74.04	62.05	25.03	22.26	66.56	57.76	457.4	441.0	410.2	364.9	1168	1022	125.2	108.7
	2	1046	957	75.11	62.55	25.41	22.53	67.55	58.33	463.0	445.8	414.9	368.2	1183	1032	127.4	110.3
	3	1059	967	76.18	63.07	25.8	22.79	68.53	58.9	468.7	450.6	419.7	371.4	1198	1042	129.6	111.8
	4	1072	976	77.26	63.61	26.18	23.05	69.52	59.49	474.4	455.5	424.4	374.6	1214	1052	131.9	113.4

Exhibit 3A.6 Comparison of smoothed and shocked simulations.

		M2PLUS		M1BPLUS		RTB		RCD		RAAA		NIASF		NIASSL	
		Smth	Shck	Smth	Shck	Smth	Shck	Smth	Shck	Smth	Shck	Smth	Shck	Smth	Shck
1969	1	622	622	468.8	468.8	5.35	5.35	5.96	5.96	6.30	6.30	8.52	8.52	-1.93	-1.93
	2	630	630	472.0	472.0	5.17	5.17	5.80	5.80	6.38	6.38	5.40	5.40	-1.90	-1.90
	3	640	640	476.0	476.0	5.06	5.06	5.66	5.66	6.46	6.46	3.56	3.56	-1.66	-1.66
	4	650	650	480.4	480.4	5.01	5.01	5.59	5.59	6.52	6.52	2.57	2.57	-1.28	-1.28
1970	1	662	662	485.4	485.4	4.99	4.99	5.57	5.57	6.57	6.57	2.11	2.11	-0.82	-0.82
	2	674	674	490.9	490.9	4.98	4.98	5.57	5.57	6.62	6.62	1.91	1.91	-0.32	-0.32
	3	688	688	496.7	496.7	4.99	4.99	5.60	5.60	6.65	6.65	1.76	1.76	0.17	0.17
	4	701	701	502.8	502.8	4.99	4.99	5.64	5.64	6.68	6.68	1.68	1.68	0.66	0.66
1971	1	715	715	508.8	508.8	5.00	5.00	5.68	5.68	6.70	6.70	1.63	1.63	1.15	1.15
	2	729	729	514.9	514.9	5.01	5.01	5.72	5.72	6.71	6.71	1.56	1.56	1.62	1.62
	3	743	743	520.9	520.9	5.02	5.02	5.76	5.76	6.73	6.73	1.44	1.44	2.07	2.07
	4	757	757	526.9	526.9	5.03	5.03	5.79	5.79	6.74	6.74	1.25	1.25	2.51	2.51
1972	1	771	771	532.9	532.9	5.04	5.04	5.82	5.82	6.75	6.75	1.01	-0.48	2.93	2.79
	2	785	784	538.9	538.0	5.05	5.04	5.83	5.76	6.76	6.80	0.72	1.27	3.33	3.53
	3	800	796	544.9	542.2	5.05	5.03	5.85	5.63	6.78	6.89	0.39	2.41	3.73	4.31
	4	815	811	551.1	548.7	5.06	5.03	5.86	5.55	6.79	6.95	0.05	1.56	4.12	4.75
1973	1	830	829	557.3	556.8	5.07	5.05	5.87	5.49	6.80	6.98	-0.30	1.03	4.51	5.26
	2	845	845	563.6	563.8	5.08	5.06	5.88	5.50	6.81	7.02	-0.65	1.51	4.90	5.97
	3	861	861	570.0	569.9	5.09	5.07	5.89	5.52	6.82	7.07	-0.99	2.06	5.30	6.73
	4	877	877	576.6	576.7	5.10	5.08	5.90	5.51	6.83	7.12	-1.33	1.79	5.72	7.31
1974	1	893	895	583.3	584.3	5.11	5.09	5.91	5.49	6.85	7.17	-1.64	0.61	6.14	7.81
	2	910	913	590.2	592.2	5.12	5.11	5.92	5.45	6.86	7.23	-1.95	1.53	6.57	8.51
	3	928	932	597.2	600.2	5.13	5.13	5.93	5.46	6.87	7.28	-2.23	0.92	7.02	9.11
	4	945	953	604.4	609.7	5.14	5.15	5.94	5.49	6.89	7.31	-2.51	1.65	7.49	9.86

Exhibit 3A.6 Continued.

		M2PLUS		M1BPLUS		RTB		RCD		RAAA		NIASF		NIASSL	
		Smth	Shck	Smth	Shck	Smth	Shck	Smth	Shck	Smth	Shck	Smth	Shck	Smth	Shck
1975	1	963	974	611.7	618.8	5.15	5.17	5.95	5.56	6.90	7.33	-2.76	1.73	7.97	10.45
	2	982	997	619.1	628.7	5.16	5.21	5.97	5.73	6.92	7.31	-3.00	-0.26	8.47	10.73
	3	1000	1019	626.7	637.8	5.17	5.24	5.98	5.88	6.93	7.28	-3.22	-1.30	9.00	11.13
	4	1020	1037	634.5	644.9	5.19	5.26	5.99	5.99	6.95	7.27	-3.41	-1.61	9.55	11.66
1976	1	1039	1056	642.4	651.8	5.20	5.27	6.00	6.06	6.97	7.28	-3.58	-2.23	10.13	12.10
	2	1060	1076	650.5	659.8	5.21	5.29	6.01	6.11	6.98	7.27	-3.72	-4.90	10.74	12.28
	3	1080	1097	658.7	667.9	5.23	5.31	6.02	6.13	7.00	7.26	-3.82	-6.05	11.38	12.61
	4	1101	1117	667.1	675.3	5.24	5.33	6.03	6.16	7.02	7.27	-3.89	-7.52	12.06	12.95
1977	1	1123	1138	675.7	683.4	5.26	5.35	6.04	6.20	7.05	7.27	-3.92	-8.93	12.78	13.34
	2	1145	1159	684.5	691.6	5.27	5.37	6.05	6.22	7.07	7.26	-3.90	-11.07	13.55	13.64
	3	1168	1181	693.4	699.8	5.29	5.39	6.05	6.26	7.09	7.27	-3.84	-12.76	14.36	13.96
	4	1191	1204	702.6	708.3	5.30	5.41	6.06	6.31	7.12	7.26	-3.72	-15.23	15.23	14.31
1978	1	1215	1226	711.9	716.5	5.32	5.43	6.07	6.33	7.15	7.27	-3.54	-16.52	16.15	14.83
	2	1239	1248	721.4	724.5	5.33	5.45	6.08	6.36	7.17	7.28	-3.31	-19.43	17.13	15.24
	3	1264	1272	731.2	733.1	5.35	5.47	6.09	6.35	7.20	7.31	-3.01	-20.86	18.17	15.84
	4	1290	1295	741.1	741.6	5.37	5.49	6.10	6.34	7.23	7.33	-2.65	-23.42	19.29	16.39
1979	1	1316	1321	751.3	751.2	5.39	5.51	6.10	6.34	7.26	7.36	-2.22	-25.69	20.47	17.04
	2	1343	1347	761.7	760.8	5.40	5.54	6.11	6.34	7.29	7.39	-1.72	-28.44	21.74	17.64
	3	1370	1374	772.2	770.9	5.42	5.57	6.12	6.36	7.33	7.43	-1.16	-31.27	23.08	18.29
	4	1399	1403	783.0	781.5	5.44	5.60	6.13	6.38	7.36	7.46	-0.53	-34.26	24.50	19.00

Exhibit 3A.7 Comparison of smoothed and shocked simulations.

		UCKNC		UCKPDQ		GNP		GNP72		YPWS		YCBT	
		Smth	Shck	Smth	Shck	Smth	Shck	Smth	Shck	Smth	Shck	Smth	Shck
1969	1	9.59	9.59	7.23	7.23	900	900	1062	1062	390.3	390.3	88.5	88.5
	2	9.76	9.76	7.08	7.08	910	910	1062	1062	395.6	395.6	87.2	87.2
	3	9.93	9.93	7.19	7.19	923	923	1067	1067	401.6	401.6	88.2	88.2
	4	10.08	10.08	6.47	6.47	940	940	1074	1074	408.0	408.0	90.9	90.9
1970	1	10.23	10.23	6.98	6.98	958	958	1083	1083	414.8	414.8	94.4	94.4
	2	10.36	10.36	7.60	7.60	977	977	1094	1094	422.1	422.1	98.0	98.0
	3	10.47	10.47	8.08	8.08	996	996	1106	1106	429.8	429.8	101.4	101.4
	4	10.57	10.57	8.68	8.68	1016	1016	1119	1119	437.9	437.9	104.7	104.7
1971	1	10.66	10.66	9.44	9.44	1036	1036	1132	1132	446.3	446.3	107.8	107.8
	2	10.74	10.74	10.12	10.12	1057	1057	1145	1145	455.0	455.0	110.8	110.8
	3	10.82	10.82	10.69	10.69	1078	1078	1159	1159	463.9	463.9	113.6	113.6
	4	10.90	10.90	11.10	11.10	1098	1098	1172	1172	473.0	473.0	116.2	116.2
1972	1	10.98	11.21	11.41	11.35	1119	1120	1186	1186	482.2	482.2	118.8	114.7
	2	11.05	11.75	11.63	11.64	1140	1145	1199	1195	491.7	490.2	121.3	124.2
	3	11.13	12.19	11.79	9.61	1162	1170	1213	1201	501.4	497.7	123.7	132.4
	4	11.21	12.52	11.91	7.11	1184	1194	1227	1209	511.2	506.6	126.2	135.5
1973	1	11.29	12.80	12.00	6.11	1206	1218	1241	1217	521.4	515.6	128.8	137.9
	2	11.37	13.13	12.07	5.34	1229	1245	1255	1225	531.8	524.3	131.4	142.7
	3	11.45	13.55	12.12	6.24	1252	1273	1269	1232	542.5	533.4	134.0	148.1
	4	11.54	14.09	12.18	7.19	1276	1301	1283	1240	553.6	543.2	136.8	153.6
1974	1	11.62	14.75	12.23	6.19	1300	1329	1298	1248	565.0	552.8	139.5	156.9
	2	11.71	15.51	12.28	5.37	1325	1357	1313	1257	576.7	562.4	142.4	167.5
	3	11.80	16.12	12.34	4.07	1351	1386	1328	1266	588.9	571.8	145.3	173.6
	4	11.89	16.57	12.39	4.69	1377	1416	1343	1275	601.4	581.2	148.3	182.5

Exhibit 3A.7 Continued.

		UCKNC		UCKPDQ		GNP		GNP72		YPWS		YCBT	
		Smth	Shck	Smth	Shck	Smth	Shck	Smth	Shck	Smth	Shck	Smth	Shck
1975	1	11.98	16.75	12.44	5.34	1405	1443	1359	1287	614.3	591.4	151.4	189.7
	2	12.08	16.77	12.48	6.63	1432	1470	1375	1300	627.7	602.1	154.6	190.6
	3	12.18	16.85	12.51	10.96	1461	1498	1391	1313	641.5	612.4	157.8	193.0
	4	12.29	17.07	12.53	13.12	1490	1527	1407	1325	655.7	622.5	161.2	198.4
1976	1	12.40	17.27	12.54	14.52	1520	1554	1423	1338	670.3	633.0	164.7	204.5
	2	12.51	17.44	12.54	14.92	1551	1582	1440	1351	685.4	643.4	168.4	205.1
	3	12.63	17.72	12.52	14.74	1583	1610	1456	1364	700.9	653.9	172.2	209.8
	4	12.75	17.99	12.50	14.22	1616	1639	1473	1377	717.0	664.4	176.2	214.7
1977	1	12.88	18.18	12.46	14.88	1649	1668	1490	1390	733.4	674.7	180.4	219.6
	2	13.01	18.37	12.41	15.51	1684	1698	1507	1404	750.4	685.4	184.9	222.9
	3	13.15	18.58	12.35	15.12	1719	1728	1524	1418	767.9	696.7	189.5	227.7
	4	13.30	18.75	12.28	15.73	1756	1759	1542	1432	785.8	707.7	194.5	230.2
1978	1	13.46	19.00	12.20	16.45	1794	1792	1559	1445	804.3	719.1	199.7	236.0
	2	13.62	19.29	12.12	16.05	1832	1826	1576	1458	823.2	730.7	205.1	238.2
	3	13.78	19.70	12.03	16.15	1872	1861	1594	1470	842.7	742.7	211.0	244.7
	4	13.96	20.12	11.94	15.12	1913	1897	1611	1483	862.7	755.0	217.1	249.1
1979	1	14.14	20.56	11.84	14.31	1956	1935	1629	1496	883.2	767.5	223.6	254.1
	2	14.33	21.10	11.75	14.10	1999	1973	1647	1509	904.2	780.7	230.4	259.0
	3	14.53	21.68	11.65	13.16	2044	2012	1664	1522	925.8	794.2	237.7	264.1
	4	14.74	22.31	11.57	13.52	2090	2052	1682	1536	947.9	807.9	245.3	269.3

APPENDIX 3B.   DETAILS OF MQEM PRICE, WAGE, AND PRODUCTIVITY EQUATIONS

This appendix presents more details about the equations of the MQEM that are analyzed in depth later on. The major price (PPNF), wage (JCMH), and productivity (QMH77) equations are further discussed at the end of this appendix using the coefficient "shares" interpretation of equation (2.5.5).

3B.1   WAGE

The rate of change of the logarithm of the private nonfarm wage index, JCMH, is dependent on a 1973 wage–price-freeze dummy variable, the lagged change in the ratio of the U.S. minimum wage to the average wage index, a lagged measure of economic slack defined as a weighted average of the lagged employment rate and the lagged rate of manufacturing-capacity utilization, and the two-quarter change in the lagged implicit consumption deflator. Lagged inflation rates of up to 10 periods are included through a two-period lagged "permanent" (i.e., smoothed) inflation-rate variable. The economic-slack variable is highly correlated with unemployment and serves the same purpose as the more traditional Phillips-curve variable. In the equations below, a superscript on a Δ indicates a difference of that amount, e.g., Δ^2 is a two-quarter difference:

$$\Delta \ln \text{JCMH}_t = 0.0107 + 0.9511 \frac{\Delta \text{WUSMIN}_t}{\text{JCMH}_{t-1}} + 0.1903 \Delta^2 \ln \text{PC}_{t-1}$$

$$+ 0.0499 \ln \left\{ \frac{2(\text{REM}_{t-1}/100) + (\text{JIPM}_{t-1}/\text{JCAP}_{t-1})}{3} \right\}$$

$$+ 0.066 \frac{\text{DTSI}_t}{\text{JCMH}_{t-1}} + 0.0096 \, \text{DFRZ1}_t$$

$$+ 0.4646 \frac{\text{RPPERM}_{t-2}}{100}, \tag{3B.1}$$

where the symbols are defined as follows:

Symbol	Type variable		Definition
	Endogenous	Exogenous	
JCMH	×		Compensation per man-hour, business nonfarm sector, 1967 = 100
WUSMIN		×	U.S. minimum wage
PC	×		Deflator for personal consumption, 1972 = 100
REM	×		Employment rate, males 20 and over
JIPM	×		Federal Reserve index of industrial production in manufacturing, 1967 = 100
JCAP	×		Index of available capacity in manufacturing
DTSI		×	Dummy for change in Social Security
DFRZ1		×	Dummy for Phase 1 of wage–price freeze
RPPERM	×		Permanent rate of inflation, quarterly rate (8-quarter smoothed rate of change of PC)

3B.2 PRICE

The pivotal price variable is PPNF, the implicit deflator for the private nonfarm GNP. It too is driven by dummy variables related to the wage–price freeze and an economic-slack variable similar to the one that appears in the wage equation, although the economic-slack variable appears with five and six quarter lags in the PPNF equation. There are also two important exogenous prices—the domestic farm-product price deflator and the price of crude materials less food, whose fluctuations in the 1970s are dominated by crude-oil prices. Another important price determinant is the smoothed unit labor cost, measured as the lagged four-quarter change in wages minus the four-quarter average of labor productivity. We have

$$\Delta \ln \text{PPNF}_t = -0.0045 + 0.0361 \, \text{DFROFF}_t + 0.0248 \Delta \ln \text{PFP}_{t-1}$$

$$+ 0.0480 \, \Delta^2 \ln \text{PCRUDE}_{t-1} - 0.0027 \left(\text{DFRZ2}_t + \text{DFRZ3}_t \right)$$

$$+ 0.0009 \left[\frac{0.6}{1 - \text{JCU}_{t-5}} + \frac{0.4}{1 - \text{JCU}_{t-6}} \right]$$

$$+ 0.1666 \left\{ \Delta^4 \ln \text{JCMH}_{t-1} - \sum_{i=1}^{4} \frac{\text{QMHT}_{t-i}}{4} \right\} \qquad (3B.2)$$

with the following definitions:

Symbol	Type variable		Definition
	Endogenous	Exogenous	
PPNF	✕		Deflator for business nonfarm GNP, 1972 = 100
DFROFF		✕	Post-price-freeze dummy
PFP		✕	Gross domestic farm-product deflator, 1972 = 100
PCRUDE		✕	WPI for crude materials less raw food and feed stocks, 1967 = 100
DFRZ2		✕	Dummy for price freeze—Phase 2
DFRZ3		✕	Dummy for price freeze—Phase 3
JCU	✕		Federal Reserve index of capacity utilization in manufacturing, 1967 = 1.00 ($\equiv$ JIPM/JCAP)
QMHT	✕		Trend productivity

There are five behavioral equations for consumption implicit price deflators: automobiles, other durables, furniture and household equipment, nondurables, and services. These equations always include the private-product nonfarm deflator PPNF, and four also contain a first-order lagged dependent variable among the explanatory variables; all equations are linear in logarithmic first differences. There is in addition an identity for the consumer price deflator calculated as current dollar consumption divided by constant-dollar consumption. This last identity enters the wage equation JCMH. We have

$$\Delta \ln \text{PCDA}_t = 0.0012 + 0.2303 \, \Delta \ln \text{PPNF}_t + 0.7450 \, \Delta \ln \text{PAUTO}_t, \tag{3B.3}$$

$$\Delta \ln \text{PCDO}_t = 0.0006 + 0.3765 \, \Delta \ln \text{PPNF}_t + 0.2259 \frac{\text{DTEX}_t}{\text{PCDO}_{t-1}}$$

$$+ 0.4343 \, \Delta \ln \text{PCDO}_{t-1}, \tag{3B.4}$$

$$\Delta \ln \text{PCDFE}_t = -0.0023 + 0.3819 \, \Delta \ln \text{PPNF}_t$$

$$+ 0.2391 \, \Delta \ln \text{PPNF}_{t-1} + 0.2648 \, \Delta \ln \text{PCDFE}_{t-1}$$

$$+ 0.1327 \frac{\text{DTEX}_t}{\text{PCDFE}_{t-1}}, \tag{3B.5}$$

$$\Delta \ln \text{PCN}_t = 0.0010 + 0.4849\,\Delta \ln \text{PPNF}_t + 0.0606\,\Delta \ln \text{PFP}_t$$

$$+\,0.0915\,\Delta \ln \text{PM}_t + 0.1641\,\Delta \ln \text{PCN}_{t-1}$$

$$+\,0.0788(1 - \text{DPGAS}_t)\,\Delta \ln \text{PGAS}_t$$

$$-\,0.002\,\text{DPGAS}_t, \tag{3B.6}$$

$$\Delta \ln \text{PCS}_t = -0.0005 + 0.2489\,\Delta \ln \text{PPNF}_t$$

$$+\,0.0714\ln\frac{\text{JCMH}_{t-1}}{\text{JCMH}_{t-5}} + 0.4392\,\Delta \ln \text{PCS}_{t-1}, \tag{3B.7}$$

$$\text{PC}_t \equiv 100\,\frac{C_t}{\text{C72}_t} \tag{3B.8}$$

with the following definitions:

Symbol	Type variable Endogenous	Exogenous	Definition
PCDA	×		Deflator for consumption of autos and parts, 1972 = 100
PAUTO		×	CPI for new autos, 1967 = 100
PCDO	×		Deflator for consumption of other durables, 1972 = 100
DTEX		×	Dummy for changes in excise taxes
PCDFE	×		Deflator for consumption of furniture and household equipment, 1972 = 100
PCN	×		Deflator for nondurable consumption, 1972 = 100
PM		×	Deflator for imports, 1972 = 100
DPGAS		×	Dummy for PGAS equation
PGAS		×	CPI for gasoline and motor oil
PCS	×		Price deflator for consumption of services, 1972 = 100
C	×		Personal consumption expenditures
C72	×		Personal consumption expenditures, 1972 $

    As suggested in the main body of the chapter, the system of price and wage equations may be strongly simultaneous, since PPNF enters into each of the consumption price equations and depends on wages through unit labor costs, while JCMH depends on the consumption deflator. Apart from exogenous price variables and capacity-utilization effects, sectoral prices and consumption prices adjust to PPNF and, in the case of the deflator for consumption of services (PCS), to JCMH as well. Since the private nonfarm GNP is approximately 80% of the total GNP, a more direct approach would have been to construct PPNF from other parts of the model through an identity and thus enforce consistency between it and other prices beyond whatever is implicit in the statistical fitting procedures. As the National Income Accounts do not allow this to happen directly, the MQEM procedure is necessarily ad hoc. These remarks are aimed at a defect in the National Income Accounts, not at the MQEM.

Other final-demand–price equations include fixed business investment in nonresidential structures, deflators for investment in residential construction, and government purchases. There is also one equation each for producer durables in production, agriculture, and "other." As with the consumption equations, PPNF and a first-order autoregressive term appear in most of these equations. Since these variables are all logarithmic first differences, they have at least a single root at or near one, a value of one being associated with borderline instability in the linearized model. We have

$$\Delta \ln \text{PINC}_t = -0.0004 + 0.7539 \Delta \ln \text{PPNF}_t$$

$$+ 0.0893 \Delta^2 \ln \text{PCRUDE}_t + 0.2698 \Delta \ln \text{PINC}_{t-1}, \quad (3\text{B}.9)$$

$$\Delta \ln \text{PIRC}_t = -0.0143 + 0.7460 \ln \left(\frac{\text{JCMH}_t}{\text{JCMH}_{t-2}} \right)$$

$$+ 0.0023 \{ 0.41 (\text{RAAA}_{t-1} - \text{RCPCD}_{t-1})$$

$$+ 0.49 (\text{RAAA}_{t-2} - \text{RCPCD}_{t-2})$$

$$+ 0.1 (\text{RAAA}_{t-3} - \text{RCPCD}_{t-3}) \}$$

$$+ 0.1068 \Delta \ln \text{PCRUDE}, \quad (3\text{B}.10)$$

$$\Delta \ln \text{PG}_t = 0.0048 + 0.7678 \Delta \ln \text{PPNF}_t$$

$$+ 0.1943 \, \text{DGPAY}_t \, \Delta \ln \left(\frac{\text{YGWS}_t}{\text{EGOV}_t} \right)$$

$$+ 0.1270 \Delta \ln \left(\frac{\text{GFD}_t + \text{GFO}_t}{\text{GFD}_t + \text{GFO}_t + \text{GSL}_t} \right), \quad (3\text{B}.11)$$

$$\Delta \ln \text{PIPDQ}_t = -0.0012 + 0.6894 \Delta \ln \text{PIPDQ}_{t-1}$$

$$+ 0.5419 \Delta \ln \text{PPNF}_t - 0.0200 \Delta \ln \text{PCRUDE}_t, \quad (3\text{B}.12)$$

$$\Delta \ln \text{PIPDAG}_t = -0.0009 + 0.5183 \Delta \ln \text{PIPDAG}_{t-1}$$

$$+ 0.7163 \Delta \ln \text{PPNF}_t, \tag{3B.13}$$

$$\Delta \ln \text{PIPDO}_t = -0.0015 + 0.4798 \Delta \ln \text{PIPDO}_{t-1}$$

$$+ 0.6322 \Delta \ln \text{PPNF}_t - 0.0672 \Delta \ln \text{PCRUDE}_t, \tag{3B.14}$$

$$\Delta \ln \text{PCPI}_t = -0.0002 + 1.1373 \Delta \ln \text{PC}_t$$

$$- 0.0004 (\text{RAAA}_{t-2} - \text{RCPCD}_{t-2})$$

$$- 0.0289 \Delta \ln \left(\frac{\text{CDA72}_t + \text{CDFE72}_t + \text{CDO72}_t}{\text{C72}_t} \right) \tag{3B.15}$$

with the following variable definitions:

Symbol	Type variables		Definition
	Endogenous	Exogenous	
PINC	×		Deflator for business fixed investment, nonresidential structures, 1972 = 100
PIRC	×		Deflator for investment in residential construction, 1972 = 100
RAAA	×		Corporate AAA bond interest rate
RCP	×		4–6-month commercial-paper rate
PG	×		Deflator for total government purchases of goods and services
DGPAY		×	Dummy for government pay raises
YGWS		×	Government wage and salary disbursements
EGOV	×		Government employment
GFD		×	Government purchases: defense
GFO		×	Government purchases: nondefense
GSL		×	Government purchases, state and local
PIPDQ	×		Deflator for business fixed investment: producer durables, other
PIPDAG	×		Deflator for business fixed investment: durables, agriculture
PIPDO	×		Deflator for business fixed investment: producer durables, other

3B.3　PRODUCTIVITY

There are three closely related productivity variables in the MQEM. QMH77, the index of output per hour of all nonfarm employees, has the most behavioral content. This equation is in log-difference form. QMH77 depends on three dummy variables: the rate of change of the constant-dollar GNP, an economic-slack variable similar to the ones in PPNF and JCMH, and smoothed nonagricultural investment. Zero–one dummy variables in first-difference equations reflect trend, so that this equation has "time" as an explanatory variable, along with many other related production equations that include neutral technical change. This productivity variable feeds into private wages and salaries and into the employment rate. We have

$$\Delta \ln \text{QMH77}_t = -0.08798 + 0.013022 \cdot \text{D5467}_t + 0.006013 \cdot \text{D6873}_t$$

$$-0.000905 \cdot \text{D79}_t - 0.072181 \ln\left(\frac{\text{JIPM}_t}{\text{JCAP}_t}\right) + 0.64693 \Delta \ln \text{GNP72}_t$$

$$+0.94466 \sum_{t=-1}^{-6} \alpha_t \ln(\text{IBF72}_t - \text{IPDAG72}_t), \tag{3B.16}$$

where

$$\alpha_{-1} = 0.10, \qquad \alpha_{-3} = 0.25, \qquad \alpha_{-5} = 0.15,$$

$$\alpha_{-2} = 0.15, \qquad \alpha_{-4} = 0.25, \qquad \alpha_{-6} = 0.10,$$

and the variables are as follows:

Symbol	Type variable Endogenous	Exogenous	Definition
QMH77	×		Index of output per hour of all nonfarm employees, 1977 = 100
D5467		×	Dummy for change in trend of productivity
D6873		×	Dummy for change in trend of productivity
D79		×	Dummy for change in trend of productivity
JIPM	×		Federal Reserve index of industrial production in manufacturing, 1967 = 100
JCAP	×		Index of available capacity in manufacturing, 1967 = 100
GNP72	×		Gross national product, 1972 $
IBF72	×		Nonresidential fixed investment, 1972 $
IPDAG72	×		Real nonresidential investment, producers' durables, agriculture, 1972 $

Current productivity growth, QHT1, is almost identical in structure to QMH77. The equation is in log-level form with identical coefficients to QMH77. The only difference between them is that the slack variable (JIPM/JCAP) is held constant at 0.8311 and the quarterly rate of growth of the constant-dollar GNP is held constant at 0.0084. This variable only enters the model via the trend growth rate of productivity QMHT, which is an annual rate smoothed value of quarterly QHT1. So, QMHT is a smoothed version of QHT1, which in turn is a smoothed version of QMH77. QMHT appears only in the PPNF equation. We have

$$\text{QHT1} = -0.08798 + 0.13022 \cdot \text{D5467}_t + 0.00613 \cdot \text{D6873}_t - 0.000905 \cdot \text{D79}_t$$

$$-0.072181 \ln 0.831102 + 0.64693 \cdot 0.008419$$

$$+0.01446 \sum_{t=-1}^{-6} \alpha_t \left(\ln \text{IBF72}_t - \ln \text{IPDAG72}_t \right), \qquad (3B.17)$$

where α_t is the same as in QMH77, and

$$\text{QMHT} = 0.5 \sum_{t=-1}^{-8} \text{QHT1}_t. \qquad (3B.18)$$

Since QMH77 has the most behavioral content, it is subsequently referred to as "the" productivity variable.

3B.4 "SHARES" INTERPRETATION OF PPNF, JCMH, AND QMH77

Elasticity-impact own-parameter responses are useful tools for investigating which of the terms on the right-hand side of an equation have the greatest influence on the dependent variable. For analysis of the three variables PPNF (nonfarm price deflator), JCMH (wage rate) and QMH77 (index of output per hour of all nonfarm employees), we first make a simple transformation: each will be elasticity scaled by its rate of change (e.g., $\Delta \ln$ PPNF for PPNF), instead of by its level. This transformation has three desirable properties:

In an economic context, the rates of change of these three variables are more interesting than their levels. See Chapter 5 for a discussion of this point.

The transformed variables have the useful property that the elasticity impact parameter responses sum to unity, which makes interpretation easier.

These three variables appear most often in the rest of the model in log-difference form, which in turn makes interpretation of other equations easier.

The transformation is described in detail in equation (2.5.25). The appropriate parameter elasticities for this case follow equation (2.5.15).

Since equations (2.5.15)–(2.5.17) require that the derivatives be evaluated at a particular time period, the following remarks are based on historical inputs for the dates 1972–1974, yielding 12 elasticity shares for each variable. PPNF is mostly driven by exogenous variables. If the shares of all exogenous variables and the intercept are summed, that total share in the rate of change of PPNF varies from −1.4 to 0.5 (recall that the sum of all terms is one). The endogenous variables contribute a relatively constant absolute value. So we conclude that most of the variation in PPNF originates in its exogenous variables. Dummy variables sometimes contribute large amounts, with absolute elasticities greater than 0.50.

JCMH receives most of its influence from the deflator for personal consumption (PC) and PC's smoothed value (RPPERM). The sum of these two shares varies between around 0.3 and 0.6, with the intercept providing most of the remaining influence. Since the sectoral price deflators that go into PC are dominated by the share of PPNF, this provides evidence that the price and wage equations are driven largely by PPNF, which in turn is driven mostly by its own exogenous variables.

QMH77 is dominated by two r.h.s. terms: smoothed nonagricultural investment and its intercept. These two impact-parameter elasticities are large (around 12.0) and opposite in sign, and suggest that QMH77 is a variable much more sensitive to variations in variables on its right-hand side than either PPNF or JCMH. So we would expect QMH77 to be much more sensitive to the rest of the model than PPNF or JCMH. A reason for this may be that while the r.h.s. terms of the JCMH and PPNF equations are mainly in rate-of-change form, the terms of QMH77 are in log-level form.

These are suggestive single-equation results that could easily change in the context of a simultaneous-equation model. In Chapter 5 we shall see that these single-equation properties are not greatly modified.

REFERENCES

Belton, T., S. Hymans, and C. Lown (1985). The Dynamics of the Michigan Quarterly Econometric Model of the U.S. Economy. In *A Regional Econometric Forecasting System: Major Economic Areas of Michigan*, Harold T. Shapiro and George A. Fulton (Eds.), Univ. of Michigan Press, Ann Arbor.

Fair, Ray C. and Dwight M. Jaffee (1972). Methods of Estimation for Markets in Disequilibrium, *Econometrica*, Vol. 40, pp. 497–514.

Friedman, Benjamin (1975). *Economic Stabilization Policy: Methods in Optimization*, North-Holland, Amsterdam.

Hicks, John R. (1937). Mr. Keynes and the "Classics," *Econometrica*, Vol. V. p. 147.

Hymans, Saul H. and Harold T. Shapiro (1974). The Structure of Properties of the Michigan Quarterly Econometric Model of the U.S. Economy, *International Economic Review*, Vol. 15, No. 3 (October).

Laffont, Jean-Jacques and A. Monfort (1979). Disequilibrium Econometrics in Dynamic Models, *Journal of Econometrics*, Vol. 11, pp. 353–361.

Modigliani, Franco (1944). Liquidity Preference and the Theory of Interest and Money, *Econometrica*, Vol. 12, p. 45.

Shapiro, Harold T. and George A. Fulton (Eds.) (1985). *A Regional Econometric Forecasting System: Major Economic Areas of Michigan*, Univ. of Michigan Press, Ann Arbor.

Stone, Richard (1970). *Mathematical Models of the Economy and Other Essays*, Chapman and Hall, London.

CHAPTER 4

Preliminary Complete
Model Dynamics

4.1 HOMOGENEOUS-DYNAMICS BACKGROUND

An initial objective in this study is to learn about the MQEM's causal dynamic structure. This will be reflected in the block-triangular structure of the matrix A_t [see equation (2A.1)] and its behavior over time. To do this we set $d\beta = 0$ and assume A to be time-invariant in

$$y_t = Ay_{t-1} + Bx_t \qquad (4.1)$$

to study the familiar initial-condition or homogeneous-dynamics recursion

$$y_{t_0+n} = A^n y_{t_0}. \qquad (4.2)$$

Properties of the matrix A have been treated analytically by Simon and Ando (1963), Ando and Fisher (1963), Gilli (1979), and Boutillier (1983), among others.[†] They have sorted out the following issues: What is the recursive structure of the matrix A? How do simultaneous blocks behave over time? By ordinary algebra, exactly recursive individual relations or exactly recursive block or block-triangular relations will be preserved as A in equation (4.2) is raised to increasing powers. But when there is weak coupling among blocks that arises from relatively small entries outside the blocks, such nearly recursive or nearly independent relationships will become more tightly coupled as n increases. Hence almost distinct blocks will ultimately merge, and we should expect to find larger simultaneous blocks as the time period increases. We plan to use this perspective in studying the MQEM's homogeneous dynamics.

[†] Boutillier's article contains a comprehensive summary and bibliography.

Block Ordering

The method used in computing block ordering is due to Tarjan (1972). Tarjan's algorithm finds a symmetric permutation that produces a lower block-triangular matrix with the important added feature that the maximum number of blocks is found. Consider, for example, the matrix

$$
A = \begin{bmatrix} 1 & 0 & 0 & 0 & 1 \\ 3 & 3 & 3 & 0 & 0 \\ 0 & 3 & 3 & 3 & 0 \\ 0 & 0 & 0 & 2 & 2 \\ 1 & 0 & 0 & 0 & 1 \end{bmatrix}.
$$

One symmetric permutation PAP^{-1}, for example, transforms A to lower block-triangular form with two blocks. Thus take

$$
P_1 = \begin{bmatrix} 1 & 0 & 0 & 0 & 0 \\ 0 & 0 & 0 & 0 & 1 \\ 0 & 1 & 0 & 0 & 0 \\ 0 & 0 & 1 & 0 & 0 \\ 0 & 0 & 0 & 1 & 0 \end{bmatrix}.
$$

Then

$$
\tilde{A}_1 = P_1 A P_1^{-1} = \left[\begin{array}{cc|ccc} 1 & 1 & 0 & 0 & 0 \\ 1 & 1 & 0 & 0 & 0 \\ \hline 3 & 0 & 3 & 3 & 0 \\ 0 & 0 & 3 & 3 & 3 \\ 0 & 2 & 0 & 0 & 2 \end{array} \right].
$$

However, another block will be formed by Tarjan's algorithm, which maximizes their number at 3. Replace P_1 by

$$
P_2 = \begin{bmatrix} 0 & 0 & 0 & 0 & 1 \\ 1 & 0 & 0 & 0 & 0 \\ 0 & 0 & 0 & 1 & 0 \\ 0 & 1 & 0 & 0 & 0 \\ 0 & 0 & 1 & 0 & 0 \end{bmatrix}.
$$

Then

$$
\tilde{A}_2 = P_2 A P_2^{-1} = \begin{bmatrix} 1 & 1 & 0 & 0 & 0 \\ 1 & 1 & 0 & 0 & 0 \\ 2 & 0 & 2 & 0 & 0 \\ 0 & 3 & 0 & 3 & 3 \\ 0 & 0 & 3 & 3 & 3 \end{bmatrix}.
$$

Initialization

Several problem-dependent decisions must be made at the beginning of linear analysis: input type and units of measurement, and the choice of time horizon and output filters. Our intention is to have as much uniformity as possible across procedures except where there are convincing reasons to override standardization. Considerable experience with an earlier version of the MQEM helped to arrive at some of the numerical magnitudes that we finally chose.

Input Type and Units of Measurement. These decisions are partly *a priori* but are also partly context-dependent. On prior grounds it seems most sensible to choose impulse inputs and observe impulse responses through time. Since the inputs in the analysis of homogeneous dynamics are initial conditions, an impulse—a one-period change that immediately reverts to its original value—does the least violence to model dynamics, as these are filtered through the matrix A and its powers. If the entire system is nonexplosive, the impulse response will decline rapidly (perhaps with oscillations) if the system is heavily damped. It will decline more slowly if dynamics are stable but slow and it will grow or fail to decline if the system is explosive.

We have also opted for elasticities rather than beta or other types of scaling. Extensive investigations of the previous version of the MQEM indicated that the broad picture was not much affected by this choice, since large elasticities and large beta responses were highly correlated. In later chapters where we utilize parameter perturbations, elasticities are preferable to beta scaling in that they avoid stochastic implications and thus remain consistent with our present nonstochastic interpretive perspective. (A stronger case could be made for beta scaling in other contexts, however.) Since we do not want different outcomes to be confounded through different choices of units, we have chosen one common measure throughout: elasticities. Thus, a 1% impulse perturbation of initial conditions will be employed here, and outputs will be measured in percentages, so that their ratio is a well-defined arc elasticity. Most results later on will also use the same procedure (1% impulse input changes, elasticity measures).

Time Horizon.   The longest period for which calculations were made is 24 quarters. In earlier, related computations we calculated results for 96 quarters, but the additional information was not particularly helpful. Since in general the matrix A_t is time-varying, calculations much beyond 24 quarters would put a severe strain on the credibility of the results. Since models such as the MQEM are seldom intended for use beyond 8 to 12 quarters, the near-term behavior is of greatest immediate interest, so that quarters 1 through 8 are the main focus of attention, while periods 12, 16 (and 24, of course) help gauge the extent of either antidamped behavior or long-term dynamic effects.

Output Filter.   We have initially chosen an elasticity filter cutoff of 0.05: in most econometric evaluations this would be thought of as conservative (i.e., small). Thus recorded results will show zeros for any magnitude below the cutoff. Since we are going to begin by exploring the block structure of the model, it is important that the near-zero off-(block)-diagonal elements be truly small, and 0.05 seems to satisfy that criterion. Often we shall be most interested in the larger values, but this conservative cutoff will provide some assurance that persistent patterns of relatively small magnitude are not overlooked. There is also empirical evidence to support the use of a cutoff in the vicinity of 0.05 in the context of evaluating homogeneous dynamics. Frequency distributions for the order-230 matrix A, 52,900 entries in all, are recorded in Exhibit 4.1 for homogeneous response elasticities in selected periods.[†]

The main purpose of presenting these distributions is to observe whether they are skewed enough to provide more information about filter cutoffs. The percentage of elasticities less then 0.05 is 96% in period 1; it drops to 81% in period 24. Thus anywhere from 4% to 19% of the largest A-entries are above this particular cutoff. Since the uses to which such models are put normally cover a span of two years or less, it is also worth recording that in periods 4 and 8, 89% and 85% of the entries lie below the cutoff. Since an elasticity near the cutoff seems too small to be interesting, an earlier conjecture—that skewed distributions would provide guidance to a manageably small informative subset—has found support here.[‡]

[†] Very large values for elasticities ordinarily reflect a violation of the standard caveat that elasticities blow up because of near-zeros in the endogenous variable [recall that $\eta = (\partial y/\partial x)x/y$]. These do not often occur.

[‡] Most of the largest values were for variables of little behavioral interest that hovered around zero. Thus extreme values of federal and state-and-local deficits (NIASF and NIASSL) and the statistical discrepancy comprise well over half of all elasticities exceeding 5 in magnitude. These comments are based on an examination of all elasticities greater than 5 in periods 1 and 5.

Exhibit 4.1 Frequency distribution of homogeneous responses of the matrix A to 1% impulse input (elasticity scale).

Interval	Period 1	2	3	4	5	6	7	8	16	24
.000–0.001	45850	40657	36827	33731	30807	28646	26748	25053	22157	22243
.001–0.01	2966	5169	6765	8083	9393	10264	11037	11762	12127	11912
0.01–0.05	1859	3358	4519	5471	6338	7056	7697	8286	9085	8754
0.05–0.10	580	1018	1334	1627	1899	2103	2312	2448	3074	3142
0.10–0.20	458	879	1223	1415	1607	1762	1840	1913	2258	2403
0.20–0.30	239	408	552	670	737	797	917	984	1077	1082
0.30–0.40	112	214	292	360	413	470	475	530	701	605
0.40–0.50	77	134	203	227	267	289	315	322	463	460
0.50–0.60	63	111	135	166	199	217	208	212	282	343
0.60–0.70	66	102	113	152	180	195	200	197	256	318
0.70–0.80	39	61	80	101	118	129	160	165	197	223
0.80–0.90	32	57	82	84	101	103	112	123	186	208
0.90–1.0	34	67	69	75	77	85	87	96	147	148
1.0–5.0	407	518	552	583	607	629	642	675	786	913
5.0–10	44	66	75	80	84	87	85	65	51	61
10–50	56	68	68	64	63	59	56	60	43	63
50–100	8	5	6	8	9	8	8	8	9	7
> 100	10	8	5	3	1	1	1	1	1	15
Total	52900	52900	52900	52900	52900	52900	52900	52900	52900	52900

4.2 BLOCK STRUCTURE

Graphics

Exhibit 4.2 shows the impact, or period-1, A-matrix elasticities. There are four segments or groups in the model. For our purposes a group is either a simultaneous block or a recursive sequence (sometimes interrupted by a small, unimportant 2×2 block which we choose to ignore). The first group is a simultaneous block of 17 equations that contains the wage variable and all of its lags, or PPNF and various consumer goods prices, and their lags. The unit wage index variable, JCMH, ties the price-wage structure together as shown by the vertical "spike" and we also observe that PPNF depends on a great many constituent or sectoral price indices. The second group of 10 equations is a recursive segment exclusively in prices from various final demand sector prices (government, consumption, investment) and their lags. In effect then there is a simultaneous price-wage block that is "earliest" in the causal structure together with a recursive set of prices that depend on the first block. As a matter of terminology, low-order groups enter earliest in the causal chain, while high-order segments depend on low-order groups.

The third 80 equation group consists of the largest simultaneous block. It is the central core of the model: GNP, consumption, income, output determination. Some investment and capacity-utilization and numerous important monetary variables are also present.

The fourth group of 123 recursive rows includes economically important variables such as many forms of investment in plant, equipment, and housing, as well as prices of investment-goods output, unit cost of capital, and consumer durables that appear naturally recursive according to widely held economic beliefs. There are also recursive constructs that depend upon the earlier endogenous variables, as well as definitions that require behavioral outputs from earlier groups.

The numerous lag definitions and definitional variables in this fourth group are consistent with two sorts of behavior. One kind of behavior is that simple definitions, such as NIASF (the Federal NIA surplus or deficit), respond to model dynamics but do not influence them. The other main possibility is that some of the lag definitions have relatively little effect on the remainder of the model.

For periods 2 through 4 the dynamic matrices in Exhibits 4.3–4.5 closely resemble the impact results. However, one new wrinkle appears: elements above the diagonal, which reflect simultaneity, become more frequent in the progression from period 1 through period 2 to period 4. This pattern of growing density (simultaneity) persists subsequently.

Period 5 differs sharply from earlier periods, as shown in Exhibit 4.6. The first three groups prior to period 5 have now merged into a single 107-equation block. The causal structure for the rows below the first block have essentially the same constituents as block 4 in earlier periods. Recursive terms that were prominent throughout the earlier periods for several definitional variables have started to disappear. Thus, in this exhibit, the lower r.h.s. diagonal elements of group 2 have begun to vanish, since lag definitions have no separate causal dynamic structure of their own and depend upon economic behavioral variables lower down the causal chain.

Periods 16 and 24 (Exhibits 4.10 and 4.11) strongly resemble periods 5 through 8 (see Exhibits 4.6–4.9). This suggests that the system has come relatively close to equilibrium by the fifth period. By period 24 we observe a tall rectangle in which behavioral equation variables, their lags, and many current identities appear at the top in the simultaneous block of 86 rows and many lagged endogenous variables and other definitions appear towards the bottom; a number of behavioral variables in final demand (durables) and monetary variables follow the simultaneous block.

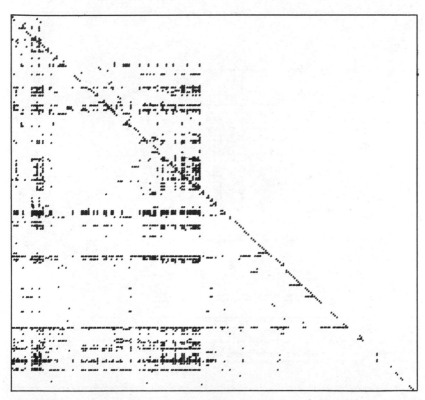

Exhibit 4.2 A matrix block structure: period 1, elasticity scale (filter level 0.05).

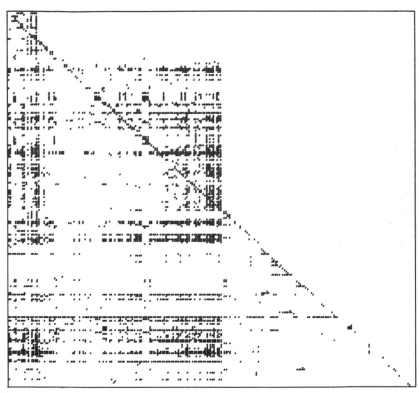

Exhibit 4.3 A matrix block structure: period 2, elasticity scale (filter level 0.05).

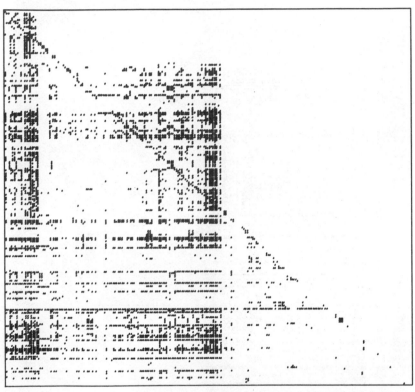

Exhibit 4.4 A matrix block structure: period 3, elasticity scale (filter level 0.05).

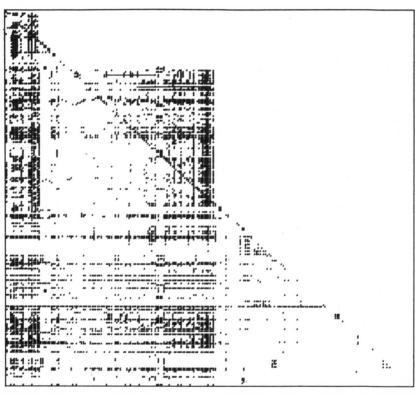

Exhibit 4.5 A matrix block structure: period 4, elasticity scale (filter level 0.05).

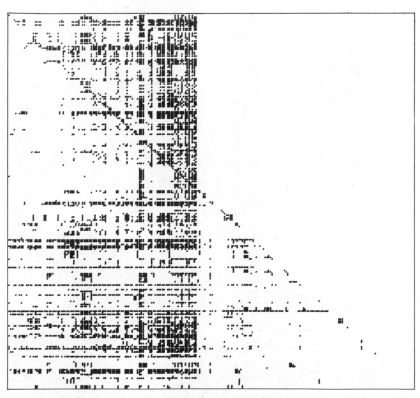

Exhibit 4.6 A matrix block structure: period 5, elasticity scale (filter level 0.05).

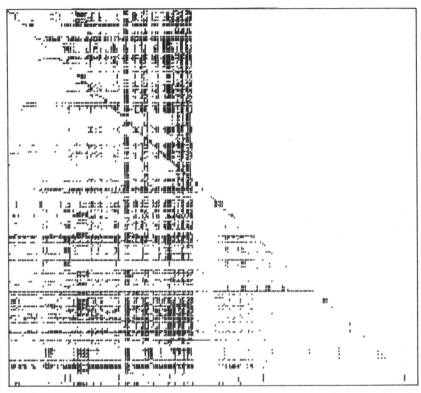

Exhibit 4.7   A matrix block structure: period 6, elasticity scale (filter level 0.05).

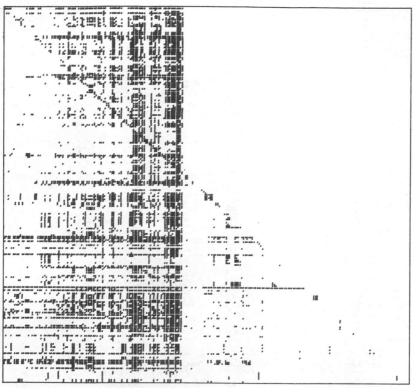

Exhibit 4.8 A matrix block structure: period 7, elasticity scale (filter level 0.05).

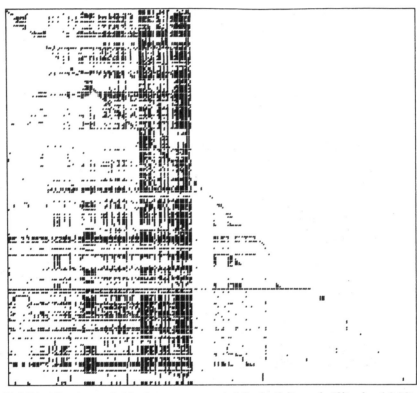

Exhibit 4.9 A matrix block structure: period 8, elasticity scale (filter level 0.05).

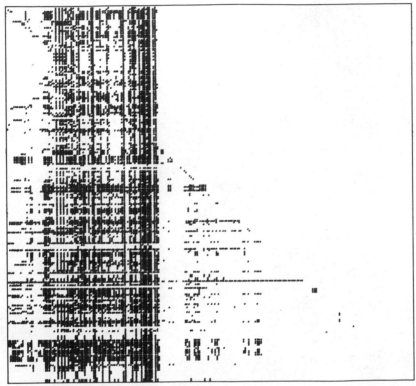

Exhibit 4.10 A matrix block structure: period 16, elasticity scale (filter level 0.05).

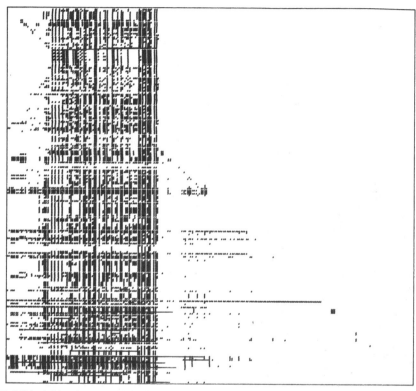

Exhibit 4.11   A matrix block structure: period 24, elasticity scale (filter level 0.05).

Broadly speaking, our results resemble other related analysis (see, e.g., Deleau and Malgrange, 1978). The analysis is in state-variable form and includes lagged-endogenous-variable definitions as current variables, instead of the more standard practice of block-ordering just current variables. However, the format of our results is similar to the usual one: a few variables appear before the main simultaneous income–demand block, which is then followed by a long "tail" of higher-order variables.

There is one major departure though. Instead of prices and wages being driven by the real sector, they appear to be of the lowest (i.e., most basic) order, at least initially, and thus drive the remainder of the equations, including the real-sector variables, becoming simultaneous with them in period 5. Thus the price–wage sector plays an unusually pivotal role. We shall explore this phenomenon more thoroughly.

Composition of Blocks

More fine detail of the block structure is shown in Exhibits 4.12–4.21. These tabulate the variable type—behavioral or construct (i.e., definitional)—and whether it is current or lagged, according to ten major economic categories. When the content is straightforward (e.g., that in Exhibit 4.12 concerned with block 1, period 1, where only wages and prices are involved), such facts have been noted, but more detailed shifts among categories across time can be gleaned from these tables.

It is immediately evident from Exhibit 4.12 that definitions dominate group 4. Behavioral variables are equally numerous in groups 3 and 4. It is also clear, for instance, that current-dollar GNP magnitudes (price-times-quantity definitions) appear predominantly in group 4. The simultaneous block grew by 13 variables in period 2, mainly as recursive dependent variables moved from group 4 into group 3. Next, skipping to period 4 (Exhibit 4.15), the large simultaneous block 3 shrinks somewhat as the "tail" group 4 increases, mainly as lag definitions are added.

The biggest change occurs in period 5, where we observe that three-fourths of prices and wages are combined in the first, simultaneous block and not in the recursive tail. Most of real investment is in the recursive tail, along with most monetary and endogenous government-expenditure variables.

Moving along to period 16 in Exhibit 4.20, we note that, compared with period 8, the large simultaneous block has diminished somewhat as the recursively dependent tail increased: most of the change occurred with current variables. This happens because real-investment and monetary

Exhibit 4.12 Composition of blocks, period 1.

Category	Block 1 Behavior Cur.	Block 1 Behavior Lag.	Block 1 Construct Cur.	Block 1 Construct Lag.	Total	Block 2 Behavior Cur.	Block 2 Behavior Lag.	Block 2 Construct Cur.	Block 2 Construct Lag.	Total
Wages and prices	6	8	1	2	17	4	4	1		9
Cost of capital										
Real aggregates						1				1
Real consumption										
Real investment										
Monetary										
Cur.-dollar GNP										
Income flows										
Taxes										
Government exp.										
Total	6	8	1	2	17	5	4	1		10

Exhibit 4.13 Composition of blocks, period 2.

Category	Block 1 Behavior Cur.	Block 1 Behavior Lag.	Block 1 Construct Cur.	Block 1 Construct Lag.	Total	Block 2 Behavior Cur.	Block 2 Behavior Lag.	Block 2 Construct Cur.	Block 2 Construct Lag.	Tota
Wages and prices	6	8	1	2	17	4	5	1		10
Cost of capital										
Real aggregates						1				1
Real consumption										
Real investment										
Monetary										
Cur.-dollar GNP										
Income flows										
Taxes										
Government exp.										
Total	6	8	1	2	17	5	5	1		11
Prior period:										
Rows added								1		1
Rows subtracted										

Exhibit 4.12   Continued

| | Block 3 | | | | | Block 4 | | | |
| Behavior | | Construct | | | Behavior | | Construct | | |
Cur.	Lag.	Cur.	Lag.	Total	Cur.	Lag.	Cur.	Lag.	Total
		1		1	4	4	4	7	19
							3	12	15
5	2	7	16	30	2	9	5	7	23
7	4			11			2		2
4	1	1		6	3	10	2	5	20
6	7	1	3	17	4	1	6	1	12
		2		2			13	2	15
5	1	2		8	1			1	2
2		2		4	5	1	2		8
		1		1	2	1		4	7
29	15	17	19	80	21	26	37	39	123

Exhibit 4.13   Continued

| | Block 3 | | | | | Block 4 | | | |
| Behavior | | Construct | | | Behavior | | Construct | | |
Cur.	Lag.	Cur.	Lag.	Total	Cur.	Lag.	Cur.	Lag.	Total
1		1		2	3	3	4	7	17
							3	12	15
5	2	7	16	30	2	9	5	7	23
7	4			11			2		2
5	2	1		8	2	9	2	5	18
6	7	1	3	17	4	1	6	1	12
		3		3			12	2	14
6	1	2	1	10					
4		2		6	3	1	2		6
1	1	1	3	6	1			1	2
35	17	18	23	93	15	23	36	35	109
6	2	1	4	13					
					6	3	1	4	14

Exhibit 4.14 Composition of blocks, period 3.

| | Block 1 | | | | | Block 2 | | | | |
| | Behavior | | Construct | | | Behavior | | Construct | | |
Category	Cur.	Lag.	Cur.	Lag.	Total	Cur.	Lag.	Cur.	Lag.	To‹
Wages and prices	6	8	1	2	17	5	6	1	2	1
Cost of capital										
Real aggregates	1				1					
Real consumption										
Real investment										
Monetary										
Cur.-dollar GNP										
Income flows										
Taxes										
Government exp.										
Total	7	8	1	2	18	5	6	1	2	1‹
Prior period:										
Rows added	1				1	1	1		2	‹
Rows subtracted						1				1

Exhibit 4.15 Composition of blocks, period 4.

| | Block 1 | | | | | Block 2 | | | | |
| | Behavior | | Construct | | | Behavior | | Construct | | |
Category	Cur.	Lag.	Cur.	Lag.	Total	Cur.	Lag.	Cur.	Lag.	Tota
Wages and prices	6	8	1	2	17	5	6	1	4	16
Cost of capital										
Real aggregates	1				1					
Real consumption										
Real investment										
Monetary										
Cur.-dollar GNP										
Income flows										
Taxes										
Government exp.										
Total	7	8	1	2	18	5	6	1	4	16
Prior period:										
Rows added									3	3
Rows subtracted									1	1

Exhibit 4.14 Continued

| | Block 3 | | | | | Block 4 | | | |
| Behavior | | Construct | | | Behavior | | Construct | | |
Cur.	Lag.	Cur.	Lag.	Total	Cur.	Lag.	Cur.	Lag.	Total
1		1		2	2	2	4	5	13
			1	1			3	11	14
4	1	7	15	27	3	10	5	8	26
7	4			11			2		2
4	1	1		6	3	10	2	5	20
6	7	1	3	17	4	1	6	1	12
		3		3			12	2	14
6	1	2	1	10					
5		2		7	2	1	2		5
1	1	1	3	6	1			1	2
34	15	18	23	90	15	24	36	33	108
1			1	2	2	2		1	5
2	2		1	5	2	1		3	6

Exhibit 4.15 Continued

| | Block 3 | | | | | Block 4 | | | |
| Behavior | | Construct | | | Behavior | | Construct | | |
Cur.	Lag.	Cur.	Lag.	Total	Cur.	Lag.	Cur.	Lag.	Total
1		1		2	2	2	4	3	11
		1	1	2			2	11	13
4	1	7	15	27	3	10	5	8	26
7	4			11			2		2
3	1	1		5	4	10	2	5	21
6	5	1	1	13	4	3	6	3	16
		3		3			12	2	14
6	1	2	1	10					
5		2		7	2	1	2		5
1	1	1	1	4	1			3	4
33	13	19	19	84	16	26	35	35	112
		1		1	1	2		5	8
1	2		4	7			1	3	4

Exhibit 4.16 Composition of blocks, period 5.

	Block 1					Block 2				
	Behavior		Construct			Behavior		Construct		
Category	Cur.	Lag.	Cur.	Lag.	Total	Cur.	Lag.	Cur.	Lag.	To
Wages and prices	12	14	3	5	34	2	2	4	4	
Cost of capital			1	1	2			2	11	
Real aggregates	5	1	7	15	28	3	10	5	8	
Real consumption	6	3			9	1	1	2		
Real investment	3	1	1		5	4	10	2	5	
Monetary	5	3	1	1	10	5	5	6	3	
Cur.-dollar GNP			2		2			13	2	
Income flows	6	1	2	1	10					
Taxes	4		2		6	3	1	2		
Government exp.			1		1	2	1		4	
Total	41	23	20	23	107	20	30	36	37	1

Exhibit 4.17 Composition of blocks, period 6.

	Block 1					Block 2				
	Behavior		Construct			Behavior		Construct		
Category	Cur.	Lag.	Cur.	Lag.	Total	Cur.	Lag.	Cur.	Lag.	Tot
Wages and prices	12	14	3	7	36	2	2	4	2	
Cost of capital			1		1			2	12	
Real aggregates	5	1	7	14	27	3	10	5	9	
Real consumption	5	3			8	2	1	2		
Real investment	3	1	1		5	4	10	2	5	
Monetary	5	2	1		8	5	6	6	4	
Cur.-dollar GNP			2		2			13	2	
Income flows	6	1	2	1	10					
Taxes	4		2		6	3	1	2		
Government exp.			1		1	2	1		4	
Total	40	22	20	22	104	21	31	36	38	12
Prior period:										
Rows added			3		3	1	1		4	
Rows subtracted	1	1		4	6				3	

Exhibit 4.18 Composition of blocks, period 7.

Category	Block 1 Behavior Cur.	Lag.	Construct Cur.	Lag.	Total	Block 2 Behavior Cur.	Lag.	Construct Cur.	Lag.	Total
Wages and prices	12	14	3	7	36	2	2	4	2	10
Cost of capital								3	12	15
Real aggregates	5	1	7	13	26	3	10	5	10	28
Real consumption	5	3			8	2	1	2		5
Real investment	3	1	1		5	4	10	2	5	21
Monetary	5	2	1		8	5	6	6	4	21
Cur.-dollar GNP			2		2			13	2	15
Income flows	6	1	2		9				1	1
Taxes	4		2		6	3	1	2		6
Government exp.			1		1	2	1		4	7
Total	40	22	19	20	101	21	31	37	40	129
Prior period:										
Rows added								1	2	3
Rows subtracted			1	2	3					

Exhibit 4.19 Composition of blocks, period 8.

Category	Block 1 Behavior Cur.	Lag.	Construct Cur.	Lag.	Total	Block 2 Behavior Cur.	Lag.	Construct Cur.	Lag.	Total
Wages and prices	12	14	3	7	36	2	2	4	2	10
Cost of capital								3	12	15
Real aggregates	5	1	6	13	25	3	10	6	10	29
Real consumption	5	3			8	2	1	2		5
Real investment	3	1	1		5	4	10	2	5	21
Monetary	6	3			9	4	5	7	4	20
Cur.-dollar GNP			2		2			13	2	15
Income flows	6	1	2		9				1	1
Taxes	5		2		7	2	1	2		5
Government exp.	1	1	1		3	1			4	5
Total	43	24	17	20	104	18	29	39	40	126
Prior period:										
Rows added	3	2			5			2		2
Rows subtracted			2		2	3	2			5

Exhibit 4.20 Composition of blocks, period 16.

Category	Block 1					Block 2				
	Behavior		Construct			Behavior		Construct		
	Cur.	Lag.	Cur.	Lag.	Total	Cur.	Lag.	Cur.	Lag.	Tota
Wages and prices	12	13	3	8	36	2	3	4	1	1
Cost of capital								3	12	1.
Real aggregates	5	1	5	10	21	3	10	7	13	3.
Real consumption	5	3			8	2	1	2		
Real investment	2		1		3	5	11	2	5	2
Monetary	3	2			5	7	6	7	4	2
Cur.-dollar GNP			2		2			13	2	1
Income flows	4	1	1		6	2		1	1	
Taxes	2		2		4	5	1	2		
Government exp.			1		1	2	1		4	
Total	33	20	15	18	86	28	33	41	42	14
Prior period:										
Rows added				1	1	10	4	2	3	1
Rows subtracted	10	4	2	3	19				1	1

Exhibit 4.21 Composition of blocks, period 24.

Category	Block 1					Block 2				
	Behavior		Construct			Behavior		Construct		
	Cur.	Lag.	Cur.	Lag.	Total	Cur.	Lag.	Cur.	Lag.	Total
Wages and prices	12	14	3	8	37	2	2	4	1	9
Cost of capital								3	12	15
Real aggregates	5	1	5	8	19	3	10	7	15	35
Real consumption	5	2			7	2	2	2		6
Real investment	2		1		3	5	11	2	5	23
Monetary	3	2			5	7	6	7	4	24
Cur.-dollar GNP			2		2			13	2	15
Income flows	5	1	1		7	1		1	1	3
Taxes	3		2		5	4	1	2		7
Government exp.			1		1	2	1		4	7
Total	35	20	15	16	86	26	33	41	44	144
Prior period:										
Rows added	2	1			3		1		2	3
Rows subtracted		1	2		3	2	1			2

variables switch among groups. Since period 24 is much the same as period 16, no further comments are needed.

Other Filter Levels

Results for three other filter levels besides 0.05 will now be discussed. For filters of 0.01 and 0.03, the model breaks into two groups from the outset: one simultaneous block of roughly 150–180 variables followed by a recursive tail. The latter (depending on the period) contains HOUSES and its lags, some investment variables, identities, and some monetary variables. In short, as is implicit in the filtering procedure, the number of groups and what they contain clearly depend on the filter level. For the very small filters just described, most variables of interest are simultaneous from the outset.

The last filter experiment was at the level 0.10, which yields a more erratic time path. Upon impact, there is a price–wage simultaneous block of 12 followed immediately by a simultaneous block of 22 entries of income and consumption and GNP72. The remainder is a long recursive tail in which most of the variables are driven by the earlier blocks and each other. Period 8 (these computations were made at longer intervals) begins with a simultaneous 38-equation block of prices, wages, and income, followed by a short recursive segment (seven equations) of a few price and monetary variables, a small simultaneous block of investment, investment prices, and lagged GNP72, and then, as always, a long recursive tail of 187 variables. More simultaneity occurs in period 16, with the largest initial block of 54 price, wage, income, and demand variables.

There is a crude logic to all of this. Clearly, small filters lead to larger initial simultaneous blocks. The causal ordering is broadly the same, but the structural breakdown (simultaneous vs. recursive segments) changes from filter to filter without strong patterns. Thus, while filtering cleans out weak simultaneity by zeroing out the small magnitudes, and helps to reveal a causal structure, it does so ambiguously, since the filter choice is ambiguous.

This observation also has a bearing on linearization. For instance, in 1979 2, a filter level of 0.10 results in block orderings for the first and for the last linearization dates which are nearly the same. Yet when the filter is dropped to 0.05, the low-order price block merges with the large simultaneous block for the last two linearization dates, but not for the first two linearization dates (to recall, the dates are 1973 2, 1975 2, 1977 2, and 1979 2). We surmise that the higher levels of capacity utilization in the latter two periods create a stronger price–capacity (and thus real-sector) interaction than in the earlier years, which had more excess capacity. Some persistent generalizations nevertheless emerge:

1. Consumer prices and wages are lowest in the causal order—or concurrent with...
2. An income-demand simultaneous block, which is in turn followed by...
3. A recursive tail of investment, investment prices, and sometimes monetary variables, together with many definitions.

4.3   HOMOGENEOUS RESPONSES: KEY ENDOGENOUS VARIABLES

In this section we describe what happens to price–wage endogenous dynamics in response to a 1% impulse in their own initial conditions. Some other variable responses are studied in the same manner. Finally, we comment on off-diagonal as distinct from "own" (i.e., diagonal) homogeneous responses of endogenous variables. This will complete our review of the homogeneous system as a prelude to subsequent analysis, all of which will involve forcing functions that operate through the homogeneous dynamics.

Wages and Prices

The first and most important observations apparent from Exhibit 4.22 concern the key price and wage variables, PPNF and JCMH. The JCMH elasticity is 1.19 on impact and then grows steadily to a peak of 1.68 in period 16, declining only slightly by period 24. Comparable behavior is evident in PPNF. It starts at about 1.10 and remains there through period 8, increasing slightly thereafter. Neither one displays dynamic stability. Stability is indicated by a response to a given impulse input that returns toward zero after the initial period. With varying degrees of severity, consumption-goods prices follow the same pattern: PCS's response nearly doubles (1.62 in period 1 and 2.82 in period 24), while all the others either remain large (i.e., above unity) throughout or even grow over the 24-quarter interval.

Prices of investment in plant or housing (PINC, PIRC) hover in the neighborhood of 1.10 throughout, while in varying degrees equipment prices reveal larger and more explosive price responses, as witnessed by the bottom three rows of Exhibit 4.22. Productivity behavior does not lie directly at the root of the problem, since the relevant productivity variables do not display any noticeably unstable dynamics.

Exhibit 4.22 MQEM homogeneous-dynamics response to own 1% impulse input (elasticity scale).[a]

Price or Wage Variable	Period 1	2	3	4	5	6	7	8	16	24
QHT1	0.0000	0.0000	0.0000	0.0000	0.0000	0.0000	0.0000	0.0000	0.0000	0.0000
QMHT	0.0000	0.0000	0.0000	0.0000	0.0000	0.0000	0.0000	0.0000	0.0000	0.0000
JCMH	1.1991	1.2181	1.2618	1.3236	1.3997	1.4685	1.5229	1.5680	1.6833	1.4981
JCMHD	0.0000	0.0000	0.0000	0.0000	0.0000	0.0000	0.0000	0.0000	0.0000	0.0000
ULC77	0.0000	0.0000	0.0000	0.0000	0.0000	0.0000	0.0000	0.0000	0.0000	0.1073
PPNF	1.0986	1.0984	1.0987	1.0996	1.1010	1.1031	1.1058	1.1094	1.1558	1.1184
PGNP	0.0000	0.0000	0.0000	0.0000	0.0000	0.0000	0.0000	0.0000	0.0000	0.0000
PC	0.0000	0.0000	0.0000	0.0668	0.0832	0.0770	0.0612	0.0000	0.0000	0.0000
PCDO	1.5448	1.7478	1.8362	1.8753	1.8931	1.9017	1.9059	1.9075	1.8820	1.8179
PCDA	1.0557	1.0557	1.0562	1.0572	1.0585	1.0600	1.0613	1.0622	1.0625	1.0534
PCDFE	1.3149	1.3877	1.4077	1.4154	1.4210	1.4270	1.4329	1.4377	1.4422	1.4008
PCN	1.2619	1.2910	1.3034	1.3209	1.3436	1.3704	1.3917	1.4050	1.3678	1.2154
PCS	1.6226	1.8400	1.9510	2.0333	2.1154	2.2084	2.3000	2.3816	2.7654	2.8045
PIPD	0.0000	0.0000	0.0000	0.0000	0.0000	0.0000	0.0000	0.0000	0.0000	0.0000
PINC	1.3884	1.4678	1.4890	1.4944	1.4955	1.4952	1.4945	1.4934	1.4672	1.4250
PIRC	1.1259	1.1256	1.1250	1.1240	1.1225	1.1205	1.1181	1.1152	1.0737	1.0023
PG	1.1300	1.1299	1.1287	1.1256	1.1200	1.1069	1.0848	1.0568	0.7876	0.5382
PCPI	1.1038	1.1037	1.1036	1.1034	1.1031	1.1027	1.1023	1.1017	1.0915	1.0679
PIBF	0.0000	0.0000	0.0000	0.0000	0.0000	0.0000	0.0000	0.0000	0.0000	0.0000
PIPDQ	1.8867	2.4171	2.7825	3.0338	3.2063	3.3243	3.4046	3.4585	3.5189	3.3762
PIPDAG	1.7026	2.0035	2.1591	2.2392	2.2802	2.3006	2.3103	2.3141	2.2831	2.1934
PIPDO	1.5979	1.8462	1.9651	2.0217	2.0484	2.0606	2.0657	2.0673	2.0421	1.9742

[a]Only responses for elasticity values greater than 0.05 appear in this table.

177

Exhibit 4.23 Homogeneous response of selected macroeconomic variables to own 1% impulse input (elasticity scale).[a]

Variable	Period 1	2	3	4	5	6	7	8	16	24
Cost of capital										
UCKNC	0.0000	0.0000	0.0000	0.0000	0.0000	0.0000	0.0000	0.0000	0.0000	0.0000
UCKPDQ	0.0000	0.0000	0.0000	0.0000	0.0000	0.0000	0.0000	0.0000	0.0000	0.0000
Real GNP										
GNP72	0.0000	−0.0634	−0.1353	−0.2246	−0.2540	−0.2757	−0.2907	−0.3084	−0.3371	−0.4055
YD72	0.0000	0.0000	0.0000	0.0000	0.0000	0.0000	0.0000	0.0000	0.0000	0.0000
M72	0.8783	0.5862	0.3815	0.2426	0.1515	0.0936	0.0580	0.0000	0.0000	0.0000
JCAP	1.1074	1.0647	1.0232	0.9826	0.9426	0.9033	0.8645	0.8265	0.5609	0.3664
JCU	0.0000	0.0000	0.0000	0.0000	0.0000	0.0000	0.0000	0.0000	0.0000	0.0000
QMH77	1.0694	1.0721	1.0743	1.0760	1.0771	1.0774	1.0771	1.0761	1.0557	1.0266
RUG	0.3977	0.1936	0.0948	0.0000	0.0000	0.0000	0.0000	0.0000	0.0000	0.0000
Real consumption										
C72	0.0000	0.0000	0.0000	0.0000	0.0000	0.0000	0.0000	0.0000	0.0000	0.0000
CDA72	0.0000	0.0000	0.0000	0.0000	0.0000	0.0000	0.0000	0.0000	0.0000	0.0000
CDO72	1.0723	0.9383	0.8214	0.7193	0.6300	0.5519	0.4835	0.4235	0.1494	0.0586
CDFE72	0.8954	0.8954	0.8305	0.7837	0.7366	0.6925	0.6502	0.6101	0.3682	0.2340
CS72	1.1670	1.1619	1.1559	1.1496	1.1422	1.1340	1.1247	1.1148	1.0407	1.0046
CN72	0.9015	0.7090	0.5638	0.4546	0.3709	0.3057	0.2538	0.2119	0.0730	0.0600

Real investment

IBF72	0.0000	0.0000	0.0000	0.0000	0.0000	0.0000	0.0000	0.0000	0.0000	0.0000
IBFPD72	0.0000	0.0000	0.0000	0.0000	0.0000	0.0000	0.0000	0.0000	0.0000	0.0000
IBFNC72	1.0350	0.9368	0.8599	0.7691	0.6836	0.6049	0.5328	0.4677	0.1521	0.0502
SINV72	1.0385	0.8988	0.7712	0.6588	0.5610	0.4771	0.4056	0.3447	0.0950	0.0000
IINV72	0.2855	0.0000	0.0000	0.0000	0.0000	0.0000	0.0000	0.0000	0.0000	0.0000
IRC72	1.2340	1.0621	0.8559	0.6750	0.5290	0.4147	0.3265	0.2594	0.0840	0.0000

Monetary

M2PLUS	1.8406	2.0979	2.2127	2.2628	2.2833	2.2905	2.2915	2.2899	2.2662	2.2362
M1BPLUS	1.4392	1.4770	1.4555	1.4219	1.3869	1.3530	1.3207	1.2900	1.0932	0.9314
RTB	0.7634	0.4263	0.2166	0.1082	0.0561	0.0000	0.0000	0.0000	0.0000	0.0000
RCD	0.4993	0.2445	0.1199	0.0586	0.0000	0.0000	0.0000	0.0000	0.0000	0.0000
RAAA	0.9346	0.8481	0.7694	0.6982	0.6336	0.5753	0.5230	0.4764	0.2456	0.1357

Cur.-dollar GNP

GNP	0.0000	0.0000	0.0000	0.0000	0.0000	0.0000	0.0000	0.0000	-0.0802	-0.1112
YPWS	1.3894	1.4826	1.5599	1.6347	1.7059	1.7727	1.8354	1.8913	2.2789	2.6302
YCBT	0.0000	0.0000	0.0000	0.0000	0.0000	0.0000	0.0000	0.0000	0.0000	0.0000

[a]Only responses for elasticity values greater than 0.05 appear in this table.

Some Other Macroeconomic Variables

GNP72 in Exhibit 4.23 follows an ever steeper downward path, beginning at -0.06 in period 2 and thereafter decreasing to -0.41 in period 24. The largest current-dollar disposable-personal-income component, private-sector wages and salaries (YPWS), follows an upward path, growing from 1.39 to about twice that rate in moving from period 1 to period 24. Apart from the unstable results noted above, selected components of real final demand (except for CS72, which appears borderline stable) exhibit a consistent pattern of nonoscillatory decay. As would be expected, because of long lags there is substantial sluggishness in investment. Consumption responses behave similarly. Only CN72 decays rapidly, while in investment the same is true only for IRC72. Still the main impression is one of stability, although sluggish responses dominate.

It is interesting to note that while the static identity GNP72 has a negative long-run response to perturbations on its own initial value, its recorded components respond positively to perturbations of their own lagged values. The reduced-form matrix A does not explicitly recognize the constraints imposed by static identities *after* t_0, although they are built into the structural equation system and hence are operative *at* t_0. If the constraints were imposed after t_0, however, the answers would be identical. When the responses of GNP72 to perturbations of all its components are summed and scaled appropriately, they are equal to the values shown for GNP72. This apparent discrepancy is a useful model diagnostic: while the consumption and investment variables have their own positive damped internal dynamics, the GNP72 identity links with the rest of the model, causing it to have negative growth. So the dynamic behavior of identities and their components can be analyzed separately. In this instance one diagnostic implication is clearly that the MQEM GNP72 identity is essential in the determination of model behavior, while in other circumstances identities can prove innocuous.

In the monetary sector, the money stocks are explosive upward, and the short-term interest rates RTB and RCD decay to zero in about one year, while long-term rates decay slowly but in stable fashion. For labor, unemployment responses are swift. QMH77, the measure of productivity relevant to employment, is explosive, remaining in the vicinity of 1.07–1.02 throughout.

Since the "own" dynamics of GNP72 components are stable and GNP72 itself is not, we confront an apparent contradiction. We believe that the answer lies in the price–wage sector. As we have seen, this sector is lower in the causal order initially and then becomes simultaneous; *its* dynamics are clearly not stable.

Homogeneous Off-Diagonal Impulse Responses

Striking results are apparent for wage–price dynamics when we consider off-diagonal impulse responses. Specifically, the effect of PPNF on $\Delta \ln$ JCMH, the rate of change of wages, is small, while the effect of $\Delta \ln$ JCMH on $\Delta \ln$ PPNF, the rate of change of the private-product deflator, is large, especially in periods 4 and 8. JCMH initial-condition perturbations strongly affect investment or consumption prices individually and in the aggregate (e.g., $\Delta \ln$ PGNP, $\Delta \ln$ PIBF), while PPNF does not. PC also strongly affects prices. Since PC enters with large weight in the wage equation, it appears that this feedback, already noted in Chapter 3, is quantitatively powerful.

We summarize our impression of the homogeneous dynamics as follows. Wage and price changes are borderline unstable. This arises in "own" homogeneous responses, while wages have their strongest impact on prices, not the reverse. That apparent almost one-way causality is *not* correct, however, since prices feed back on wages through PC. We shall endeavor to pinpoint this feedback loop more precisely in subsequent chapters.

REFERENCES

Ando, Albert and F. M. Fisher (1963), Near-Decomposability, Partition and Aggregation, and the Relevance of Stability. In *Essays on the Structure of Social Science Models*. (A. Ando, F. M. Fisher, and H. Simon, Eds.), MIT Press, Cambridge, MA. [Reprinted from *International Economic Review*, Vol. 4, No. 1 (January 1963).]

Boutillier, Michel (1983), The Concept of Reading as Analysis of Macroeconomic Models. In *Fourth IFAC/IFORS/IIAAS Conference on the Modelling and Control of National Economies and the 1983 SEDC Conference on Economic Dynamics and Control* (Tamer Basar, Ed.), Preprints, McGregor and Werner, Washington, DC.

Gilli, Manfred (1979), *Étude et Analyse des Structure Causales dans les Modèles Économique*, Editions Peter Lang, Berne.

Simon, Herbert and A. Ando (1963), Aggregation of Variables in Dynamic Systems. In *Essays on the Structure of Social Science Models* (A. Ando, F. M. Fisher, and H. Simon, Eds.), MIT Press, Cambridge, MA. [Reprinted from *Econometrica*, Vol. 2a, No. 2 (April 1961).]

Tarjan, Robert (1972), Depth First Search and Linear Graph Algorithms, *SIAM Journal of Computing*, Vol. 1, pp. 146–160.

CHAPTER 5

Multiplier and Parameter Perturbations in the MQEM

The methods developed in Chapter 2 will now be applied in order to learn about important variables and coefficients. We consider the impact on selected variables of changes in all the model's parameters and exogenous variables. Most emphasis has been given to PPNF, JCMH, and QMH77.[†] Since our focus is the analysis of inflation, we chose PPNF, the most inclusive price variable, and one which enters into most other price equations. Also, JCMH is the private-sector wage rate as well as a major factor in PPNF's unit-labor-cost variable. Price–wage interactions obviously deserve special attention. Equally, since (transformations of) the basic productivity variable, QMH77, directly affects unit labor costs in PPNF, it too has been singled out.[‡]

Section 5.1 of this chapter is about multipliers: exogenous prices, fiscal variables, and monetary-policy variables. Partial root responses use aggregates of the root decomposition described in Chapter 2 to indicate root–exogenous-variable coupling. Next, Section 5.2 extends the interpretation of parameter-perturbation elasticities in the context of particular nonlinearities which occur repeatedly in the MQEM's structural equations (exactly parallel consequences arise for multipliers). Then parameter-perturbation responses are used to identify the important structural elements. Although only the three main variables are dealt with in much detail, a graphic summary shows that a much larger number of important elements are also

---

[†]Although this analysis focuses on a subset of three variables, little information about the total model is lost. From our analysis of all the model's responses, a surprising result was that if a perturbation (especially for parameters) was important in one part of the model, it tended to be important in many sectors. This seems to be a consequence both of the tight interconnections in the MQEM, mainly through identities, and of well-defined properties of certain equations that make them influential.

[‡]The reader should review Appendix 3B for detailed equation structure.

pinpointed. Partial root decompositions associated with parameter perturbations are used to isolate the roots with important implications for the MQEM's dynamic structure. Section 5.3 discusses the properties of some roots that prior analysis has indicated are most heavily involved with interesting price–wage–productivity behavior. The chapter conclusion, Section 5.4, provides an overall summary. The reader may find it easiest to start there before plunging into the detailed report that perforce makes up most of this chapter. An appendix describes some detailed technical issues about conditioning and root sensitivities.

5.1 MULTIPLIERS

Only a few exogenous variables are significant for the issues at hand. The important exogenous prices are farm prices (PFP) and other raw material prices (PCRUDE), whose movement is dominated by petroleum prices. The usual financial policy instruments, the monetary base MBASE and the discount rate RDIS, are relevant for our purposes as well. There are also three pertinent fiscal variables: state and local government expenditure on goods and services (GSL), nonmilitary federal outlays for expenditure on goods and services (GFO), and federal government wages and salaries (YGWS). Federal military outlay (GFD) had much the same effect as nonmilitary outlay and therefore has not been discussed separately. All remaining multiplier computations were made. None of the other exogenous variables had broad influences on the three main variables, PPNF, JCMH, and QMH77,[†] or on most other variables in the model.[‡]

Exogenous Price Multipliers

Exhibits 5.1 and 5.2 summarize as elasticities what happens when impulse inputs for PFP and PCRUDE multipliers are calculated for the linearized MQEM. Prices, wages, and productivity are measured as changes in logarithms (designated as DL or $\Delta \ln$) to reflect percentage rates of change, for reasons given in Section 5.2. The largest multiplier effects are completed by period 4 for PFP and period 6 for PCRUDE, a comment based on the fact that

[†]All of the productivity, price, and wage variables have been transformed from levels to rates of change. This transformation is described in detail in the context of parameter perturbations later in this chapter. Transformed variables are identified by a prefix $\Delta \ln$ or DL (for "delta log").

[‡]Two other exogenous variables, PAUTO and YPINT (automobile prices and personal interest payments), were next in importance and could have been included in the discussion. Since their intrinsic economic interest is less than that of the variables listed, they were excluded from the text.

Exhibit 5.1 Multiplier elasticity response to PFP impulse.

Variable	Period 1	2	3	4	5	6	7	8	12	16	24
Productivity											
Δ ln QHT1			−0.04	−0.11	−0.19	−0.20	−0.10	0.05	0.09	−0.04	0.02
Δ ln QMHT					−0.02	−0.04	−0.07	−0.09		0.11	
Δ ln QMH77	−0.89		0.82	0.32	0.18	0.05		−0.01	−0.03		−0.01
Prices and wages											
Δ ln JCMH		0.36	0.16	−0.12	−0.10	−0.05	−0.03	−0.02	−0.06	−0.02	
Δ ln JCMHD	−3.99	2.64	1.82	0.01	−0.23	−0.16	−0.04	0.04	−0.09		
Δ ln ULC77	0.66	0.61	−0.29	−0.42	−0.28	−0.11	−0.04	−0.02	−0.08	−0.03	
Δ ln PPNF		3.97	−3.83	0.18	0.14	0.08	−0.09	−0.16	−0.03	−0.03	
Δ ln PC	3.75	−1.80	−1.39	−0.24	0.02	0.06	−0.02	−0.08	−0.03	−0.03	
Δ ln PCDO		1.83	−0.98	−0.34	−0.08		−0.04	−0.09	−0.03	−0.03	
Δ ln PCDA		1.45	−1.41	0.07	0.05	0.03	−0.03	−0.06	−0.01	−0.01	
Δ ln PCDFE		4.15	−0.32	−2.34	−0.36	0.07	−0.01	0.21	−0.07	−0.06	−0.01
Δ ln PCN	10.78	−6.87	−3.19	−0.43		0.05	−0.04	−0.09	−0.02	−0.02	
Δ ln PCS		0.74	−0.35	−0.06	0.04	0.07		−0.06	−0.04	−0.04	−0.01
Δ ln PIPD		2.74	−1.19	−0.49	−0.17	−0.03	−0.07	−0.14	−0.06	−0.05	−0.01
Δ ln PINC		3.17	−2.21	−0.45	−0.01	0.06	−0.05	−0.14	−0.04	−0.03	
Δ ln PIRC		0.44	0.67	0.11	−0.24	−0.17	−0.10	−0.08	−0.11	−0.04	−0.02
Δ ln PIBF		2.85	−1.52	−0.50	−0.11	0.02	−0.06	−0.14	−0.05	−0.04	−0.01
Δ ln PIPDQ		1.89	−0.53	−0.28	−0.12	−0.05	−0.07	−0.12	−0.08	−0.05	−0.02
Δ ln PIPDAG		2.38	−1.07	−0.44	−0.15	−0.03	−0.07	−0.13	−0.05	−0.04	−0.01
Δ ln PIPDO		3.23	−1.57	−0.60	−0.18	−0.02	−0.08	−0.16	−0.06	−0.04	−0.01
Δ ln PGNP	2.19	−0.15	−1.51	−0.15	0.01	0.04	−0.03	−0.09	−0.03	−0.03	
Δ ln PG		2.23	−2.16	0.10	0.08	0.05	−0.05	−0.09	−0.02	−0.02	
Δ ln PCPI	4.03	−1.91	−1.48	−0.29	0.08	0.06	−0.02	−0.08	−0.03	−0.03	
Cost of capital											
UCKNC		0.03	0.01								
UCKPDQ		0.02	−0.43		−0.03	−0.04	0.39	−0.03	0.04	0.02	

184

Real GNP components

GNP72			−0.01						
YD72		−0.01	−0.01						
M72				−0.01					
SERVE72									
JCAP		−0.02	−0.01						
JCU									
QMH77									
RUG	0.05	0.10	0.08	0.04	0.02	0.01			

Real consumption

C72	−0.01		−0.02						
CDA72									
CDO72	0.01								
CDFE72									
CS72									
CN72	−0.03	−0.01							

Real investment

IBF72			−0.01	−0.01					
IBFPD72			−0.01	−0.01					
IBFNC72			−0.01						
SINV72									
IINV72		−0.14	−0.15	−0.04		0.02	0.02	0.02	0.01
IRC72									

Monetary

M1BPLUS									
M2PLUS									
RTB						0.02			
RCD		−0.03	−0.02						
RAAA		0.01	0.01						

Current-dollar GNP

GNP									
YPWS									
YCBT	−0.04	0.08	−0.03			0.01	0.01		

185

Exhibit 5.2 Multiplier elasticity response to PCRUDE impulse.

Variable	Period 1	2	3	4	5	6	7	8	12	16	24
Productivity											
Δ ln QHT1				-0.08	-0.22	-0.37	-0.43	-0.24	0.28	-0.06	0.10
Δ ln QMHT						-0.04	-0.09	-0.15	-0.09	0.13	0.08
Δ ln QMH77	-0.02	-1.39	-0.14	1.58	0.67	0.33	0.08	-0.08	-0.04	0.01	-0.03
Prices and wages											
Δ ln ICMH			0.21	0.26	-0.04	-0.13	-0.07	-0.04	-0.04	-0.03	
Δ ln ICMHD		-2.60	-0.34	2.81	0.49	-0.18	-0.15	-0.05	-0.02		
Δ ln ULC77	0.02	1.00	0.46	-0.64	-0.50	-0.42	-0.16	-0.01	-0.04	-0.04	
Δ ln PPNF		7.24		-7.02	0.16	0.14	0.06	-0.10	-0.05	-0.04	
Δ ln PC		2.45	0.73	-2.15	-0.53	-0.09		-0.03	-0.05	-0.04	-0.01
Δ ln PCDO		3.34	1.45	-2.63	-1.06	-0.39	-0.14	-0.11	-0.07	-0.04	
Δ ln PCDA		2.65		-2.60	0.06	0.05	0.02	-0.04	-0.02	0.02	
Δ ln PCDFE		7.57	6.63	-5.44	-5.65	-1.22	-0.17	-0.10	-0.16	-0.08	-0.01
Δ ln PCN		3.89	0.64	-3.70	-0.52		0.03	-0.05	-0.04	-0.03	
Δ ln PCS		1.35	0.60	-1.04	-0.37	-0.09		-0.02	-0.06	-0.05	-0.01
Δ ln PIPD	-8.61	9.20	4.69	-2.35	-1.12	-0.51	-0.24	-0.19	-0.14	-0.07	-0.01
Δ ln PINC	14.17	9.60	-11.29	-8.64	-2.19	-0.47	-0.08	-0.10	-0.07	-0.05	-0.01
Δ ln PIRC	13.17	-12.98	0.31	0.73	0.42	-0.14	-0.26	-0.21	-0.11	-0.07	-0.02
Δ ln PIBF	-0.80	9.22	-0.74	-4.42	-1.48	-0.48	-0.14	-0.16	-0.13	-0.06	-0.01
Δ ln PIPDQ	-2.63	4.25	2.92	-1.34	-0.84	-0.51	-0.32	-0.26	-0.17	-0.08	-0.02
Δ ln PIPDAG		4.35	2.24	-3.04	-1.47	-0.67	-0.31	-0.22	-0.11	-0.06	-0.01
Δ ln PIPDO	-13.00	12.53	5.95	-2.84	-1.22	-0.46	-0.17	-0.16	-0.12	-0.06	-0.01
Δ ln PGNP	0.54	2.77	0.38	-2.71	-0.40	-0.08	-0.01	-0.06	-0.06	-0.04	
Δ ln PG		4.07		-3.98	0.09	0.08	0.03	-0.06	-0.03	-0.03	
Δ ln PCPI		2.67	0.86	-2.37	-0.67	-0.13	0.01		-0.05	-0.04	-0.01
Cost of capital											
UCKNC	0.09	0.16	0.10	0.03			0.77	0.77	0.07	0.02	
UCKPDQ	-0.02	0.02	-0.75	-0.78		-0.03					

186

Real-GNP components

	1	2	3	4	5	6	7	8	9
GNP72	−0.01	−0.02							
YD72	−0.03	−0.03							
M72	−0.02	−0.02	−0.01						
SERVE72									
JCAP									
JCU	−0.02	−0.03	−0.03	−0.01					
QMH77									
RUG	0.09	0.18	0.14	0.08	0.03	0.01	0.01	0.01	−0.01

Real consumption

	1	2	3	4	5	6	7	8	9
C72		−0.01							
CDA72		−0.04	−0.03						
CDO72		−0.02	−0.02	−0.01					
CDFE72		−0.01	−0.02	−0.01					
CS72									
CN72	−0.01	−0.02							

Real investment

	1	2	3	4	5	6	7	8	9
IBF72				−0.02	−0.02	−0.01			
IBFPD72				−0.02	−0.02	−0.01			
IBFNC72			−0.01	−0.03	−0.03	−0.02			
SINV72									
IINV72	−0.01	−0.24	−0.29	−0.09	0.02	0.03	0.04	0.01	−0.02
IRC72				0.02	0.02	0.01		0.02	−0.01

Monetary

	1	2	3	4	5	6	7	8	9
M1BPLUS	−0.01	−0.01		0.02					
M2PLUS	−0.01	−0.01		0.02					
RTB	−0.02	−0.02		0.01					
RCD	−0.06	−0.09	−0.04	0.05	0.07	0.03			
RAAA	0.02	0.04		0.02					

Current-dollar GNP

	1	2	3	4	5	6	7	8	9
GNP	0.01								
YPWS	0.01	0.01							
YCBT	−0.12	0.24	0.19	−0.03	0.01	0.02	0.02		

no elasticity exceeds unity thereafter. Raw-material prices have consequences for prices only and do not spill over into real or monetary variables. The elasticities often alternate in sign, which is a direct consequence of the differenced form used to describe the price equations in the MQEM, largely for statistical convenience.

From an examination of PFP effects in Exhibit 5.1, large but nearly offsetting responses are apparent in periods 2 and 3 for $\Delta \ln$ PPNF (row 7). These are followed by small but persistent damped oscillations. The effect on wages, $\Delta \ln$ JCMH (row 4), is positive on balance—sizably so in periods 2 and 3. Then there is a sequence of smaller negative responses that partially counteract the positive initial impact. $\Delta \ln$ PCN has the largest positive initial response to PFP, but this is mostly offset by period 4. While in Exhibit 5.2 time patterns of response to PCRUDE are slower than those for PFP, the tendency to have a net cumulative influence close to zero by period 8 is again manifest, as large initial effects are shortly compensated by subsequent opposite responses.

Fiscal-Policy Multipliers

Impulse multipliers for state and local government expenditures and nonmilitary federal outlays are shown in Exhibits 5.3 and 5.4. State and local expenditures have larger effects than federal. However, there is less effective discretionary control over expenditures at the state and local level. While there could be some implications for the design of federal grant-in-aid policy,[†] this difference in behavior is otherwise unimportant. $\Delta \ln$ PPNF reacts with a delay to an impulse in GSL. The response then attains a maximum in period 7 and trails off. $\Delta \ln$ JCMH has two peaks. There is "one of its own" in period 2 through 5, and a later, smaller one·that probably is induced through PC, which persists through period 12. Some sectoral prices are powerfully influenced through period 12 (see the investment deflators and some for consumption). The $\Delta \ln$ PGNP response is a first-difference "sawtooth" in periods 1 and 2, followed by a steady positive buildup to an elasticity of 0.78 in period 7, which damps out by period 12. Endogenous monetary responses to fiscal impulses are negligible. While the effect on GNP72 decays rapidly to zero by period 5, the response of RUG (global unemployment) is predictably negative through period 6 but positive thereafter. The net effect of the impulse in GSL is to reduce unemployment permanently. Since GFO and YGWS largely mirror GSL although with less

---

[†] Intergovernmental financing is a complicated matter, so this observation needs to be reviewed in a more detailed study.

intensity, we shall not comment on them further. Exhibits 5.4 and 5.5 tabulate their consequences.

Some lesser aspects of multipliers deserve mention. First, the minimum wage variable WUSMIN has a large effect on $\Delta \ln$ JCMH that nets to zero because of first-differencing. WUSMIN's impact on $\Delta \ln$ PPNF nets to zero for related reasons, but in periods 2 and 6 (elasticities $+0.68$, -0.63, respectively), because of the functional form of the unit-labor-cost variable in the PPNF equation. Second, export quantities X72 have a moderate positive elasticity effect (0.12 to 0.42) from period 5 through period 8 on $\Delta \ln$ PPNF.

Monetary-Instrument Multipliers

Monetary variables naturally induce different behavior. The monetary base has no effect on PPNF through the sixth period (see Exhibit 5.6). Thereafter MBASE's influence builds to a small maximum of 0.11 by period 12 and then diminishes. $\Delta \ln$ JCMH registers quite small positive effects from MBASE, beginning in period 3. Offsets are not complete, i.e., an impulse leaves a "permanent" long-term effect. The delayed effect of MBASE on $\Delta \ln$ PPNF from investment components is also apparent, IINV72 and IRC72 in particular. Real measures of aggregates (e.g., GNP72) are barely affected. Exhibit 5.7 for RDIS shows qualitatively similar results to MBASE, that is, it affects the same variables with comparable magnitudes.[†]

Monetary exogenous-variable MBASE and RDIS impulses naturally affect endogenous monetary variables, interest rates in particular. Short-term interest-rate responses are of the expected sign. These fade within four or five periods. Long-term rate responses are weaker and stretch out over a longer interval as a consequence of the term structure relations. Prices also react, but with a delay. $\Delta \ln$ PIRC registers strongly on impact, but its response has died out by period 7. Productivity-growth effects are oscillatory. These do not damp out fully, but on balance respond negatively to MBASE.

Standard Multipliers: A Summary

Let us summarize the main linear multiplier outcomes. PFP and PCRUDE have some influence on productivity, but do not cut across economic sectors into final demand or monetary variables. They noticeably affect prices and the wage rate, although because of cancellation, their small net impact is

[†]Obviously, if the monetary authorities could exert greater influence on RDIS than on MBASE, quantitative results would need to be interpreted accordingly. While for institutional reasons this is not true in the United States, the reader is reminded that the discussion in Chapter 2 on "interesting variations" in scaling bears directly on this aspect of interpretation.

Exhibit 5.3 Multiplier elasticity response to GSL impulse.

Variable	Period 1	2	3	4	5	6	7	8	12	16	24
Productivity											
Δ ln QHT1			1.03	1.91	2.91	2.35	0.33	−1.67	−1.19	0.30	−0.04
Δ ln QMHT				0.13	0.37	0.77	1.11	1.19	−0.22	−1.88	0.30
Δ ln QMH77	20.95	−20.52	−5.62	−2.55	−1.69	−0.17	0.21	0.37	0.64	0.33	0.21
Prices and wages											
Δ ln JCMH		0.48	0.41	0.24	0.14	0.08	0.09	0.12	0.09	0.03	−0.03
Δ ln JCMHD		1.01	0.75	0.30	0.01	−0.44	−0.58	−0.35	0.12	0.12	0.02
Δ ln ULC77	−15.60	15.66	4.63	2.13	1.34	0.24	0.01	−0.02	−0.18	−0.09	−0.11
Δ ln PPNF			0.16	0.30	0.38	1.20	1.39	0.91	0.02	−0.10	−0.05
Δ ln PC		−0.02	0.09	0.19	0.27	0.59	0.73	0.59	0.10	−0.01	−0.03
Δ ln PCDO			0.08	0.17	0.25	0.67	0.94	0.83	0.10	−0.07	−0.05
Δ ln PCDA			0.06	0.11	0.14	0.45	0.53	0.35		−0.04	−0.03
Δ ln PCDFE			0.17	0.45	0.69	1.60	2.50	2.34	0.19	−0.16	−0.08
Δ ln PCN			0.09	0.18	0.24	0.70	0.88	0.65	0.03	−0.07	−0.04
Δ ln PCS			0.08	0.19	0.28	0.49	0.58	0.49	0.14	0.03	−0.03
Δ ln PIPD		−0.22	0.27	0.29	0.60	1.01	1.46	1.37	0.28	−0.07	−0.06
Δ ln PINC			0.13	0.27	0.38	1.06	1.39	1.09	0.06	−0.10	−0.05
Δ ln PIRC		0.61	1.12	0.79	0.45	0.27	0.22	0.31	0.34	0.13	−0.03
Δ ln PIBF		−0.20	0.22	0.97	−0.02	1.03	1.41	1.24	0.22	−0.07	−0.06
Δ ln PIPDQ			0.08	0.20	0.31	0.78	1.19	1.24	0.42		−0.07
Δ ln PIPDAG			0.10	0.23	0.35	0.89	1.29	1.20	0.20	−0.08	−0.06
Δ ln PIPDO			0.13	0.30	0.45	1.17	1.65	1.49	0.20	−0.11	−0.07
Δ ln PGNP	−4.21	4.24	0.19	0.29	0.24	0.64	0.78	0.61	0.10	−0.02	−0.04
Δ ln PG	−11.61	11.77	0.09	0.17	0.22	0.69	0.80	0.53	0.01	−0.06	−0.04
Δ ln PCPI	−0.02	−0.49	0.29	0.36	0.37	0.67	0.80	0.65	0.07	−0.03	−0.04
Cost of capital											
UCKNC				−0.02		0.02	0.03	0.04	0.05	0.04	0.02
UCKPDQ					−0.05	−0.08	−0.21	−0.34	−0.15	0.09	0.10

Real-GNP components

GNP72	0.22	0.07	0.04	0.02	0.03	0.03	0.02	0.02	0.01	0.01	0.01	
YD72	0.09	0.04	0.04	0.04	0.08	0.05	0.03	0.03	0.02	0.03	0.02	0.01
M72	0.10	0.15	0.13	0.10								
SERVE72	0.03											
JCAP	0.30	0.25	0.01	0.02	0.02	0.02	0.02	0.02	0.02	0.01	0.01	
JCU	0.12		0.14	0.07	0.02	−0.01	−0.02	−0.03	−0.03	−0.02	−0.02	−0.01
QMH77			−0.03	−0.04	−0.05	−0.05	−0.05	−0.04	−0.04	−0.03	−0.02	
RUG	−1.32	−1.28	−0.70	−0.31	−0.12	−0.05	0.06	0.10	0.15	0.09	0.06	

Real consumption

C72	0.02	0.04	0.03	0.02	0.02	0.02	0.01	0.01	0.01	0.01	0.01	
CDA72		0.30	0.17	0.08	0.03	0.02	0.01	0.01		0.03	0.02	
CDO72	0.06	0.03	0.03	0.04	0.03	0.03	0.03	0.02	0.02	0.02	0.02	
CDFE72	0.04	0.04	0.04	0.04	0.04	0.03	0.03	0.02	0.02	0.02	0.02	
CS72	0.01											
CN72	0.03	0.02	0.03	0.03	0.03	0.03	0.02	0.02	0.01	0.01	0.02	

Real investment

IBF72		0.13	0.16	0.13	0.04	0.03	0.02	0.01	0.02			
IBFPD72		0.12	0.16	0.17	0.05	0.04	0.03	0.02	−0.01			
IBFNC72		0.13	0.17	0.06	0.03	0.02	0.01					
SINV72		0.05	0.06	0.06	0.06	0.05	0.05	0.04	0.02	0.01		
IINV72	0.17	3.86	0.86	0.13	−0.14	−0.34	−0.38	−0.26	−0.10	−0.03		
IRC72		0.02	0.02	0.02	0.02	0.03	0.03	0.05	0.04	0.02		

Monetary

M1BPLUS	0.04	0.05	0.03	0.02								
M2PLUS	0.04	0.05	0.03	0.02								
RTB	−0.03											
RCD	−0.03											
RAAA					−0.02		0.01	0.02	0.02			

Current-dollar GNP

GNP	0.19	0.07	0.04	0.03	0.01	0.01	0.02	0.02	0.02	0.03	0.02	
YPWS	0.17	0.09	0.08	0.07	0.07	0.06	0.06	0.06	0.05	0.05	0.05	
YCBT	0.97	0.20	−0.07	−0.13	−0.10	−0.06	−0.04					

191

Exhibit 5.4 Multiplier elasticity response to GFO impulse.

Variable	Period 1	2	3	4	5	6	7	8	12	16	24
Productivity											
Δ ln QHT1			0.14	0.26	0.39	0.31	0.03	−0.25	−0.16	0.05	
Δ ln QMHT	2.86	−2.81		0.02	0.05	0.10	0.15	0.16	−0.05	−0.26	0.05
Δ ln QMH77			−0.78	−0.36	−0.23	−0.01	0.04	0.07	0.09	0.04	0.03
Prices and wages											
Δ ln JCMH		0.07	0.06	0.03	0.02		0.01	0.02	0.01		
Δ ln JCMHD		0.14	0.10	0.04		−0.06	−0.08	−0.05	0.02	0.02	
Δ ln ULC77	−2.13	2.14	0.64	0.30	0.18	0.02		−0.01	−0.03	−0.01	−0.01
Δ ln PPNF			0.02	0.04	0.05	0.16	0.19	0.12		−0.02	
Δ ln PC			0.01	0.03	0.04	0.08	0.10	0.08			
Δ ln DOPCDO			0.01	0.02	0.03	0.09	0.13	0.11			
Δ ln PCDA				0.02	0.02	0.06	0.07	0.05		−0.01	
Δ ln PCDFE			0.02	0.06	0.09	0.22	0.34	0.32	0.02	−0.03	−0.01
Δ ln PCN			0.01	0.02	0.03	0.09	0.12	0.09		−0.01	
Δ ln PCS			0.01	0.03	0.04	0.07	0.08	0.07	0.02		
Δ ln PIPD		−0.03	0.04	0.04	0.08	0.14	0.20	0.18	0.03	−0.01	
Δ ln PINC			0.02	0.04	0.05	0.14	0.19	0.15		−0.02	
Δ ln PIRC		0.07	0.13	0.09	0.05	0.03	0.02	0.04	0.04	0.01	
Δ ln PIBF		−0.03	0.03	0.13		0.14	0.19	0.17	0.02	−0.01	
Δ ln PIPDQ			0.01	0.03	0.04	0.11	0.16	0.17	0.05		
Δ ln PIPDAG			0.01	0.03	0.05	0.12	0.17	0.16	0.02	−0.02	
Δ ln PIPDO			0.02	0.04	0.06	0.16	0.22	0.20	0.02	−0.02	
Δ ln PGNP	0.77	−0.77	0.02	0.04	0.03	0.09	0.11	0.08			
Δ ln PG	3.47	−3.48	0.01	0.02	0.03	0.09	0.11	0.07		−0.01	
Δ ln PCPI		−0.07	0.05	0.06	0.05	0.09	0.11	0.09			
Cost of capital											
UCKNC											
UCKPDQ							−0.03	−0.04	−0.02	0.02	0.01

Real-GNP components

	1	2	3	4	5	6	7	8	9	10
GNP72	0.03									
YD72	0.01									
M72	0.01	0.02	0.02	0.01	0.01					
SERVE72										
JCAP										
JCU	0.04	0.03	0.02	0.02						
QMH77	0.02									
RUG	−0.18	−0.17	−0.09	−0.04	−0.01		0.01	0.02	0.02	0.01

Real consumption

	1	2	3	4	5	6	7	8	9	10
C72										
CDA72		0.04	0.02							
CDO72										
CDFE72										
CS72										
CN72										

Real investment

	1	2	3	4	5	6	7	8	9	10
IBF72							0.02	0.02	0.02	
IBFPD72							0.02	0.02	0.02	
IBFNC72							0.02	0.02		
SINV72										
IINV72	0.02	0.53	0.12	0.01	−0.03	−0.05	−0.06	−0.06	−0.04	−0.01
IRC72										

Monetary

	1	2	3	4	5	6	7	8	9	10
M1BPLUS										
M2PLUS										
RTB	0.02	0.01								
RCD	0.02	0.02	0.01							
RAAA										

Current-dollar GNP

	1	2	3	4	5	6	7	8	9	10
GNP	0.04									
YPWS	0.02	0.01	0.01							
YCBT	0.15	0.03	0.01				−0.01	−0.02	−0.02	−0.01

Exhibit 5.5 Multiplier elasticity response to YGWS impulse.

Variable	Period 1	2	3	4	5	6	7	8	12	16	24
Productivity											
Δ ln QHT1			0.12	0.32	0.54	0.61	0.38		−0.47	−0.05	
Δ ln QMHT				0.02	0.06	0.13	0.21	0.27	0.07	−0.42	0.05
Δ ln QMH77	2.69	−0.52	−1.77	−0.91	−0.66	−0.41	−0.21	−0.21	0.14	0.09	0.04
Prices and wages											
Δ ln JCMH		0.04	0.07	0.07	0.05	0.04	0.03	0.03	0.02	0.01	
Δ ln JCMHD	0.01	0.09	0.13	0.12	0.06		−0.06	−0.08		0.03	
Δ ln ULC77	−2.01	0.44	1.37	0.73	0.52	0.32	0.18	0.17	−0.04	−0.02	−0.02
Δ ln PPNF			0.01	0.04	0.04	0.13	0.22	0.23	0.04	−0.02	−0.01
Δ ln PC	−0.01	−0.02	0.02	0.02	0.04	0.07	0.12	0.13	0.06	−0.01	
Δ ln PCDO				0.02	0.04	0.07	0.14	0.17	0.02		
Δ ln PCDA				0.01	0.02	0.05	0.08	0.09			
Δ ln PCDFE			0.01	0.05	0.10	0.19	0.34	0.44	0.13	−0.03	−0.02
Δ ln PCN				0.02	0.04	0.08	0.13	0.15	0.03	−0.01	
Δ ln PCS				0.02	0.04	0.07	0.10	0.11	0.05	0.01	
Δ ln PIPD		−0.03		0.04	0.08	0.13	0.21	0.27	0.11		−0.01
Δ ln PINC				0.03	0.06	0.12	0.21	0.24	0.06	−0.02	−0.01
Δ ln PIRC		0.05	0.15	0.18	0.15	0.11	0.08	0.07	0.08	0.04	
Δ ln PIBF		−0.02		0.12	0.07	0.10	0.21	0.25	0.10		−0.01
Δ ln PIPDQ				0.02	0.04	0.09	0.17	0.22	0.14	0.02	−0.01
Δ ln PIPDAG				0.03	0.05	0.10	0.18	0.23	0.10		−0.01
Δ ln PIPDO				0.04	0.07	0.13	0.24	0.29	0.11	−0.01	−0.01
Δ ln PGNP	0.05	−0.02		0.04	0.05	0.08	0.12	0.14	0.05		
Δ ln PG				0.02	0.03	0.07	0.13	0.13	0.03	−0.01	
Δ ln PCPI	−0.05	−0.53	0.48	0.07	0.07	0.10	0.13	0.18	0.04		
Cost of capital											
UCKNC											
UCKPDQ						−0.01	−0.02	−0.05	−0.06		0.02

194

Real-GNP components

GNP72	0.03	0.03	0.02	0.01						
YD72	0.18	0.01								
M72	0.01	0.02	0.03	0.03	0.02	0.02	0.02	0.01		
SERVE72	0.02									
JCAP										
JCU	0.02	0.05	0.04	0.03	0.03	0.01	0.02	−0.01		
QMH77	0.02	0.01								
RUG	−0.15	−0.26	−0.23	−0.16	−0.10	−0.06	−0.03	−0.01	0.04	0.03	0.02

Real consumption

C72	0.04	0.04	0.01	0.01						
CDA72	0.33	0.04	0.02					−0.03		
CDO72	0.12	0.02	0.02	0.01	0.01					
CDFE72	0.09	0.05	0.04	0.03	0.02	0.01				
CS72	0.02									
CN72	0.06	0.02	0.02	0.02	0.01	0.01	0.01			

Real investment

IBF72	0.02	0.03	0.03	0.02	0.01	0.01				
IBFPD72	0.01	0.03	0.04	0.03	0.02	0.01	0.01			
IBFNC72	0.02	0.03	0.02	0.02	0.01					
SINV72	0.01	0.01	0.01							
IINV72	0.02	0.35	0.45	0.20	0.10	0.02	−0.03	−0.05	−0.07	−0.03	−0.01
IRC72	0.01	0.02	0.03	0.03	0.02	0.02	0.01	0.01		

Monetary

M1BPLUS										
M2PLUS										
RTB										
RCD								−0.01	−0.01	
RAAA										

Current-dollar GNP

GNP	0.03	0.03	0.02	0.01	0.02	0.01	0.01	0.01		
YPWS	0.02	0.02	0.02	0.01	0.01	0.01				
YCBT	−0.36	0.12	0.05	0.02				−0.01		

Exhibit 5.6 Multiplier elasticity response to MBASE impulse.

Variable	Period 1	2	3	4	5	6	7	8	12	16	24
Productivity											
Δ ln QHT1		0.38	0.36	0.06	0.17	0.35	0.53	0.56	-0.39	-0.42	0.02
Δ ln QMHT						0.03	0.08	0.15	0.30	-0.13	-0.21
Δ ln QMH77				0.10	-0.37	-0.40	-0.44	-0.39	-0.06	0.13	0.10
Prices and wages											
Δ ln JCMH				0.02	0.03	0.04	0.04	0.04	0.03	0.01	-0.01
Δ ln JCMHD			0.02	0.04	0.06	0.07	0.05	0.02	-0.02		
Δ ln ULC77		-0.28	-0.24	-0.03	0.30	0.32	0.33	0.29	0.07	-0.04	-0.06
Δ ln PPNF						0.02	0.05	0.08	0.11	0.01	-0.04
Δ ln PC						0.01	0.03	0.05	0.07	0.02	-0.02
Δ ln PCDO						0.01	0.03	0.05	0.10	0.02	-0.03
Δ ln PCDA							0.02	0.03	0.04		-0.02
Δ ln PCDFE					0.01	0.03	0.07	0.13	0.23	0.05	-0.05
Δ ln PCN						0.01	0.03	0.05	0.08	0.01	-0.03
Δ ln PCS						0.01	0.03	0.04	0.06	0.03	-0.02
Δ ln PIPD			-0.01			0.02	0.06	0.09	0.15	0.05	-0.04
Δ ln PINC				-0.01		0.02	0.04	0.08	0.12	0.02	-0.04
Δ ln PIRC		0.47	0.68	0.31	0.11	0.05	0.03	0.02	0.01	0.04	-0.04
Δ ln PIBF				0.01	0.03	0.04	0.04	0.06	0.13	0.07	-0.04
Δ ln PIPDQ						0.01	0.03	0.06	0.15	0.04	-0.04
Δ ln PIPDAG						0.02	0.04	0.07	0.14	0.04	-0.04
Δ ln PIPDO						0.02	0.05	0.09	0.16	0.04	-0.05
Δ ln PGNP		0.03	0.03	0.02	0.01	0.02	0.03	0.05	0.07	0.02	-0.02
Δ ln PG						0.01	0.03	0.05	0.06		-0.02
Δ ln PCPI		-0.09	-0.26	-0.08	0.06	0.03	0.05	0.07	0.10	0.03	-0.02
Cost of capital											
UCKNC	-0.10		-0.03	-0.03	-0.02	-0.02	-0.02	-0.02	-0.06	-0.03	
UCKPDQ	-0.11		-0.03	-0.03	-0.03	-0.02	-0.02	-0.03	-0.06	-0.03	0.03

Real-GNP components

	1	2	3	4	5	6	7	8	9	10
GNP72		0.01	0.01	0.01	0.01	0.02	0.02			
YD72										
M72		0.01	0.01	0.02	0.02	0.02	0.02			
SERVE72										
JCAP			0.02	0.02	0.02	0.02	0.01			
JCU		0.01	0.02	0.02	0.02	0.02	0.01			
QMH77										
RUG	−0.02	−0.07	−0.11	−0.13	−0.13	−0.11	−0.09		0.05	0.04

Real consumption

	1	2	3	4	5	6	7	8	9	10
C72										
CDA72	0.05	0.06	0.07	0.03	0.02	0.02	0.02			
CDO72					0.02	0.02	0.02			
CDFE72	0.01	0.01	0.02	0.02	0.02	0.02	0.02	0.01		
CS72										
CN72										

Real investment

	1	2	3	4	5	6	7	8	9	10
IBF72		0.02	0.02	0.03	0.03	0.03	0.02			
IBFPD72		0.02	0.03	0.03	0.03	0.02	0.02			
IBFNC72		0.01	0.02	0.02	0.02	0.02	0.01			
SINV72										
IINV72		0.07	0.14	0.18	0.15	0.12	0.08	−0.04	−0.06	−0.02
IRC72	0.03	0.09	0.10	0.09	0.08	0.05	0.04	−0.01	−0.01	

Monetary

	1	2	3	4	5	6	7	8	9	10
M1BPLUS	0.02	0.02	0.02	0.02	0.02	0.01	0.01			
M2PLUS										
RTB	−0.94	−0.13	−0.05	−0.01						
RCD	−0.92	−0.21	−0.10	−0.04	−0.01					
RAAA	−0.19	−0.06	−0.05	−0.05	−0.04	−0.04	−0.03	−0.02		

Current-dollar GNP

	1	2	3	4	5	6	7	8	9	10
GNP			0.01	0.01	0.01	0.01				
YPWS			0.01	0.01	0.01	0.01	0.01			
YCBT	0.02	0.04	0.05	0.04	0.03	0.02	0.01	0.01		

Exhibit 5.7 Multiplier elasticity response to RDIS impulse.

Variable	Period 1	2	3	4	5	6	7	8	12	16	24
Productivity											
Δ ln QHT1				-0.09	-0.24	-0.47	-0.65	-0.59	0.59	0.35	-0.03
Δ ln QMHT					-0.01	-0.04	-0.11	-0.20	-0.28	0.25	0.14
Δ ln QMH77		-0.61	-0.40	0.05	0.69	0.50	0.47	0.36	-0.02	-0.15	-0.09
Prices and wages											
Δ ln ICMH			-0.01	-0.03	-0.04	-0.04	-0.04	-0.03	-0.02		0.01
Δ ln ICMHD			-0.03	-0.06	-0.08	-0.07	-0.04		0.02	-0.01	
Δ ln ULC77		0.44	0.26	-0.09	-0.53	-0.39	-0.35	-0.27	-0.03	0.05	0.06
Δ ln PPNF					-0.01	-0.03	-0.06	-0.11	-0.09		0.03
Δ ln PC					-0.01	-0.02	-0.04	-0.06	-0.07		0.02
Δ ln PCDO						-0.02	-0.04	-0.07	-0.09		0.03
Δ ln PCDA						-0.01	-0.02	-0.04	-0.04		0.02
Δ ln PCDFE					-0.02	-0.04	-0.09	-0.04	-0.22	-0.01	0.05
Δ ln PCN						-0.02	-0.04	-0.17	-0.07		0.03
Δ ln PCS						-0.02	-0.03	-0.07	-0.06		0.02
Δ ln PIPD			0.02	0.01		-0.03	-0.08	-0.05	-0.15	-0.02	0.04
Δ ln PINC					-0.01	-0.03	-0.06	-0.12	-0.11	-0.03	0.04
Δ ln PIRC		-0.74	-0.87	-0.14	0.06	0.03		-0.10	-0.02		0.04
Δ ln PIBF			-0.01	-0.01	-0.04	-0.05	-0.04	-0.08	-0.13	-0.02	0.04
Δ ln PIPDQ						-0.02	-0.04	-0.08	-0.15	-0.05	0.04
Δ ln PIPDAG						-0.02	-0.05	-0.09	-0.13	-0.02	0.04
Δ ln PIPDO					-0.01	-0.03	-0.06	-0.12	-0.16	-0.02	0.05
Δ ln PGNP		-0.04	-0.04	-0.01		-0.02	-0.04	-0.06	-0.07		0.03
Δ ln PG		0.14	0.37			-0.02	-0.04	-0.06	-0.06		0.02
Δ ln PCPI					-0.16	-0.05	-0.06	-0.09	-0.09	-0.02	0.02
Cost of capital											
UCKNC	0.16	-0.03	0.03	0.03	0.02	0.02	0.02	0.01			
UCKPDQ	0.17	-0.03	0.03	0.03	0.02	0.02	0.02	0.03	0.07	0.02	-0.04

Real-GNP components

	1	2	3	4	5	6	7	8	9	10
GNP72			−0.01	−0.01	−0.01					
YD72		−0.01			−0.02	−0.02	−0.01			
M72			−0.01	−0.02	−0.02	−0.01				
SERVE72										
JCAP										
JCU		−0.02	−0.03	−0.03	−0.02	−0.02	−0.01			
QMH77				−0.02	−0.02	−0.01				
RUG	0.04	0.10	0.15	0.14	0.12	0.10	0.07	−0.02	−0.05	−0.04

Real consumption

	1	2	3	4	5	6	7	8	9	10
C72		−0.02	−0.08	−0.01	−0.01	−0.01	−0.01			
CDA72	−0.07	−0.08	−0.08	−0.08	−0.01	−0.01	−0.01	−0.01		
CDO72	−0.02	−0.02	−0.02	−0.02	−0.02	−0.02	−0.02			
CDFE72					−0.02	−0.02	−0.02	−0.01		
CS72										
CN72										

Real investment

	1	2	3	4	5	6	7	8	9	10
IBF72		−0.01	−0.02	−0.03	−0.03	−0.03	−0.02			
IBFPD72		−0.01	−0.02	−0.04	−0.04	−0.03	−0.02			
IBFNC72			−0.02	−0.02	−0.02	−0.02	−0.02	−0.01		
SINV72										
IINV72		−0.11	−0.20	−0.21	−0.14	−0.09	−0.04	0.06	0.06	0.02
IRC72	−0.05	−0.12	−0.12	−0.09	−0.06	−0.04	−0.02	0.01	0.01	

Monetary

	1	2	3	4	5	6	7	8	9	10
M1BPLUS	−0.06	−0.03	−0.02	−0.02	−0.01	−0.01	−0.01	0.01		
M2PLUS	−0.02									
RTB	1.48	−0.21	−0.10	−0.05	−0.03	−0.02	−0.01	−0.01		
RCD	1.45	−0.08	−0.05	−0.03	−0.02	−0.02	−0.01	−0.01		
RAAA	0.30	0.06	0.05	0.04	0.04	0.03	0.03	0.01		

Current-dollar GNP

	1	2	3	4	5	6	7	8	9	10
GNP		−0.01	−0.01	−0.01	−0.01					
YPWS			−0.01	−0.01	−0.01					
YCBT	−0.03	−0.05	−0.06	−0.04	−0.03	−0.01	−0.01			

restricted to the short run, as their importance attenuates by period 5. The strongest responses, individually and across sectors, originate with fiscal variables. Productivity reacts strongly, with oscillations, and does not damp out. Wage rate-of-change responses are persistently positive, while $\Delta \ln$ PPNF has a delayed but strong reaction that has almost vanished by period 16. Finally, monetary-policy variables have delayed effects that lead to persistent long-run price responses.

Exhibit 5.8 Partial elasticity root multiplier response of $\Delta \ln$ PPNF: filter 0.10, 1% initial impulse.

Root Information			Partial Multiplier Responses					
Root Index	Root Mag.	Imag. Comp.	Period 2	4	8	12	16	24
36	0.96	0.05	0.11		−0.18	−0.26	−0.28	−0.22
38	0.93		0.23	0.19	0.14			
45	0.79	0.28	−3.70	−0.75	0.90	0.17		
47	0.77	0.11	0.91	0.29				
52	0.71	0.43	−0.69	−0.98	0.21			
53	0.69	0.35	−0.84	−0.13				
54	0.69	0.60	0.86	−2.19	0.12			
56	0.66	0.50	0.73	−0.25				
57	0.65	0.01	−0.18					
58	0.64	0.63	−2.56	0.59				
59	0.63	0.52	0.25	0.63				
61	0.63	0.19	3.50	1.24				
62	0.62	0.60	−2.72	0.68				
63	0.61	0.58	3.66	−1.34				
64	0.61	0.23	−2.78	−0.20	0.16			
65	0.60	0.55	3.46	−0.48	0.15			
66	0.60	0.43	3.82	1.35	−0.16			
67	0.60	0.32	3.34	−0.52	−0.11			
68	0.60		−3.47	−1.21	−0.14			
69	0.59	0.48	3.74	−3.17	0.32			
70	0.59	0.59	3.27	−1.14	−0.13			
71	0.58	0.11	2.89	0.86				
72	0.58	0.57	1.95	−0.44				
73	0.57	0.44	−6.08	1.42	−0.19			
74	0.56	0.54	1.27	−0.28				
75	0.54	0.23		−0.21				
76	0.53		1.05	0.29				
87	0.41	0.36	−0.27					

Exhibit 5.9 Partial elasticity root multiplier response of $\Delta \ln$ JCMH: filter 0.10, 1% initial impulse.

Root Information			Partial Multiplier Responses					
Root Index	Root Mag.	Imag. Comp.	Period 2	4	8	12	16	24
36	0.96	0.05	0.12			−0.10	−0.13	−0.14
38	0.93		0.13	0.11				
45	0.79	0.28	0.10	−0.24	−0.15			
46	0.78		−0.17	−0.10				
47	0.77	0.11	0.35	0.31	0.15			
52	0.71	0.43		−0.18				
53	0.69	0.35	0.26	0.67				
54	0.69	0.60	−0.66	0.70				
56	0.66	0.50	0.27					
58	0.64	0.63	1.26	−0.63	−0.11			
59	0.63	0.52	4.68	−1.17	0.29			
61	0.63	0.19	−0.48					
62	0.62	0.60		−0.18				
63	0.61	0.58	0.72	−0.48				
64	0.61	0.23	0.99	0.27				
65	0.60	0.55	0.75	−0.35				
66	0.60	0.43	−1.10	0.54				
67	0.60	0.32	0.50	−0.28				
68	0.60		−1.29	−0.45				
69	0.59	0.48	−3.54	1.40	−0.19			
70	0.59	0.59	−1.16	0.43				
71	0.58	0.11	−0.32					
72	0.58	0.57	−3.52	0.67				
73	0.57	0.44	13.18	−4.23	0.52			
74	0.56	0.54	−7.32	1.34	−0.11			
75	0.54	0.23	3.09	3.47	0.10			
76	0.53		−5.84	−1.62	−0.12			
88	0.36	0.31	0.35					
89	0.34		−0.31					

Partial Root Multiplier Responses

While according to equation (2.3.10) it is possible to decompose responses by root and variable, we have found it more informative to sum elasticity responses for a particular endogenous variable (in each period) across exogenous variables associated with a particular root. This aggregation, midway between the full-blown decomposition and the total multiplier,

Exhibit 5.10 Partial elasticity root multiplier response of $\Delta \ln$ QMH77: filter 0.10, 1% initial impulse.

Root Information			Partial Multiplier Responses					
Root Index	Root Mag.	Imag. Comp.	Period 2	4	8	12	16	24
36	0.96	0.05	0.39	0.46	0.56	0.60	0.58	0.43
44	0.84		−0.12					
45	0.79	0.28	−0.71	−2.60	−1.03	0.34	0.20	
46	0.78		−0.37	−0.23				
52	0.71	0.43	−1.53	0.64				
53	0.69	0.35	−0.14	0.26				
54	0.69	0.60	−4.84	1.66	−0.59			
56	0.66	0.50	0.64	0.69	−0.11			
57	0.65		−0.41	−0.18				
58	0.64	0.63	0.73	0.16	0.17			
59	0.63	0.52	5.89	−3.68	0.57			
61	0.63	0.19	−18.60	−3.81	0.95	0.19		
62	0.62	0.60	3.21	−0.52	0.17			
63	0.61	0.58	0.58	1.31	0.37			
64	0.61	0.23	1.94	−0.64	−0.24			
65	0.60	0.55	3.50	1.27	0.39			
66	0.60	0.43	−7.06	2.04	−0.28			
67	0.60	0.32	−5.04	−2.74	0.30			
68	0.60		4.04	1.47	0.19			
69	0.59	0.48	−16.11	6.42	−0.97			
70	0.59	0.59	5.05	−1.89	−0.25			
71	0.58	0.11	4.63	1.17				
72	0.58	0.57	−0.98	−0.46	−0.21			
73	0.57	0.44	19.52	−8.01	1.00	−0.10		
74	0.56	0.54	−6.55	0.72	−0.22			
75	0.54	0.23	−2.37	1.04	0.15			
76	0.53		−6.25	−1.80	−0.15			
79	0.50		0.13					
81	0.48		1.37	0.32				
84	0.46	0.03	−6.40	−1.61				
86	0.43		0.53					
87	0.41	0.36	−37.19	1.00	−0.19			
88	0.36	0.31	−46.24	4.58	−0.11			
89	0.34		−18.96	−2.22				
90	0.33	0.05	132.90	8.78				

successfully captures important dynamic aspects of responses without excessive detail. Exhibits 5.8–5.10 contain multipliers of this sort for $\Delta \ln$ PPNF, $\Delta \ln$ JCMH, and $\Delta \ln$ QMH77. Sensitivities of important roots to individual coefficients of the linearized model are described at the end of this chapter.

Many roots in Exhibit 5.8 for $\Delta \ln$ PPNF, the majority of them imaginary, have large elasticities in the short run, that is, for periods 2 and 4. The roots most influential on impact include root 73, which is relatively small, and root 45, which is relatively large. Of the two, root 45 persists above the cutoff level of 0.10 through period 12. Other large short-run partial elasticity effects drop below the cutoff following period 8. By period 8 all such responses are less than ± 1.0. Only root 36, with a magnitude of 0.96 (and a small imaginary component), persists into period 24. It has a small, slowly diminishing magnitude.

Root 73 is also strongest on impact for $\Delta \ln$ JCMH, while roots 76 and 59 (real and imaginary, respectively) are also sizable in period 2. Once again, only root 36 barely exceeds the cutoff in periods 12 through 24 according to Exhibit 5.9.

Rather different and more responses are in evidence for $\Delta \ln$ QMH77. According to Exhibit 5.10, six roots between 74 and 88 have above-cutoff values in the short run that are *not* influential for either prices or wages. A second main difference is that the short-run productivity elasticities are substantially larger than for the other two principal variables. Yet another difference is that root 36 has a small persistent elasticity for $\Delta \ln$ QMH77, throughout the entire time range explored, that lies in the interval 0.38–0.60. In the longer-term analysis, root 45 is above the cutoff through period 16. A basic similarity among the three is that most partial root elasticities have sharply diminished by period 8, and most have dropped beneath the cutoff by period 12.

Another informative way to scan the root–multiplier association is to rank the net root response from largest to smallest absolute value. This has been done in Exhibits 5.11–5.13 in which each entry is a root index number whose position is set by its rank size within a given period. Since there is no absolute cutoff, different aspects of behavior are now apparent. For instance, the largest two roots (1 and 2 respectively) become of increased importance in periods 12, 16, and 24, as one should expect, although small coefficients or net offsets have effectively reduced the influence of many large roots. Thus, large root magnitudes alone are not automatic grounds for long-run dominance. Root 73 controls the early periods for $\Delta \ln$ JCMH and is also high in the rankings for the other two variables. The difference between $\Delta \ln$ QMH77 and the price–wage pair is revealed most clearly in the early periods. The important roots initially (periods 2 and 4) for productivity are among the very smallest (i.e., have high indices) and are disjoint from

Exhibit 5.11   Ranked partial elasticity root multiplier response of $\Delta \ln$ PPNF.[a]

Rank	Period 2	4	8	12	16	24
1	−73	−69	−45	−36	−36	−36
2	−66	−54	−69	−45	−45	38
3	−69	−73	−52	38	38	1
4	−45	−66	−73	−47	−47	33
5	−63	−63	−36	−54	33	32
6	−61	−61	−66	33	32	−45
7	68	68	−64	−52	1	2
8	−65	−70	−65	32	−54	−11
9	−67	−52	68	−58	2	3
10	−70	−71	38	−61	42	8
11	−71	−45	−70	1	−58	4
12	−64	−62	−54	−63	−11	5
13	−62	−59	−67	−67	40	42
14	−58	−58	−53	−62	44	−47
15	−72	−67	−47	−73	8	40
16	−74	−65	−58	−66	3	−21
17	76	−72	−56	−69	−64	44
18	−47	−47	−62	68	4	−54
19	−54	76	−71	−70	46	9
20	−53	−74	33	−53	−59	41
21	−56	−56	32	−56	−65	7
22	−52	−75	−59	42	−62	−52
23	−87	−64	1	2	−66	35
24	−59	38	−61	−59	5	10
25	38	−53	76	44	−56	37

[a] Negative signs mark imaginary roots.

the significant roots for the other two variables. Indices in the range 87–90 occupy the four largest productivity net root influences, while root indices in the range 45–75 have the four greatest influences on period-2 prices and wages. From period 8 onward roots in the same size range (generally different ones, however) predominate.

We summarize specific facts about the partial root elasticities as follows. Root 36 has the greatest long-term influence for all three key endogenous variables. Root 45 has strong intermediate-run effects for prices and productivity and noticeable but lesser effects on $\Delta \ln$ JCMH. Root 73 has a large influence through period 8 for all variables. Many different roots are

Exhibit 5.12 Ranked partial elasticity root multiplier response of Δ ln JCMH.[a]

Rank	Period 2	4	8	12	16	24
1	−73	−73	−73	−36	−36	−36
2	−74	−75	−59	38	38	1
3	76	76	−69	−73	−45	38
4	−59	−69	−47	−47	1	33
5	−69	−74	−45	−59	33	32
6	−72	−59	76	−75	32	2
7	−75	−54	−58	−53	40	40
8	68	−72	−74	−74	−47	−45
9	−58	−53	−75	−45	2	−11
10	−70	−58	38	40	−54	35
11	−66	−66	−54	−69	−53	−57
12	−64	−63	−66	−54	46	44
13	−65	68	−62	1	−73	3
14	−63	−70	68	−72	44	41
15	−54	−65	−70	33	35	46
16	−67	−47	−63	46	−72	5
17	−61	−67	−72	32	−11	42
18	−88	−64	−36	−58	41	37
19	−47	−45	−61	76	48	22
20	−71	−62	−53	−66	−74	−21
21	89	−52	46	44	42	10
22	−56	38	−52	2	−63	−53
23	−53	46	−64	68	−66	24
24	46	−56	40	−62	−59	48
25	91	−88	−71	−70	68	9

[a] Negative signs mark imaginary roots.

relevant for periods 2 and 4, including roots 73 and 69, which have significant standing in the rankings for all three variables. The relative net root ranks differ noticeably among all three variables. While several roots are common, most dynamics originate from different roots for each.

On a more general level, two further comments are warranted. First, the mere fact that a root is large does not mean that it dominates dynamic behavior. Second, only a few characteristic roots are strongly influential. Their influence depends on particular time spans and endogenous variables as well as the analytical perspective (multiplier vs. parameter perturbation), a matter which becomes obvious in the following section.

Exhibit 5.13   Ranked partial elasticity root multiplier response of $\Delta \ln$ QMH77.[a]

Rank	Period 2	4	8	12	16	24
1	− 90	− 90	− 45	− 36	− 36	− 36
2	− 88	− 73	− 73	− 45	− 45	33
3	− 87	91	− 69	− 61	33	32
4	91	− 69	− 61	− 73	32	− 45
5	− 73	− 88	− 54	− 69	38	1
6	89	− 61	− 59	33	1	− 11
7	− 61	− 59	− 36	32	− 54	38
8	− 69	− 67	− 65	− 54	40	3
9	− 66	− 45	− 63	− 62	− 11	35
10	− 74	89	− 67	− 58	− 52	40
11	− 84	− 66	− 66	− 66	46	5
12	76	− 70	− 70	− 52	35	4
13	− 59	76	− 64	38	44	22
14	− 70	− 54	− 74	46	42	8
15	− 67	− 84	− 72	− 72	3	42
16	− 54	68	68	− 74	− 73	44
17	− 71	− 63	− 87	− 59	− 59	41
18	68	− 65	− 62	− 70	− 63	46
19	− 65	− 71	− 58	− 65	− 65	2
20	− 62	− 75	76	40	− 58	7
21	− 75	− 87	− 75	68	41	− 52
22	− 64	− 74	− 88	44	5	9
23	− 52	− 56	− 56	42	4	− 54
24	81	− 52	− 84	− 53	22	6
25	− 72	− 64	46	1	− 66	20

[a] Negative signs mark imaginary roots.

5.2   PARAMETER PERTURBATIONS

Interpretation of Parameter-Perturbation Elasticities

Elasticities have proven their worth in many contexts. One main use is to remove units of measurement in order to ease subsequent interpretation. Understanding them in a nonlinear econometric model whose equations have different functional forms requires further explanation. The MQEM behavior equations share a common characteristic: although l.h.s. variables are often nonlinear, the equations are linear in their coefficients, so that our attention is directed to that case. Explanatory variables, on the other hand,

Exhibit 5.14 Impact parameter elasticities for alternative functional forms.

Equation	Functional Form	Sum of Impact Elasticities
(1)	$y_t = \gamma_0 + \gamma_1 x_{1t} + \gamma_2 x_{2t} + \cdots$	1
(2)	$\Delta \ln y_t = \gamma_0 + \gamma_1 x_{1t} + \gamma_2 x_{2t} + \cdots$	$\Delta \ln y_t$
(3)	$\Delta y_t = \gamma_0 + \gamma_1 x_{1t} + \gamma_2 x_{2t} + \cdots$	$\Delta y_t / y_t$
(4)	$\ln y_t = \gamma_0 + \gamma_1 x_{1t} + \gamma_2 x_{2t} + \cdots$	$\ln y_t$

can be in original units, first differences, logarithms, reciprocals, and so on. As it turns out, this does not matter for our immediate interpretive needs. Exhibit 5.14 contains impact elasticities for the principal equation forms. These were calculated with methods explained in Chapter 2, Section 5 for parameter elasticities. Beginning with the completely linear case in row 1,[†] each equation is always linear in the coefficients and (possibly transformed) r.h.s. variables, while the dependent variable has four different expressions. All MQEM equations fall into one of these categories. Note that the corresponding sums of impact elasticities in the last column are quite different.[‡] Since for a given endogenous l.h.s. variable the linear (in coefficients and variables) r.h.s. structure is symmetric in variable or parameter perturbations, the following comments about parameters apply equally to multipliers.

While simultaneity and dynamics modify single-equation impact elasticities in multiple-equation systems, in practice strong-impact feedbacks are rare, so that single equations convey relevant implications, especially for the earlier periods. Recalling an earlier proposition from Chapter 2, impact elasticities are highly informative in that they establish the base from which elasticity dynamics propagate endogenous variables into future periods.[§]

Most MQEM price or wage equations have been estimated as first differences of logarithms. The first-difference transformation is used to circumvent some unwanted effects that trends in the data can exert on the estimates, although we have seen that it is not innocuous for multiplier responses. We now show differencing also complicates the interpretation of

---

[†]While composite or other transformed r.h.s. variables will not have exactly symmetric responses unless the perturbation is done on the transformed variable (as distinct from an element of the transformation), the immediately following discussion is still qualitatively relevant.

[‡]See Section 2.5 for further explanation.

[§]See Section 2.5 and text in the vicinity of equations (2.5.8) and (2.5.9) as well as Appendix 2A for discussion of this point.

elasticities.[†] Thus equation (2) in Exhibit 5.14 was used repeatedly throughout the MQEM, especially for prices and wages, with the ensuing impact elasticities summing to $\Delta \ln y_t$. This closely approximates the percentage rate of change when these changes are small, so that most historical price or wage impact elasticities for the U.S. economy fall below 0.10. Therefore impact wage–price parameters are small by construction.

We believe that this definitional consequence of the MQEM estimation procedure and mechanical extraction of *level* elasticities is misleading when applied to the study of inflation, since $\Delta p_t / p_t$ or $\Delta w_t / w_t$ best describes inflationary behavior. Hence, calculation of elasticities for p_t, w_t *levels* from equations with a l.h.s. variable such as $\Delta \ln p_t$ does not convey the requisite information. To investigate rates of change, we have defined new variables such as $z_t \equiv \Delta \ln p_t$.[‡] These definitions have no independent behavior and are driven by the associated behavior equation (see Exhibit 3.2 for a list). This transparent expedient causes the "new" endogenous variable's single-equation impact elasticities to sum to unity according to functional form (1) in Exhibit 5.14 and measure the elasticity or sensitivity of inflation, not the price level. Mathematically, the only change is that the denominator p_t used in elasticity scaling is replaced by z_t. Furthermore, those impact elasticities are then on a comparable basis with the majority of MQEM equations, which are linear, like functional form (1). We have chosen to make the same sort of definitional change of variables for productivity.[§] For similar reasons rates of productivity growth are inherently more interesting than the corresponding levels in studying economic behavior. All other equations remain as originally specified.

The difference between the impact elasticities based on functional forms (2) and (3) will be small so that for prices and wages at least, the extensive remarks just made about (2) apply equally to (3). The last functional form (4) matters in two equation types: in the monetary-sector definitions of liquidity stocks, and for the import equation. Given the units chosen by the MQEM modelers, impact elasticities for liquidity and imports are, as should be expected by now, the largest in the MQEM.

Elasticity sensitivities are also affected when autoregressive corrections are incorporated into the equation structure. This occurs several times in the MQEM. The consequences are indicated in Exhibit 5.15. Our comments for autocorrelation-corrected equations will be restricted to the first two func-

---

[†]This complication and our treatment of it are described in the text following equation (2.5.24).
[‡]See equation (2.5.25).
[§]Since productivity appears as a transformed variable in PPNF, this comment is correct for QMH77 but does not apply in the same way to QMHT, which is the transformation entering the PPNF equation (see Appendix 3B for details).

Exhibit 5.15 Impact parameter elasticities, functional form, and autoregressive errors.

	Functional Form and Error Process[a]	Sum of Impact Elasticities
(1)	$y_t = \gamma_0 + \gamma_1 x_{1t} + \gamma_2 x_{2t} + \cdots + u_t$ $u_t = \rho u_{t-1} + \varepsilon_t$	$1 - \dfrac{\rho y_{t-1}}{y_t}$
(2)	$\Delta \ln y_t = \gamma_0 + \gamma_1 x_{1t} + \gamma_2 x_{2t} + \cdots + u_t$ $u_t = \rho u_{t-1} + \varepsilon_t$	$\Delta \ln y_t - \dfrac{\rho \ln y_{t-1}}{\ln y_t}$
(3)	$\Delta y_t = \gamma_0 + \gamma_1 x_{1t} + \gamma_2 x_{2t} + \cdots + u_t$ $u_t = \rho u_{t-1} + \varepsilon_t$	$\dfrac{\Delta y_t}{y_t} - \dfrac{\rho y_{t-1}}{y_t}$
(4)	$\ln y_t = \gamma_0 + \gamma_1 x_{1t} + \gamma_2 x_{2t} + \cdots + u_t$ $u_t = \rho u_{t-1} + \varepsilon_t$	$\ln y_t - \rho \ln y_{t-1}$

[a] It is assumed as usual that $|\rho| < 1$ and ε_t is i.i.d.

tional forms. When autoregressive corrections have been used in estimation, it is correct, especially when forecasting, to include autoregressive error structure directly in the model equations. When the autoregressive parameter is positive and large (i.e., close to one) and the dependent variable is relatively smooth, so that y_{t-1}/y_t is approximately 1, there is substantial attenuation in sensitivity from one toward zero for functional forms (1) and (2). The effects are surprisingly large. The rationale is, quite simply, that large output sensitivities to parameter perturbations can be counteracted by persistence generated through the error process. Clearly, this initial reduction in sensitivity will be overcome and later swamped if there are strong internal elasticity dynamics, as long as $|\rho| < 1$.

Empirical Results of Parameter Perturbations

As a convenient way to summarize parameter perturbation, we shall initially describe major results in two categories. The first group of results includes elasticity responses for "own dynamics" to an impulse perturbation, that is, own autoregressive terms. These often exert a powerful influence on endogenous variables. The second set of results (for a given endogenous variable) will be about large endogenous responses for the remaining coefficient perturbations. The equations are identified in the first column by the endogenous variable in whose equation the perturbed coefficient appears, in the second column by the coefficient symbol, and in the third column by the coefficient's *coterm*,[†] that is, a single variable in the simplest case of no transformation and/or combinations of variables in more complex situations, whose coefficient is being perturbed. The variable names are explained in Chapter 3.

Results are reported only for above-cutoff elasticity responses to a 1% impulse parameter change. In order to capture most nontrivial effects, we have chosen a conservative elasticity cutoff of 0.10 for periods 2, 4, 8, 12, 16, and 24. For reasons described in the previous section, we have normalized some variables to have a unit impact elasticity by using the construct $z_t = \Delta \ln p_t$ so that, for example, the price variable appears as $\Delta \ln$ PPNF.

PPNF: *Private Nonfarm Deflator.* The preponderance of large responses of $\Delta \ln$ PPNF to own-dynamics parameter perturbations is from final demand: four consumption sectors, four investment sectors, and imports. Parameters in manufacturing production and capacity also matter, as do the three monetary variables RTB, RAAA, and M1BPLUS. These comments are based on Exhibit 5.16.

The impact elasticities are plausibly small and attain a peak eight quarters later. Consumption effects have largely attenuated after period 12. Investment in plant and manufacturing capacity (capital stock) reach a maximum around period 8, and RAAA effects have a maximum in period 12. M1BPLUS peaks in period 16. Some responses persist into period 24. Thus influences on $\Delta \ln$ PPNF begin, albeit with some delay, with final demand and then shift to investment and monetary variables. Enough impulse responses remain strong for long periods to lend further credence to the concept of borderline inflationary instability.[‡]

Notably missing from the own dynamics but present in other coterms are two equations that *a priori* affect PPNF, wage rate (JCMH), and productivity (QMH77). The JCMH intercept A1.0 shows up in period 2, but has dissipated after period 5. An investment term B1.4 in QMH77, which also appears in QMHT, has moderate consequences through period 12 that decline afterwards. Parameters in the import (M72) equation and some other final demands (CN72 especially) have sizable elasticity magnitudes through period 8. Many lagged investment terms appear in periods 6–12. However, the largest elasticities are elsewhere, principally imports (C13), nondurable demand (C6), and the index of industrial production for manufacturing (F2).

[†] The word *coterm* has been created to fill a verbal lacuna which arises in describing elements of an equation.

[‡] In the previous chapter, long-term, persistent consequences of initial conditions raised serious questions about the stability of price–wage dynamics.

Lags for a money-demand (E16) component and for the money supply (E2) are relatively strong in period 12 and afterwards.

The dominant coterms are final-demand variables (e.g., GNP72), disposable personal income, and final sales in the nonmonetary sectors. Intercepts also appear several times. Intercept impulses can be interpreted as one-time random shocks to the l.h.s. endogenous variable, or what they are quite literally, a one-time change in a particular exogenous variable, the intercept. When the l.h.s. variable is a first difference, the intercept represents a trend term. In the monetary sector a M1BPLUS-to-RTB effect appears relevant, as well as RDIS and MBASE influences.

Thus we have arrived at an economically consistent picture of how parameter perturbations are informative about the behavior of $\Delta \ln$ PPNF. The process begins with wages in the short run. Then the emphasis shifts in the middle term to GNP components, especially imports and consumption demand. In the long run, $\Delta \ln$ PPNF responds mainly to monetary and investment variables. The effects are sluggish and persistent as the important underlying dynamics shift from sector to sector. While the coefficients of the autoregressive terms from other equations tend to dominate responses for a given equation such as PPNF, other coefficients also count, mainly aggregate output (sometimes averaged), and intercepts.

"Partial characteristic-root decompositions," described algebraically by equation (2.3.10), will now be used to decompose each period's parameter response into weights (entries from C), characteristic roots, and coefficient changes. The latter are single initial-period 1% perturbations. By summing across all $\Delta \ln$ PPNF responses for one root in a given period, we obtain a convenient summary measure of the *net* impact of that characteristic root–period outcome for the variable in question. This amounts to reporting the net effect of components of equation (2.3.10) by individual roots, as we have already done for multipliers.

Exhibit 5.17 contains 34 results in all for which the $\Delta \ln$ PPNF response exceeded the cutoff 0.10.[†] These have been tabulated from the largest to smallest root magnitudes. As algebraic logic dictates (barring exceptional C matrix elements), small roots only matter in the short run. Thus, with just one exception, the 20 smaller imaginary roots, ones with magnitude less than 0.70, had only nominal influence beyond period 4. Some root magnitudes between 0.70 and 0.80 were influential through period 12, while those in excess of 0.80 in numerous instances showed up strongly through periods 16 or 24. Oscillatory-root influences disappear beyond period 4 except for imaginary roots 45, 54, 56, and 66 among the 20 imaginary characteristic-root

---

[†] While arbitrary, this cutoff captures one-third of the root total, which should be adequate to give a fair picture of what is happening.

Exhibit 5.16 Parameter-perturbation elasticity responses of Δ ln PPNF.

| L.H.S. | Coef. | Coterm | Equation Elements | | | | | | | | | | |
			Period 1	2	3	4	5	6	7	8	12	16	24
QMH77	B1.0	Intercept							0.11	0.16	0.24	0.22	0.17
	B1.4(−2)	Non-agr. invest. (−2)							−0.14	−0.15			
	B1.4(−3)	Non-agr. invest. (−3)						−0.13	−0.23	−0.24	−0.16		
	B1.4(−4)	Non-agr. invest. (−4)				−0.11	−0.16	−0.22	−0.23	−0.24	−0.16		
	B1.4(−5)	Non-agr. invest. (−5)				−0.11	−0.16	−0.22	−0.23	−0.13			
	B1.7	Non-agr. invest.: average						−0.13	−0.14	−0.14	−0.19	−0.17	−0.14
JCMH	A1.0	Intercept		0.27	0.27	0.27	0.29						
PPNF	A2.0	Intercept	−0.68										
	A2.5	JIPM/JCAP: Weighted ave.	0.82										
	A2.6	Rate of change JCMH − QMH77	0.83										
M72	C13.0	Intercept				0.21	0.38	0.83	1.46	1.76	0.78		−0.10
	C13.1	ln GNP72			−0.10	−0.33	−0.60	−1.31	−2.32	−2.80	−1.25	−0.12	0.16
	C13.3	ln M72(−1)			−0.10	−0.33	−0.60	−1.31	−2.32	−2.79	−1.25	−0.12	0.16
JCAP	F3.0	Intercept						−0.21	−0.28	−0.28	−0.30	−0.28	−0.21
	F3.3	Nonres. invest.						−0.14	−0.19	−0.19	−0.20	−0.19	−0.14
	F3.4	Capacity × nonres. invest.							−0.11	−0.11	−0.12	−0.11	
	F3.5	ln JCAP(−1)					0.11	0.38	0.52	0.52	0.55	0.52	0.39
JIPM	F2.0	Intercept						−0.40	−0.37	−0.17			
	F2.1	FSMF72			0.15	0.22	0.26	1.30	1.22	0.57	0.20		
	F2.5	JIPM(−1)			0.17	0.24	0.28	1.39	1.30	0.61	0.21		
	F2.6	CN72				0.14	0.16	0.80	0.74	0.35	0.12		
	F2.7	FSNMF72						0.11	0.10				
CDO72	C5.4	CDO72(−1)					0.12	0.11	0.17	0.20	0.15		
CDFE72	C4.6	CDFE72(−1)					0.12	0.29	0.45	0.52	0.46	0.30	0.11
CN72	C6.0	Intercept					0.12	0.29	0.47	0.53	0.24		
	C6.2	YD72(−1)					0.11	0.27	0.44	0.50	0.22		

	Eq.	Regressor	(1)	(2)	(3)	(4)	(5)	(6)	(7)	(8)
CDAO72	C6.3	PCN(−1)/PC(−1)			0.26		−0.21	−0.35	−0.39	−0.17
	C6.5	CN72(−1)			0.47		1.10	1.79	2.03	0.90
CDAO72	C3.6	CDAO72(−1)				0.10	0.15	0.17	0.10	
AUTOS	C1.2	AUTOS(−1)				0.12	0.19	0.19		
IBFNC72	C9.4	IBFNC72				0.22	0.34	0.38	−0.41	−0.49
IINV72	C10.1	FS72(−1) − SERVE72(−1)	0.10	0.16	0.18	0.71	0.66	0.21	−0.17	−0.12
	C10.2	SINV72(−1)		−0.13	−0.15	−0.58	−0.54	−0.17	0.14	
IRC72	C11.5	IRC72(−1)			0.17	0.40	0.67	0.82	0.55	0.17
	C11.6	IRC72(−2)					−0.15	−0.18	−0.12	
IPDO72	C14.1	IPDO72				0.25	0.37	0.36	0.55	−0.14
	C14.4	Depr. − inv. tax credit				0.14	0.20	0.20	−0.12	
IPDQ72	C19.1	IPDO72(−1)					0.11			
	C19.2	GNPAVEQ(−2)		0.14	0.34	0.49	0.44	−0.22	−0.44	−0.26
	C19.3	GNPAVEQ(−3)		−0.13	−0.31	−0.45	−0.40	0.20	0.40	0.24
M1BPLUS	E16.1	M1BPLUS(−1)/M2PLUS(−1)					−0.17	−0.78	−1.03	−0.58
	E16.2	M1BPLUS(−2)/M2PLUS(−2)						0.16	0.22	0.12
RTB	E2.0	Intercept						0.20	0.11	0.12
	E2.4	ln RDIS						−0.40	−0.21	−0.11
	E2.5	ln RDIS(−1)						0.22	0.11	
	E2.6	ln MBASE						0.42	0.22	0.12
	E2.7	ln M1BPLUS			−0.60	−0.31	−0.17	−0.15	0.10	−0.13
	E2.8	ln RTB(−1)						−0.11	0.19	
RCD	E15.1	RTB						−0.14	−0.24	−0.10
	E15.8	RCD(−1)							−0.12	
RAAA	E11.8	RAAA(−1)					0.19	0.55	0.55	0.28
	E11.7	PPNF/PPNF(−2)					0.10	0.30	0.30	0.15
	E11.2	RTB(−1)							−0.12	−0.12
	E11.1	RTB							0.12	0.12
	E11.0	Intercept						−0.29	−0.29	−0.14
YPDIV	D7.2	YPDIV(−1)							0.13	

Exhibit 5.17 Partial elasticity parameter perturbation-root response of $\Delta \ln$ PPNF: filter 0.10, 1% initial impulse.

Root Information			Partial Parameter Responses					
Root Index	Root Mag.	Imag. Comp.	Period 2	4	8	12	16	24
32	1.00		−0.75	−0.73	−0.68	−0.61	−0.54	−0.42
33	1.00		1.33	1.29	1.20	1.07	0.94	0.72
36	0.96	0.05	3.18	2.09	0.41	−0.64	−1.17	−1.32
37	0.94		0.13	0.12				
38	0.93		0.98	0.83	0.58	0.40	0.26	0.12
39	0.91		−0.95	−0.78	−0.51	−0.33	−0.20	
42	0.88		−1.08	−0.82	−0.47	−0.26	−0.14	
45	0.79	0.28	−5.77	−1.80	1.12	0.33	−0.11	
46	0.78		0.22	0.13				
47	0.77	0.11	4.20	2.86	0.98	0.22		
48	0.77		0.88	0.50	0.16			
50	0.74	0.01	−5.53	−2.92	−0.80	−0.21		
51	0.71		0.92	0.45	0.11			
52	0.71	0.43	−2.93	0.47				
53	0.69	0.35	0.19	0.12				
54	0.69	0.60	4.89	−1.96	0.51			
55	0.69		−0.12					
56	0.66	0.50	−2.08	−1.00	0.11			
57	0.65	0.01	2.05	0.86	0.15			
58	0.64	0.63	1.55	−0.63				
59	0.63	0.52	−0.58	0.27				
61	0.63	0.19	1.40	0.45				
62	0.62	0.60	−2.78	0.78				
63	0.61	0.58	0.26					
64	0.61	0.23	0.44	−0.31				
65	0.60	0.55	0.51	0.30				
66	0.60	0.43	−1.31	0.90	−0.11			
67	0.60	0.32	1.22	0.48				
68	0.60		0.82	0.29				
69	0.59	0.48	0.54	−0.73				
70	0.59	0.59		−0.13				
71	0.58	0.11	−1.23	−0.29				
72	0.58	0.57	0.29					
73	0.57	0.44	−0.64					

pairs.[†] Pronounced long-term effects are concentrated in the large real roots, with the exception of imaginary root 45. Borderline explosive characteristic roots 32 and 33 matter a great deal to $\Delta \ln$ PPNF in period 24 (although they have partially offsetting effects), and real root 36 seems to induce borderline instability with a 0.96 magnitude.[‡]

JCMH: *Private-Sector Wage.* Exhibit 5.18 for $\Delta \ln$ JCMH (the counterpart of Exhibit 5.16 for $\Delta \ln$ PPNF) does not include price-equation influences, although a few wage-equation parameters had consequences for $\Delta \ln$ PPNF. This suggests one-way causation. Several consumption sectors (CN72 especially) and imports (M72) matter strongly through period 12; so do parameters for manufacturing output, JIPM. Autoregressive consumption-sector parameters prominently influence $\Delta \ln$ JCMH. In contrast to $\Delta \ln$ PPNF, elasticity responses for $\Delta \ln$ JCMH are considerably smaller; the latter often exceed unity, while the former never exceed 0.80.

There are also longer-term effects from lagged residential construction (IRC72(−1)) and manufacturing capital stock (JCAP). Lags from the monetary-sector equations M1BPLUS and RAAA are especially prominent. Examination of several of the lags suggests borderline instability, since their impulse input effects have not damped out by period 16 or 24—see especially JCAP(−1), RAAA(−1), and M1BPLUS(−1)/M2PLUS(−1).

Other coefficient-change responses in Exhibit 5.18 also appear. Parameters in the inventory and manufacturing-output equations have relatively strong initial impacts that soon vanish. Imports (equation C13) have a strong negative influence from the outset that lasts through period 16. Another sort of behavior is indicated for IPDQ72 (equation C19), equipment investment in the nonagricultural sector. It has two coterms that contain six-period moving averages of constant-dollar GNP lagged two and three periods respectively, as indicated by C19.2 and C19.3. These terms are opposite in sign but equal in magnitude, which suggests that output accelerator effects on investment feed into $\Delta \ln$ JCMH. The responses are only moderate and damp down after period 5. JCAP's intercept in equation F3 (i.e., capital stock's intercept in manufacturing output) displays undamped behavior, and so does the first-order lag in the same equation, all with low above-cutoff elasticities. RDIS and MBASE have a moderate influence on $\Delta \ln$ JCMH through the RTB (money supply) equation in periods 8 and/or 12. Other monetary influences, except in the RAAA equation, are weak.

[†] We do not believe that imaginary parts less than 0.05 are "really" oscillatory: the periodicity is much too long to have economic meaning.
[‡] Only one negative real root, number 68, shows up in the $\Delta \ln$ PPNF penumbra and then only through period 4.

Exhibit 5.18 Parameter-perturbation elasticity response of $\Delta \ln \text{JCMH}$

L.H.S.	Coeff.	Coterm (Equation Elements)	Period 1	2	3	4	5	6	7	8	12	16	24
QMH77	B1.0	Intercept									0.11	0.12	0.12
JCMH	A1.0	Intercept	0.78										
	A1.2	$(\ln \text{PC}(-1) - \ln \text{PC}(-3))$	0.19										
	A1.3	$\frac{2}{3}(\text{REM}(-1)/100) + \frac{1}{3}(\text{JCU}(-1))$	−0.24										
	A1.6	RPPERM	0.24										
M72	C13.0	Intercept		0.19	0.43	0.50	0.47	0.40	0.34	0.31	0.28	0.17	
	C13.1	$\ln \text{GNP72}$		−0.30	−0.68	−0.80	−0.75	−0.64	−0.54	−0.50	−0.45	−0.26	
	C13.3	$\ln \text{M72}(-1)$		−0.30	−0.68	−0.80	−0.75	−0.64	−0.54	−0.50	−0.45	−0.26	
JCAP	F3.0	Intercept									−0.12	−0.13	−0.12
	F3.5	$\ln \text{JCAP}(-1)$		0.10	0.10	0.11	0.11	0.12	0.13	0.16	0.21	0.24	0.23
JIPM	F2.0	Intercept		−0.14									
	F2.1	FSMF72		0.46	0.20	0.10			0.11	0.15	0.12		
	F2.5	$\text{JIPM}(-1)$		0.49	0.22	0.11			0.12	0.16	0.12		
	F2.6	CN72		0.28	0.12								
CDFE72	C4.6	$\text{CDFE72}(-1)$			0.13	0.14	0.15	0.15	0.15	0.16	0.18	0.16	

CN72	C6.0	Intercept		0.13	0.16	0.15	0.13	0.11	0.10			
	C6.2	YD72(−1)		0.13	0.15	0.14	0.12	0.10	0.10			
	C6.3	PCN(−1)/PC(−1)			−0.12	−0.11						
	C6.5	CN72(−1)	0.26	0.52	0.60	0.57	0.49	0.42	0.40	0.34	0.18	−0.22
IBFNC72	C9.4	IBFNC72		0.11	0.13	0.14	0.13	0.11	0.10			
IINV72	C10.1	FS72(−1) − SERVE72(−1)	0.31	0.18								
	C10.2	SINV72(−1)	−0.25	−0.14								
IRC72	C11.5	IRC72(−1)		0.19	0.23	0.24	0.23	0.21	0.20	0.19	0.13	
IPDO72	C14.1	IPDO72		0.12	0.12	0.10						
IPDQ72	C19.2	GNPAVEQ(−2)	0.11	0.17	0.16	0.13						−0.15
	C19.3	GNPAVEQ(−3)	−0.10	−0.15	−0.15	−0.12						0.13
M1BPLUS	E16.1	M1BPLUS(−1)/M2PLUS(−1)					−0.11	−0.16	−0.21	−0.38	−0.47	−0.43
	E16.2	M1BPLUS(−2)/M2PLUS(−2)									0.10	
RTB	E2.4	ln RDIS					−0.11	−0.13	−0.13			
	E2.6	ln MBASE					0.12	0.14	0.13			
	E2.7	ln M1BPLUS				−0.13	−0.17	−0.19	−0.19	−0.14		
RAAA	E11.8	RAAA(−1)					0.11	0.14	0.16	0.22	0.24	0.18
	E11.7	PPNF/PPNF(−2)								0.12	0.13	
	E11.0	Intercept								−0.11	−0.12	

Exhibit 5.19 Partial elasticity parameter-perturbation root responses of $\Delta \ln$ JCMH: filter 0.10, 1% initial impulse.

Root Information			Partial Parameter Responses					
Root Index	Root Mag.	Imag. Comp.	Period 2	4	8	12	16	24
32	1.00		−0.30	−0.30	−0.28	−0.27	−0.25	−0.22
33	1.00		0.51	0.50	0.47	0.44	0.42	0.37
35	0.96		0.14	0.13	0.11			
36	0.96	0.05	1.99	1.43	0.55		−0.46	−0.76
37	0.94		0.11					
38	0.93		0.56	0.48	0.34	0.25	0.17	
39	0.91		−0.39	−0.32	−0.22	−0.15		
40	0.90		0.15	0.12				
42	0.88		−0.21	−0.16				
45	0.79	0.28	0.35	−0.22	−0.22			
46	0.78		−0.39	−0.23				
47	0.77	0.11	−2.14	−1.01				
48	0.77		−1.09	−0.63	−0.21			
50	0.74	0.01	3.22	1.71	0.48	0.13		
51	0.71		−0.39	−0.19				
52	0.71	0.43	−0.61					
53	0.69	0.35	0.31					
54	0.69	0.60	−1.58	0.43	−0.17			
56	0.66	0.50	0.62	−0.52	0.10			
57	0.65	0.01	−0.60	−0.25				
58	0.64	0.63	0.21					
59	0.63	0.52	1.54	0.25				
61	0.63	0.19	−0.15					
62	0.62	0.60	−0.22	−0.12				
63	0.61	0.58	0.15					
64	0.61	0.23	−0.41					
65	0.60	0.55	0.46					
66	0.60	0.43	−0.94	−0.11				
67	0.60	0.32	0.39					
68	0.60		0.31	0.11				
69	0.59	0.48	−0.69	0.35				
70	0.59	0.59	0.22					
72	0.58	0.57	−0.62	0.19				
73	0.57	0.44	1.50	−0.26				
75	0.54	0.23	0.16					
76	0.53		−0.42	−0.12				

In summary, the $\Delta \ln$ JCMH responses broadly resemble those of $\Delta \ln$ PPNF. While the significant equations are often the same, the coefficients often differ. With few exceptions, own dynamics are much stronger than other terms for $\Delta \ln$ JCMH, but not for $\Delta \ln$ PPNF.

Exhibit 5.19, the JCMH counterpart of Exhibit 5.18 for PPNF, has a comparable number of above-cutoff root results. Root 36 for $\Delta \ln$ PPNF shows possibilities of explosive oscillations while analogous though weaker results appear for $\Delta \ln$ JCMH. Roots 32 and 33, partially offsetting once more, also persist into the long run. Except for root 36, little else persists.

In the medium run (periods 8 and 12), roots 36 and 50 show up. Roots 47, 50, and 54 are associated with large responses in the initial periods recorded in the first two columns.

QMH77: *Labor Productivity.* Labor-productivity growth is more sensitive to parameter perturbations than either $\Delta \ln$ JCMH or $\Delta \ln$ PPNF, which is reflected by the numbers of roots, equations, and parameters and the response size. Potentially unstable impulse responses appear in several own lag patterns (see Exhibit 5.20). Autoregressive terms for CN72, manufacturing output (C6.5), have a peak elasticity in period 1, and remain strong through period 8. These perturbations cause oscillations in the $\Delta \ln$ QMH77 response. Parameters in equations for the investment variables IBFNC72, IRC72 and for manufacturing capacity (capital stock) JCAP, together with long-term interest rates RAAA and money supply M1BPLUS, lead to strong productivity responses through period 24.

Summarizing results on QMH77 in Exhibit 5.20 for coefficients apart from lagged dependent variables is difficult, since there are so many. Some of the period 1 responses are extremely large, but by period 2 have more plausible values. Other noteworthy results are these. The intercept response of QMH77 (row B1.0) remains sizable throughout the 24 periods. Parameters for CN72 have a pronounced influence, especially through period 8, and oscillate thereafter. One generalization that does emerge is that the rest of the model has its strongest effects on QMH77 from investment. IPDQ72 has the same accelerator effect (C19.2, C19.3) that was observed for $\Delta \ln$ JCMH. Perturbations of permanent income and its lags (see rows I1.1–I1.11(−5)), especially when the latter are combined, clearly have an influence in $\Delta \ln$ QMH77. These permanent income terms enter several final-demand equations strongly, especially auto retail sales (C1), other real auto consumption (C3), and real consumption of furniture and household equipment (C4). M72, another important final-demand equation, has coefficients that significantly influence QMH77 throughout. Large and highly persistent monetary responses are also apparent.

Exhibit 5.20 Parameter-perturbation elasticity response of $\Delta \ln \text{QMH}_{77}$.

L.H.S.	Coeff.	Coterm	Period 1	2	3	4	5	6	7	8	12	16	24
		Equation Elements											
QMH77	B1.0	Intercept	-14.59	0.52	0.10		-0.23	-0.32	-0.37	-0.42	-0.36	-0.30	-0.25
	B1.2	Dummy	1.00										
	B1.4(-1)	Non-agr. invest. (-1)	1.17										
	B1.4(-2)	Non-agr. invest. (-2)	1.75										
	B1.4(-3)	Non-agr. invest. (-3)	2.90	-0.10					0.10				
	B1.4(-4)	Non-agr. invest. (-4)	2.89	-0.10									
	B1.4(-5)	Non-agr. invest. (-5)	1.73										
	B1.4(-6)	Non-agr. invest. (-6)	1.15										
	B1.5	ln JCU	1.78										
	B1.6	(ln GNP72 - ln GNP72(-1))	1.20										
	B1.7	Non-agr. invest.: average	11.58	-0.41			0.19	0.26	0.29	0.33	0.29	0.24	0.20
PPNF	A2.0	Intercept	0.11										
	A2.5	JIPM/JCAP: Weighted ave.	-0.14										
	A2.6	Rate of change JCMH - QMH77	-0.14										
PG	A11.0	Intercept	-0.11										
PG	A11.1	(ln PPNF - ln GNP72(-1))	-0.11										
YPERM72	I1.1	Earned income		1.88	-2.66	-0.32	0.13	0.20	0.31	0.27	0.13		
	I1.1(-1)	Earned income (-1)		1.49	-2.10	-0.25	0.10	0.16	0.24	0.21	0.10		
	I1.1(-2)	Earned income (-2)		1.17	-1.65	-0.20		0.13	0.19	0.17			
	I1.1(-3)	Earned income (-3)		0.93	-1.31	-1.16		0.10	0.15	0.13			
	I1.1(-4)	Earned income (-4)		0.73	-1.04	-0.13			0.12	0.11			
	I1.1(-5)	Earned income (-5)		0.58	-0.82								

Rotated table (coefficients by column). Columns are numbered C1–C11 in left-to-right reading order.

Eq.	Variable	C1	C2	C3	C4	C5	C6	C7	C8	C9	C10	C11
M72												
C13.0	Intercept	9.59	1.68	−5.15	−6.13	−5.78	−4.61	−3.33	−2.25	0.31	0.84	0.50
C13.1	ln GNP72	−15.25	−2.67	8.20	9.74	9.20	7.33	5.29	3.58	−0.49	−1.33	−0.79
C13.3	ln M72(−1)	−15.24	−2.67	8.19	9.73	9.19	7.32	5.29	3.58	−0.49	−1.33	−0.79
C13.4	Dummy	−0.20	0.11	0.13	0.12	0.12	0.12	0.10				
SERVE72												
F1.1	ΔCS72			0.11	0.11	0.12	0.12	0.12	0.12	0.10		
JCAP												
F3.0	Intercept	0.59	0.56	0.55	0.54	0.55	0.58	0.60	0.61	0.56	0.51	0.35
F3.3	Nonres. invest.	0.40	0.38	0.37	0.37	0.37	0.39	0.41	0.41	0.38	0.34	0.24
F3.4	Capacity × nonres. invest.	0.24	0.23	0.22	0.22	0.22	0.23	0.24	0.24	0.23	0.20	0.14
F3.5	ln JCAP(−1)	−1.09	−1.03	−1.00	−0.99	−1.00	−1.06	−1.10	−1.11	−1.03	−0.93	−0.65
JIPM												
F2.0	Intercept	1.45	0.55	0.20								
F2.1	FSMF72	−4.77	−1.81	−0.65	−0.24	−0.12	−0.29	−0.30	−0.14	0.18	0.18	0.21
F2.4	IINV72	−0.26										
F2.5	JIPM(−1)	−5.09	−1.94	−0.69	−0.26	−0.13	−0.31	−0.32	−0.15	0.19	0.19	0.23
F2.6	CN72	−2.91	−1.11	−0.40	−0.15		−0.18	−0.18		0.11	0.11	0.13
F2.7	FSNMF72	−0.40	−0.15									
CDO72												
C5.0	Intercept	0.22										
C5.2	Weighted sum: PCDO/PC	−0.23				−0.10	0.11					
C5.3	YD72(−1)	0.24				−0.10	−0.11					
C5.4	CDO72(−1)	1.18	−0.40	−0.51	−0.55	−0.50	−0.44	−0.37	−0.13			
CDFE72												
C4.0	Intercept	−0.26				0.10						
C4.1	YPERM72(−1)	0.42		−0.15	−0.16	−0.15	−0.14	−0.13				
C4.2	Time × YPERM72(−1)	−0.23										
C4.3	YD72 − YPERM72(−1)	0.25										
C4.4	3 × IRC72 + 0.7 × IRC72(−1)	0.12										
C4.6	CDFE72(−1)	3.29	−0.78	−0.78	−1.14	−1.27	−1.21	−1.13	−1.03	−0.60	−0.30	

Exhibit 5.20 Continued

Equation Elements

L.H.S.	Coeff.	Coterm	Period 1	2	3	4	5	6	7	8	12	16	24
CS72	C7.0	Intercept	0.31										
CN72	C6.0	Intercept	-5.19	-0.64	-1.77	-1.95	-1.90	-1.50	-1.10	-0.76		0.27	0.16
	C6.1	$\Delta(1/\text{YD72})$	0.11										
	C6.2	YD72(-1)	4.89	-0.60	-1.66	-1.84	-1.79	-1.41	-1.03	-0.72		0.25	0.15
	C6.3	PCN(-1)/PC(-1)	-3.84	0.47	1.31	1.44	1.41	1.11	0.81	0.56		-0.20	-0.12
	C6.5	CN72(-1)	19.85	-2.45	-6.76	-7.46	-7.27	-5.73	-4.20	-2.91	0.30	1.02	0.61
CDAO72	C3.0	Intercept	-0.35	0.14		0.13	0.13	0.11					
	C3.2	YPERM72(-1)	0.37	-0.14		-0.14	-0.13	-0.11					
	C3.4	PGAS × JGPM/PC	0.28	-0.11		-0.10							
	C3.6	CDAQ72(-1)	1.30	-0.50	-0.35	-0.48	-0.47	-0.40	-0.33	-0.26			
AUTOS	C1.0	Intercept	0.38	-0.12	-0.18	-0.16	-0.14						
	C1.1	YPERM72(-1)	0.70	-0.22	-0.34	-0.31	-0.26	-0.18	-0.11				
	C1.2	AUTOS(-1)	1.61	-0.51	-0.77	-0.70	-0.59	-0.40	-0.25	-0.14			
	C1.4	Auto-related prices	-0.16										
IBFNC72	C9.0	Intercept	0.14										
	C9.2	Depr. × GNP72	0.57										
	C9.3	Weighted sum: UCKNC/PPNF	-0.26										
	C9.4	IBFNC72	3.57	0.34	-0.43	-0.59	-0.58	-0.38	-0.13		0.13	0.19	0.17
	C9.5(-2)	GNP72, Cost cap. (-2)	0.12								0.82	1.21	1.05

Eq.	Code	Variable											
IINV72	C10.0	Intercept	-1.05	1.28	0.28	-0.38	0.15	0.69	0.70	0.68	0.45	0.12	
	C10.1	FS72(-1) − SERVE72(-1)	9.39	-11.37	-2.53	0.31	-0.12	-0.56	-0.57	-0.55	-0.37		
	C10.2	SINV72(-1)	-7.65	9.26	2.06								
	C10.3	IINV72(-1)	0.20	-0.24									
IRC72	C11.0	Intercept	0.27										
	C11.2(-1)	RAAA(-1) − RCD(-1)	0.27	-0.14	-0.14	-0.15	-0.14	-0.12					
	C11.2(-2)	RAAA(-2) − RCD(-2)	0.32	-0.16	-0.18	-0.17	-0.14						
	C11.3	YD72: Weighted sum	0.58	0.11	-0.17	-0.29	-0.33	-0.30	-0.25	-0.11	-0.19		
	C11.4	Relative price of housing	-0.23	0.11	0.13	0.12							
	C11.5	IRC72(-1)	4.77	0.92	-1.42	-2.39	-2.70	-2.47	-2.04	-1.60	-0.28	0.21	0.22
	C11.6	IRC72(-2)	-1.06	-0.20	0.32	0.53	0.60	0.55	0.45	0.36			
IPDO72	C14.0	Intercept	-0.55	0.13	0.22	0.19	0.15	-0.54	-0.26	-0.12	0.27	0.26	
	C14.1	IPDO72	3.29	-0.78	-1.32	-1.15	-0.89						
	C14.4	Depr. − inv. tax credit	1.81	-0.43	-0.73	-0.63	-0.49	-0.30	-0.14				
	C14.5	(ln GNP72(-1) − ln GNP72(-4))	0.13										
IPDAG72	C15.3	IPDAG72(-1)	0.27	-0.13	-0.15	-0.14	-0.10						
IPDQ72	C19.0	Intercept	-0.18										
	C19.1	IPDO72(-1)	1.18	-0.25	-0.42	-0.33	-0.22		0.29	0.20	0.18		
	C19.2	GNPAVEQ(-2)	5.47	-1.17	-1.93	-1.54	-1.04	-0.43	0.91	0.83	0.44		
	C19.3	GNPAVEQ(-3)	-5.00	1.07	1.76	1.40	0.95	0.39	-0.27	-0.83	-0.75	-0.40	
	C19.5	IBFNC72(-1)	0.27										
M1BPLUS	E16.1	M1BPLUS(-1)/M2PLUS(-1)	-0.30	-0.74	-1.05	-0.91	-0.50	-0.67	0.62	2.05	1.92	0.46	
	E16.2	M1BPLUS(-2)/M2PLUS(-2)		0.16	0.22	0.19	0.11	-0.13	-0.43	-0.41			
RTB	E2.0	Intercept	0.35	0.53	0.38	-0.16	-0.49	-0.67	-0.71	-0.22	0.18	0.19	
	E2.4	ln RDIS	-0.67	-1.03	-0.73	0.31	0.96	1.31	1.38	0.43	-0.35	-0.38	
	E2.5	ln RDIS(-1)	0.37	0.57	0.41	-0.17	-0.53	-0.73	-0.77	-0.24	0.19	0.21	
	E2.6	ln MBASE	0.72	1.11	0.78	-0.33	-1.03	-1.40	-1.48	-0.46	0.37	0.40	

Exhibit 5.20 Continued

L.H.S.	Coeff.	Coterm	Period 1	2	3	4	5	6	7	8	12	16	24
		Equation Elements											
	E2.7	ln M1BPLUS		-1.02	-1.57	-1.11	-0.47	1.45	1.98	2.09	0.65	-0.53	-0.57
	E2.8	ln RTB(-1)		-0.19	-0.30	-0.21		0.28	0.38	0.40	0.12	-0.10	-0.11
RCD	E15.1	RTB		-0.53	-0.61	-0.31	0.38	0.57	0.71	0.72	0.31		
	E15.2	RTB(-1)		0.21	0.24	0.12	-0.15	-0.23	-0.28	-0.29	-0.12		
	E15.8	RCD(-1)		-0.27	-0.30	-0.16	0.19	0.29	0.36	0.36	0.16		
RAAA	E11.8	RAAA(-1)		0.57	0.83	0.73		-0.35	-0.75	-1.06	-1.45	-1.10	-0.41
	E11.7	PPNF/PPNF(-2)		0.31	0.45	0.40		-0.19	-0.41	-0.58	-0.78	-0.60	-0.22
	E11.2	RTB(-1)		-0.12	-0.18	-0.16			0.16	0.23	0.31	0.24	
	E11.1	RTB		0.13	0.18	0.16			-0.17	-0.24	-0.32	-0.25	
	E11.0	Intercept		-0.29	-0.43	-0.38		0.18	0.39	0.55	0.75	0.57	0.21
YPWS	D1.1	(ln JCMH - ln JCMH(-1))	0.11										
	D1.2	(ln GNP72 - ln GNP72(-1))	0.11										
YPDIV	D7.2	YPDIV(-1)	0.41	0.31		-0.10	-0.20	-0.26	-0.28	-0.30	-0.23	-0.11	

Exhibit 5.21 Partial elasticity parameter-perturbation root response of $\Delta \ln$ QMH77: filter 0.10, 1% initial impulse.

Root Information			Partial Parameter Responses					
Root Index	Root Mag.	Imag. Comp.	Period 2	4	8	12	16	24
32	1.00		1.07	1.09	1.13	1.17	1.19	1.12
33	1.00		−2.10	−2.13	−2.20	−2.27	−2.29	−2.14
35	0.96		0.63	0.60	0.54	0.49	0.43	0.31
36	0.96	0.05	0.74	1.44	2.53	3.22	3.51	3.04
38	0.93		−0.29	−0.26	−0.20	−0.16	−0.12	
39	0.91		−0.19	−0.16	−0.12			
40	0.90		−0.18	−0.15	−0.11			
41	0.89		0.18	0.14				
42	0.88		−1.53	−1.21	−0.77	−0.49	−0.30	−0.11
43	0.86		−0.12					
44	0.84		−0.12					
45	0.79	0.28	0.61	−2.92	−1.71	0.33	0.31	
46	0.78		−0.84	−0.53	−0.21			
47	0.77	0.11	−0.37	−0.19				
48	0.77		−1.33	−0.80	−0.29	−0.11		
50	0.74	0.01	−0.75	−0.40	−0.12			
51	0.71		−1.32	−0.68	−0.18			
52	0.71	0.43	3.39	1.43	−0.51	0.13		
53	0.69	0.35	0.19					
54	0.69	0.60	−3.92	−0.66	−0.44	0.15		
55	0.69		1.19	0.58	0.14			
56	0.66	0.50	6.19	−1.79	0.50	−0.12		
57	0.65	0.01	4.96	2.18	0.42			
58	0.64	0.63	−1.36	0.49				
59	0.63	0.52	3.90	−0.48	0.24			
61	0.63	0.19	−6.69	−1.05	0.43			
62	0.62	0.60	3.54	−0.75	0.13			
63	0.61	0.58	−0.67	0.28				
64	0.61	0.23	0.63	0.78				
65	0.60	0.55	−1.87	1.45				
66	0.60	0.43	−3.90	−0.96	0.13			
67	0.60	0.32	1.71	−0.35				
68	0.60		−0.96	−0.35				
69	0.59	0.48	−3.17	1.60	−0.22			
70	0.59	0.59	−0.51					
71	0.58	0.11	−1.49	−0.21				
72	0.58	0.57	−0.65	0.15				
73	0.57	0.44	2.37	−0.54				
76	0.53		−0.45	−0.13				
79	0.50		0.17					
81	0.48		2.94	0.69				
82	0.48		0.13					
83	0.48		−1.03	−0.24				
84	0.46	0.03	6.54	1.66				
86	0.43		−1.06	−0.20				
87	0.41	0.36	7.16	−2.88				
88	0.36	0.31	2.27	0.89				
89	0.34		0.50					
90	0.33	0.05	−34.47	−5.24				

Net elasticity effects of roots 32–36 for $\Delta \ln$ QMH77 in Exhibit 5.21 continue throughout the 24 quarters. Some large short-run responses in periods 2 and 4 are also present. We suppose the latter to be associated with widely observed cyclical labor productivity, while the former are more closely linked to the long-run trend in productivity. The three largest elasticity long-run responses appear for roots 32, 33, and 36. These are not only sizable but show few signs of diminishing. Roots 35 and 42, on the other hand, are still big in period 24 but display very gradual decay after period 4.

Nearly all roots numbered above 62 (with magnitude 0.62) have large initial effects that diminish rapidly. In a later section of the chapter we shall establish which equations primarily drive the observed dynamic behavior.

Exhibit 5.22 Ranked partial elasticity parameter-perturbation response of $\Delta \ln$ PPNF.[a]

Rank	Period 2	4	8	12	16	24
1	−45	−50	33	33	−36	−36
2	−50	−47	−45	−36	33	33
3	−54	−36	−47	32	32	32
4	−47	−54	−50	38	38	38
5	−36	−45	32	39	39	39
6	−52	33	38	−45	42	42
7	−62	−56	−54	42	−45	1
8	−56	−66	39	−47	−50	−11
9	−57	−57	42	−50	37	37
10	−58	38	−36	−52	−11	35
11	−61	42	48	37	1	8
12	33	−62	−57	48	35	34
13	−66	39	−56	−11	−52	−45
14	−71	−69	−66	35	34	−47
15	−67	32	51	1	−54	3
16	42	−58	−52	−54	48	10
17	38	48	37	−57	8	−21
18	39	−67	−58	51	−47	9
19	51	−52	−64	34	−21	−50
20	48	51	−69	−62	41	7
21	68	−61	−65	41	3	40
22	32	−64	−67	8	10	41
23	−73	−65	46	46	40	2
24	−59	−71	35	40	43	48
25	−69	68	−59	−66	51	5

[a] Negative signs mark imaginary roots.

Ranked Root Effects and Parameter Perturbations

Relative rankings according to the absolute values of net root effects for the three basic variables are presented in Exhibits 5.22–5.24. Roots 32, 33, and 36 are highly influential for all three variables in periods 12, 16, and 24. Root 33 is also toward the top in period 8, but these pervasively relevant roots often partly cancel each other, as we have seen earlier.

The most noticeable differences occur in the earliest two periods. Thus, wages and prices have net root effects in common (roots appearing in the top half of the ranks), except root 45, which matters for $\Delta \ln$ PPNF but not $\Delta \ln$ JCMH. A second noteworthy aspect of these exhibits is that $\Delta \ln$ QMH77 root behavior is not the same as that of prices and wages. For periods 2 and

Exhibit 5.23   Ranked partial elasticity parameter-perturbation response of $\Delta \ln$ JCMH.[a]

Rank	Period 2	4	8	12	16	24
1	− 50	− 50	− 36	33	− 36	− 36
2	− 47	− 36	− 50	32	33	33
3	− 36	− 47	33	38	32	32
4	− 54	48	38	39	38	38
5	− 59	− 56	32	− 50	39	35
6	− 73	33	− 45	35	35	39
7	48	38	39	− 36	− 47	1
8	− 66	− 54	48	48	37	37
9	− 69	− 69	− 54	− 47	− 50	40
10	− 72	39	35	37	− 45	42
11	− 56	32	− 56	42	42	34
12	− 52	− 73	42	40	40	− 21
13	− 57	− 57	− 47	46	48	− 47
14	38	− 59	46	1	1	− 11
15	33	46	40	− 54	34	10
16	− 65	− 45	37	− 56	46	− 45
17	76	51	− 62	− 59	41	41
18	− 64	− 72	− 59	41	− 21	22
19	51	42	51	− 52	10	− 50
20	− 67	35	− 57	34	− 11	3
21	39	40	− 69	− 45	− 52	2
22	46	− 62	− 73	51	44	48
23	− 45	76	− 52	− 53	− 54	9
24	− 53	68	− 53	44	43	46
25	68	− 66	41	− 57	22	44

[a] Negative signs mark imaginary roots.

Exhibit 5.24   Ranked partial elasticity parameter-perturbation response of $\Delta \ln$ QMH77.[a]

Rank	Period 2	4	8	12	16	24
1	− 90	− 90	− 36	− 36	− 36	− 36
2	91	− 45	33	33	33	33
3	− 87	− 87	− 45	32	32	32
4	− 61	− 57	32	35	35	35
5	− 84	33	42	42	− 45	42
6	− 56	91	35	− 45	42	− 21
7	− 57	− 56	− 52	38	38	38
8	− 54	− 84	− 56	− 54	− 21	− 11
9	− 59	− 69	− 54	− 52	39	22
10	− 66	− 65	− 61	− 56	− 11	− 45
11	− 62	− 36	− 57	48	40	3
12	− 52	− 52	48	39	22	1
13	− 69	42	− 59	− 57	41	39
14	81	32	− 69	46	48	8
15	− 73	− 61	46	40	3	40
16	− 88	− 66	38	− 61	46	34
17	33	− 83	51	− 21	1	41
18	− 65	48	55	41	− 56	7
19	− 67	− 64	− 62	− 11	8	9
20	42	− 62	− 66	22	− 52	10
21	− 71	81	39	51	34	37
22	− 58	51	− 50	− 59	43	31
23	48	− 54	40	− 62	− 57	20
24	51	35	− 84	55	− 54	43
25	55	55	41	− 50	44	5

[a] Negative signs mark imaginary roots.

4 the 10 largest net root effects for prices and wages lie in the root-index range 36–72, while for productivity the range is 33–90. Several larger net $\Delta \ln$ QMH77 ranks lie above root index 65 while most of the lower root indices (ones with larger magnitude) apply to $\Delta \ln$ PPNF and $\Delta \ln$ JCMH.

A Graphical Summary

An overview of parameter perturbation for the 53 representative variables from the entire model[†] can be gleaned from Exhibits 5.25–5.29 for periods 1, 4, 8, 12, and 24. Elasticity responses above 0.10 are dots, while those

[†] These are described in Chapter 4.

below 0.10 are blank. The rows correspond to the 53 variables, while the columns correspond to all 395 coefficients in the model. The coefficients are in the same order as the rows for the retained equations, while omitted equation coefficients are grouped by the same sectors.

On impact, according to Exhibit 5.25, several clear impressions emerge. First, prices and wages mainly have a diagonal pattern which indicates that "own" coefficient perturbations matter most. The two exceptions are three coefficients in the PPNF equation that permeate all prices and wages except $\Delta \ln$ PIRC and $\Delta \ln$ JCMH. In addition, JCMH coefficients affect productivity ($\Delta \ln$ QMH77) and $\Delta \ln$ PIRC. Second, there are few initial effects from wage–price–productivity parameter perturbations on other sectors. Third, productivity especially, but also some prices and wages (especially ULC77, unit labor cost), are influenced by final demand. Fourth, monetary-sector coefficients only affect other monetary variables and the cost of capital. Fifth, the diagonal pattern observed for prices and wages also prevails elsewhere, but not quite as strongly. Thus, at impact, there are relatively few simultaneous feedbacks or any other kind of cross-equation links.

When we arrive at period 4 in Exhibit 5.26, a change in the overall pattern has emerged, which becomes stronger through time. The diagonal pattern has substantially weakened. While coefficients in the price–wage–productivity sector fail to influence the rest of the economy, this sector is subject to influence from everywhere else, including the monetary sector. The pattern is noticeably more "vertical," that is, particular coefficients now have pervasive consequences for many other parts of the economy.

In period 8, according to Exhibit 5.27, productivity affects wages and prices. The latter are now even more strongly linked to the remainder of the economy. While for periods 12 and 24 in Exhibits 5.28 and 5.29 there are many fewer above-cutoff responses, the vertical pattern becomes even stronger. The wage–price–productivity sector is more widely influenced than any other segment, and as time progresses, the dominant monetary–investment influence once again appears prominently.

5.3   ROOTS

Attention will now be directed to characteristic roots. An abbreviated preview appears in Exhibit 5.30. Nearly 40% of the magnitudes (counting each complex pair as an entity) exceed 0.90, a fact that is associated with sluggish or mildly explosive dynamics. Most imaginary roots—which happen to be particularly relevant for price dynamics—are concentrated in the more swiftly responding, smaller roots.

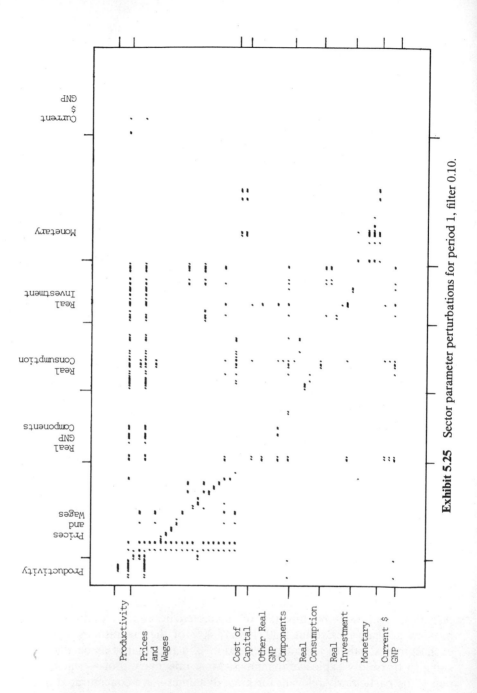

Exhibit 5.25 Sector parameter perturbations for period 1, filter 0.10.

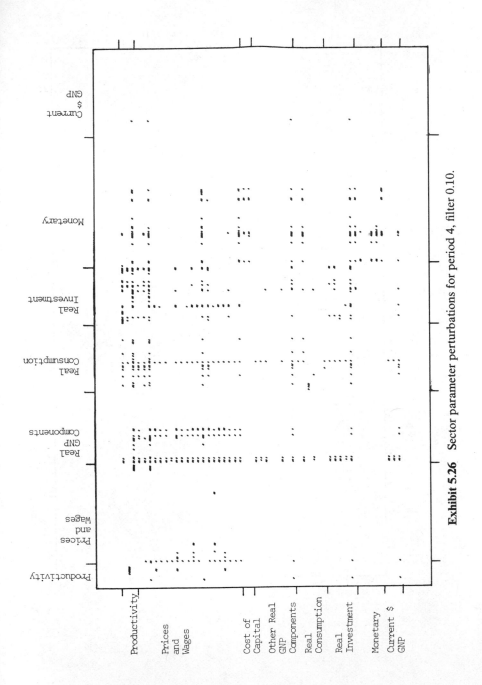

Exhibit 5.26 Sector parameter perturbations for period 4, filter 0.10.

231

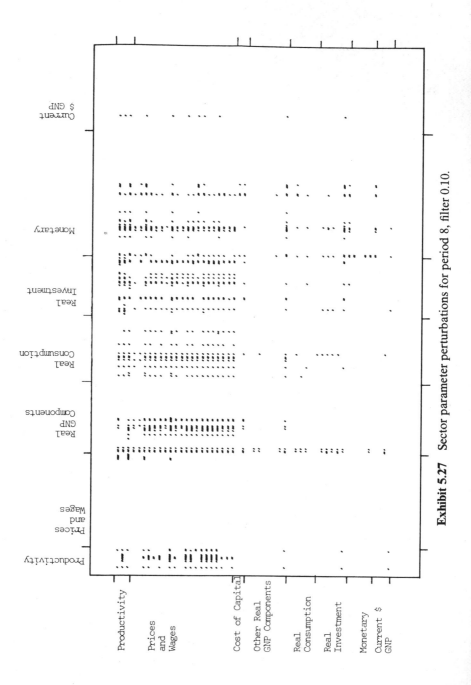

Exhibit 5.27 Sector parameter perturbations for period 8, filter 0.10.

232

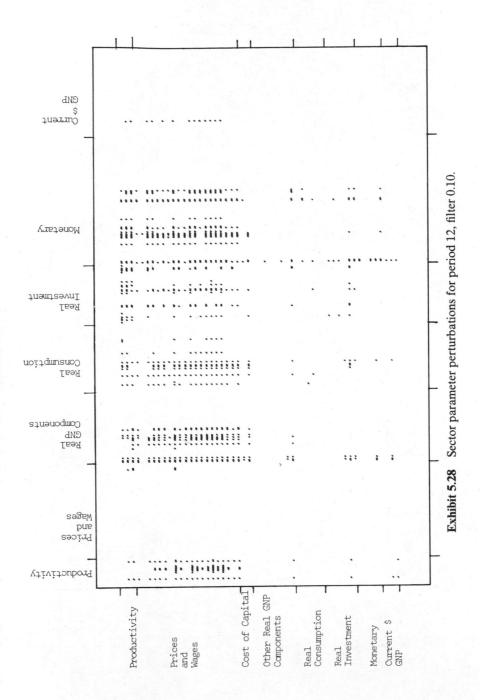

Exhibit 5.28 Sector parameter perturbations for period 12, filter 0.10.

233

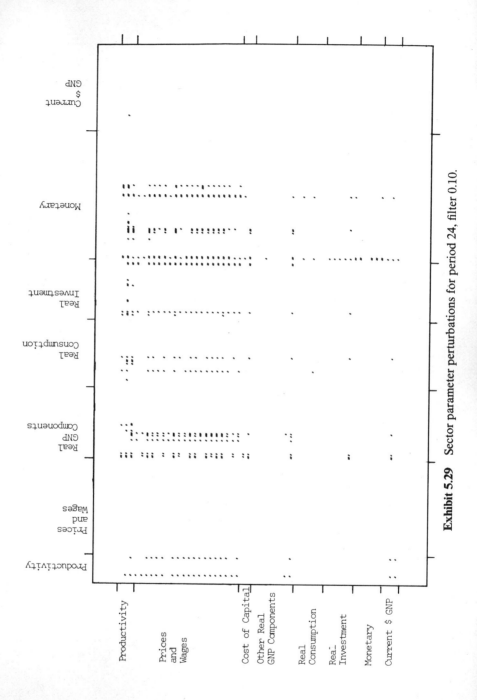

Exhibit 5.29 Sector parameter perturbations for period 24, filter 0.10.

234

Exhibit 5.30   MQEM characteristic-root summary for the matrix A.[a]

Root Magnitude	Total	Real	Imaginary Pairs
1.01–1.036	10	10	0
0.99–1.01	23	21	2
0.90–0.99	7	6	1
0.80–0.89	4	4	0
0.70–0.79	8	4	4
0.60–0.69	13	2	11
0.50–0.59	13	3	10
0.40–0.49	9	7	2
0.32–0.39	3	1	2
	90	58	32

[a] These roots are above the cutoff 0.327. See discussion in Appendix 2B concerning equation (2B.5.10).

Since the homogeneous part of many MQEM relations is linear (in coefficients) first- or second-order difference equations, it is simple to treat each in isolation and extract its characteristic roots. If there is minimal simultaneous interaction, the roots thus obtained will be extremely close to those calculated by LIMO for the complete system. When, additionally, the root sensitivities [see equation (2.3.11)] are dominated by terms from the same homogeneous difference equation, we can confirm the success of both the matching and the isolation of that particular equation. It is possible, as we next explain, to complete this pair of operations successfully for a large number of roots. There remains an interesting root subset, however, for which this cannot be done, and it is these roots which are heavily involved in the simultaneous core of the model.

Exhibit 5.31 presents the first and second characteristic roots[†] for individual equations, and Exhibit 5.32 shows the actual equation assignment and full MQEM root information. For instance, the single isolated root for PPNF is 1.00696 (Exhibit 5.31, row 5), and this is very close to the value of 1.0067, for MQEM root 16, for which PPNF root sensitivities were dominant; so we "assigned" this MQEM root to PPNF. The question immediately arises, why didn't this root—or root 7 for JCMH, with a comparable story—show up in earlier analyses? The answer has to do with levels vs. rates of change. Recall from Chapter 4 that borderline instability was

[†] No higher-order roots are needed according to the MQEM specification.

Exhibit 5.31 Single-equation characteristic roots of MQEM.

Variable	Root 1	Root 2
Productivity and Employment		
RUG	0.4771	0
RUM	0.96745	0.016918
QMH77	1.00577	0
Prices and Wages		
JCMH	1.01361	0
PPNF	1.00696	0
PCDO	1.00543	0.436405
PCDA	1.00395	0
PCDFE	1.00274	0.265135
PCN	1.00588	0.165041
PCS	1.0108	0.442015
PINC	1.00609	0.271638
PIRC	1.00782	0
PG	1.00939	0
PCPI	1.00743	0
PIPDQ	1.01028	0.69225
PIPDAG	1.0065	0.523455
PIPDO	1.05693	0.429363
Other Real GNP Components		
M72	0.737571	0
AUTOS	0.64293	0
JCAP	0.970331	0.01041
JIPM	0.43127	0
SERVE72	1	−0.11033
Real Investment		
IPDQ72	0.68843	0
IPDAG72	0.653512	0.231488
IPDO72	0.70811	0
IRC72	0.77722	0.31457
IINV72	0.2224	0
IBFNC72	0.88927	0
SINV72	1	0
Real Consumption		
CN72	0.76502	0
CDFE72	0.947409	−0.213149
CDAO72	0.84711	−0.26405
CDAN72	0.998662	−0.495162

Exhibit 5.31 Continued

Variable	Root 1	Root 2
Real Consumption		
CDO72	0.88652	0
CS72	1	0
Income Flows		
YOL	1.03213	0.487976
YPWS	1.02128	0
YUNB	0.976261	0
YFP	1.01552	0
YNFP	1.01381	0
YPDIV	0.94171	0
YCP	1	0
GINTF	0.999999	0.481581
TP	1	0
TIBF	1	0
TIBSL	1	0
TSIF	1.01754	0
TSIP	1.01737	0
TCF	0.8593	0
TCSL	1	0
TPSL	1	0
Monetary Sector		
M1BPLUS	1.00837	0.271288
M2PLUS	1.02246	0.460585
RTB	0.43623	0.312881
RAAA	0.90921	0
RCD	0.49012	0
RCP	0.6269	0
RG5	0.74419	0
GCBDD	0.76018	0
MRAM	1	0
GDEBTP	1	0

reported for price- and wage-level homogeneous dynamics, which is consistent with these root magnitudes. But when we look at rates of change (i.e., inflation magnitudes) over the time horizons we consider long enough for the purposes to which models such as this are put, only roots with indexes 32 and higher matter. In short, while asymptotically the rates of change establish levels, other aspects of model behavior are more influential on

Exhibit 5.32 Assignment of roots in MQEM according to single equation roots and root sensitivities.

Root Index	Real Part	Imaginary Part	Magnitude	Period	Wilkinson Condition	Assignment
1	1.036	0	1.036	0	2.2E + 03	YOL
2	1.027	0	1.027	0	3.4E + 03	YPWS
3	1.021	0	1.021	0	1.1E + 04	M22PLUS
4	1.017	0	1.017	0	2.0E + 03	TSIF
5	1.017	0	1.017	0	1.9E + 03	TSIP
6	1.015	0	1.015	0	661.11	YFP
7	1.014	0	1.014	0	4.9E + 03	YNFP
8	1.013	0	1.013	0	4.6E + 04	JCMH
9	1.012	0	1.012	0	8.9E + 04	GINTF
10	1.01	0	1.01	0	2.4E + 03	PG
11	1.008	0.005	1.008	1.4E + 03	2.9E + 04	PCS
12	1.008	0	1.008	0	565.695	PIPDAG
13	1.008	0	1.008	0	5.2E + 03	PIPDQ
14	1.008	0	1.008	0	7.6E + 03	PIPDQ/PIRC
15	1.007	0	1.007	0	2.085	PCPI
16	1.007	0	1.007	0	1.2E + 04	PPNF
17	1.006	0	1.006	0	2.7E + 03	PINC
18	1.006	0	1.006	0	1.8E + 03	PCDO
19	1.005	0	1.005	0	2.3E + 03	PIPDO
20	1.004	0	1.004	0	8.3E + 03	PCDA
21	1.004	0.002	1.004	4.0E + 03	5.2E + 04	QMH77/SERVE72
22	1.002	0	1.002	0	3.6E + 04	YCP
23	1	0	1	0	2.3E + 03	TP
24	1	0	1	0	9.5E + 03	TIBF
25	1	0	1	0	1.811	TSCL
26	1	0	1	0	1.158	MRAM
27	1	0	1	0	103.097	TIBSL
28	1	0	1	0	3.7E + 03	CS72

29	1	0	1	0	7.4E + 04	YP/TPSL
30	1	0	1	0	3.1E + 03	GDEBP
31	0.999	0	0.999	0	4.7E + 03	CDAN72
32	0.997	0	0.997	0	2.1E + 04	
33	0.996	0	0.996	0	9.4E + 03	
34	0.976	0	0.976	0	36.329	YUNB
35	0.964	0.051	0.964	118.027	124.453	RUM
36	0.955	0	0.956	0	9.0E + 03	YPDIV
37	0.942	0	0.942	0	2.6E + 03	
38	0.929	0	0.929	0	3.0E + 04	CDFE72
39	0.915	0	0.915	0	4.7E + 04	CDFE72
40	0.904	0	0.904	0	1.2E + 04	
41	0.888	0	0.888	0	267.829	CDO72
42	0.881	0	0.881	0	882.873	IBFNC72
43	0.859	0	0.859	0	10.582	TCF
44	0.841	0	0.841	0	955.458	CDAO72
45	0.738	0.281	0.79	17.264	3.6E + 03	
46	0.781	0	0.781	0	9.8E + 03	IRC72
47	0.764	0.113	0.772	42.627	7.3E + 03	
48	0.767	0	0.767	0	2.0E + 03	CN72
49	0.76	0	0.76	0	11.946	GCBDD
50	0.738	0.008	0.738	570.678	4.0E + 03	M72/RG5
51	0.708	0	0.708	0	579.035	IPDO72
52	0.561	0.429	0.706	9.622	2.3E + 03	
53	0.597	0.354	0.694	11.745	1.5E + 03	
54	0.353	0.597	0.694	6.061	2.3E + 03	
55	0.693	0	0.693	0	1.3E + 03	PIPDQ
56	0.43	0.504	0.663	7.268	2.0E + 03	
57	0.654	0.007	0.654	611.168	3.4E + 03	IPDAG72/AUTOS
58	0.101	0.629	0.637	4.452	2.3E + 03	
59	0.352	0.525	0.632	6.412	2.1E + 03	
60	0.627	0	0.627	0	1	
61	0.596	0.192	0.626	20.106	4.6E + 03	RCP

Exhibit 5.32 Continued

Root Index	Real Part	Imaginary Part	Magnitude	Period	Wilkinson Condition	Assignment
62	−0.148	0.601	0.619	3.469	3.1E + 03	
63	0.19	0.584	0.614	5	2.4E + 03	
64	−0.561	0.232	0.607	2.285	2.8E + 03	
65	−0.239	0.55	0.6	3.173	3.0E + 03	
66	−0.422	0.426	0.6	2.671	4.1E + 03	
67	−0.506	0.316	0.597	2.432	3.0E + 03	
68	−0.596	0	0.596	0	2.2E + 03	
69	−0.349	0.478	0.592	2.853	6.1E + 03	
70	−0.039	0.59	0.592	3.839	2.9E + 03	
71	−0.568	0.108	0.579	2.128	2.4E + 03	
72	0.094	0.569	0.576	4.464	1.8E + 03	
73	−0.357	0.439	0.566	2.788	5.0E + 03	
74	−0.136	0.542	0.558	3.458	1.7E + 03	
75	−0.492	0.227	0.542	2.319	1.3E + 03	
76	−0.531	0	0.531	0	1.4E + 03	
77	0.522	0	0.522	0	212.976	PIPDAG
78	−0.292	0.418	0.509	2.882	71.357	HOUSES
79	−0.497	0	0.497	0	138.026	CDAN72
80	0.482	0	0.482	0	236.904	PIPDO
81	0.478	0	0.478	0	5.2E + 03	YOL
82	0.477	0	0.477	0	254.824	GINTF
83	0.477	0	0.477	0	2.9E + 03	RUG
84	0.46	0.032	0.461	89.442	4.2E + 03	M2PLUS
85	0.437	0	0.437	0	821.815	PCDO
86	0.427	0	0.427	0	1.4E + 03	RTB
87	0.203	0.356	0.41	5.964	5.2E + 03	
88	−0.18	0.312	0.36	2.999	6.9E + 03	
89	−0.339	0	0.339	0	6.4E + 03	
90	0.324	0.05	0.327	41.154	1.6E + 03	

rates of change for shorter time intervals. Thus, while rates of change ultimately determine levels, the reverse is not true.

Largest Roots

While few of the largest roots are heavily involved in price–wage–productivity multipliers or parameter perturbations, in Exhibit 5.32[†] there are 33 root magnitudes (counting an imaginary pair as one root) of 0.99 or greater. This is noteworthy in itself, so we comment briefly on root parameter sensitivities with respect to (linearized) model coefficients [see Chapter 2, equation (2.3.11) and its discussion] measured as elasticities. Each entry of the modulus root-sensitivity tables is a percentage change of the characteristic root in response to a 1% change in an entry of the matrix A. Similarly, the associated period table records the percentage change of the period of the root with respect to elements of A.

The largest two roots of 1.0357 and 1.0279 are related to income "filler" equations. Such filler equations are usually autoregressively driven national-income components that are needed to fill in the income side of the basic national-income accounting identity (i.e., Σ incomes $\equiv \Sigma$ outputs). There is seldom adequate theory for such equations, and ad hoc, "plausible" correlates are selected. This kind of equation appears in most econometric forecasting models. The largest root has dominant sensitivities 1.456 and -0.685 for YOL (other labor income) for lags 1 and 2 in the YOL equation, according to Exhibit 5.33. In this and similar root-sensitivity tables, the largest 10 elasticities, provided they are above 0.05, have been recorded.

The first-order lag sensitivity for YPWS (private wages and salaries) has a sizable entry (0.67) in the YPWS equation. The second largest root has larger YPWS than YOL lag sensitivities but otherwise strongly resembles the biggest root (see also Exhibit 5.33). While such "filler" equations appear innocuous, we conjecture that their presence may introduce inertia (or possibly explosiveness) into the model that could adversely affect its response to exogenous variables and influence its longer-run behavior. The third largest root has large sensitivities for M2BPLUS from the money demand equation. The remaining roots above unity are most strongly influenced by autoregressive price terms.

Multiple roots of unity for roots 23–30 mainly originate in tax equations. The former are usually defined by the MQEM modelers as the linear first differences in a tax-receipt variable explained by a first difference in an appropriate tax base. This structure automatically generates a unit root. These multiple roots did not impair solution accuracy (see Appendix 5A),

---

[†]See Appendix 5A for the interpretation of the Wilkinson condition number.

Exhibit 5.33 Sensitivity of roots 1 and 2 with respect to *A*.

Modulus of Root 1

	GNP72(−1)	JCAP(−1)	JCMH(−1)	PG(−1)	YOL(−1)	YPERM72(−1)	YPWS(−1)	YOL(−2)	YPERM72(−2)	Sum
CDAN72						0.089			−0.081	0.027
JCAP	−0.094									−0.100
JCMH		−0.151								−0.155
PG			−0.096							−0.098
YOL					2.192			−0.701		1.490
YPWS							0.670			0.645
YOL(−1)	−0.095				−0.701					−0.701
Sum	−0.143	−0.100	−0.155	−0.098	1.490	−0.003	0.645	−0.701	−0.011	

Modulus of Root 2

	CS72(−1)	GNP72(−1)	JCAP(−1)	JCMH(−1)	PCS(−1)	SERVE72(−1)	YOL(−1)	YPWS(−1)	YOL(−2)	Sum
CS72	0.096									0.097
JCAP		−0.142								−0.149
JCMH			−0.242							−0.245
PCS				−0.095						−0.067
SERVE72						−0.090				−0.105
YOL							0.688		−0.222	0.464
YPWS		−0.170						1.367		1.306
YOL(−1)							−0.221			−0.221
Sum	0.097	−0.170	−0.149	−0.245	−0.067	−0.105	0.464	1.306	−0.221	

although the condition number of A was inflated as a consequence. The random walk thus created might have adverse long-term implications, but the short-run uses of the model weaken the negative connotations of this equation form.[†]

Indeed, all 30 roots of magnitudes 1.0 and above share the common attribute of originating in equations where $y_t = y_{t-1} + \cdots$ or $\log y_t = \log y_{t-1} + \cdots$, and further autoregressive terms may also be included. Thus the difference (or log difference) dominates the unit and above-unit roots. Furthermore, associated root sensitivities reflect the same basic structure. None of these roots are influential in either multipliers or parameter perturbations. Thus, these differenced equations affect model levels as shown in the homogeneous dynamics of Chapter 4 (see Exhibit 4.22). Rate-of-change dynamics are associated with regular autoregressive terms in behavior equations.

Next, we consider roots that were prominent in either multipliers or parameter perturbations. We do so in terms of the following three groups: roots that are common in both multipliers and parameter perturbations, those that are influential mainly for multipliers, and those that dominate parameter perturbations. Since many roots are relevant in one way or another, we have selected a handful and describe their characteristics, either because they are especially important or because they are in some loose sense representative of a cluster of related roots.

Common Roots

Two roots have particular relevance in that they control the long-run responses for parameter perturbations and multipliers. These are root 36 (with a small imaginary part) and root 45, having respective magnitudes of 0.96 and 0.79 in Exhibits 5.34 and 5.35. Root 36 appears closely related to prices and wages, especially the imaginary components. Lagged JCAP is relatively important in the real part, but by far the largest elasticities occur among the imaginary elements, where lagged wages overwhelm the other, quite large elasticities. Exhibit 5.35 for root 45 is less interpretable, although some important aspects are apparent. Specifically, investment and investment-driving variables are prominent (IRC72, IPDQ72 and GNPAVEQ, UCEAVEQ respectively), together with final demand: GNP72 and YPERM. Several prices emerge among the larger imaginary elasticities. These aspects figure

---

[†] While there may be adequate reasons to estimate equations this way, the modelers could and probably should revert to levels after estimation and thus eliminate the unit root. This produces a static equation, which had been their original intention. It is also the correct way to calculate estimated-tax payments.

Exhibit 5.34 Sensitivity of root 36 with respect to *A*.

Modulus

	CS72(-1)	JCAP(-1)	M1BPLUS(-1)	PCN(-1)	PCS(-1)	PG(-1)	PINC(-1)	YPWS(-1)	PCS(-2)	Sum
CS72	0.140									0.133
JCAP		0.346								0.335
M1BPLUS			0.176							0.135
PCN				0.125						0.127
PCS					-0.381				0.145	-0.204
PG						0.303				0.298
PINC							0.260			0.200
YPWS								-0.282		-0.260
PCS(-1)					0.129					0.129
Sum	0.133	0.335	0.135	0.127	-0.204	0.298	0.200	-0.260	0.129	

Period

	JCMH(-1)	PC(-1)	PCN(-1)	PCS(-1)	JCMH(-2)	JCMH(-3)	JCMH(-4)	PCS(-2)	Sum
JCMH	19.483								18.424
PCN			10.921						8.804
PCS				24.843				-7.866	16.587
JCMH(-1)	-5.332								-5.332
JCMH(-2)					-4.821				-4.821
JCMH(-3)						-4.821			-4.821
JCMH(-4)							-4.838		-4.838
PC(-1)		-4.625							-4.625
PCS(-1)								-7.703	-7.703
Sum	18.424	-1.735	8.804	16.587	-5.332	-4.821	-4.821	-7.703	

Exhibit 5.35 Sensitivity of root 45 with respect to A.

Modulus

	GNP72(-1)	IRC72(-1)	YPERM72(-1)	GNPAVEQ(-2)	GNPAVEQ(-3)	UCEAVEQ(-4)	YPERM72(-2)	Sum
AUTOS			-0.063				0.077	-0.002
IPDQ72		-0.055		-0.067	0.059	0.056		0.007
IRC72				0.091				0.006
GNPAVEQ(-2)	0.065							0.091
GNP72(-1)								0.065
UCEAVEQ(-4)						-0.076		-0.076
YPERM72(-1)			0.078					0.078
Sum	0.099	0.006	0.002	0.004	0.091	0.010	0.078	

Period

	IPDO72(-1)	IRC72(-1)	PCN(-1)	PPNF(-1)	YPWS(-1)	PPNF(-2)	PPNF(-3)	UCEAVEQ(-4)	UCEAVEQ(-5)	Sum
IPDO72	0.217									0.281
IPDQ72									-0.251	0.080
IRC72		0.457								0.348
PCN			-0.236							-0.174
PPNF				0.523						0.366
YPWS					-0.240					-0.137
PPNF(-1)				-0.211						-0.211
PPNF(-2)						-0.237				-0.237
PPNF(-3)							-0.186			-0.186
UCEAVEQ(-4)								-0.230		-0.230
Sum	0.281	0.348	-0.174	0.366	-0.137	-0.211	-0.237	-0.109	-0.230	

Exhibit 5.36 Sensitivity of root 58 with respect to A.

Modulus

	JCMH(−1)	JCMH(−2)	JCMH(−3)	JCMH(−4)	PC(−2)	PC(−3)	PC(−7)	PC(−8)	PC(−9)	Sum
RPPERM	0.052								0.052	0.049
JCMH(−1)		0.052								0.052
JCMH(−2)			0.052							0.052
JCMH(−3)				0.052						0.052
JCMH(−4)					0.051					0.052
PC(−2)						0.052				0.051
PC(−3)							0.056			0.052
PC(−7)								0.056		0.056
PC(−8)									0.052	0.052
Sum	0.004	0.052	0.052	0.052	0.049	0.051	0.050	0.056	0.052	

Period

	JCMH(−1)	PCN(−1)	PCS(−1)	JCMH(−2)	JCMH(−3)	JCMH(−5)	Sum
PC		0.027	0.038			−0.057	0.012
PCN		−0.022				0.024	0.008
PCS			−0.049			0.043	−0.002
JCMH(−1)	0.016						0.016
JCMH(−2)				0.016			0.016
JCMH(−3)					0.016		0.016
Sum	0.020	0.008	−0.002	0.016	0.016	0.016	

Exhibit 5.37 Sensitivity of root 69 with respect to *A*.

	Modulus										
	IBF72(−2)	IBF72(−4)	IBF72(−5)	IBF72(−6)	JCMH(−5)	QHT1(−6)	QHT1(−8)	QMHT(−2)	QMHT(−3)	UCEAVEQ(−5)	Sum
IBF72										0.069	0.054
PC					−0.106				−0.125		−0.040
QHT1				0.090							0.054
QMHT							0.064	0.097			0.054
IBF72(−2)	0.065										0.065
IBF72(−4)		0.074									0.074
IBF72(−5)			0.090								0.090
QHT1(−6)						0.065					0.065
Sum	0.056	0.016	0.074	0.090	−0.038	0.042	0.064	0.039	0.059	0.035	

	Period				
	IBF72(−5)	JCMH(−5)	QMHT(−3)	QMHT(−4)	Sum
PC		0.094	0.050	−0.128	−0.018
PCN		−0.030	−0.029	0.052	0.007
PCS		−0.051		0.034	0.001
PPNF				0.049	0.009
QHT1	−0.039				0.007
Sum	−0.019	−0.015	−0.002	0.018	

prominently in earlier discussions. We were not able to unambiguously assign these roots to particular equations, however.

Other common roots, mostly imaginary, come in index clusters: $\{52, 54, 58, 59, 61, 62\}$, $\{69, 71, 72, 73\}$, and $\{84, 87, 88, 90\}$. Roots 58, 69, and 87 were somewhat arbitrarily selected as representatives from these three clusters, more to indicate the nature of the roots with different magnitudes rather than for their typicality. These imaginary roots appear in Exhibits 5.36–5.38. Exhibit 5.36 for root 58 has long lags in JCMH and PC, and more generally is linked with price block behavior. This points strongly to the wage equation, which has long lags in RPPERM.

The next root, number 69 in Exhibit 5.37, has mainly aggregate investment and averaged productivity in its large-sensitivity modulus elasticities. The same variables appear in the imaginary part, and mainly affect prices. This points clearly to the PPNF equation as the principal influence on this root.

The very rapid root 87 in Exhibit 5.38 requires a somewhat longer interpretation. The lagged average GNP and lagged average cost of capital are part of the IPDQ72 equation (C19), which was prominent in earlier parameter perturbations. The lagged productivity term also enters the

Exhibit 5.38   Sensitivity of root 87 with respect to A.

			Modulus			
	GNPAVEQ(-2)	GNPAVEQ(-3)	QMHT(-4)	UCEAVEQ(-4)	UCEAVEQ(-5)	Sum
FS72		1.060			-1.031	0.032
GNP72	1.023					0.162
IBF72		-1.540			1.729	-0.002
YD72	1.068		-1.007	-1.008		0.147
YPWS	-1.243			1.221		-0.150
Sum	-0.001	-0.002	0.000	0.000	0.002	

		Period		
	GNPAVEQ(-3)	QMHT(-4)	UCEAVEQ(-5)	Sum
GNP72	-2.191		2.266	-0.068
IBF72	1.551		-1.395	-0.004
PC		-1.492		-0.000
YD72	-2.605	1.478	2.622	-0.067
YPWS	2.576		-2.683	0.088
Sum	-0.002	-0.000	0.002	

Exhibit 5.39 Sensitivity of root 66 with respect to *A*.

Modulus

	IBF72(−5)	IBF72(−6)	JCMH(−5)	QHT1(−7)	QHT1(−8)	QMHT(−3)	QMHT(−4)	UCKPDQ(−4)	UCKPDQ(−5)	Sum
PC			−0.084				0.102			−0.019
PCN							−0.051			−0.000
QHT1		0.065								0.039
QMHT					0.061					0.039
UCEAVEQ									0.067	0.044
IBF72(−5)	0.065									0.065
QHT1(−7)				0.061						0.061
QMHT(−3)						0.053				0.053
UCKPDQ(−4)								0.067		0.067
Sum	0.019	0.065	−0.017	0.036	0.061	0.032	0.053	0.039	0.067	

Period

	IPDQ72(−1)	IBF72(−4)	IBF72(−5)	JCMH(−5)	QMHT(−2)	QMHT(−3)	QMHT(−4)	UCEAVEQ(−5)	Sum
IBF72	0.016							−0.019	−0.004
PC				0.022	0.015	−0.035	0.039		0.010
PPNF							−0.016		0.002
QHT1		0.024	−0.015						−0.004
IBF72(−4)		−0.019							−0.019
Sum	0.006	0.005	−0.019	0.009	−0.001	−0.009	0.001	−0.006	

Exhibit 5.40   Sensitivity of root 67 with respect to *A*.

Modulus

	IBF72(−5)	IBF72(−6)	QHT1(−7)	QHT1(−8)	QMHT(−4)	Sum
PC					−0.065	−0.011
PPNF					0.053	0.012
QHT1		0.055				0.036
QMHT				0.053		0.036
IBF72(−5)	0.055					0.055
QHT1(−7)			0.053			0.053
Sum	0.020	0.055	0.031	0.053	0.048	

Period

	IBF72(−3)	IBF72(−4)	IBF72(−5)	JCMH(−5)	QMHT(−2)	QMHT(−3)	QMHT(−4)	Sum
PC				0.014	−0.013	0.023	−0.030	−0.002
PCN							0.010	0.001
PPNF						−0.016	0.018	0.002
QHT1	−0.010	0.018	−0.013					0.001
Sum	−0.001	0.010	−0.009	−0.002	0.005	−0.002	0.008	

cost-of-capital variables. These in turn affect final demand, especially investment and income, as shown in the row designations. This holds for both real and imaginary sensitivities. Exhibit 5.39 for root 66 has a short story: its sensitivities are for investment-related variables, which in turn drive some prices and investment.

Multiplier Roots

Roots 67 and 75, both imaginary, primarily drive multipliers and have the low magnitudes 0.60 and 0.54 respectively. These come from the root index sets $\{63, 64, 67\}$ and $\{74, 75, 76, 81, 89\}$. They are shown in Exhibits 5.40 and 5.41. For the first, investment lags feed into PPNF via productivity, and PPNF is an argument in the price equations PCN and PCS. More generally, these are important in the consumption deflator PC. A similar pattern emerges for root 75 in Exhibit 5.41.

Parameter-Perturbation Roots

We explore the roots mainly connected to parameter perturbations in the root sets $\{32, 33, 38, 39, 42, 47, 48\}$ and $\{56, 57, 65, 66, 68, 70\}$. The main slow roots are 32 and 33, which we have not been able to assign uniquely to

Exhibit 5.41 Sensitivity of root 75 with respect to A.

	Modulus				
	JCMH(−5)	QMHT(−2)	QMHT(−3)	QMHT(−4)	Sum
PC	0.832	−0.243	0.510	−0.882	0.068
PCN	−0.202		−0.210	0.340	0.001
PCS	−0.355			0.219	−0.055
PPNF				0.237	−0.000
Sum	0.068	0.000	0.001	0.000	

	Period				
	PCS(−1)	QMHT(−1)	JCMH(−5)	QMHT(−2)	QMHT(−4)	Sum
PC	0.038	0.045	−0.182	−0.049	0.123	−0.005
PCN			0.059		−0.069	0.001
PCS	−0.036		0.099		−0.041	0.006
Sum	0.006	0.001	−0.003	0.001	0.002	

Exhibit 5.42 Sensitivity of root 47 with respect to *A*.

Modulus

	IPDO72(−1)	IPDQ72(−1)	IRC72(−1)	M1BPLUS(−1)	PCS(−1)	PIPDQ(−1)	PPNF(−1)	IRC72(−2)	PPNF(−2)	Sum
IPDO72	−0.112									−0.106
IPDQ72		0.206								0.244
IRC72			−0.330							−0.215
M1BPLUS				−0.138						−0.085
PCS					−0.094					−0.033
PIPDQ						−0.089				−0.037
PPNF							−0.183			−0.134
IRC72(−1)			0.097					0.101		0.097
PPNF(−2)									0.130	0.130
Sum	−0.106	0.244	−0.215	−0.085	−0.033	−0.037	−0.134	0.097	0.052	

Period

	IPDO72(−1)	IPDQ72(−1)	IRC72(−1)	PCS(−1)	JCMH(−5)	PCS(−2)	UCEAVEQ(−4)	UCEAVEQ(−5)	Sum
IPDO72	0.632								0.804
IPDQ72		0.639							0.479
IRC72			1.007						0.937
PCS				1.427		−0.525			0.800
PPNF					0.386				0.335
PCS(−1)				−0.474					−0.474
UCEAVEQ(−4)							0.966	−1.123	−1.295
Sum	0.804	0.479	0.937	0.800	−0.115	−0.474	−0.206	−1.295	

a particular equation, in part because of poor conditioning, a technical problem discussed in Appendix 5A. Root 38 has been assigned to CDFE72, root 42 to IBFNC72, and root 48 to CN72. While root 47 has not been assigned, it appears to be primarily driven by investment according to Exhibit 5.42. In the next index set {56,..., 70}, only root 57 has been assigned: to IPDAG and AUTOS. The remainder of the unassigned roots clearly belong to the simultaneous central part of the model. With some exceptions, durables, mostly investment or investment costs, predominate.

Summary

Root sensitivities convey a large amount of information, although at times their diffuseness makes interpretation difficult. Nevertheless, in view of the basic fact that there are 279 state variables in the matrix A, most of the time only a small handful of coefficients appear relevant in a particular root. Finally, some roots are, when viewed through their sensitivities, dedicated to (or originated from) one or a few equations.

5.4 SUMMARY

While interim evaluations have been made along the way in this chapter, an unavoidable mass of detail was generated. This summary is intended to supply a more concise perspective.

1. Multipliers convey quite different information from parameter perturbations. The most striking difference is in their dynamic behavior. Multiplier impulse responses decline rapidly, with few noticeable effects after period 8, while numerous parameter-perturbation impulse responses remain strong even 24 periods after the initial shock. It thus appears that the model is less stable relative to its own endogenous structure than it is to exogenous variables.

2. A small subset of exogenous variables or coefficients matter for price, wage, and productivity rates of change. We noted from the block recursive structure information in the previous chapter that many prices and wages are initially lower (more basic) in the block triangular structure than the real-demand, "Keynesian"-plus-monetary sector. The two sectors merge in period 4 into a large simultaneous block. It is encouraging that numerous equations drop out completely, while many others are compressible in the sense that they have neither significant multiplier nor parameter effects. The details of nonlinear model compression based on the preceding linear information are explained in the next chapter.

3. For multipliers, fiscal effects are more pronounced than either exogenous prices or monetary-policy instruments. Exogenous price effects damp

out quickly and fiscal effects last longest, while monetary effects are of intermediate duration.

4.   Parameter perturbations are more complex. Initially wages feed into prices, although the reverse does not seem to happen. In the medium term, coefficients of final consumption demand are pronounced. In the long run, monetary-equation parameters (especially those associated with the private long-term bond rate) and investment (causally linked to long-term interest rates) dominate the wage–price–productivity complex.

5.   Among parameter perturbations, autoregressive terms clearly dominate other coefficients. Almost half of the larger parameter-perturbation responses are associated with first-order lags.

6.   One interesting approach to roots is to establish which roots in individual linear homogeneous equations are extremely close to ones in the full model. If very close matching (less than 1% difference) is accompanied additionally by dominant-root sensitivities for that equation, the assignment or identification of root origins in particular equations and their relative isolation can both be determined. While this is possible for many individual equations, a subset of influential roots that are important to the simultaneous core of the model cannot be assigned in this way. This "negative" result is informative about model structure.

7.   Characteristic-root information often illuminates dynamic structure. We have chosen to look at characteristic roots in three ways. First, we have seen which roots are most influential for particular endogenous variables of interest by looking at the largest net partial root decompositions. Second, we have extracted the largest individual exogenous variable–root or parameter–root sensitivities from the full partial root decomposition to locate the most important exogenous variable or parameter effects. Third, we have found which parameters in the matrix A have the largest root-associated sensitivities (elasticities). Different roots count more at some times than others, and different roots matter more for some variates than others, so that some unexpected insights into the sources of model dynamics have emerged from these various explorations.

APPENDIX 5A.   CONDITIONING AND THE RELIABILITY OF RESULTS

5A.1   CONDITIONING CONCEPTS

This appendix investigates the reliability of the tools of the book. From the tests used below, we conclude that linear systems analysis applied to the MQEM is reliable and stable enough for the purposes of this monograph.

Reliability is measured in two ways. First, using techniques borrowed from the literature of numerical analysis, the sensitivity of the characteristic roots to small changes in the original problem is bounded by the appropriate condition numbers. The most fundamental reference for this class of problems is Wilkinson (1965). The second test compares the perturbation responses of the linearized model with solutions attained by an alternative method (simulation). The two independent solution methods provide answers that are close.

Condition Number for Solution of Characteristic Roots

The solution of a system of equations may be sensitive to small perturbations in its coefficients. If the system is extremely sensitive to small changes in the original problem, the solution may be unstable or unreliable; small rounding errors that would not affect the solution of a stable problem may cause computational inaccuracy. To assess how sensitive a solution is relative to a certain problem, it is helpful to have an index of sensitivity that provides a bound on the rate of change of the solution with respect to perturbations to the system. For many matrix applications, the appropriate index of sensitivity is the condition number, a measure of the "condition" of the problem under consideration. The appropriate condition number differs according to the type of problem.

The traditional condition number familiar in economics has been the spectral condition number $k(A)$ (defined below), which is a measure of the sensitivity of the solution vector x of the equation

$$Ax = b, \qquad (5A.1.1)$$

where A is a matrix and b is a column vector. This condition number is also known as the condition number relative to inversion of the matrix A. The upper bound of the magnitude of change in x due to changes in A or b is simply the change in A or b times the condition number. The best condition number is $k(A) = 1$, and results become potentially less reliable as it increases. For a discussion of conditioning and its relation to regression, see Belsley, Kuh, and Welsch (1980, p. 100).

The conditioning problem of decomposing the matrix A into a system of characteristic roots and vectors is different. The conditioning of equation (2.3.4) of Chapter 2 (reproduced here for convenience),

$$AR = R\Lambda, \qquad (5A.1.2)$$

is related, not to $k(A)$, but to the condition number $k(R)$ of the matrix R, where A = the $G \times G$ dynamics matrix dy_t/dy_{t-1}.

R = a $G \times G$ square matrix whose columns are the right characteristic vectors of A.

Λ = a $G \times G$ diagonal matrix whose elements are the characteristic roots of A.[†]

The stability of the solution of equation (5A1.2) depends on the condition number $k(R)$ (Wilkinson, 1965).

The notion of the sensitivity of the magnitude of the elements of a matrix requires some measure of matrix size. A useful measure of the size of a matrix is a matrix norm,[‡] which is analogous to the length of a vector (neither depends on the dimension of the matrix or vector). The norm can be used to compare the relative sizes of matrices in the same sense that one vector can be longer than another. The following norms will be used in this appendix: Euclidean (or spectral), l_1 and Frobenius. These are defined as follows:

Euclidean norm,

Vector
$$\|R\|_E = \max \frac{z'R'Rz}{z'z}, \qquad (5A.1.3a)$$

Matrix
$$\|z\|_E = \sqrt{z'z}. \qquad (5A.1.3b)$$

l_1 norm,

Vector
$$\|R\|_1 = \max_j \sum_i |r_{ij}|, \qquad (5A.1.3c)$$

Matrix
$$\|z\|_1 = \sum_i |z_i|. \qquad (5A.1.3d)$$

Frobenius norm,

Matrix
$$\|R\|_F = \left(\sum_i \sum_j (r_{ij})^2 \right)^{1/2} = \sqrt{\mathrm{Trace}(R^T R)}. \qquad (5A.1.3e)$$

[†] These matrices are discussed in Chapter 2; a mathematical presentation is in Appendix 2B.
[‡] A norm is a measure of the magnitude of a matrix or vector. An elementary introduction to norms is in Bellman (1970), and a more advanced presentation is in Wilkinson (1965).

Some properties of these norms that are used implicitly in this appendix are

$$\|R\|_E \le \|R\|_F \le n^{1/2}\|R\|_E, \qquad (5A.1.3f)$$

$$n^{-1/2}\|R\|_1 \le \|R\|_E \le n^{1/2}\|R\|_1 \qquad (5A.1.3g)$$

(where R is an $n \times n$ matrix).

The problem we want to solve is the calculation of characteristic roots:

$$R^{-1}AR = \Lambda. \qquad (5A.1.4)$$

Suppose instead we are solving the neighboring problem

$$R^{-1}(A + \varepsilon B)R = \Lambda^*, \qquad (5A.1.5)$$

where B is an arbitrary $G \times G$ matrix whose elements b_{ij} are all less than one, ε is the magnitude of the scalar perturbation[†] to the system, and Λ^* is the $G \times G$ matrix of perturbed characteristic roots. The intuitive notation is that if the change in the characteristic root matrix Λ is extremely sensitive to perturbation ε, then the solution of the problem is ill conditioned and the results based on it may be unreliable. The upper bound of the sensitivity of individual roots to perturbation ε is

$$|\lambda_i - \lambda_i^*| < \varepsilon \cdot k(R) \cdot \|B\|_E, \qquad (5A.1.6)$$

where the spectral norm of B satisfies $\|B\|_E < G$ by construction (recall that B is a $G \times G$ matrix), and where the product of the spectral norm of the right characteristic vector matrix and the spectral norm of its inverse,

$$k(R) = \|R\|_E \cdot \|R^{-1}\|_E, \qquad (5A.1.7)$$

is defined as the spectral condition number of R. Note that for a given matrix B and perturbation ε the bound on the magnitude of change of the characteristic roots is a linear function of the condition number $k(R)$.[‡]

It is important to note that since the matrix R of right characteristic vectors is not unique (each column can be scaled by an arbitrary factor), $k(R)$ is not unique either. Wilkinson (1965) defines the spectral condition

---

[†] The perturbation ε may be interpreted as errors introduced by roundoff in calculations with finite-precision arithmetic.

[‡] By contrast, the condition number for solution of equation (5A.1) is the spectral condition number of the matrix A. The two conditioning problems have no simple relationship.

number of A with respect to its characteristic-root problem to be the *smallest* $k(R)$ for all permissible R.

A condition-number estimate calculated by the LIMO algorithm is described in a paper by Cline, Moler, Stewart, and Wilkinson (1979). This approximation does not require the matrix inverse (which saves considerable cost). Instead, the system

$$Rz = y \tag{5A.1.8}$$

is solved for the vector z, with the vector y chosen so that $\|z\|_1/\|y\|_1$ is as large as possible. The details of the choice of vectors z and y are beyond the scope of this appendix, but are described in the paper cited above. Since

$$\frac{\|z\|_1}{\|y\|_1} \cong \|R^{-1}\|_1, \tag{5A.1.9}$$

the condition number of R is then estimated as

$$\tilde{k}(R) = \frac{\|R\|_1\|z\|_1}{\|y\|_1} \cong \|R\|_1 \cdot \|R^{-1}\|_1. \tag{5A.1.10}$$

Apart from roundoff errors,

$$\tilde{k}(R) \le k(R). \tag{5A.1.11}$$

Although there are no rigorous results to show the accuracy with which $\tilde{k}(R)$ estimates the true condition number $k(R)$, Cline and his colleagues claim that experimentally the ratio $\tilde{k}(R)/k(R)$ is almost always greater than 0.1 for well-conditioned matrices, and if $k(R)$ is in the range 10^8–10^{12}, the ratio is often 0.99. However, there is no guarantee that the estimated condition number is this accurate. Since only the order of magnitude usually matters in assessing conditioning, this approximation should be adequate for the purposes at hand.

For computations with 16-digit accuracy, a condition number $k(R)$ of the order of 10^8 is a reasonable limit beyond which computations could become unreliable because of roundoff error. A condition number of this magnitude is common with medium-size econometric models, although with careful design of the model (see below) and the solution algorithm (see Appendix 2B, Sections 2B.5 and 2B.10) conditioning difficulties can be mitigated.

Wilkinson Condition Numbers and Sources of Ill-Conditioning in R

Although the matrix of right characteristic vectors may be near to being a defective matrix (i.e., without a full set of characteristic vectors), this near-singularity of R may be caused by a small subset of right characteristic vectors. Wilkinson condition numbers help to isolate the subsets of vectors that contribute to ill-conditioning in R.

Wilkinson condition numbers are a measure of the sensitivity of the individual characteristic roots to small perturbations of A, in the same manner that $k(R)$ in equation (5A.1.6) is an index of the sensitivity of the entire matrix Λ:

$$|\lambda_h - \lambda_h^*| \ \text{cond}(\lambda_h) \cdot \|B\|_E. \tag{5A.1.12}$$

Thus, Wilkinson condition numbers $\text{cond}(\lambda_h)$ can isolate which portions of R contribute to instability in Λ. The terms "well-conditioned root" and "ill-conditioned root" below refer to the degree to which inclusion of the root (and corresponding pair of right and left characteristic vectors) changes the conditioning of the system. See Appendix 2B, Section 2B.9 for a more detailed presentation. The most helpful discussions of Wilkinson condition numbers appear in Chan, Feldman, and Parlett (1977) and Golub and Wilkinson (1976).

These condition numbers have two useful interpretations. The first is that for simple roots (i.e., nonmultiple roots) the Wilkinson condition number is

$$\text{cond}(\lambda_n) = \frac{\|l_h\|_E \cdot \|r_h\|_E}{l_h' r_h}, \tag{5A.1.13}$$

which reproduces equation 2B.9.1. Remembering that $l_h' r_h = 1$, we see that this reduces to the reciprocal of the cosine of the angle between right and left characteristic vectors for a particular root λ_h:

$$\text{cond}(\lambda_h) = \frac{1}{\cos \Theta_h}. \tag{5A.1.14}$$

A root is well conditioned if the angle between right and left vectors is zero, and becomes progressively more ill conditioned as the angle between them increases. Extremely ill-conditioned roots have angles approaching 90°. As

Wilkinson (1965) indicates, it is impossible for the angle between one root's pair of vectors to be 90°, because in all the other pairs of vectors the left vector is perpendicular to the right vector in question.[†] So a root is well conditioned when the Wilkinson condition number is one (the angle between vectors is zero) and becomes progressively less well conditioned as the condition number increases (as the angle between right and left characteristic vectors increases).

The second interpretation of Wilkinson condition numbers is based on the derivatives of the roots with respect to the entries of the matrix A. These are discussed extensively in Appendix 2B, Section 2B.8. In their unscaled form, these are simply the (i, j)th individual elements of the matrix created from the outer product of the right and left characteristic vectors:

$$\frac{\partial \lambda_h}{\partial a_{ij}} = \left(r_h l_h' \right)_{ij}. \qquad (5A.1.15)$$

However, the entire outer-product matrix can be viewed as a projection matrix into the space of the right characteristic vector associated with that root. Defining this spectral projection matrix[‡]

$$P_h = r_h l_h', \qquad (5A.1.16)$$

it is shown in Chan, Feldman, and Parlett (1977) that the Wilkinson condition number for the root λ_h is the Frobenius norm of the spectral projection matrix:

$$\text{cond}(\lambda_h) = \|P_h\|_F = \left(\sum_j \sum_i (p_{ij})^2 \right)^{1/2}. \qquad (5A.1.17)$$

This second interpretation of the Wilkinson condition number may be generalized to clusters of ill-conditioned roots. Clusters of roots may be identified that have similar spectral projection matrices. A pair of ill-condi-

---

[†] In an arbitrary $N \times N$ matrix any one vector can only be perpendicular to at most $N - 1$ others. Since by construction the left characteristic vector l_h is perpendicular to the $N - 1$ right characteristic vectors r_i, $i \neq h$, it is impossible for l_h to be perpendicular to r_h.
[‡] The columns of P_h are simply r_h weighted by the individual elements of l_h. P_h is of rank one, and any matrix multiplied on the left by P_h will be the projection of that matrix into the space of r_h.

tioned roots may have projection matrices that project into nearly parallel spaces but in opposite directions.

In evaluating equation (5A.1.12) or other interpretations of cond(λ_h), condition numbers should not be viewed in isolation. Ill-conditioned roots occur in pairs (or clusters), so that a perturbation in the matrix A may lead to opposite and almost equal changes in that pair (or cluster) of roots. This means that looking at only individual Wilkinson condition numbers may lead one to overstate the sensitivity of the matrix Λ, since most of the changes in a λ_h may be canceled by changes in neighboring roots.

Finally, a useful connection exists between $k(R)$ and Wilkinson condition numbers. If the right and left characteristic vectors are normalized so that their lengths are equal to the square roots of the Wilkinson condition numbers, the sum of Wilkinson condition numbers will be an upper bound on the minimum condition number $k(R)$. Wilkinson (1965) defines the appropriate condition number to be the smallest value of $k(R)$ for all permissible R, and this rescaling of the length of right and left characteristic vectors by their Wilkinson condition numbers is one permissible transformation. With this rescaled $\hat{R}$ and $\hat{R}^{-1}$ we have

$$
\begin{aligned}
k(\hat{R}) &= \|\hat{R}\|_E \cdot \|\hat{R}^{-1}\|_E \\
&\leq \|\hat{R}\|_F \cdot \|\hat{R}^{-1}\|_F = \left(\sum_1^n \text{cond}(\lambda_i)\right)^{1/2} \left(\sum_1^n \text{cond}(\lambda_i)\right)^{1/2} \\
&= \sum_1^n \text{cond}(\lambda_i).
\end{aligned}
\tag{5A.1.18}
$$

Thus the sum of Wilkinson condition numbers is an upper bound on $k(\hat{R})$; this sum is often more useful than the condition-number estimate $\tilde{k}(R)$.

Error Analysis

The preceding analysis focused on the stability of the characteristic roots λ_h under small changes in the original matrix A. This problem is of interest both because the roots are themselves of interest and because if the characteristic-root problem is ill conditioned, the matrix $R\Lambda^n L^T$ may not be close to A^n. This second issue is focused on directly here.

Suppose that the calculated characteristic roots and vectors are a correctly rounded set for a matrix near A:

$$
R\Lambda L^T = A^* = A + E.
\tag{5A.1.19}
$$

Ideally one would like to obtain bounds on $\|E\|$ to assess the closeness of the decomposed A-matrix to the original A. Unfortunately, this is a problem without a clean analytic solution.

A more direct approach for our purposes is to use an alternative method to calculate the perturbation responses. A linearized model created from the original model was simulated by Newton's method using the TROLL simulator. Perturbation responses were calculated by perturbing the model and comparing the perturbed with the baseline simulation. The TROLL simulator has been shown to be highly accurate when it was compared with well-coded alternative solution algorithms, and it performs well with ill-conditioned models (Costenoble, 1981). The simulated results are thus analogues.

Since the two models are mathematically equivalent, the responses to perturbing each should be identical. Any divergence in the solutions will be due to roundoff error and may become more pronounced as the system becomes progressively more ill conditioned.

5A.2 MQEM'S CONDITIONING

The conditioning of the characteristic-root–vector decomposition of the MQEM is high but within acceptable bounds. Ill-conditioned portions of the problem can be located in the original structure of the MQEM. In this section we isolate the portions of the right-characteristic-vector matrix that contribute to ill-conditioning and show how the ill-conditioned parts affect the conditioning of the whole problem. Next, the computed characteristic vectors are shown to be stable for calculations with different root cutoffs.[†] Finally, a linear simulation model constructed from the linearized coefficients of the MQEM is perturbed in a manner exactly analogous to LIMO, and the results show that the deterioration caused by ill-conditioning is small enough to be neglected in this application of LIMO.

Conditioning of the Matrix of Right Characteristic Vectors

The condition-number estimate $\tilde{k}(R)$ of the right-characteristic-vector matrix for the roots above 0.327 is 1.95×10^7, and the sum of Wilkinson condition numbers was 6.8×10^5. This root cutoff was used to generate the results in the bulk of this book. The partial characteristic decomposition

---

[†] Recall from Appendix 2B, Section 2B.5, that the algorithm calculates characteristic vectors only for characteristic roots above a specified modulus. In brief, the algorithm: (1) partitions the matrix A into known zero and unknown roots, (2) transforms the unknown-root portion into upper Schur form with the roots on the diagonal ordered according to descending modulus, (3) partitions the Schur submatrix into above- and below-cutoff-root sections, and (4) calculates characteristic vectors for the above-cutoff roots.

only calculates characteristic vectors for roots greater than a given magnitude; it is discussed in Appendix 2B, Section 2B.5. The MQEM's condition number, while high, did not appear to degrade the results obtained. One reason is that all calculations were done in double precision with extended-precision inner products; another reason is that much of the right-vector matrix was not associated with ill-conditioning.

To get a better picture of the conditioning of the MQEM, we have calculated the condition numbers of the characteristic-root problem for a variety of root cutoffs. Two different measures of conditioning are used: $\tilde{k}(R)$ (the estimated condition number of the right-characteristic-vector matrix), and the sum of the Wilkinson condition numbers. According to equation (5A.1.18), the sum of Wilkinson condition numbers is an upper bound on the conditioning of the system and is probably the more informative measure. In the plots of Exhibit 5A.1, we see that although these indices are roughly proportional for root cutoffs greater than 0.5, they diverge for smaller root cutoffs. This divergence sharply increases as the root cutoff is decreased from 0.327 to 0.30 (see Exhibit 5A.2 for tabulated values).

One interesting pattern in both Exhibits 5A.1 and 5A.2 is the increasing estimated condition number $\tilde{k}(R)$ as the root cutoff increases past 0.60. Since many ill-conditioned roots are near unity in magnitude, the ill-conditioned portions of the matrix R are not affected by the root cutoff until it reaches 0.99. The sum of Wilkinson condition numbers is stable over this range. We conclude that the deletion of sets of ill-conditioned roots can cause a large change in the conditioning of R.

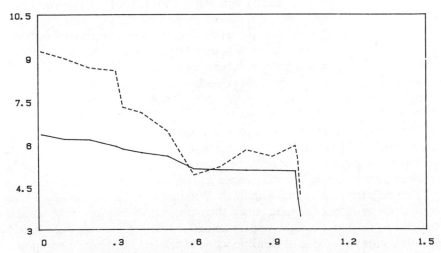

Exhibit 5A.1 Sum of Wilkinson condition numbers (solid line) and $\tilde{k}(R)$ (dashed line) vs. root-cutoff magnitude.

Exhibit 5A.2   Comparison of $\tilde{k}(R)$ and sums of Wilkinson condition numbers.

Root Cutoff	$\tilde{k}(R)$	Sum of Wilkinson Condition Numbers	Roots Above Cutoff[a]
0.01	1,690,000,000	2,259,260	106
0.10	976,000,000	1,546,194	101
0.20	452,000,000	1,448,280	98
0.30	357,000,000	860,749	92
0.327	19,500,000	679,437	90
0.40	12,400,000	510,990	87
0.50	2,870,000	381,927	78
0.60	82,349	133,573	65
0.70	158,089	122,013	52
0.80	608,967	116,865	44
0.90	360,263	114,554	40
0.99	863,266	110,052	33
1.00	290,041	11,643	22
1.01	13,416	2,809	10

[a] Complex root pairs count as one root.

Wilkinson Condition Numbers

The Wilkinson condition numbers isolate the ill-conditioned parts of the right-characteristic-vector matrix with respect to its roots. These condition numbers are displayed with their roots in Exhibit 5.32 (Chapter 5). The most ill-conditioned roots are those with either near-unit real components or negative real components. Also, roots with huge periodicities are associated with high Wilkinson condition numbers, so these periodicities (which have no economic meaning) are probably due more to ill-conditioning than to the behavioral structure of the model. A table of characteristic roots sorted by Wilkinson condition numbers is presented in Exhibit 5A.3.

The reason that the near-unit roots are the major source of ill-conditioning is obvious: these near-multiple roots are associated with characteristic vectors having a small acute angle between them. All these roots originate in first-differenced or log-first-differenced equations.

The negative real roots with high Wilkinson condition numbers also contribute to ill-conditioning, since their projection matrices have similar structures, so that the right vectors associated with these roots are nearly parallel. This shows that ill-conditioned root clusters need not be composed of roots with nearly identical magnitudes.

Exhibit 5A.3 Characteristic roots sorted by Wilkinson condition number.

Root Index	Real Part	Imaginary Part	Magnitude	Period	Wilkinson Condition
9	1.012	0	1.012	0	89312.9
29	1	0	1	0	73948.0
21	1.004	0.002	1.004	4020.05	51950.9
39	0.915	0	0.915	0	47027.2
8	1.013	0	1.013	0	45596.7
22	1.002	0	1.002	0	36386.1
38	0.929	0	0.929	0	29889.9
11	1.008	0.005	1.008	1368.45	28555.9
32	0.997	0	0.997	0	21294.4
40	0.904	0	0.904	0	12361.8
16	1.007	0	1.007	0	11705.9
3	1.021	0	1.021	0	10745.9
46	0.781	0	0.781	0	9792.03
24	1	0	1	0	9506.53
33	0.996	0	0.996	0	9447.66
36	0.955	0.051	0.956	118.027	9042.46
20	1.004	0	1.004	0	8314.71
14	1.008	0	1.008	0	7586.04
47	0.764	0.113	0.772	42.627	7339.8
88	−0.18	0.312	0.36	2.999	6940.34
89	−0.339	0	0.339	0	6364.25
69	−0.349	0.478	0.592	2.853	6134.36
87	0.203	0.356	0.41	5.964	5242.65
13	1.008	0	1.008	0	5194.77
81	0.478	0	0.478	0	5152.1
73	−0.357	0.439	0.566	2.788	5011.72
7	1.014	0	1.014	0	4880.57
31	1	0	1	0	4718.92
61	0.596	0.192	0.626	20.106	4608.95
84	0.46	0.032	0.461	89.442	4176.99
66	−0.422	0.426	0.6	2.671	4092.5
50	0.738	0.008	0.738	570.678	3968.63
28	1	0	1	0	3650.8
45	0.738	0.281	0.79	17.264	3611.94
2	1.027	0	1.027	0	3437.41
57	0.654	0.007	0.654	611.168	3382.29
30	1	0	1	0	3070.61
62	−0.148	0.601	0.619	3.469	3069.11
65	−0.239	0.55	0.6	3.173	3018.69
67	−0.506	0.316	0.597	2.432	2975.04
83	0.477	0	0.477	0	2931.74

Exhibit 5A3   Continued

Root Index	Real Part	Imaginary Part	Magnitude	Period	Wilkinson Condition
70	−0.039	0.59	0.592	3.839	2894.15
64	−0.561	0.232	0.607	2.285	2814.69
17	1.006	0	1.006	0	2658.17
37	0.942	0	0.942	0	2552.94
71	−0.568	0.108	0.579	2.128	2447.27
10	1.01	0	1.01	0	2445.84
63	0.19	0.584	0.614	5	2441.76
58	0.101	0.629	0.637	4.452	2349.11
23	1	0	1	0	2333.37
19	1.005	0	1.005	0	2316.41
54	0.353	0.597	0.694	6.061	2281.3
52	0.561	0.429	0.706	9.622	2254.46
1	1.036	0	1.036	0	2226.48
68	−0.596	0	0.596	0	2169.04
59	0.352	0.525	0.632	6.412	2130.35
48	0.767	0	0.767	0	2022.1
56	0.43	0.504	0.663	7.268	2015.22
4	1.017	0	1.017	0	1990.26
5	1.017	0	1.017	0	1921.66
18	1.006	0	1.006	0	1827.0
72	0.094	0.569	0.576	4.464	1821.55
74	−0.136	0.542	0.558	3.458	1718.27
90	0.324	0.05	0.327	41.154	1552.47
53	0.597	0.354	0.694	11.745	1475.81
86	0.427	0	0.427	0	1400.06
76	−0.531	0	0.531	0	1388.57
75	−0.492	0.227	0.542	2.319	1315.61
55	0.693	0	0.693	0	1295.92
44	0.841	0	0.841	0	955.458
42	0.881	0	0.881	0	882.873
85	0.437	0	0.437	0	821.815
6	1.015	0	1.015	0	661.111
51	0.708	0	0.708	0	579.035
12	1.008	0	1.008	0	565.695
41	0.888	0	0.888	0	267.829
82	0.477	0	0.477	0	254.824
80	0.482	0	0.482	0	236.904
77	0.522	0	0.522	0	212.976
79	−0.497	0	0.497	0	138.026
35	0.964	0	0.964	0	124.453
27	1	0	1	0	103.097

Exhibit 5A3 Continued

Root Index	Real Part	Imaginary Part	Magnitude	Period	Wilkinson Condition
78	−0.292	0.418	0.509	2.882	71.357
34	0.976	0	0.976	0	36.329
49	0.76	0	0.76	0	11.946
43	0.859	0	0.859	0	10.582
15	1.007	0	1.007	0	2.085
25	1	0	1	0	1.811
26	1	0	1	0	1.158
60	0.627	0	0.627	0	1

Although there are many clusters of ill-conditioned roots that we could study, we shall focus on roots 32 and 33 (see Exhibit 5A.4), which have opposite and almost equal partial decomposed values in parameter-perturbation responses. Using the interpretation of these root-sensitivity tables as projection matrices[†] into the space of the right characteristic vectors associated with these two roots, we see that the right vectors are nearly parallel, although in opposite directions. This geometric fact is easily seen because the spectral projection matrix for root 32 is $P_{32} \cong (-1)P_{33}$. Thus, $r_{32} \cong (-1)r_{33}$. So, although the elasticity sensitivities of each of these roots are high, it is misleading [as Wilkinson (1965) has pointed out] to inspect only one root at a time. A small change in the A matrix entry for d PCS/d PCS(−1) (see Chapter 3 for variable definitions) has a large negative impact on root 32, but as root 33's response will be positive and almost equal in magnitude, the net effect on the system of characteristic roots and vectors may be negligible.

The origin of this root pair in the original structural equations is simple to identify. The only important difference between the root sensitivities in terms of the important A-matrix coefficients is that in root 32 YCP is influential, whereas in root 33 it is ULC77. ULC77 enters the model only in the YCP equation, which is a linear first-differenced equation with most of its terms (including ULC77) in differenced form. A perturbation in ULC77 will affect other parts of the model, but the corresponding perturbation included in YCP will cause most of these responses to net to zero.

[†] The projection-matrix interpretation holds strictly only for unscaled root-sensitivity matrices, but since all root-sensitivity matrices are scaled similarly, we retain the elasticity form to ease interpretation. All root sensitivities presented in this appendix are modulus root sensitivities.

Exhibit 5A.4 Modulus sensitivities of roots 32 and 33 with respect to *A*.

Root 32

	GINTF(−1)	JCMH(−1)	M1BPLUS(−1)	PCDFE(−1)	PCN(−1)	PCS(−1)	PINC(−1)	YCP(−1)	PCS(−2)	Sum
GINTF	−1.586	0	0	0	0	0	0	0	0	−1.064
JCMH	0	−1.127	0	0	0	0	0	0	0	−1.109
M1BPLUS	0	0	−1.652	0	0	0	0	0	0	−1.315
PCDFE	0	0	0	2.591	0	0	0	0	0	2.038
PCN	0	0	0	0	3.357	0	0	0	0	2.858
PCS	0	0	0	0	0	−10.363	0	0	3.201	−7.114
PINC	0	0	0	0	0	0	−1.392	0	0	−1.086
YCP	0	0	0	0	0	0	0	0.919	0	0.915
PCS(−1)	0	0	0	0	0	3.179	0	0	0	3.179
Sum	−1.064	−1.109	−1.315	2.038	2.858	−7.114	−1.086	0.915	3.179	

Root 33

	GINTF(−1)	JCMH(−1)	M1BPLUS(−1)	PCDFE(−1)	PCN(−1)	PCS(−1)	PINC(−1)	ULC77(−1)	PCS(−2)	Sum
GINTF	1.127	0	0	0	0	0	0	0	0	0.755
JCMH	0	0.892	0	0	0	0	0	0	0	0.876
M1BPLUS	0	0	3.133	0	0	0	0	0	0	2.491
PCDFE	0	0	0	−1.648	0	0	0	0	0	−1.295
PCN	0	0	0	0	−2.393	0	0	0	0	−2.035
PCS	0	0	0	0	0	7.963	0	0	−2.463	5.46
PINC	0	0	0	0	0	0	1.168	0	0	0.91
YCP	0	0	0	0	0	0	0	−1.032	0	−0.458
PCS(−1)	0	0	0	0	0	−2.445	0	0	0	−2.445
Sum	0.755	0.876	2.491	−1.295	−2.035	5.46	0.91	−1.035	−2.445	

Geometrically, if we add the two projection matrices together, we get roughly a projection onto the space of YCP and UCL77, with the other terms canceling. This is a common occurrence among the near-unit roots. We conclude that the main source of ill-conditioning in the model is the presence of first-differenced equations in the dynamic structure of the model.

Another interesting case concerns three roots (87, 88, 89) that form an ill-conditioned cluster but are not numerically close (magnitudes 0.410, 0.360, and 0.312, respectively). It is displayed in Exhibit 5A.5. The last two have negative real components, and the first two have large imaginary

Exhibit 5A.5 Modulus root sensitivities of roots 87, 88, 89 with respect to A.

| | Root 87 | | | | | |
	GNPAVEQ(−2)	GNPAVEQ(−3)	QMHT(−4)	UCEAVEQ(−4)	UCEAVEQ(−5)	Sum
FS72	0	1.06	0	0	−1.031	0.032
GNP72	1.023	0	0	0	0	0.162
IBF72	0	−1.54	0	0	1.729	−0.002
YD72	1.068	0	−1.007	−1.008	0	0.147
YPWS	−1.243	0	0	1.221	0	0.15
Sum	−0.001	−0.002	0	0	0.002	

| | Root 88 | | | |
	GNPAVEQ(−3)	QMHT(−4)	UCEAVEQ(−5)	Sum
FS72	−2.036	0	1.9	−0.045
GNP72	3.494	0	−3.316	0.129
IBF72	0	0	1.545	−0.001
YD72	3.875	1.577	−3.73	0.171
YPWS	−3.172	0	3.02	−0.107
Sum	−0	−0	0	

| | Root 89 | | | | |
	GNPAVEQ(−2)	GNPAVEQ(−3)	UCEAVEQ(−4)	UCEAVEQ(−5)	Sum
GNP72	0	−4.953	0	5.309	0.123
IBF72	0	4.264	0	−4.57	0.001
YD72	−2.787	−7.612	2.988	8.159	0.183
YPWS	0	5.043	0	−5.405	−0.121
Sum	−0	−0	0	0	

components. Note that in each of these the columns of lagged endogenous variables sum to zero and that there is a great deal of cancellation between roots. The explanation for this is straightforward: most of the current-period endogenous variables (the rows) are static identities that link different sectors of the model. The responses of these static identities to a perturbation in coefficients may be large over a particular root, but net to zero when the individual root responses are summed.

We see from this cluster of roots that the investment accelerator terms have large influences on the above identities that net to zero, and that this in turn creates conditioning difficulties when characteristic roots and vectors are calculated. So it appears that the linking of sectors of econometric models through static identities is a major cause of ill-conditioning for the type of analysis performed here.

So the nearness of R to being a defective matrix may be due to a near-multiple root where it is difficult for the algorithm to distinguish between two or more roots (which often occurs with first-differenced equations), or where there are many links between equations via static identities. Cancellation due to tight behavioral coupling in the model did not seem to be a source of ill-conditioning. The roots that were most severely affected were isolated by their high Wilkinson condition numbers, and were arranged in clusters according to the structure of their spectral projection matrices.

Empirical Link Between Wilkinson and Matrix Condition Number $\tilde{k}(R)$

As mentioned above, if the characteristic vectors were normalized appropriately, the sum of Wilkinson condition numbers would be an upper bound on the condition number for inversion of the right-vector matrix R. In Exhibit 5A.1 these two quantities were seen to be related, but links between individual Wilkinson condition numbers and the conditioning index $\tilde{k}(R)$ were not shown. Exhibit 5A.6 shows the relationship between the Wilkinson condition numbers generated by a root cutoff of 0.01 and the change in condition numbers $\tilde{k}(R)$ between different root cutoffs (their levels are tabulated in Exhibit 5A.2). Since the Wilkinson condition numbers can be viewed in a heuristic way as proportional to the rate of change of $k(R)$ with respect to changes in the root cutoff, both graphs should have a similar structure.

If the two graphs of Exhibit 5A.6 are read right to left, they are seen to have a qualitatively similar structure until the root cutoff magnitude is less than 0.3.[†] Especially significant is the large change in both graphs between

---

[†] There is a "spike" in the change in $\tilde{k}(R)$ where the cutoff passes the near-unit root magnitudes, analogous to the "spike" in Wilkinson condition numbers for these magnitudes. This is not apparent because of the scale of the ordinate. See Exhibit 5A.2 for this pattern.

root magnitudes of 0.3 and 0.327 (the latter is the root cutoff used for the perturbation analysis elsewhere in this book). So some portions of the matrix R contribute to ill-conditioning more than others, and for a range of root magnitudes the Wilkinson condition numbers identify these ill-conditioned portions.

For root cutoffs less than 0.3, the two indices diverge. This is possibly not very important, as $\tilde{k}(R)$ is greater than 10^8, and the algorithm may not be reliable in this range. Since the sum of Wilkinson condition numbers is an upper bound on the minimum $k(R)$, this sum becomes the more useful index.

Another interesting pattern can be seen by comparing the Wilkinson condition numbers of Exhibit 5A.6 with $\log \tilde{k}(R)$ in Exhibit 5A.1. Note that $\tilde{k}(R)$ drops sharply between root cutoffs of 0.327 and 0.6, although none of the roots in this range are associated with extremely large Wilkinson

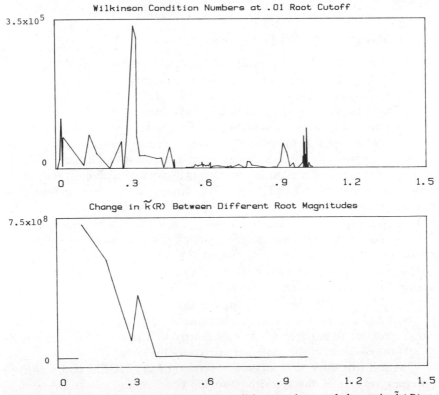

Exhibit 5A.6 Comparison of Wilkinson condition numbers and change in $\tilde{k}(R)$ for different root magnitudes.

condition numbers. Since many of these roots were important in the parameter perturbations and multiplier experiments of Chapter 5, this apparent discrepancy needs explanation. Their root-sensitivity matrices are similar, indicating that they are an ill-conditioned cluster of roots associated with price–productivity–investment behavior. So the deletion of any single root from this cluster need not have had a large influence on $\tilde{k}(R)$ (as the Wilkinson condition numbers are not large), but the deletion of the entire cluster improves $\tilde{k}(R)$ by three orders of magnitude.

Wilkinson condition numbers have proven to be a useful tool in isolating the poorly conditioned portions of the right-vector matrix when the characteristic roots associated with the conditioning problem form a very small cluster. As the number of roots in a poorly conditioned cluster increases, the Wilkinson condition numbers are a less reliable guide to which portions of the right-vector matrix are the source of conditioning problems. In this case, the spectral projection matrices P_h must be examined individually to identify these clusters.

The Stability of Characteristic Vectors

To test the sensitivity of the results of this book relative to ill-conditioning, characteristic vectors were calculated for two different root cutoffs, 0.1 and 0.5. The condition numbers $\tilde{k}(R)$ were 1.34×10^8 and 6.30×10^6, respectively. Root sensitivities were compared for a number of different roots. If the system's solutions were sensitive to the conditioning of the system, it would be expected that the results of the root-sensitivity comparison would be very sensitive, as these matrices contain element-by-element multiplications of the pair of characteristic vectors associated with each root. Four roots are compared in Exhibit 5A.7. The first three columns in the upper part are the root's index, magnitude, and periodicity, which are the same for both sets of vectors. The fourth column is the Wilkinson condition number for the root cutoff 0.1, and the fifth column is the ratio of the Wilkinson condition numbers for the two cutoffs. The lower part of Exhibit 5A.7 contains descriptive statistics of the matrix of differences between the cutoff vectors 0.1 and 0.5. The maximum difference between these root sensitivities is around 10^{-7}. From this test, it appears that for a given set of characteristic roots and a given Schur matrix, changing the dimension of the characteristic-vector problem (from an $N \times N$ matrix to a lower-order one) hardly affects the elements of the characteristic-vector matrices.

This test was done with an earlier version of the MQEM and a slightly different version of the algorithm, so the conditioning of the problem is slightly different from the results presented earlier in this appendix. The

Exhibit 5A.7 Differences between root sensitivities at root cutoffs 0.1 and 0.5.

Root Index	Magnitude	Root Information Period	Wilkinson Condition	W. Cond. Ratio[a]
1	1.030	0	1.7E3	1.56
23	1	0	1.9E5	1.00
33	0.997	0	2.4E4	3.80
40	0.915	0	6.1E4	1.71

Descriptive Statistics of Root Sensitivities[b]			
Minimum	Maximum	Mean	Std. Dev.
0	0	0	0
0	0	0	0
$-1.2E-7$	$1.7E-7$	$2.2E-12$	$8.4E-10$
$-3.7E-9$	0	$-5.0E-14$	$1.4E-11$

[a](Cutoff-0.1 value)/(cutoff-0.5 value).
[b]Absolute difference between values for cutoffs 0.1 and 0.5.

algorithm modifications should not have affected the analytic properties observed here.

Comparison of Results with Perturbed Model Simulation

Another check for how the conditioning of the characteristic-root–vector decomposition may have influenced the results is to use an alternative calculation procedure. A simultaneous-equation version of the MQEM was constructed with the same linearized coefficients that were used in the characteristic-root and vector calculations. This model was perturbed and the output scaled in a manner exactly analogous to LIMO, so the results are directly comparable. Exhibit 5A.8 contains selected parameter-perturbation responses to the autoregressive coefficient $c_{6.5}$ in the CN72 (nondurable consumption) equation, and Exhibit 5A.9 contains responses to perturbations of the exogenous variable GFO (federal government purchases, other). Both were 1% impulse perturbations in 1973 2.

Although the conditioning of the system appears high, no qualitative results have changed, and the magnitudes by which the solutions differ is small for the purposes of this book.

Exhibit 5A.8 LIMO and linear MQEM elasticity responses to identical perturbations: 1% perturbation of coefficient C6.5.[a]

LIMO *Response*

	Period 1	2	3	4	5	6	7	8	12	16	24
Δ ln PPNF				0.26	0.47	1.10	1.79	2.03	0.90		−0.16
Δ ln JCMH		0.26	0.52	0.60	0.57	0.49	0.42	0.40	0.34	0.18	
Δ ln QMH77	19.85	−2.45	−6.76	−7.46	−7.27	−5.73	−4.20	−2.91	0.30	1.02	0.61
CN72	0.77	0.61	0.48	0.38	0.31	0.26	0.21	0.17			
IINV72	0.15	3.55	3.41	2.64	1.83	1.04	0.43		−0.76	−0.57	−0.19
RUG	−1.16	−2.03	−2.18	−1.95	−1.59	−1.21	−0.87	−0.56	0.23	0.38	0.28

MQEM *Response*

	Period 1	2	3	4	5	6	7	8	12	16	24
Δ ln PPNF				0.26	0.46	1.12	1.82	2.07	0.93		−0.13
Δ ln JCMH		0.26	0.52	0.61	0.58	0.50	0.44	0.41	0.37	0.19	
Δ ln QMH77	20.16	−2.35	−6.79	−7.58	−7.45	−5.91	−4.36	−3.06	0.27	1.00	0.58
CN72	0.79	0.62	0.49	0.40	0.32	0.27	0.22	0.18	0.10		
IINV72	0.15	3.60	3.48	2.72	1.90	1.10	0.47		−0.76	−0.58	−0.19
RUG	−1.18	−2.08	−2.24	−2.02	−1.66	−1.28	−0.92	−0.61	0.21	0.36	0.27

[a]Only elasticities greater than 0.10 appear in this exhibit.

Exhibit 5A.9 LIMO and linear MQEM elasticity responses to identical perturbations: 1% perturbation of exogenous variable GPO.[a]

LIMO *Response*

	Period 1	2	3	4	5	6	7	8	12	16	24
Δ ln PPNF			0.02	0.04	0.05	0.16	0.19	0.12	0.01	−0.02	
Δ ln JCMH		0.07	0.06	0.03	0.02		0.01	0.02			
Δ ln QMH77	2.86	−2.81	−0.78	−0.36	−0.23	−0.01	0.04	0.07	0.09	0.04	0.03
CN72											
IINV72	0.02	0.53	0.12	0.01	−0.03	−0.05	−0.06	−0.06	−0.04	−0.01	
RUG	−0.18	−0.17	−0.09	−0.04	−0.01		0.01	0.02	0.02	0.01	

MQEM *Response*

	Period 1	2	3	4	5	6	7	8	12	16	24
Δ ln PPNF			0.02	0.04	0.04	0.15	0.18	0.11	−0.03		−0.01
Δ ln JCMH		0.07	0.05	0.03	0.01		0.02		0.03		−0.03
Δ ln QMH77	2.82	−2.79	−0.80	−0.37	−0.25	−0.02	0.03	0.06	0.09	0.03	0.01
CN72											
IINV72	0.02	0.52	0.11	0.01	−0.03	−0.06	−0.06	−0.06	−0.04	−0.02	−0.01
RUG	−0.18	−0.17	−0.09	−0.04	−0.01	0.01	0.02	0.03	0.03	0.03	0.03

[a] Only elasticities greater than 0.01 appear in this exhibit.

Comparison of Conditioning of Original MQEM with MINI 1

In Chapter 6, a "mini MQEM" is constructed based largely on the parameter perturbations of Chapter 5. The root structure of this model (MINI 1) is presented in Exhibit 6.10. While this compressed model has dynamic behavior almost identical with the original MQEM, MINI 1 is better conditioned. The Wilkinson condition numbers of MINI 1 in Exhibit 6.10 are much smaller than MQEM's in Exhibit 5.32 (Chapter 5). Also, the estimated condition number for inversion of MINI 1's right-characteristic-vector matrix was on the order of 10^5 instead of 10^7, and the sum of Wilkinson condition numbers was 3.1×10^4 instead of 6.8×10^5. The difference in model structure that matters in the context of conditioning is that many of the first-differenced equations that are a source of the MQEM's conditioning difficulties were not included in MINI 1. Many of the MQEM's tight behavioral links also appear in MINI 1, which indicates that these links are not the major sources of conditioning problems. Finally, the success of MINI 1 in replicating much of the dynamic behavior of the MQEM supports the techniques used in this book, and reinforces our belief that the MQEM's conditioning has not adversely affected their usefulness for our analytic objectives.

5A.3   CONCLUSIONS

This appendix has investigated the conditioning of the MQEM and the effect of conditioning on the results of this book. While it appears that the solutions are ill conditioned, the extent of degradation is acceptable for the answers sought. Further, three findings are reported that may be useful to those who plan to use similar techniques.

First, it is possible to isolate the poorly conditioned parts of the right-characteristic-vector matrix R in two distinct senses. The ill-conditioned roots are isolated by the Wilkinson condition number and by the associated root-sensitivity matrices. Also, these results point to the use of both first-differenced equations and static identities in the original model as the source of most of the R-matrix conditioning difficulties. Model builders in the future may wish to avoid using either of these when it is not required for structural reasons.

Second, the partial decomposition algorithm that generated the results of this book has proven to be stable enough despite conditioning difficulties.

Third, the perturbation responses that underlie most of the analysis of this book are quite close to the simulation behavior of a linearized version of the MQEM, which further increases confidence in the reliability of the algorithm.

We thus arrive at the general conclusion that ill-conditioning is not an insurmountable problem, and that the techniques of linear systems analysis used in this monograph are useful, fairly stable tools. Further, the sources of ill-conditioning in econometric models appear to be well defined. Some of these problems could readily be avoided in the future.

REFERENCES

Bellman, Richard (1970). *Introduction to Matrix Analysis*, 2nd edition, McGraw-Hill, New York.

Belsley, David A., Edwin Kuh, and Roy E. Welsch (1980). *Regression Diagnostics: Identifying Influential Data and Sources of Collinearity*, Wiley, New York.

Chan, S. P., R. Feldman, and B. N. Parlett (1977). "Algorithm 517: A Program for Computing the Condition Numbers of Matrix Eigenvalues Without Computing Eigenvectors [F2], *ACM Transactions on Mathematical Software*, Vol. 3, No. 2, pp. 186–203.

Cline, A. K., C. B. Moler, G. W. Stewart, and J. H. Wilkinson (1979). An Estimate for the Condition Number of a Matrix, *SIAM Journal of Numerical Analysis*, Vol. 16, No. 2, pp. 368–375.

Costenoble, S. (1981). Mimeo, MIT, Center for Computational Research in Economics and Management Science.

Golub, G. H. and J. H. Wilkinson (1976). Ill-Conditioned Eigensystems and the Computation of the Jordan Canonical Form, *SIAM Review*, Vol. 18, No. 4, pp. 578–619.

Wilkinson, J. H. (1965). *The Algebraic Eigenvalue Problem*, Oxford, U.P., Oxford.

CHAPTER 6

Reduced Models
and the MQEM

This chapter brings together diverse elements from earlier chapters. Smaller macromodels derived from the MQEM are constructed, mainly from the analysis in Chapter 5. These are intended to make understanding price, wage, and productivity behavior easier and, where practical, other economic sectors as well. First the process of moving from the MQEM to the principal reduced version, MINI 1, is explained. MINI 1's equations and coefficients were mainly selected according to influential parameters and secondarily from exogenous-variable perturbations for the three main equations. Simulation comparisons with common inputs are the main way to corroborate how effectively linear system methods pick out accurate (relative to the MQEM) compressed models. Besides these comparisons of simulation paths, three multipliers are computed (for one exogenous price, one fiscal, and one monetary-policy variable) and analogous comparisons undertaken. In addition some characteristic-root properties of MINI 1 are examined.

Another compressed model, MINI 4, is created using block ordering information from Chapter 4. To recall the MQEM's recursive structure, a simultaneous price–wage block was the most basic in the initial four periods, after which that block merged with the Keynesian demand (plus accounting identity plus monetary) block. Several other compressed-model criteria were applied, which did not work out. One of these, MINI 2, was created using $\Delta \ln$ PPNF sensitivities only, ignoring those for $\Delta \ln$ JCMH and $\Delta \ln$ QMH77. Finally, a MINI 3 corroborative attempt was made with a model based on short- and long-run dynamics extracted from MINI 2. Influential $\Delta \ln$ PPNF sensitivities from investment and monetary variables first appear in period 5. These equations were suppressed from MINI 3 in an effort to devise a short-run compressed model, which did not succeed.

278

6.1 MODEL REDUCTION PROCESS

Static-Identity Removal

As one preliminary, we eliminated seven particularly simple, uninteresting static identities. Four of these were in the final-demand (consumption–investment) sector. A total of 49 identities remain, along with the original 61 behavioral equations, so this nominally altered version of the complete MQEM has 110 equations. The number of equations in any model is a matter of choice, since an arbitrary number of static "convenience" identities can be incorporated. This somewhat leaner starting set seemed more relevant for our purposes.

Model Reduction

Exhibit 6.1 records the final results of equation reduction for MINI 1: half the behavioral equations remain, along with a third of the identities.[†] The last third of Exhibit 6.1 shows in relative terms where changes occurred. Most of the behavior equations in consumption and investment remain, whereas most of the income-sector behavior equations disappear. Half of the fourteen wage–price behavior equations were eliminated, as were six of seven price–wage identities. As a last highlight, five of eleven monetary-sector equations stay while all its six identities vanish. The broad impression is that, relative to our objectives, the reduced version of the MQEM is a model driven by final demand with a condensed monetary sector, and for the analysis of inflation, of course, the central price–wage–productivity elements.

We next describe the process of creating MINI 1. First, "primary" equations—PPNF, JCMH, and QMH77—were kept intact. It might be argued that all equations in the model should be treated the same and that by leaving the three equations unchanged we are biasing the results in our favor. But since the model is a set of simultaneous dynamic equations, their interaction with the remainder of the model can significantly modify behavior. If, however, the model is only weakly coupled and if cross-equation dynamics are weak, then the compressed-model results are bound to be close to those of the full model. This still serves our purpose, which is to arrive at a compressed model that closely mimics the responses of the original large model. Earlier analysis suggests that by period 4 the equations are becoming coupled, so that this issue probably is not critical here. Second, other

[†] It is obvious that the left-hand side of a static identity can only provide information about behavior contained in r.h.s. behavioral variables. While static identities are often convenient summaries, most interest obviously attaches to behavior equations.

Exhibit 6.1 MQEM equations remaining in MINI 1.

Sector	MQEM			MINI 1			Equations Remaining in MINI 1 (%)		
	Behavior	Identity	Total	Behavior	Identity	Total	Behavior	Identity	Total
Wages and prices	14	7	21	7	1	8	50	14	38
Productivity and employment	3	3	6	1	2	3	33	66	50
Consumption and investment	15	19	34	14	8	22	93	42	65
Income flows	15	14	29	2	5	7	13	35	24
Monetary	11	6	17	5	0	5	45	0	29
Output composition	3	0	3	3	0	3	100	—	100
Total	61	49	110	32	16	48	52	33	44

equations and/or parameters were retained that had a sensitivity elasticity for parameter perturbations or multipliers exceeding 0.10 in at least one of the three central equations. The equations for which such variables appeared on the left-hand side were retained, although some of their coefficients were eliminated (with minor exceptions) unless they exceeded the standard elasticity minimum, 0.10, for one of the three central equations.

The exceptions mentioned parenthetically above are few in number. They mainly occur where their inclusion is needed to complete the model. Indirect links between an influential coefficient or variables (ones that satisfied the 0.10 elasticity criterion, or which appeared in one of three basic equations) include two productivity variables: QHT1 and a smoothed version of it, QMHT, which appears in the PPNF equation. These in turn are derived from the behavioral equation QMH77, which exerts strong influences that were noted in the previous chapter. Other direct links were needed to complete the IPDQ72 equation: C72 to satisfy the definition of GNP72, and UCKPDQ to complete the definition of UCEAVEQ. Similarly, YP and TP (personal income and personal taxes) were required to construct YD (disposable income) and YD72 (its constant-dollar version) or YPERM72 (its moving average), since the two constant-dollar personal-income variables were associated with influential coefficients in the YPDIV and YPWS equations (dividend, and private wage plus salary equations).

Several other variables were also retained for completeness that otherwise were uninfluential. To construct YD72, PC (which originally was made up of all consumption prices indexes, half of which were eliminated) was necessary to deflate YD to obtain YD72, and PC is also part of the JCMH equation. In this and similar instances we propose a simple, naive, mechanical rule to create the missing variable. Thus PC was defined to be a weighted average of PCS and PCN, which are the main consumption price equations that remain in the reduced model. Similarly, the algebraic sum of TSIP, YFP, YNFP, and YOL (income sources or tax payments) is an element of personal income YP. This sum was defined to be proportional to YPWS plus YGWS (private plus public wage and salary income).[†] Finally, CDAN72, which was *not* influential, is part of C72. It is defined to be proportional to CDAO72, which *is* influential and hence included in the reduced model. So in these instances, "pseudobehavioral" relations replace the original relation for uninfluential variables.

Exhibit 6.2 contains the percent of remaining variables and the percentage of remaining coefficients in MINI 1 compared with the MQEM, offering much the same impression as Exhibit 6.1. Final demand (i.e.,

---

[†] The employment rate REM and the two unemployment variables, RUG and RUM, were related to influential coefficients and retained by setting them constant: they thus become part of the intercept.

Exhibit 6.2 Percentage of variables and coefficients retained in MINI 1 relative to the MQEM.

Sector	Variables (%)	Coefficients (%)
Wages and prices	38	51
Productivity and employment	59	29
Consumption and investment	59	67
Income flows	18	15
Monetary	29	49
Output composition	65	69
Total	40	50

consumption and investment) is the largest sector, reinforcing the impression that the MQEM remains substantially what it started out to be two decades ago, a final demand model. The monetary sector loses a high proportion of variables, but the retained equations are long ones, so that the coefficient proportion drops much less.

Exhibit 6.3 shows further details about the coefficient structure of MINI 1. The first two columns show that 68 + 9 = 77 of the 116 remaining coefficients were kept as a direct consequence of the linear sensitivity analysis. The remaining 39 coefficients are there for other reasons. First, indirect links across sectors must be completed. Second, basic accelerator behavior in investment or consumer durables led to inclusion of "companion" terms where only one of the rate of change variables had an influential parameter. Third, some terms in JCMH and PPNF were retained to complete these two equations as originally specified, even though they were not influential. Fourth, PPNF stayed in any other remaining price equation that had at least one influential coefficient or multiplier term, to preserve the originally specified structure of the internal price dynamics.

At this stage it is impressive that so few equations matter for inflation behavior even when we apply what seems to be a conservative criterion (an elasticity response ≥ 0.1 in at least one period) and retain other relations for reasons of model completeness. For the central inflation relations, half the behavior equations and two-thirds of the definitions are redundant. The uneven distribution of the remainder—some price and monetary equations and most of final demand—already conveys much information about the full model's structure. Other facets of the MQEM, especially how influential dynamic responses migrate from sector to sector as the time span lengthens, were described in the previous chapter.

Exhibit 6.3   Reasons for retaining coefficients in MINI 1.

Sector	Source of Influence			
	Parameter	Multiplier	Other	Total
Wages and prices	3	8	11	22
Productivity and employment	1		3	4
Consumption and investment	33	1	14	48
Income flows	3		4	7
Monetary	19		7	26
Output composition	9			9
Total	68	9	39	116

Functional Form

As matters turned out, certain types of equations were extremely influential
and were retained in MINI 1, while others were uninfluential and therefore
eliminated. Two distinct forces operate in making an equation influential
according to the criterion of parameter perturbations: the functional form
of the equation, and the degree of cancellation among the "own" parameter
perturbations in summing to the constraint described in Exhibit 5.14. The
most influential equations were those in log-level form, followed by those in
linear-level, log-difference, and linear-difference forms. Because of the units
chosen by the MQEM modelers, log-level parameter-perturbation constrained impact elasticities happen to sum to values 2–3 times the constraint
for the linear-level form (which is one), and the differenced-equation values
are always far smaller.

This explains what might otherwise appear to be anomalies in our
sensitivity results. For example, CS72 [consumption of services, the largest
single component of C72 (consumption)] and CDAN72 (new-auto consumption) are the only two consumption equations without influential parameters, but they are also the only two consumption equations in linear-difference form. The income sector is constructed mostly of log-differenced
equations, and this sector retained only 13% of its equations in MINI 1. M72 is
among the most influential equations in the model, and it is in log-level
form.

Although the equation's impact elasticity parameter perturbations are
constrained to sum to a well-defined magnitude, in any particular equation
there may be a greater or lesser degree of cancellation in adding up the
individual perturbations. So, if the absolute value of the sum of impact
parameter perturbations is much larger than the arithmetic (i.e., constrained) sum, the equation may be an influential one in the model,
depending on the linkages that exist between equations. While certain

function forms may have desirable estimation properties, these functional forms may have unintended deterministic model properties.

6.2 COMPARATIVE MODEL BEHAVIOR

The comparison between the MQEM and its MINI 1 counterpart will be done in several ways over the period 1973 2 to 1980 4. Two graphical comparisons—time plots, and percentage differences—will be used to visually judge the size of divergences. Simulations for these comparisons are based on common inputs (exogenous variables, initial conditions). The first set will be based upon smoothed inputs. These were described in Chapter 3, and used to obtain the smoothed outputs of the MQEM prior to linearization. Their merit for purposes of comparison has a comparable rationale, namely, that transitory variations of inputs will not obscure normal model behavior. Further, since the selection criteria for influence that led to MINI 1 used smooth inputs, it seems reasonable to make comparisons in the same framework.

A second set of comparisons involves endogenous variables with two sets of historical inputs for the MINI model and a single set of inputs for the MQEM. The latter are the full set of exogenous variables—including dummy variables—that were originally assembled at the University of Michigan to estimate and simulate the model. The two sets of exogenous variables for MINI 1 include one with, and one without, dummy variables. Their contrasting behavior enables us to evaluate how much dummy variables influence model behavior. As it happens, some important short-run movements in many key endogenous variables are heavily affected by the dummy variables.

The third set of comparisons involves multipliers based on smoothed inputs only for one exogenous price, one exogenous federal expenditure, and one monetary-policy variable.

In the remainder of the chapter we shall concentrate on time plots of eight major variables: $\Delta \ln$ PPNF, $\Delta \ln$ JCMH, $\Delta \ln$ QMH77, RTB, GNP72, C72, IBFNC72, and IINV72. Bar graphs of average percentage differences for a more inclusive set of variables are in Appendix 6A. These latter graphs are composed of the centered percentage differences for each simulated endogenous variable at each point in time, which are then averaged over four successive quarters. Most interest in quarterly models is in their first-two-year behavior; the first two bars (years) convey this information.

As described in Chapter 2, if the original and reduced-model time paths are close, information contained in the linear procedures is corroborated. More concretely, if the price–wage–productivity behavior in both original and reduced versions shows small discrepancies, our methods have served their main purpose. If, in addition, other important variables also show small discrepancies, a second objective has been achieved, which is to arrive at a reduced model with acceptable behavior (judged relative to the original model).

MINI 1 **Smooth Inputs**

Smooth exogenous variables are used for the first comparison of full- and compressed-model simulations. The graphs in Exhibit 6.4 for the selected eight variables show highly similar movements and levels, so that the "corroborative" evaluation (Section 2.4) is favorable. MINI 1 tracks the full MQEM especially closely for $\Delta \ln$ PPNF and $\Delta \ln$ QMH77 throughout the 24 quarters and does only slightly worse with $\Delta \ln$ JCMH. The major macroeconomic aggregates GNP72, C72, and IINV72 track well. RTB also shows similar movements in both versions, since at their worst, discrepancies are only 30 basis points. IBFNC72 alone shows a rapidly growing divergence between the two models, but even for it, the first 10 to 12 quarters appear reasonably close. Since MINI 1 paths are generally so close to MQEM ones, we have confirmed that the excluded equations and coefficients were unimportant in

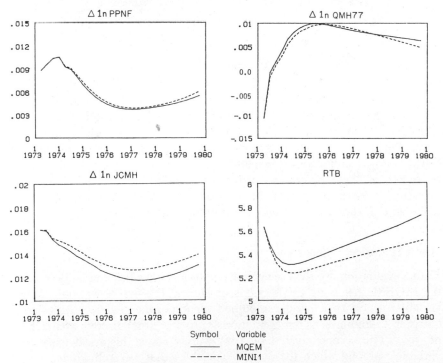

Exhibit 6.4   Time paths of MQEM and MINI 1 endogenous variables: smooth inputs.

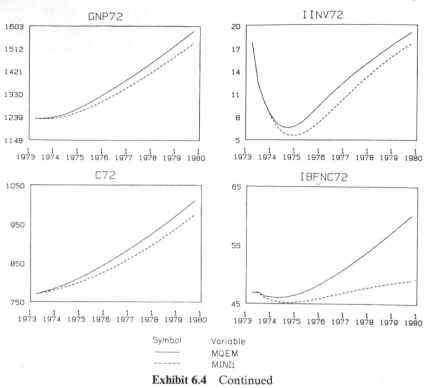

Exhibit 6.4   Continued

this context. Sometimes the graphical percentage differences in Appendix 6A are large because the denominator is extremely small; this is especially true for $\Delta \ln$ QMH77. Exhibit 6.A.1 covers a wide span of variables, 28 altogether, a few of which track poorly. FSNMF72 is a prominent example, but it is an exception to the generally good performance across all sectors. In terms of these percentage errors, sectoral price rates of change for investment, especially $\Delta \ln$ PIPDQ and $\Delta \ln$ PIRC, have large discrepancies, while on the whole consumption deflators show acceptable performance.

MINI 1 Historical Comparisons

In this evaluation, we shall see how well MINI 1 tracks the simulation path of the MQEM. There are two versions of MINI 1. The first is without dummy variables. In constructing the smoothed version of the model as described in Chapter 3, dummies, as representations of (often large) discrete events, have no role. The second version of MINI 1 uses actual historical exogenous variables, among which the dummy variables that were eliminated in the smoothing process are reintroduced. Exhibit 6.5 has time paths for the

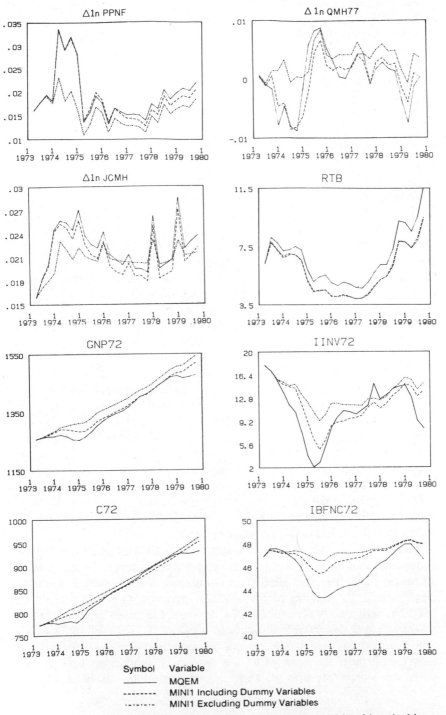

Exhibit 6.5 Time paths of MQEM and MINI 1 endogenous variables: historical inputs.

selected subset of variables. The dummy variables have a critical effect from 1973 2 through 1975 2 on price, wage, and productivity rates of change, but a lesser impact thereafter. During the oil-shock-plus-recession period the magnitudes of price changes are far off when dummies are excluded, even though the direction of change is correct. The same remark applies to the other two major variables. There may be a model-related connection, since upward-biased productivity can lead to downward biases in unit labor costs and hence also in $\Delta \ln$ PPNF. The time pattern of $\Delta \ln$ JCMH with and without dummy variables has the same direction of bias, but the magnitude is smaller. The short-term interest rate RTB is unaffected by dummy variables.

As an experiment, we ran a modified single-equation simulation of a version of $\Delta \ln$ PPNF in which the same l.h.s. variable $\Delta \ln$ PPNF remains, but only dummy variables plus intercept appear on the right-hand side. Variables with economic content, such as smoothed unit labor cost and capacity utilization, were dropped. This equation was compared with the full MQEM historical simulations. The simulation paths of $\Delta \ln$ PPNF from the full model and this single equation were extremely close, for the following, quite transparent reason. PPNF much of the time had a nearly constant rate of growth, so that when the dummies are set to zero the intercept equals that steady growth rate. But unusual historical events such as the oil price shock and its aftermath, partially coinciding with the wage–price-freeze dummy variables of the early 1970s, pick up most of the large swings in percentage changes of PPNF. Thus, the ability to distinguish economically meaningful variables is swamped by dummy variables. In this sense comparisons which exclude dummy variables are more informative about systematic economic behavior. Dummy variables should be considered as stochastic shocks that at times dominate the price-level movement.

Smooth aggregates like GNP72 and C72 are barely affected by the dummies. While the MQEM shows C72 to be nearly constant throughout the initial two-year period, both versions of MINI 1 increase more or less regularly throughout the entire recorded 24 quarters. The dummy-variable versions of cyclical variables like IINV72 and IBFNC72 are considerably closer to the full MQEM including dummy variables, as we should expect to happen according to the discussion in the previous paragraph.

Multipliers for the three main endogenous variables and three principal exogenous variables—PCRUDE, GFO, and MBASE—were also computed as additions to the previous simulation comparisons. Each exogenous variable was given a 1% impulse perturbation in period 1 (1973 2) for both the MQEM and MINI 1. The difference between the cases of perturbed and smooth exogenous-variable simulations is calculated for each of 24 quarters and graphed in Exhibit 6.6. Several observations are evident. First, and most important, the time paths are extremely similar, so that for these variables MINI 1 captures all the important mechanisms of the MQEM.

Second, endogenous-variable responses are not particularly sensitive to exogenous variables. For example, price impulse perturbations of order 10^{-2} cause responses that are of order 10^{-4} or 10^{-5}. Third, responses to PCRUDE are short-lived for $\Delta \ln$ PPNF and $\Delta \ln$ QMH77, but last 16 quarters for $\Delta \ln$ JCMH. Fourth, the responses to fiscal or monetary exogenous-variable changes of $\Delta \ln$ PPNF and $\Delta \ln$ JCMH appear moderately unstable, since after several years of zero response and apparent return to equilibrium after the

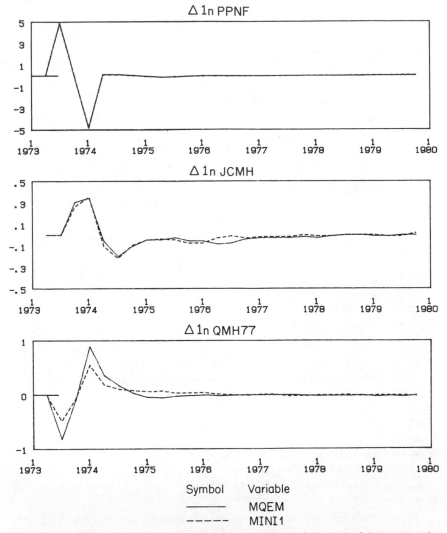

Exhibit 6.6   Time paths of selected multiplier effects on $\Delta \ln$ PPNF, $\Delta \ln$ JCMH, and $\Delta \ln$ QMH77. Responses to 1% perturbations of PCRUDE.

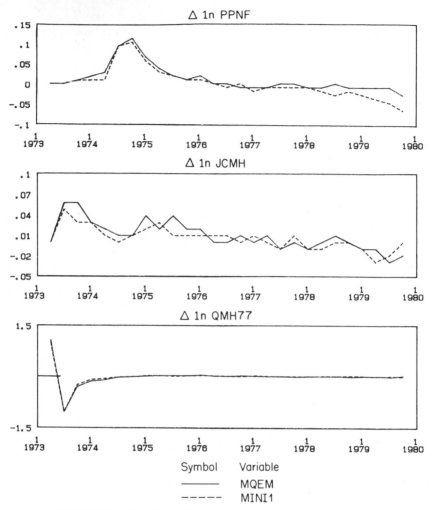

Exhibit 6.6 Continued. Responses to 1% perturbations of GFO.

initial shock, $\Delta \ln$ PPNF and $\Delta \ln$ JCMH start to wander apart. Since the scale is so small, these indications are tentative. Neither MINI 2 nor MINI 3 (see introductory remarks) was an acceptable reduced model, since explosive behavior occurred too frequently for us to believe that these still further condensed versions of the MQEM correctly reflected the original model's behavior.

We are thus left with the provisional conclusion that MINI 1 is close to the most condensed version of the MQEM that we can obtain. The approaches suggested for MINI 3 and MINI 4 seem reasonable and might yield good results

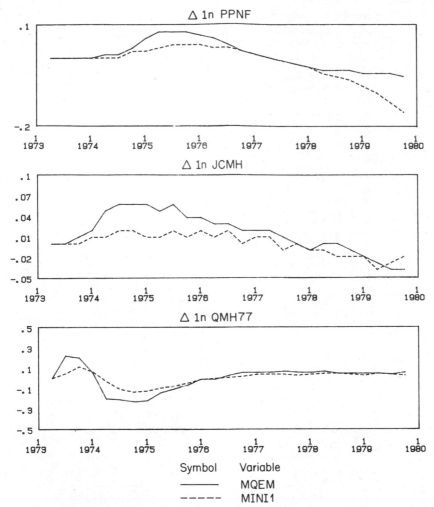

Exhibit 6.6 Continued. Responses to 1% perturbations of MBASE.

for models other than the MQEM. The notion of corroboration has proven to be more complex in implementation than in concept.

MINI 1 Dynamic Properties

A brief review of the dynamic properties of MINI 1 is in order. In comparison with the MQEM, it has about half the total number of roots, 51 in all, above the root cutoff 0.30 that was used for both models. Half of these are isolated equations that can be uniquely associated with the full set of MINI 1 roots. Unlike the MQEM, of the remaining 26 "simultaneous" imaginary roots,

Exhibit 6.7 MINI 1 and MQEM frequency distribution of root magnitudes.

Magnitude	MINI 1	MQEM
0.30–0.34	0.00	0.02
0.35–0.39	0.02	0.01
0.40–0.44	0.02	0.03
0.45–0.49	0.06	0.07
0.50–0.54	0.06	0.04
0.55–0.59	0.10	0.10
0.60–0.64	0.18	0.09
0.65–0.69	0.08	0.06
0.70–0.74	0.06	0.03
0.75–0.79	0.06	0.06
0.80–0.84	0.02	0.01
0.85–0.89	0.06	0.03
0.90–0.94	0.06	0.04
0.95–0.99	0.10	0.16
1.00–1.05	0.14	0.24
Root total	51.00	90.00

Exhibit 6.8 MINI 1 and MQEM frequency distributions of root periodicities.

Periodicity	MINI 1	MQEM
0–9	0.61	0.64
10–19	0.14	0.09
20–29	0.00	0.00
30–39	0.04	0.00
40–49	0.00	0.06
50–59	0.00	0.00
60–69	0.00	0.00
70–79	0.00	0.00
80–89	0.00	0.03
90–99	0.00	0.00
≥ 100	0.21	0.18
Imaginary roots	28.00	33.00

nine were assignable to sets of equations or variables on the basis of the root sensitivities. Clearly, a favorable consequence of simplification is the easier interpretation of the compressed model. In the MQEM, comparable root sensitivities were so diffuse and included so many different economic sectors that it was impossible to sort out their origins.

Broadly speaking, the root magnitudes are similar in their structure and size distribution, according to Exhibit 6.7. One difference between the two models is that there are proportionately fewer unit and near-unit roots in MINI 1, since perturbation analysis eliminated many income-by-source and tax first-difference equations that cause the unit roots. The relative distributions of root periodicities in the MQEM and MINI 1 are much the same according to Exhibit 6.8.

More details on root assignments appear in Exhibits 6.9 and 6.10 for MINI 1, which correspond to Exhibits 5.31 and 5.32 for the MQEM. These show, respectively, the single-equation roots and the assigned origins based on magnitude and root sensitivities. While the differences in MINI 1 between single-equation roots and the full counterparts are larger than in the MQEM, the dominating root sensitivities are so clear that we are convinced

Exhibit 6.9 Single-equation characteristic roots of MINI 1.

Variable	Root 1	Root 2
Productivity and Employment		
QMH77	0.989563	0
Prices and Wages		
JCMH	1.01563	0
PPNF	1.0082	0
PCN	1.0088	0.167116
PCS	1.01307	0.443836
PIRC	1.0215	0
PG	1.01157	0
PIPDQ	1.00713	0
Other Real GNP Components		
M72	0.725981	0
AUTOS	0.64293	0
JCAP	0.970535	0.010319
JIPM	0.43127	0
SERVE72	1	0

Exhibit 6.9   Continued

Variable	Root 1	Root 2
Real Investment		
IPDQ72	0.68843	0
IPDAG72	0.653512	0.231488
IPDO72	0.70811	0
IRC72	0.77722	0.31457
IINV72	0.2207	0
IBFNC72	0.88927	0
SINV72	1	0
Real Consumption		
CN72	0.76502	0
CDFE72	0.9362	0
CDAO72	0.80692	0
CDO72	0.88652	0
CS72	1	0
Income Flows		
YPWS	1.01075	0
YPDIV	0.94171	0
TP	1	0
Monetary Sector		
M1BPLUS	1	0.27193
M2PLUS	1.01754	0
RTB	0.36919	$\pm i0.145$
RAAA	0.90921	0
RCD	0.49012	0

that few assignment errors were made. Because MINI 1 has more simultaneity that the MQEM, its full model roots differ from its single equation roots to a greater extent. One difference of some interest is that it is now possible to assign the major-monetary sector variables RTB and RAAA, since the monetary sector is separate from the large simultaneous block of which it is a part in the MQEM.

Broadly speaking, there are few surprises and many similarities between the original and the compressed model. The gain in interpretability of the roots, a direct result of MINI's small scale, is a clear benefit.

Exhibit 6.10 Assignment of roots in MINI 1 according to single-equation roots and root sensitivities.

Real Index	Real Part	Imaginary Part	Magnitude	Period	Wilkinson Condition Number	Assignment
1	1.021	0	1.021	0	300.486	PIRC
2	1.018	0	1.018	0	1310.190	M2PLUS
3	1.017	0.001	1.017	6357.220	1829.070	PCS/YPWS
4	1.010	0	1.010	0	105.704	PG
5	1.009	0	1.009	423000	1320.070	PPNF/PCN
6	1.007	0	1.007	0	18.271	PIPDQ
7	1.005	0.010	1.005	623.737	1181.100	
8	1	0	1	0	5.095	TP
9	1	0	1	0	5.781	SERVE72
10	1	0	1	0	122.130	CS72
11	0.989	0	0.989	0	1.786	QMH77
12	0.966	0.004	0.966	1482.330	1905.620	
13	0.946	0	0.946	0	1526.850	
14	0.942	0	0.942	0	15.584	YPDIV
15	0.904	0	0.904	0	350.878	RAAA
16	0.891	0	0.891	0	698.364	IBFNC72
17	0.889	0	0.889	0	743.020	IBFNC72
18	0.881	0.018	0.881	304.830	1343.010	
19	0.791	0.146	0.805	34.364	675.663	
20	0.797	0	0.797	0	198.695	CDAO72
21	0.776	0.008	0.776	644.958	206.459	IRC72
22	0.694	0.296	0.755	15.571	436.466	
23	0.745	0	0.745	0	69.573	CN72
24	0.563	0.439	0.714	9.486	578.701	
25	0.706	0	0.706	0	131.665	IPDO72

Exhibit 6.10 Continued

Real Index	Real Part	Imaginary Part	Magnitude	Period	Wilkinson Condition Number	Assignment
26	0.445	0.512	0.678	7.350	621.001	
27	0.671	0	0.671	0	637.362	M72
28	0.316	0.589	0.669	5.830	792.404	
29	0.654	0	0.654	0	121.318	IPDAG72
30	0.647	0	0.647	0	403.962	AUTOS
31	0.524	0.361	0.636	10.428	33.165	PCS
32	0.205	0.594	0.629	5.075	912.720	
33	0.082	0.602	0.608	4.377	925.587	
34	−0.339	0.502	0.606	2.901	932.781	
35	−0.038	0.604	0.605	3.845	1018.780	
36	−0.511	0.323	0.605	2.438	905.315	
37	−0.248	0.550	0.603	3.150	951.979	
38	−0.135	0.587	0.603	3.496	1053.080	
39	−0.432	0.416	0.600	2.646	848.250	
40	−0.556	0.225	0.599	2.279	915.207.	
41	0.269	0.525	0.590	5.728	72.528	
42	−0.586	0	0.586	0	863.290	
43	−0.573	0.108	0.584	2.126	853.512	
44	−0.015	0.525	0.525	3.927	27.524	
45	−0.268	0.443	0.518	2.970	28.967	
46	0.509	0	0.509	0	1317.930	RCD
47	−0.435	0.244	0.498	2.390	22.122	
48	−0.495	0	0.495	0	29.269	
49	0.464	0	0.464	0	1043.900	JIPM
50	0.377	0.140	0.403	17.656	706.846	RTB
51	0.307	0.208	0.371	10.550	337.274	

MINI 4

MINI 4 is based upon the block orderings observed with a 0.05 filter for homogeneous impulse responses. These show a simultaneous block of 11 equations that include JCMH, PPNF, JCAP, and eight other sectoral deflators. Their content is indicated in Exhibit 6.11. This simultaneous block is lowest (most basic) in the block ordering until period 5, when it (with some other price equations) merges with the simultaneous 84-equation Keynesian-plus-monetary block. Given that structure, we hypothesize that for at least the first four to six periods the isolated simultaneous block will mimic its MQEM counterpart very closely, but thereafter this block in isolation will deviate increasingly from the MQEM. Comparative time paths for smoothed inputs are shown in Exhibit 6.12, and for historical inputs, including dummies, are shown in Exhibit 6.13 for selected variables: $\Delta \ln$ PPNF, $\Delta \ln$ JCMH, $\Delta \ln$ PC, and $\Delta \ln$ PIPDO. The other variables, not shown here to save space, display the same qualitative behavior.

If the hypothesized behavior is observed, it will corroborate the usefulness of filtered data for block ordering. For the smoothed data in Exhibit 6.11, tracking is extremely close in the first four to six periods and moderately close until period 12; then sharp divergences begin to appear. For the historical data in Exhibit 6.12, where exogenous variables and dummies in individual equations are strongly influential, the two versions of this block are very close through period 12 and then gradually drift apart. This experiment, which is not a strong one, can be·considered a success.

Exhibit 6.11 MQEM equations remaining in MINI 4.

Sector	Number of Equations		
	Behavior	Identity	Total
Wages and prices	7	1	8
Productivity and employment	0	1	1
Consumption and investment	0	0	0
Income flows	0	0	0
Monetary	0	0	0
Output composition	2	0	2
Total	9	2	11

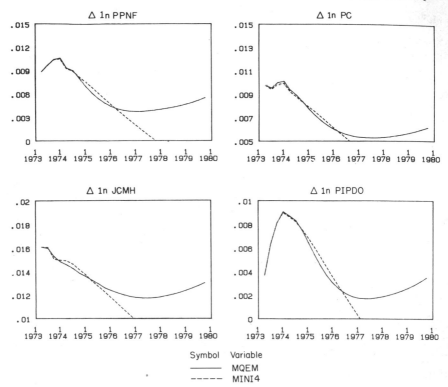

Symbol   Variable
————   MQEM
– – – –   MINI4

Exhibit 6.12   Time paths of MINI 4 and MQEM: smooth inputs.

6.3   RECAPITULATION

We began this book several years ago. The basic motivation has been
recounted—a belief that large macroeconomic models are impossible to
understand with existing methods, while at the same time, it is likely that
their most significant elements are few in number. Linear systems methods
seemed to possess the power and versatility to solve the dilemma posed by
large-model opaqueness obscuring a small number of critical components.
One necessary missing ingredient to test these beliefs was tractable, accurate
computer code that could be applied to macromodels. This led to a
three-year effort to build the TROLL task LIMO.

Next, the MQEM, as representative of thoughtfully conceived middle-size
macroeconomic models, appears well suited to our methodological needs. It
is large enough to be far from transparent. It is not a toy model, but rather
one that has been used regularly for macroeconomic forecasts and policy
analysis. The model's authors, Saul Hymans and Philip Howrey, were most

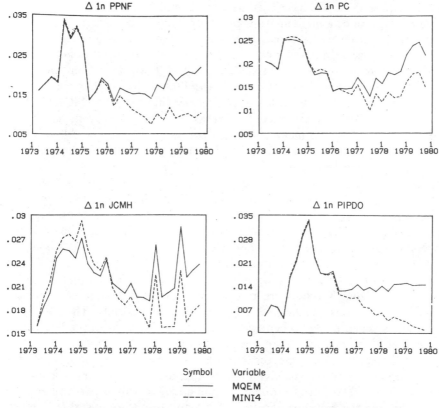

Exhibit 6.13   Time paths of MINI 4 and MQEM: historical inputs.

cooperative in making their model available and in responding to our questions, thus reducing misconceptions on our part. They bear no responsibility, however, for the analysis or its conclusions.

We also wanted to have a substantive economic focus. Looking at an interesting topic serves the dual purpose of learning more about a matter of current interest and understanding how the methods apply to a meaningful problem. Finally, these various elements must be fashioned into a reasonable sequence of analytical steps. The nature of one such general approach is sketched in Chapter 2. To the best of our ability these steps have been implemented in Chapters 3, 4, 5, and the first two sections of this chapter.

We believe the results fulfill some aspirations voiced in Chapter 1. There, the hope was expressed that the methods proposed would serve to strengthen agreement among econometricians and model users on rules of evidence. We believe that valid methods, some well-known if seldom applied and others less well-known, have been used in the inflation wage–price–productivity nexus. Since a preliminary exploration supported a belief that nonlinearities are often weak, concentration on linear systems analysis and its implications seemed warranted. To the extent that MINI 1 successfully reproduces many of the responses of the full MQEM, the content of linear analysis has been at least partially corroborated. In another context—a model with about 570 equations and 800 states (in contrast to MQEM's 117 equations and 321 states) used to forecast regional refinery demand and supply—linear systems methods yielded accurate and interpretable results.[†] Thus even much larger models than the MQEM are potentially amenable to these systems methods.

A second hope advanced in Chapter 1 was to employ methods that go beyond the inevitable black-box nature of multiplier analysis, however instructive it is for many purposes. We believe that some other procedures, parameter perturbations especially, in conjunction with characteristic-root decompositions, go directly to model structure and that their use is complementary, not competitive with multipliers.

At the outset, Chapter 2 proposes several logical sequences that might be pursued. Obviously others are possible and at times preferable. Furthermore, the methods yield valuable information sporadically. Their value is problem-specific, so that other aspects of the MQEM or other models would have placed the analysis in a quite different light.

Let us summarize some of the main results, starting with recursive structure and homogeneous dynamics in Chapter 4. The recursive structure revealed by a 0.05 filter for one-at-a-time initial-condition perturbations is this: through the first four quarters, wages and prices are lowest (i.e., more basic) in the causal ordering, including a simultaneous wage–price block and a recursive segment of other prices and price lags. This part of the model feeds into the main large "Keynesian" block consisting of final demand plus national-accounting-related variables plus monetary relations, which is in turn followed by a long tail composed of monetary and investment variables together with more lag identities. From period 5 onward the initial wage–price blocks merge with the Keynesian block, so that thereafter the model has two blocks: the large one just described, and a recursive tail, with some behavioral and many definitional lag equations. A second property emerged from the homogeneous dynamics. These naturally rely on wage–price–productivity levels (or differences from baseline path), a proposition that follows naturally from the basic dynamic equation (2.2.10).

[†] TROLL Translation and Analysis of IFFS, Sensitivity Analysis of Refinery Model, October 1983, MIT Center for Computational Research in Economics and Management Science, Cambridge, MA (unpublished).

In essence, JCMH and PPNF, the wage level and the nonfarm-private-product price deflator respectively, along with a number of other prices, display borderline instability. This proposition is a consequence of the fact that impulse inputs have not dissipated by period 24, retaining throughout elasticities in the range 0.8–2.0 that appear soon after the initial impact. Thus, while rates of change in the key variables are not explosive according to later analysis, levels are on the borderline within the MQEM structure.

Most results of linear system analysis are reported in Chapter 5. Linear multiplier analysis yields straightforward results that a handful of exogenous variables—several fiscal- and monetary-policy variables along with food prices and crude material prices (crude oil mainly)—are the most significant ones; these have swift dynamics, so that their effects have largely terminated after six to eight quarters. Through parameter perturbations we have uncovered the most revealing information about the inflationary structure of the MQEM. We noted that wage parameter perturbations affect prices, while price effects on wages are much weaker. In the medium term inflation rates are most sensitive to consumption final demand, while in the longer term consumption effects on prices die down, but monetary and investment parameters most prominently influence price and wage rates of change.

There is no simple way to summarize information contained in characteristic roots. We were able to isolate a subset that was associated with influential exogenous variables or parameters and thus related these roots to the specific dynamics described above. Computation of root sensitivities with respect to linearized-equation parameters often led to the identification of an equation as the primary source of particular roots. This was feasible when the equations were relatively isolated, but we found some key roots that were not, and believe this subset is most relevant to the simultaneous dynamics of the model. Also, the root dynamics associated with each aspect of the price–wage–productivity trio tended to differ, with the productivity dynamics distinctly swifter and different from prices and wages.

The notion of corroboration, described in Chapter 2, utilizes the kinds of information extracted by previous characteristic-root–vector analysis to eliminate coefficients and/or equations that were least important. This leads to a compressed version of the full MQEM. We described this process in the first two sections of this chapter, which led to MINI 1, a model which successfully mimics much price–wage–productivity behavior of the MQEM, and most of the remaining sectors as well. MINI 1 was about half the size of the MQEM. Other efforts to apply more stringent criteria that would further pare down equations and coefficients produced smaller models that failed to mimic the MQEM satisfactorily, leading us to conjecture that MINI 1 is approximately the most compact version of the MQEM that still works.

We view this study as a beginning. While interesting and even surprising results sometimes emerged, there are undoubtedly other aspects of this approach which could have been applied to better advantage. We hope that others will find this attempt promising enough to delve into macro or other models in a similar spirit, to isolate what really makes them tick.

APPENDIX 6A.   MINI 1 AND MQEM: ANNUAL AVERAGE PERCENTAGE DIFFERENCE

6A.1   SMOOTHED INPUTS

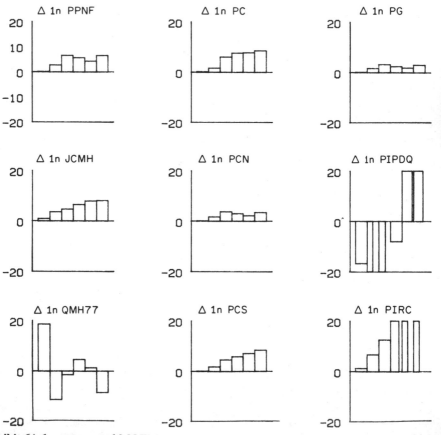

Exhibit 6A.1   MINI 1 and MQEM: annual average percentage difference—smoothed inputs.

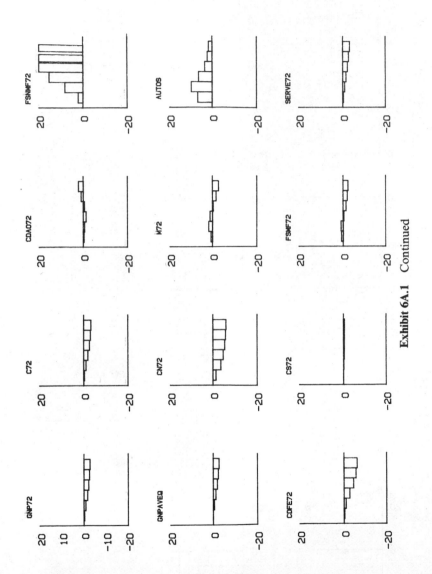

Exhibit 6A.1 Continued

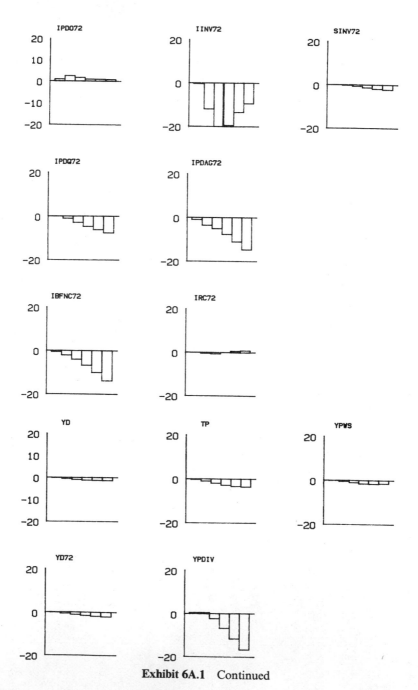

Exhibit 6A.1 Continued

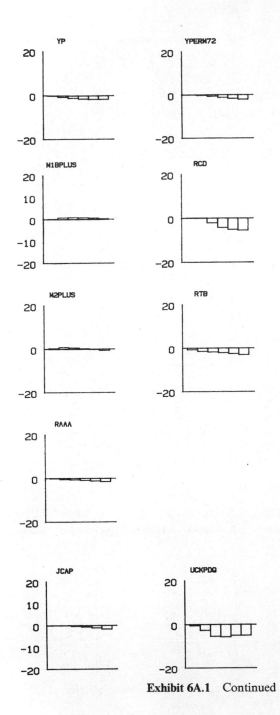

Exhibit 6A.1 Continued

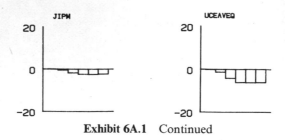

Exhibit 6A.1 Continued

6A.2 HISTORICAL INPUTS INCLUDING DUMMY VARIABLES

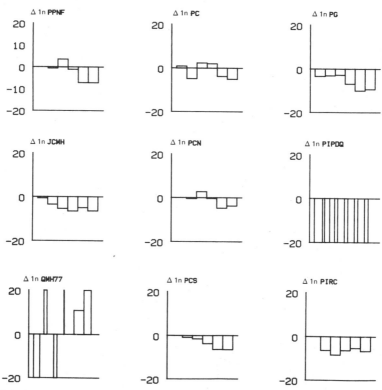

Exhibit 6A.2 MINI 1 and MQEM: annual average percentage difference—historical inputs including dummy variables.

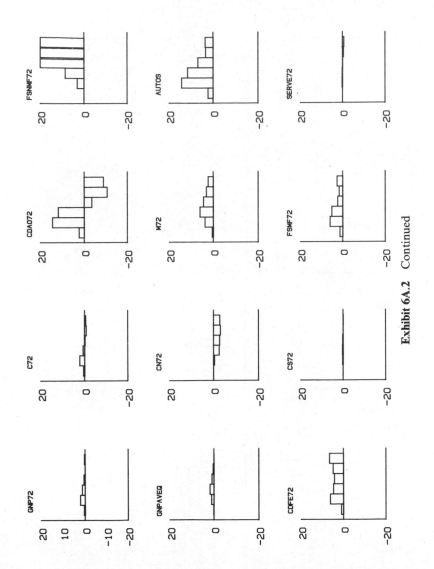

Exhibit 6A.2 Continued

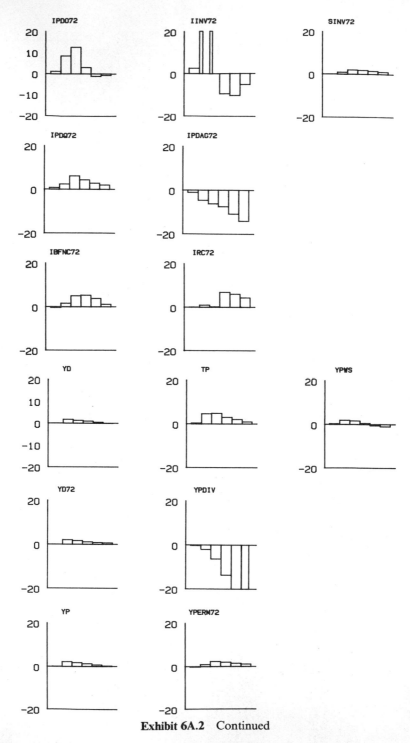

Exhibit 6A.2 Continued

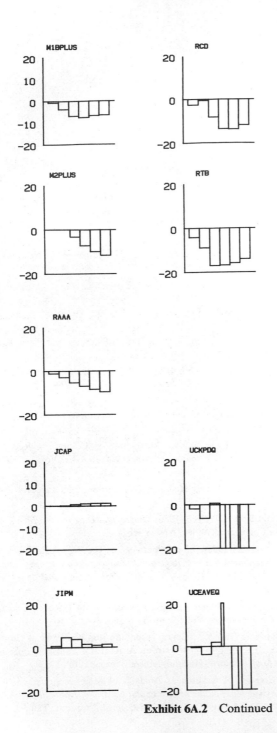

Exhibit 6A.2　Continued

Bibliography

Adelman, Irma and Frank L. Adelman (1959). The Dynamic Properties of the Klein–Goldberger Model, *Econometrica*, Vol. 27, pp. 596–625.

Ando, Albert and F. M. Fisher (1963). Near-Decomposability, Partition and Aggregation, and the Relevance of Stability. In *Essays on the Structure of Social Science Models*, A. Ando, F. M. Fisher, and H. A. Simon (Eds.), MIT Press, Cambridge, MA [Reprinted from *International Economic Review*, Vol. 4, No. 1 (January)].

Ando, Albert, Franklin M. Fisher, and Herbert A. Simon (1963). *Essays on the Structure of Social Science Models*, MIT Press, Cambridge, MA.

Aoki, Masano (1976). *Optimal Control and System Theory in Dynamic Economic Analysis*, American Elsevier, New York.

Artus, Patrick, Guy Laroque, and Gilles Michel (1984). Estimation of a Quarterly Macroeconomic Model with Quantity Rationing. In *Conference Proceedings of International Seminar on Recent Developments in Macroeconomic Modeling* (Paris), Pierre Malgrange and Pierre Alain Muet (Eds.), Blackwell, Oxford, 1984.

Bartels, R. H. and G. W. Stewart (1972). Algorithm 432, the Solution of the matrix equation AX-SB = C, *Communications of the Association for Computing Machinery*, Vol. 15, No. 9, pp. 820–826.

Baumol, William (1979). *Economic Dynamics: An Introduction*, 3rd edition, MacMillan, New York.

Bavely, Connice A. and G. W. Stewart (1979). An Algorithm for Computing Reducing Subspaces by Block Diagonalization, *SIAM Journal of Numerical Analysis*, Vol. 16, No. 2, pp. 359–367.

Bellman, Richard (1970). *Introduction to Matrix Analysis*, 2nd edition, McGraw-Hill, New York.

Belsley, David A., Edwin Kuh, and Roy E. Welsch (1980). *Regression Diagnostics: Identifying Influential Data and Sources of Collinearity*, Wiley, New York.

Belton, T., S. Hymans, and C. Lown (1985). The Dynamics of The Michigan Quarterly Econometric Model of the U.S. Economy. In *A Regional Econometric Forecasting System: Major Economic Areas of Michigan*, Harold T. Shapiro and George A. Fulton (Eds.), Univ. of Michigan Press, Ann Arbor.

Benassy, Jean Pascal (1977). On Quantity Signals and the Foundations of Effective Demand Theory, *Scandanavian Journal of Economics*, Vol. 79, pp. 147–168.

Bergstrom, Rex and Clifford Wymer (1976). A Model of Disequilibrium Neoclassical Growth and Its Application to the United Kingdom. In Bergstrom, A. R. (Ed.), *Statistical Inference in Continuous Time Economic Models*, North-Holland, Amsterdam, pp. 267–327.

Boutillier, Michel (1983). The Concept of Reading as Analysis of Macroeconomic Models. *Fourth IFAC/IFORS/IIAAS Conference on the Modeling and Control of National Economies and the 1983 SEDC Conference on Economic Dynamics and Control*, Preprints, Tamer Basar

(Ed.), McGregor and Werner, Washington.

Chan, S. P., R. Feldman, and B. N. Parlett (1977). "Algorithm 517: A Program for Computing the Condition Numbers of Matrix Eigenvalues Without Computing Eigenvectors [F2], *ACM Transactions on Mathematical Software*, Vol. 3, No. 2, pp. 186–203.

Chow, Gregory (1975). *Analysis and Control of Dynamic Economic Systems*, Wiley, New York.

Cline, A. K., C. B. Moler, G. W. Stewart, and J. H. Wilkinson (1979). An Estimate for the Condition Number of a Matrix, *SIAM Journal of Numerical Analysis*, Vol. 16, No. 2, pp. 368–375.

Costenoble, S. (1981). Mimeo, MIT, Center for Computational Research in Economics and Management Science.

Deleau, Michel and Pierre Malgrange (1978). *L'Analyse Des Modeles Macro Economiques Quantitatifs*, Economica, Paris.

Deleau, Michel and Pierre Malgrange (1976). Analysis of Macroeconometric Dynamic Models, *Colloques Internationaux du CNRS*, No. 259.

Deleau, Michel, Pierre Malgrange, and Pierre Alain Muet (1984). A Study of Short Run and Long Run Properties of Macroeconomic Dynamic Models by Means of an Aggregative Core Model. In *Conference Proceedings of International Seminar on Recent Developments in Macroeconomic Modeling*, Pierre Malgrange and Pierre Alain Muet (Eds.), Blackwell, Oxford 1984.

Duesenberry, J., G. Fromm, L. Klein, and E. Kuh (Eds.) (1965). *The Brookings Quarterly Econometric Model of the United States*, Rand McNally, Chicago; North Holland, Amsterdam.

Duff, I. S. (1981). Algorithms for Obtaining a Maximum Transversal, *ACM Transactions on Mathematical Software*, Vol. 7, No. 3, pp. 315–330.

Duff, I. S. and J. K. Reid (1978). An Implementation of Tarjan's Algorithm for Block Triangularization of a Matrix, *ACM Transactions on Mathematical Software*, Vol. 4, No. 2, pp. 137–147.

Fair, Ray C. (1980). Estimating the Predictive Accuracy of Econometric Models, *International Economic Review*, Vol. 21 (June).

Fair, Ray and Dwight Jaffee (1972). Methods of Estimation for Markets in Disequilibrium, *Econometrica*, Vol. 40, pp. 497–514.

Flamm, David S. and Robert A. Walker (undated). Corrections to Algorithm 506: HQR 3 . . . , mimeo.

Friedman, Benjamin (1975). *Economic Stabilization Policy: Methods in Optimization*, North-Holland, Amsterdam.

Frisch, Ragner (1933). Propagation Problems and Impulse Problems in Dynamic Economics. In *Economic Essays in Honor of Gustav Cassel*, London.

Gandolfo, Giancarlo (1981). *Qualitative Analysis and Econometric Estimation of Continuous Time Dynamic Models*, North-Holland, Amsterdam.

Gelb, Arthur (Ed.) (1974). *Applied Optimal Estimation*, MIT Press, Cambridge, MA.

Gilli, Manfred (1979). *Étude et Analyse des Structure Causales des Modèles Économiques*, Editions Peter Lange, Berne.

Golub, G. H. and J. H. Wilkinson (1976). Ill-Conditioned Eigensystems and the Computation of the Jordan Canonical Form, *SIAM Review*, Vol. 18, No. 4, pp. 578–619.

Gordon, Robert J. (1981). Output Fluctuations of Gradual Price Adjustment, *Journal of Economic Literature*, Vol. XIX, pp. 493–530 (June).

Hazelwinkel, M. and A. H. G. Rinnoy Kan (Eds.) (1982). *Current Developments in the Interface: Economics, Econometrics, Mathematics*, D. Reidel, Dordrecht.

Hicks, John R. (1937). Mr. Keynes and the "Classics," *Econometrica*, Vol. V, p. 147.

Howrey, Philip (1972). Dynamic Properties of a Condensed Version of the Wharton Model. In B. G. Hickman (Ed.), *Econometric Models of Cyclical Behavior*, Vol. 2, NBER New York, pp. 601–663.

Hymans, Saul H. and Harold T. Shapiro (1974). The Structure and Properties of The Michigan Quarterly Econometric Model of the U.S. Economy, *International Economic Review*, Vol. 15, No. 3 (October).

Keynes, John M. (1936). *The General Theory of Employment, Interest and Money*, MacMillan, New York.

Klein, L. R. and Arthur S. Goldberger (1955). *An Econometric Model of the United States 1929–1952*, North-Holland, Amsterdam.

Kuh, Edwin and John Neese (1982). Parameter Sensitivity, Dynamic Behavior and Model Reliability: An Initial Exploration with the MQEM Monetary Sector. In *Proceedings of the Econometric Society European Meeting 1979, Selected Econometric Papers—in Memory of Stefan Valavanis*, E. G. Charatsis (Ed.), The Athens School of Economics and Business Science, Athens.

Laffont, Jean-Jacques and A. Monfort (1979). Disequilibrium Econometrics in Dynamic Models, *Journal of Econometrics*, Vol. 11, pp. 353–361.

Liu, C. L. and J. W. S. Liu (1975). *Linear System Analysis*, McGraw-Hill, New York.

Lucas, Robert E. (1976). Econometric Policy Evaluation: A Critique. In *The Phillips Curve and Labor Markets* (Vol. 1 of a Supplementary Series to the *Journal of Monetary Economics*), K. Bruner and A. H. Meltzer (Eds.), pp. 19–46.

Lucas, Robert E. (1981). Tobin and Monetarism, *Journal of Economic Literature*, Vol. XIX, pp. 558–567 (June).

Malinvaud, Edmond (1977). *The Theory of Unemployment Reconsidered*, Blackwell, Oxford.

Modigliani, Franco (1944). Liquidity Preference and the Theory of Interest and Money, *Econometrica*, Vol. 12, p. 45.

Moler, C. and C. Van Loan (1978). Nineteen Dubious Ways to Compute the Exponential of a Matrix, *SIAM Review*, Vol. 20, No. 4.

Pagan, A. R. and J. H. Shannon (1983). Sensitivity Analysis for Linearized Computable General Equilibrium Models, mimeo, Australian National University.

Quandt, Richard E. (1982). Econometric Disequilibrium Models (with discussions by D. F. Hendry, A. Monfort, and J.-F. Richard and reply by Quandt), *Communications in Statistics: Econometric Reviews*, Vol. 1, No. 1, pp. 1–63, Marcel Dekker, New York.

Samuelson, Paul A. (1939). Interactions between the Multiplier Analysis and the Principle of Acceleration, *The Review of Economics and Statistics*, pp. 75–78 (May).

Sargent, Thomas J. (1976). A Classical Macroeconomic Model for the United States, *Journal of Political Economics*, Vol. 84, No. 2, pp. 207–237.

Sargent, Thomas J. (1979). *Macroeconomic Theory*, Academic, New York.

Shapiro, Harold T. and George A. Fulton (Eds.) (1985). *A Regional Econometric Forecasting System: Major Economic Areas of Michigan*, The University of Michigan Press.

Shiller, Robert J. (1978). Rational Expectations and the Dynamic Structure of Macroeconomic Models, A Critical Review, *Journal of Money and Credit*, 4, pp. 1–44.

Simon, Herbert and A. Ando (1963). Aggregation of Variables in Dynamic Systems. In *Essays on the Structure of Social Science Models*, A. Ando, F. M. Fisher, and H. A. Simon (Eds.), MIT Press, Cambridge, MA [reprinted from *Econometrica*, Vol. 2a, No. 2 (April 1961)].

Sims, Christopher (1980). Macroeconomics and Reality, *Econometrica*, Vol. 48, pp. 1–48 (January).

Sims, Christopher (1982). Scientific Standards in Econometric Modeling. In *Current Developments in the Interface*: *Economics, Econometrics, Mathematics*, M. Hazelwinkel and A. H. G. Rinnoy Kan (Eds.), Reidel, Dordrecht, pp. 317–340.

Slutzky, Eugen (1937). The Summation of Random Causes as the Source of Cyclic Processes, *Econometrica*, Vol. 5, p. 105.

Smith, B. T., J. M. Boyle, J. H. Dongarra, B. S. Garbow, Y. Ikebe, V. C.. Klema, and C. B. Moler (1976). *Matrix Eigensystem Routines, EISPACK Guide*, 2nd edition, Springer, New York.

Stewart, G. W. (1976). Algorithm 506 HQR3 and EXCHNG: Fortran Subroutines for Calculating and Ordering the Eigenvalues of a Real Upper Hessenberg Matrix [F2], *ACM Transactions on Mathematical Software*, Vol. 2, No. 3, pp. 275–280.

Stone, Richard and Murray Croft (1959). *Social Accounting and Economic Models*, Bowes & Bowes, London.

Stone, Richard (1970). *Mathematical Models of the Economy and Other Essays*, Chapman and Hall, London.

Tarjan, Robert (1972). Depth First Search and Linear Graph Algorithms, *SIAM Journal of Computing*, Vol. 1, pp. 146–160.

Tobin, James (1977). Macroeconomic Models and Policy. In *Frontiers of Quantitative Economics*, M. D. Intrilligator, (Ed.), Vol. IIIb; Contributions to Economic Analysis, Vol. 106, pp. 560–573.

Tobin, James (1980). *Asset Accumulation and Economic Activity*: *Reflections on Contemporary Economic Theory*, Yrao Johansson Lectures, Blackwell, Oxford.

Tobin, James (1983). Macroeconomics Under Debate, Cowles Foundation Discussion Paper No. 669, Yale University.

Wilkinson, J. H. (1965). *The Algebraic Eigenvalue Problem*, Oxford U.P., Oxford.

Wolter, Jurgen (1980). Business Cycle Stabilization Policies in a Small Econometric Model of the FRG, *European Economic Review*, Vol. 14, pp. 9–43.

Zellner, Arnold and Stephen C. Peck (1973). Simulation and Experiments with a Quarterly Macroeconomic Model of the U.S. Economy. *Econometric Studies of Macro and Monetary Relations*, In A. A. Powell and R. A. Williams (Eds.), North Holland, Amsterdam pp. 149–168.

Index

(*continued from front*)